"McNamara's decisions were not alwa[...]
book by two of his former Whiz Kids de[...]
usually were based on 'explicit criteria[...]
Decisions by the military services are often compromises to protect
'various institutional, parochial or other vested interests.'"
—*New York Times*, March 1971

"Makes a superb contribution to public understanding of the
critical and volatile McNamara years. It is not written as the
definitive 'insider history' of that era; but it is the best view we've
had so far of how McNamara decisions were shaped, told in sharp
detail by men who helped frame some of his most difficult choices.
The authors make an articulate, convincing plea for sanity—
for more analysis, instead of 'appeals to authority'—in defense
decision-making. Their logic is exciting, their candor is refreshing,
and their clarity of expression (simple but elegant English)
make the book a delight to read."
—*Armed Forces Journal*, February 1971

"Well written . . . [this book] is more than a ringing defense
of systems analysis. It reveals new aspects of in-fighting within
the Pentagon, particularly over Vietnam. . . . To his credit,
Enthoven's concern goes beyond the status and trappings
accorded the systems analysts. The larger issue is what kind of
manager a defense secretary elects to be, for that choice will
determine how he uses systems analysis."
—*Business Week*, January 1971

"A great deal of nonsense is written about the Pentagon
and military decision making in this country. This is a book
that tells, probably better than any other, just how it is
possible to come to a reasonable compromise with that
unanswerable question, *How Much is Enough?*"
—*Evening Star*, Washington, DC, March 1971

HOW MUCH IS ENOUGH?

Shaping the Defense Program 1961–1969

ALAIN C. ENTHOVEN

K. WAYNE SMITH

How Much Is Enough? Shaping the Defense Program, 1961–1969 was originally published by Harper & Row, Publishers, Inc., in 1971. This RAND edition reflects the original layout with the addition of an introduction to the new edition and a new foreword.

Library of Congress Cataloging-in-Publication Data

Enthoven, Alain C., 1930–
    How much is enough? : shaping the defense program, 1961–1969 /
Alain C. Enthoven, K. Wayne Smith.
      p. cm.
    "CB-403."
    Includes bibliographical references and index.
    ISBN 0-8330-3826-5 (pbk. : alk. paper)
    1. Military planning—United States—History—20th century. 2. Military administration—United States—History—20th century. 3. United States—Armed Forces—Cost control—History—20th century. 4. United States. Dept. of Defense—History—20th century. I. Smith, K. Wayne. II. Title.

U153.E58 2005
355'.033573'09046—dc22

2005018910

The RAND Corporation is a nonprofit research organization providing objective analysis and effective solutions that address the challenges facing the public and private sectors around the world. RAND's publications do not necessarily reflect the opinions of its research clients and sponsors.

RAND® is a registered trademark.

Cover design by Eileen Delson La Russo

Published 2005 by the RAND Corporation
1776 Main Street, P.O. Box 2138, Santa Monica, CA 90407-2138
1200 South Hayes Street, Arlington, VA 22202-5050
201 North Craig Street, Suite 202, Pittsburgh, PA 15213-1516
RAND URL: http://www.rand.org/
To order RAND documents or to obtain additional information, contact Distribution Services: Telephone: (310) 451-7002;
Fax: (310) 451-6915; Email: order@rand.org

To the memory of Charles J. Hitch, founding Chief of the Economics Division at the RAND Corporation and father of the Planning, Programming, and Budgeting System.

To Robert S. McNamara, Secretary of Defense 1961–1968, the brilliant leader who made it happen.

Last, but not least, to our wives.

Introduction to the New Edition

Resource allocation issues have long loomed large in Department of Defense (DoD) deliberations. As such, they continue to be the subjects of much of the RAND Corporation's research on behalf of the DoD. *How Much Is Enough?* grew out of our early experience in fashioning workable methods for systematically evaluating the choices posed in allocating resources. It is being brought back into print by RAND now as both a classic account of the application of new and powerful means of analysis and a cautionary history of the controversies that inevitably arose from those efforts. The question and the lessons of *How Much Is Enough?* are fully applicable in today's national security environment, where new challenges and new technologies further complicate the allocation of resources entrusted to the DoD. The book was originally funded by RAND, and this edition includes a new foreword by Under Secretary of Defense for Acquisition, Technology, and Logistics Kenneth J. Krieg and Under Secretary of Defense for Personnel and Readiness David S. C. Chu.

James A. Thomson, President and CEO, RAND Corporation
Michael D. Rich, Executive Vice President, RAND Corporation

Foreword to the New Edition

We are honored by the opportunity to write a foreword to this new edition of *How Much Is Enough?* A work of enduring value and lasting relevance, it is both a classic account of the application of powerful ideas to the problem of managing the Department of Defense (DoD) and a cautionary history of the controversies inspired by that successful effort. Our hope is to provide its readers an appreciation of its ideas, the way in which they were applied, how they have continued to shape the nation's defenses, and why they are as powerful today as they were in 1961.

As *How Much Is Enough?* recounts, Robert S. McNamara took office in 1961 convinced that the Secretary of Defense, rather than the services, should control the evaluation of military needs and should choose among alternatives for meeting those needs. He was determined to exercise the previously little-used powers that Congress had given the Secretary to integrate the nation's defenses into a coherent whole. His device was a new system for allocating defense resources, the Planning, Programming, and Budgeting System (PPBS), which was based on the six deceptively simple fundamental ideas described in Chapter Two:

- Decisions should be based on explicit criteria of national interest, not on compromises among institutional forces.

- Needs and costs should be considered simultaneously.
- Major decisions should be made by choices among explicit, balanced, feasible alternatives.
- The Secretary of Defense should have an active analytic staff to provide him with relevant data and unbiased perspectives.
- A multiyear force and financial plan should project the consequences of present decisions into the future.
- Open and explicit analysis, available to all parties, should form the basis for major decisions.

We submit that these principles constitute the foundation for sound management of any public institution, and we affirm that their application is painful. It requires the hard collaboration that leads to real choices; forbids the easy consensus that comes from splitting differences; forces attention onto the future consequences of present decisions; and illuminates the opportunity costs we incur when we decide to commit limited resources to a particular purpose. This discipline is the foundation of sound decisionmaking. It also sharpens differences, raises anxieties, and imposes great responsibilities on the decisionmakers.

The record leaves no doubt that the problems Robert McNamara addressed were important ones or that he reached, and enforced, hard decisions on difficult issues, often at the expense of weapons systems that were deeply grounded in the cultures of the military services. Both the decisions themselves and the assertion of the authorities of the Secretary of Defense deeply offended elements of the senior military leadership and the Congress. It is thus no wonder that the PPBS, and in particular the analyses on which McNamara relied (and the analysts responsible for preparing them), came under attack. If anything, the authors understate the rancor of those attacks: Despite later modifications intended to restore the services' autonomy and satisfy congressional concerns, that rancor persisted strongly into the 1980s and festers in some quarters today.

Notwithstanding attacks to the contrary, the analyses on which McNamara relied were of the very highest quality. The work, performed by McNamara's office of Systems Analysis, was presented in Draft Presidential Memorandums (DPMs), some of which are described in *How Much Is Enough?* In all, 93 DPMs were prepared in the eight Kennedy-Johnson years. Several have since been declassified, and one, the November 1962 DPM on Strategic Retaliatory Forces, has been cleared for public release. (It can be found on the web site of the DoD Office of Program Analysis and Evaluation, www.ra.pae.osd.mil/ra/servlet/economics.) The DPMs share five hallmarks: They place primary emphasis on the *definition of the objective*, rather than on calculations of precise quantities; they consider the full range of alternative means for achieving the objective; they focus on identifying the most *cost-effective* means for achieving the objective; they consider a range of assumptions and offer a range of results, rather than single point solutions; and they carefully and explicitly identify the roles of analysis and judgment. For example, the Strategic Retaliatory Forces DPM identified the strategic objective as deterrence (rather than the creation of a first-strike capability), reviewed the full span of the nation's nuclear forces, and adjusted the mix of forces to increase their collective deterrent value, chiefly by enlarging the (most expensive and most effective) ballistic missile submarine force. McNamara's decisions in the DPM shaped the nuclear triad that supported the strategic policy of the United States for the duration of the Cold War. The document itself, which put fully into practice the concept of capability-based planning that has recently received renewed attention, is a classic of analysis.

Time has vindicated the PPBS. Most of the decisions that inspired great controversy in the 1960s are taken as bedrock defense policy today, and the methods adopted with such pain have become embedded as the DoD's approach to defining and resolving issues. Despite lengthy debate over its merits, every Secretary of Defense since Robert McNamara has seen fit to rely on the PPBS, shaping it to his management style and to the circumstances of his time. We do not suggest that it has always worked effectively; we do conclude that it remains the DoD's primary method for identifying and resolving major programmatic issues.

How Much Is Enough? poses, however, a more demanding test. In Chapter Five, Enthoven and Smith wrote:

But the continuation of something called PPBS and the survival of the Systems Analysis office and the other tools that make the system work are not the important thing. The important question is the substance of DoD management, not the appearance. Here, as of early 1970, the signs were mixed.

The last DPM was written in 1968. In 1969, the incoming Secretary of Defense, Melvin R. Laird, restored to the military departments the responsibility for identifying future needs and undertook to shape the defense program by providing guidance to the departments and having his staff evaluate their responses to that guidance. This approach has remained the practice since, with recurrent debates over how much guidance the Secretary of Defense should provide and how much review the Secretary's staff should undertake.

Since 1969 there have been four important trends in the forces that influence the defense program: first, increased congressional engagement in the management of the DoD (the Defense Appropriations Act grew from 16 pages in 1968 to 435 pages in 2003); second, further improvements in the military services' analytic capabilities; third, increased advocacy for subelements of the defense program by a greatly expanded Office of the Secretary of Defense; and fourth, increased engagement in shaping the defense program by the Joint Staff and the commanders of major joint commands. The effect of the first three changes has been to shape the defense program in terms of the interests of particular constituencies and to focus debate on issues at the margins of those interests. This tendency has been partially offset by the increased influence of the joint community.

The adjustments in the defense program since the end of the Cold War illustrate strengths and weaknesses in the performance of the current version of the PPBS. On a positive note, investments in mobility forces and special operations forces have increased proportionately over the period, while investments in strategic retaliatory forces have declined. Less creditably, many weapons systems initiated during the Cold War continued in development—without entering production—through the 1990s, and it is only recently that the DoD has begun turning to a systematic review to determine which of them are likely to prove useful against the challenges the nation now faces and can foresee.

We leave the record for others to judge but think it, on the whole, favorable. As we will argue, recent modifications in the PPBS have the potential to strengthen its performance further. First, however, we will present the evidence that the fiscal realities we now face make the principles of the PPBS as relevant and needful today as they were in 1961.

The costs of meeting the nation's commitments to provide economic security and adequate health care to an aging population have already begun to impose hard choices on discretionary spending, and they will continue to do so. In 1964, the defense program accounted for 44 percent of all federal expenditures and social security and health insurance, together, for 18 percent. Today, those proportions are reversed: In 2004, defense accounted for 19 percent of federal outlays and social security and health insurance, together, for 47 percent. Given current benefit levels and absent sizable tax increases, the costs of social security and health insurance will grow to about 58 percent of federal outlays by 2025. This reality will impose on future Secretaries of Defense enormous pressures to demonstrate the cost-effectiveness of the defense program.

Within the defense budget, growth in personnel costs will impose added pressures on other accounts. In 1964, the annual cost to the DoD budget of an active-duty military work year was $41,900 in today's dollars. By 2005, that figure had climbed to $77,300—an increase of 84 percent. Thus, while the number of people on active duty shrank by 46 percent over the interval (from 2.7 million in 1964 to 1.6 million in 2005), the cost of maintaining the force *increased* by 3 percent (from $119 billion in 1964 to $123 billion in 2005).[1] This trend, too, can be expected to continue, as the military services compete with the civil sector for highly capable men and women. The pressures this competition will exert on the DoD's business and investment accounts will be compounded by the need to modernize the defense infrastructure and the imperative of maintaining readiness.

Unless the DoD can reduce the costs of its business practices, the pressures will fall principally on the investment accounts. At the same time, the investment accounts will generate budgetary pressures of their own, as the ever greater technical complexity of new weapons continues to lengthen system development times and increase their unit costs.

Under these circumstances, future Secretaries of Defense will need to exert skillful control over DoD spending in two ways: On the one hand, they will need to guide the selection of new weapons programs and to decide the programs' futures early in their development if per-

---

[1] The total cost of military personnel, which includes retirement, health care, and veterans' benefits, far exceeds the costs to the DoD budget, and it has grown faster. The total cost to the treasury of an active-duty work year was $60,200 in 1964 and is $140,700 today—an increase of 134 percent.

formance falls short of expectations; on the other, they will be challenged to create compelling rationales for the necessary changes in the total business structure of the DoD.

The opportunity costs of deciding to cancel systems late in development are staggering. For example, $6.2 billion in today's dollars was spent on the Crusader artillery system, which was canceled in 2001 after 18 years of development. Likewise, every dollar devoted to the continuation of inefficient or unnecessary business practices is a dollar denied to modernization, to readiness, or both.

This is going to be a painful business for future Secretaries, for the military services, and for the Congress. Every major weapon system has proponents in the DoD who are deeply committed to its survival and success, as well as advocates in the Congress. The political costs of cancellation can be very high. Similarly, DoD business practices have proven very difficult to change. Although they are known to be inefficient, they perform necessary functions, and each has constituencies inside and outside the DoD.

As we move through another era of significant change in the nation's defenses, we are drawn again to the need for strategic choices. If, in this regard, we could offer one corollary to the seminal question of *How Much Is Enough?* it would be: *How much risk are we willing to take?* The problem facing future Secretaries will be to decide what is best, not just how much is enough—and to defend those decisions. The original principles of the PPBS provide the only credible means of arriving at the necessary decisions and the only sustainable basis for defending them. This broad juxtaposition of needs and costs thus forces us back to the six simple and profound ideas laid out in Chapter Two.

Given these realities, it is promising that recent modifications in the PPBS reemphasize its original principles. In 2003, Secretary Donald R. Rumsfeld chartered the Joint Defense Capabilities Study, of which he asked three things: a way to ensure that programs would be conceived and developed jointly; a reduction in the noise level of the annual process of guidance and review; and increased influence for the combatant commanders in shaping the defense program. The study recommended a planning process in which needs and costs would be considered simultaneously, with the full participation of all affected parties (including the Office of the Secretary of Defense); clear alternatives for meeting the requirements would be presented to DoD top management for review; and the Secretary's decisions on the issues would be conveyed to the DoD as mandatory, DPM-like guidance.[2]

The new process was used for the first time in 2004, in the development of the defense program for fiscal years 2006–2011. It succeeded in reducing the noise level of the programming process and, though hampered by a late start and the difficulties always encountered in installing new procedures, partially succeeded in bringing major issues forward for the Secretary's review. We believe that this approach, which implements the fundamental ideas of the original PPBS, holds great promise and that Secretaries of Defense will sorely need it (or something like it) to shape the defense program under the economic pressures of the coming decades.

One final word: We have been privileged to lead, under three presidents, the office Alain Enthoven created. We have tried to continue the work he started because we believe it to be essential to the national defense. We further believe that *How Much Is Enough?* remains, after 35 years, a beacon for those who think seriously about these problems.

June 27, 2005

Kenneth J. Krieg
David S.C. Chu

Dr. Chu is Under Secretary of Defense for Personnel and Readiness; he was Director and later Assistant Secretary of Defense for Program Analysis and Evaluation from 1981 to 1993. He previously served in government as Assistant Director of the Congressional Budget Office for National Security and International Affairs. He was commissioned in the United States Army in 1968, served on active duty until 1970, and resigned with the rank of captain in 1974.

Mr. Krieg is Under Secretary of Defense for Acquisition, Technology, and Logistics; he was Director for Program Analysis and Evaluation from July 2003 to June 2005. He previously served in government as Executive Secretary to the DoD Senior Executive Council, as Executive Assistant to the Deputy Secretary of Defense, and as a member of the National Security Council and White House staffs.

---

[2] The study was led by the Honorable E. C. "Pete" Aldridge, who had recently retired from the position of Under Secretary of Defense for Acquisition, Technology, and Logistics. Aldridge had previously served as Secretary of the Air Force (1986–1988), as Under Secretary of the Air Force (1981–1986), and as Director of Planning and Evaluation during Secretary Rumsfeld's first tour (1975–1977).

Preface

This book was written for three main purposes. The first is to record some of the valuable lessons regarding strategy, force, and financial planning learned in the 1950's and 1960's and applied in the 1960's in the hope that, by doing so, they will not have to be relearned in the 1970's. The second is to make a case for what we believe to be the proper role of the Secretary of Defense: that is, personally to grasp the strategic issues and provide active leadership in developing a defense program that sensibly relates U.S. foreign policy, military strategy, defense budgets, and the choice of major weapons and forces. The third is to increase public understanding of the uses of analysis in defense decision making and to help build support for its increased use. If successful, our effort will contribute to a more effective and economical defense program for the United States.

The subjects this book deals with are highly controversial and emotional under the best of circumstances. They are doubly so in view of the current public concern over the war in Southeast Asia, the costs of defense, and national priorities. We are somewhat concerned that, given this climate, the extreme partisans of one or another point of view may misinterpret what we have written or attempt to use portions of it out of context. Accordingly, we want to establish certain points at the outset, even though most of them are made clearly in the book. First, in order to explain what the Secretary of Defense needs to do his job well, we must discuss frankly the institutional limitations and biases of military recommendations regarding requirements for weapons and forces. But in doing so, we distinguish clearly between organizations and individuals; our concern and criticisms are directed at the product of the organizations, not at the individuals who make them up. Our point is simply that the organizations and processes with which military planners work—like most nonmilitary organizations—have important impacts on their recommendations which ought to be understood and accepted for what they are.

Second, the differences we describe between independent civilian analysts and career military officers, between the Systems Analysis office and the Military Services, between concern for the national interest and concern for parochial interests, though real and important, are differences of degree, not of kind. To say that civilian analysts can have more career and intellectual independence than career military officers is not to say that there are no (or even few) objective and vigorously independent military officers; rather it is to say only that it is more difficult for them to be so. To point out the institutional limitations and pressures on those who work in the Services is not to say that there are no such limitations and pressures on those who work in the Office of the Secretary of Defense. We have emphasized certain differences in this book largely to make a point; the similarities are just as numerous and also important.

Finally, we have tried in this book to be fair. We are well aware, however, that the fact that we worked for the Secretary of Defense influences our point of view regarding the issues we discuss. When we took a stand on these issues it was because we believed strongly that we were right. But we recognize that there was (and still is) room for honest differences of opinion and that those who differed with us did so in the belief that they were right. And we are not so foolish as to claim total objectivity or infallibility. We made our value judgments and we made our share of mistakes, some of which we discuss in this book.

The ideas and events described in this book are products of the contributions of many people. We would like particularly to acknowledge our debt of gratitude to some of them here.

Our first debt of gratitude is to Robert S. McNamara, Secretary of

Defense from 1961 to 1968, whose vision of how the Defense Department ought to be run is one of the main subjects of the book. His strength and his courage in making needed reforms against tremendous opposition have earned him a unique place of honor in the history of the Executive Branch of government. The public knows him for the extraordinary power of his mind and the strength of his will. We who worked for him know him as a warm and humane man, a demanding but appreciative leader.

Second only to McNamara in the importance of his contributions to the development of the Planning-Programming-Budgeting System in the Department of Defense was Charles J. Hitch, Assistant Secretary of Defense (Comptroller) from 1961 to 1965, and "the father of PPBS." Charlie Hitch was the main architect of the system and provided the able leadership that saw it through to reality.

We are indebted to Presidents Kennedy and Johnson, each of whom knew about the Systems Analysis office, personally and publicly recognized its contributions, and provided the political support without which the office would have been ineffective (and probably nonexistent).

The necessary condition for the existence of a good program analysis office in any organization is that the leaders of the organization understand the need for the office and use its analyses as an important tool in their decision making even in the face of strong pressures to do otherwise. In this regard we want to thank the other men for whom we worked: Secretary of Defense Clark Clifford and Deputy Secretaries Roswell Gilpatric, Cyrus Vance, and Paul Nitze. It would be difficult to find a comparable group of such distinguished and capable men.

We owe a great deal to our colleagues in the Systems Analysis office, an unusually talented group of men who gave generously of themselves to produce a great deal of analytical work of high quality. Mentioning a few of the leaders of the office necessarily means leaving out many other very able men. However, special mention should be made of Russell Murray II, the Principal Deputy Assistant Secretary of Defense for Systems Analysis, whose calm and evident integrity brought many a stormy controversy to a reasoned conclusion, and Harold Asher, William Brehm, Charles DiBona, Stephen Enke, Arthur Herrington, Victor Heyman, Fred Hoffman, Laurence Lynn, Merton J. Peck, Daniel Rathbun, Herbert Rosenzweig, Charles Rossotti, Dieter Schwebs, Ivan Selin, Jacob Stockfisch, and Robert Valtz. We are particularly grateful to the more than one hundred military officers who served with us in the Systems Analysis office. They brought a tremendous knowledge of military operations and organization as well as excellent analytical skills. More importantly, they joined us as individuals, not as "representatives" of their particular Service.

We also want to acknowledge gratefully the civilian and military leaders of the Services who joined us in debate on many complex and controversial issues. We are thinking particularly of Secretaries Stanley Resor, Paul Ignatius, and Harold Brown and our military counterparts responsible for the program analysis work in the Services and the Joint Staff. These men displayed courage in distinguishing the best from the less meritorious proposals of their Services and ably defending the best. They provided us with stimulation, challenge, and ideas. We are particularly grateful to them for their commitment to the idea of reasoned debate of the issues, rather than emotional appeals.

We are indebted to a number of members of the Congress for their support and encouragement over the years. In particular, we want to thank Senator Henry M. Jackson. "Scoop" Jackson saw the need for many of the management reforms described in this book, provided the forum for discussion of the problems of defense organization and management, and explained and defended to his colleagues in the Senate Armed Services Committee the role of and need for the Systems Analysis office. Much of the credit for the Committee's strong stand against abolition of the Systems Analysis office belongs to him.

We want to thank those friends and colleagues who read and commented on various parts or drafts of the book. We have greatly benefited from their advice and counsel, even though we sometimes chose not to follow it. In addition to some already mentioned above, they include: Richard Enthoven Sr., Richard Fryklund, Phil Goulding, William Kaufmann, Robert Komer, Richard Moorsteen, Malcolm Palmatier, Randy Revelle, John Rubel, John Seigle, William Snyder, George Stigler, W. G. T. Turtle, Rudolph Winnacker, and Charles Wolf, Jr. Of course, all errors of fact or interpretation are ours, not theirs.

Last, but definitely not least, the ladies. A special debt is owed to Geneva M. Coleman, who served us both so well, working more than sixty hours a week for eight years, turning out prodigious amounts of excellent work. Always loyal, always effective, women like Genny are the unsung heroines who make the wheels of government turn. Ann

Harper and Sylvia Frick typed the many drafts of our manuscript quickly and well under pressure. Our wives, Rosemary Enthoven and Audrey Smith, had to forgo our company many evenings and weekends for years, while we were in the Pentagon and later while we wrote the book. We like to think that was a sacrifice for them, and we are grateful for their patience.

April 22, 1970   *Alain C. Enthoven*
                                   K. Wayne Smith

With gratitude, we acknowledge Dr. Vance Gordon's role in identifying the need for a new edition of this book, finding a publisher, and securing the support of the Under Secretaries of Defense. Dr. Gordon has long been the keeper of the flame of PPBS principles.

June 27, 2005   *Alain C. Enthoven*
                                   K. Wayne Smith

Contents

Tables

"You cannot make decisions simply by asking yourself whether something might be nice to have. You have to make a judgment on how much is enough."

ROBERT S. MCNAMARA
April 20, 1963

1

Unfinished Business, 1961

Introduction

The defense budget is today a matter of increasing public debate and concern. For a decade after Sputnik, however, the public mood in the United States was one of support for almost anything proposed in the name of national security. During this period, the Secretary of Defense was under constant pressure to spend more money than he believed necessary. In practically every conflict between the Secretary of Defense and the Congress over spending, the Congress wanted to spend more. The Armed Services Committees were rarely challenged by the rest of the Congress. Their main theme was that the military leaders are the experts; they know best what the nation needs for national defense; any reduction from what they recommend means risking the nation's security; and such shortfalls must be exposed and attacked as such.

Now the national mood has changed. Frustration over the war in Vietnam, concern over urgent domestic needs, the enormous costs of new weapon systems, and inflation are leading more and more people to question not only military needs and spending but also some of the foundations on which U.S. national security policy has rested for two decades. The Congress, reflecting the changing mood,

1

is cutting military spending below what many leaders of the Department of Defense (DoD) believe is necessary. Expressions of concern over Communist military threats are being treated with new-found skepticism. Proposals for drastic reductions in the U.S. military posture are being debated seriously. Prominent voices are being heard attacking the military, questioning their judgment and even their integrity. People are choosing sides; the middle ground seems to be eroding.

This book attempts to make a case for the middle ground. We do not believe that the nation's military needs are necessarily what the Joint Chiefs of Staff say they are. Nor should domestic needs, however stated, have an overriding priority. It is for the President and the Congress to decide the over-all allocation. As for the formulation of military needs, at the strategic level there is no such thing as a "pure" military requirement, only alternatives with varying risks and costs attached. Choosing among these alternatives is the main job of the Secretary of Defense. To him more than to any other individual falls the task of determining the nation's military needs and then explaining and defending his conclusions. In reaching his conclusions, obviously he must obtain advice and information from his military advisers, who are, with rare exceptions, men of high intelligence and integrity. Less obvious but just as important in our view, he must also obtain information and advice from civilians who have given serious study to the matter of military requirements and whose careers and points of view are independent of the military establishment.

This book is about two main ideas. The first concerns the proper role of the Secretary of Defense. The statutory authority of the Secretary of Defense, as it exists today, was defined by a series of laws beginning with the National Security Act of 1947 and ending with the Department of Defense Reorganization Act of 1958. Each of these laws represented a major step in the integration of the defense establishment and the consolidation of power in the hands of the Secretary of Defense. Only as recently as 1958, however, did the law clearly give the Secretary of Defense the authority to determine the force structure of the combatant commands, to supervise all research and engineering activities of the Department, and to transfer, reassign, abolish, and consolidate combatant functions. Without that authority, the work we describe in this book could not have been done.

Within the framework of the 1958 Act, two broad schools of thought have emerged as to how the Secretary should exercise his authority. One, which might be called the "traditional" view, holds that once the President and the Congress have determined how much money can be spent on defense, the job of the Secretary of Defense is to allocate this total among the Services, to see that they live within the financial limits, and to arbitrate disputes among the military leaders. But basically, according to this view, it is the Joint Chiefs of Staff and the Services who should decide how the money is to be spent, with minimum civilian supervision of only the obviously "civilian" aspects of the program such as science and technology, production, personnel, and finance. The civilians should keep away from such military matters as strategy and force requirements.

The opposing school, to which the authors belong, holds that foreign policy, military strategy, defense budgets, and the choice of major weapons and forces are all closely related matters of basic national security policy. And the principal task of the Secretary of Defense is personally to grasp the strategic issues and provide active leadership to develop a defense program that sensibly relates all these factors. In short, his main job is to shape the defense program in the national interest. In particular, it is his job to decide what forces are needed.

Of course, these two views as outlined here are only points on a spectrum of opinion. The views of many individuals lie somewhere between.

Secretaries Thomas Gates, Robert McNamara, and Clark Clifford held the latter view—which might be called the "active management" view. In his year as Secretary of Defense, Gates appeared to be moving in the direction of active leadership. In a significant departure from previous practice, he met regularly with the Joint Chiefs of Staff to review disputed issues. And he established a Joint Strategic Targeting Planning Staff whose job was to coordinate all U.S. long-range nuclear attacks by all commands. That decision, which seems a matter of obvious common sense today, was so controversial at the time that one of the Service Chiefs personally appealed to President Eisenhower to overrule the Secretary. But while apparently moving in the direction of active leadership, Gates, who became Secretary of Defense only in the last year of the Eisenhower administration, had neither the necessary time nor the management tools to exercise the authority conferred on him by the 1958 Act. That opportunity was left primarily to McNamara, who believed he should exercise his statutory authority fully. How he did so is one of the main subjects of this book.

During his year as Secretary of Defense, Clifford devoted the bulk of his attention to the Vietnam war, turning the day-to-day management of the Defense Department over to the Deputy Secretary. However, his retention of the entire McNamara management system, his strong support of the Systems Analysis office, and his vigorous role in the Vietnam strategy debate attest to his support of the active management view.

Despite the efforts of Gates, Clifford, and McNamara in particular, the active management view is not widely accepted today. There is still strong opposition to it. For example, in 1968 and 1969, the Chairman of the House Armed Services Committee tried to abolish the Office of the Assistant Secretary of Defense for Systems Analysis on the grounds that he believed the Secretary should not have a civilian-led staff of analysts advising him on matters of strategy and force requirements. Yet, for reasons we set forth in Chapter 3, the Secretary cannot exercise active leadership effectively in these areas without such a staff.

Much of the debate over specific issues is rooted in this basic disagreement over the Secretary's proper role. Thus, the two views are not just points in a historical trend; they also represent foundations for continuing controversy over how the Defense Department is to be managed.

Why should the Secretary of Defense provide active leadership in the determination of military strategy and force requirements? (In the Defense Department, the word "requirement" is generally used to mean the quantity of a weapon system or the amount of force that is needed to support the foreign policy of the United States.) Basically, for two reasons. First, as we noted earlier, foreign policy, military strategy, the choice of major weapons and forces, and defense budgets are all closely related matters of basic national security policy. At least at the level of decisions made in Washington, there are no "pure" military requirements. All issues of requirements involve political, economic, diplomatic, and technical factors as well as military ones. The Secretary of Defense cannot do his part in making and carrying out national security policy without active involvement in requirements issues.

Second, there is the matter of probable biases and inevitable institutional pressures on the military leaders who would shape the defense program under the traditional view. Picture, if you will, a man who has spent his entire adult life in the Air Force, flying bombers and leading bomber forces. Bombers are his professional commitment and his expertise. His chances for promotion, public recognition, and success, and those of the officers serving under him, are largely tied to the continued importance of bombers. He believes strongly in what he is doing; that is one of the main reasons he does it well. Now suppose—as happened in the late 1950's and early 1960's—that the development of the intercontinental ballistic missile (ICBM) makes bombers highly vulnerable and less useful as the nation's chief means of deterrence. The nation's needs shift from bombers to missiles. The Polaris missile-firing submarine is developed, and the nation's needs further shift from the Air Force to the Navy. It is no reflection on the honor, patriotism, or dedication of such a man to say that it is unreasonable to expect him to be objective about the shift of the strategic mission from bombers to missiles and from the Air Force to the Navy.

The traditional approach to dealing with this problem has been to say that this man must be made to compromise and reach agreement with another man who has spent a similar career in aircraft carriers. Not surprisingly, the easiest thing for them to agree on is *more* bombers and *more* carriers, and this, more often than not, is what happens. So this approach, rather than solving the problem, simply builds in pressures for more and more spending and creates another problem: that of spiraling and unmet military requirements. Before 1961, the response to this situation was for the Secretary of Defense to impose and enforce a financial limit without seriously involving himself in the matter of needs. There are at least two basic defects to this approach. First, it might just happen that more bombers and more carriers *are* needed. Second, there is no reason to suppose that, faced with this financial limit, the "bomber general" and the "carrier admiral" will agree to cut back their preferred weapons to make room for Polaris submarines. Their tendency will be to agree on bombers and carriers, especially to the extent that the matter depends on "judgment" rather than on explicit criteria of national need. Powerful institutional forces push them in that direction. And Polaris, being new, is not likely to be represented at the bargaining table.

This problem is not unique to bombers and carriers. It pervades the defense decision-making process. Nor is it a problem peculiar to defense planning. The same thing happens in universities. Does anyone expect the classics professor to be objective about a cut in his departmental budget in response to a shift in student interest from classics to physics? The same thing happens in hospitals among specialists dividing up the floor space and facilities. The same thing happens in civilian branches of government and in business. In short, the institutional factors working against the national interest in the defense establishment have their counterparts in all walks of life.

We believe that the only satisfactory answer to the problem is for the Secretary of Defense personally to shape the defense program in the national interest—to study the problems of strategy, force requirements, and budgets in detail, to explain and defend his conclusions to the Congress and the public, and to supervise the execution of his decisions. The Secretary of Defense, directly responsible to the President, and through the President to the nation as a whole, sits in the best place to do this. As McNamara once put it: "The Secretary of Defense—and I am talking about any Secretary of Defense—must make certain kinds of decisions, not because he presumes his judgment to be superior to [that of] his advisers, military or civilian, but because his position is the best place from which to make these decisions."[1] *

Military advice to the Secretary of Defense is essential. But the Secretary should not ask the military to do his job for him. And the Congress and the public should not assume that something is wrong if the Secretary doesn't always accept their advice.

To do this job effectively, the Secretary needs both management tools and independent staff assistance. In this book, we describe the

* Notes begin on page 339.

principal management tools developed during the years 1961–1968. We also describe the role played by the Systems Analysis office during this period.

The second main idea of the book is closely related to the first. The problems of military strategy and force requirements, though complex, can be grasped, analyzed, and understood. They can be importantly, even if not wholly, quantified. Satisfactory answers can and should be found through a combination of judgment and analysis. Defense issues can and should be decided on their merits. They need not and should not be approached solely on the basis of unaided personal judgment or on the personal authority or credibility of any particular set of advisers. In this book, we describe some of the analyses of force requirements done during the years 1961–1968.

Finally, a word about the book's general perspective. This book is concerned largely with the process of planning military strategy, forces, and budgets in the Defense Department, with specific emphasis on the role of the Systems Analysis office in that process. We discuss some of the shortcomings in this process before 1961, the major changes made by McNamara, and some important areas of unfinished business in 1969. The book is not intended to be, nor is it, a complete history of the McNamara years. Strategy, force, and financial planning are only one of the Secretary of Defense's many areas of responsibility. He also has responsibilities in the fields of foreign policy, military operations, defense procurement, financial management, personnel policies, research and development, and public affairs. Decisions and innovations were made, policies developed, and actions taken in each of these areas which were as important and controversial as the ones we discuss. The book is not about them because we have chosen to limit ourselves to matters with which we were directly involved and for which we were directly responsible when we were, respectively, Assistant Secretary of Defense for Systems Analysis and Special Assistant to the Assistant Secretary. For that reason, we do not discuss important events of the times, such as the Bay of Pigs invasion, the Cuban missile crisis, or the seizure of the *Pueblo*. Similarly, we are not qualified to write a firsthand account of such matters as the initial TFX decisions, the major decisions of the Vietnam war, or the cost overruns on the C-

5A, though we do comment briefly on each of these. We point this out now so there will be no confusion over where the reader is headed. Some may consider the world of military strategy, force planning, and budgets to be less exciting than the world of military operations and international crises, but it lies close to the heart of what much of national security policy is all about.

Some Areas of Unfinished Business in 1961

Between 1947 and 1961 substantial progress was made in improving the organization and legal structure of the U.S. defense establishment. The Office of the Secretary of Defense was created and gradually strengthened as a center-seeking force to counter the centrifugal thrust of the three Services. The Secretary's role slowly evolved from that of a relatively powerless arbiter to that of a major participant in the decision process. A unified budget structure was developed, encompassing all the funds for the Defense Department in a manageable number of appropriations. The process of welding the three separate Services into a workable whole had begun. The legal foundations were laid for strengthening DoD management in a number of areas. These accomplishments would be impressive under any conditions; they are doubly so in the face of the rapid political, economic, and technological changes taking place at home and abroad during this period. Despite this progress, however, there was much unfinished business in defense management in 1961, just as there was eight years later. At issue was not the men, many of whom were exceptionally able and made lasting contributions to the Defense Department; it was the philosophy, structure, and techniques of the Department's management system.

The need for further improvement in certain areas of Defense Department management, particularly budgeting, was widely recognized by 1961. President Eisenhower's farewell remarks concerning the potential dangers of the military-industrial complex marked the culmination of almost a decade of growing concern over defense management. The criticism was broadly based, originating from officials in the Executive Branch, members of the Congress, senior military officials, and private citizens. The lines of dissent and the reasons for them varied. Many critics stressed the importance to national security of assuring better integration of strategy, force planning, and budgets; others, the importance of correcting obvious imbalances in the force structure; others, the need to eliminate costly duplication in research and development (R&D) programs; and still others, the need for a more rational approach to making decisions on expensive weapon systems.

Inadequate Means for Central Leadership

A major piece of unfinished business was the lack of recognition of the responsibility of the Secretary of Defense for shaping the defense program in the national interest and the development of adequate means to permit him to do so. Defense decision making was predominantly committee decision making, reflecting the necessary compromises among the Department's various institutional and other vested interests. The Services held on to their traditional missions, which often corresponded to what they had been doing in the past and not necessarily to the changing national need. The system was conservative and resistant to change—especially to change that threatened vested interests. For example, the Air Force was dominated by the advocates of strategic air power, who had little interest in tactical air power. In fact, the Tactical Air Command was a poor cousin, and it tried to emulate the Strategic Air Command (SAC) by developing an overseas theater-based nuclear delivery capability, a kind of "junior SAC," rather than taking seriously the task of preparing to provide air support for the Army in a conventional war. To change Air Force thinking and build up tactical air power would require strong outside pressure. Indeed, in the early 1960's the Air Force resisted increases in tactical air forces decided upon by the Secretary of Defense for fear that they would come out of SAC's budget. Similarly, the more traditional branches in the Army resisted the innovations posed by helicopter mobility; again, in the early 1960's it took strong leadership from the Secretary of Defense to bring about the airmobile division. There were, of course, important innovations in the 1950's—the ICBM and the Polaris system, for example. But, for the most part, either these were extensions of existing missions and forces, and thus threatened no vested interests, or they were approved on the strength of (1) the fact that they were obvious, clear-cut matters of national importance and (2) the existence of strong pressure from the Congress and elsewhere outside DoD in their support.

The Secretary of Defense's role was still seen largely as that of a judge, not a leader. Even a Secretary of Defense who wanted to lead found it difficult, for he lacked the necessary information and control systems.

This situation persisted despite the fact that the need for increased central direction had been recognized in every defense reorganization act since World War II. The clear intent of these acts was to pull together into one place and into a few hands the major decision-making tasks on defense policy. Recognition of the need for a strong Secretary of Defense grew out of the lessons of combined land, sea, and air operations in World War II and Korea, the growing pressures for economy and efficiency, the strict controls on the use of force dictated by the risks of nuclear conflict, and the effects of rapid technological change. The United States could not afford independent military departments, each viewing the over-all security problems of the United States from its own perspective and developing force structures and weapon systems accordingly. For over two decades, members of the Congress and Presidents of both parties repeatedly demanded increased central control, both military and civilian.

But as of 1961, such centralization as existed was clearly unsatisfactory. The Services remained essentially independent entities. Each Service based its planning and force structures on a unilateral view of priorities and how a future war might be fought. Each had its own intelligence net (and intelligence estimates), its own supply system, its own ballistic missile programs. Each Service emphasized its own missions at the expense of joint missions. Each Service attempted to lay the groundwork for an increased share of the budget in future years. Each Service tried to protect the over-all size of its own force structure, sometimes at the cost of readiness and real combat capability. All decisions on these matters were made by dedicated military and civilian leaders, who were convinced that by acting in the best interests of their own Service they were acting in the best interests of the nation as well. But the result was not always balanced and adequate military forces. In 1961, for instance, the airlift furnished by the Air Force and the sealift furnished by the Navy were not sufficient for the timely movement of reinforcements planned by the Army to meet an attack in Europe. The Army was counting on close air support in a nonnuclear war, but the Tactical Air Command of the Air Force was concentrating almost exclusively on aircraft and ordnance for use in theater nuclear wars. And in all Services the maintenance of inventories of supplies required to support combat operations had been sacrificed to permit procurement of technologically advanced but operationally unreliable weapon systems.

Defense Budgeting

Another major piece of unfinished business concerned defense budgeting practices. The defense budget was far from the vital policy instrument it should have been. Rather than a mechanism for integrating strategy, forces, and costs, it was essentially a bookkeeping device for dividing funds between Services and accounts and a blunt instrument for keeping a lid on defense spending. The information contained in the defense budget was primarily useful for day-to-day administration of the hundreds of departments and agencies in DoD. It was not very useful for helping the President, members of the Congress, and the Secretary of Defense to establish priorities and choose between competing programs. In fact, by focusing their attention on individual appropriation titles such as procurement or construction or personnel rather than major missions such as strategic retaliatory forces or continental air defense forces, it detracted from making such judgments.

By the late 1950's, criticisms of defense budgeting practices were particularly severe. The Rockefeller Report on the problems of U.S. defense, published in 1958, recommended that a start be made toward a budgetary system that "corresponds more closely to a coherent strategic doctrine." "It should not be too difficult . . ." the report argued, "to restate the presentation of the Service budgets, so that instead of the present categories of 'procurement,' 'operation and maintenance,' 'military personnel,' etc., there would be a much better indication of how much goes, for example, to strategic air, to air defense, to anti-submarine warfare, etc."[2]

In his book *The Uncertain Trumpet,* former Army Chief of Staff General Maxwell D. Taylor expressed similar views about the then current DoD budget practices:

This method of budget-making by service has the serious defect of obscuring the impact of the budget upon the functional categories of the forces. In other words, the three services develop their forces more or less in isolation from each other, so that a force category such as the strategic retaliatory force, which consists of contributions of both the Navy and the Air Force, is never viewed in the aggregate. Similarly, it is impossible to tell exactly how much continental air defense is being obtained from the defense budget since this is another category to which several services contribute. In other words, we look at our forces horizontally when we think of combat functions but we view them vertically in developing the defense budget.[3]

Senator Lyndon B. Johnson, then Chairman of the Senate Preparedness Investigating Subcommittee, pointed out the consequences of having a budget focused on unrelated items of expenditure rather than on the major missions of the Defense Department:

Two of the members of the Joint Chiefs of Staff agree that too much money is being spent during fiscal year 1959 for defense against manned bombers, yet the Department of Defense had no specific figures as to how much was being devoted to continental air defense in the 1960 budget. Furthermore, despite all the glowing statements and promises concerning unification in the Department of Defense, the testimony before this and other committees clearly shows that the 1960 budget was never considered, nor were decisions made, on a functional basis for the Department of Defense as a whole but rather decisions were made on a service-by-service basis in relation to individual expenditure targets.[4]

Many critics of defense budgeting practices hoped that more meaningful fiscal presentations would permit more rational use of resources. The House Appropriations Committee, one of the severest critics of defense budgeting practices before 1961, recommended the following:

The Joint Chiefs of Staff should look at what is available for what purposes and attempt to match it with the needs. As an example, the Joint Chiefs should take a look at the combined forces of the Marine Corps and the Army. It is not a question of combining the Army and Marine Corps.

It is merely a question of looking at the combined strength and the combined capability of these two great forces in making the final determination as to what our ground force should be providing for our commitments throughout the world.[5]

Perhaps the key reason for the limited usefulness of the defense budget was the fact that defense budgeting was, in effect, conceived as being largely unrelated to military strategy. The two were treated as almost independent activities. They were carried out by different people, at different times, with different terms of reference, and without a method for integrating their activities. The strategy and forces were thought to be essentially military matters, while the budget was thought to be mainly a civilian matter. Force planning was done for several years into the future, by military men, on a mission-oriented basis, by the Services with attempts at coordination by the JCS organization. Financial planning was done one year at a time, largely by civilians, in terms of object classes of expenditures such as personnel and procurement, through the Service and DoD Comptroller organizations. This gap between strategy and forces, on the one hand, and budgets, on the other, posed a serious obstacle to rational defense planning.

In addition, defense budgets represented essentially predetermined, arbitrary ceilings in the sense that they did not follow from decisions about strategy, military needs, and weapon systems. Starting with the Truman administration and continuing under Eisenhower, the President, relatively early in the budget cycle, provided guidance to the Secretary of Defense on the size of the defense budget which he thought economically and politically feasible for the next fiscal year. The problem was that this figure was usually arrived at by simply estimating the government's total revenues, then deducting fixed payments (such as interest on the national debt and payments to veterans), the estimated costs of domestic programs, and expenditures on foreign aid. Whatever "remained" was then allocated to the military.[6] The strategic implications of these budget guidelines were not explicitly and systematically considered. Once the President had decided on an acceptable defense budget, the Secretary of Defense then determined and enforced a fixed percentage among the Services. Largely because the fractions set in each year's budget guidelines were an extrapolation of the fractions in the previous budget, from 1954 to 1961 the allocations remained remarkably constant at about 47 percent for the Air Force, 29 percent for the Navy and Marine Corps, and 24 percent for the Army. Each Service in turn fixed allocations among its various components in accordance with its internal institutional pressures and its own interpretation of the guidance on national strategy and priorities infrequently set forth by the National Security Council in a paper called Basic National Security Policy (BNSP).

Difficulties beset the entire procedure. BNSP was a vague and general document that provided little real guidance on how defense dollars should be spent. General Taylor summarized the document's weakness as follows:

[It is] so broad in nature and so general in language as to provide limited guidance in practical application. In the course of its development, the sharp issues in national defense which confront our leaders have been blurred in conference and in negotiation. The final text thus permits many different interpretations. The protagonists of Massive Retaliation or of Flexible Response, the partisans of the importance of air power or of limited war, as well as the defenders of other shades of military opinion, are able to find language supporting their divergent points of view. The "Basic National Security Policy" document means all things to all people and settles nothing.[7]

The results of requirements planning done without explicit regard to costs, and budget planning done without explicit regard to needs, were absolutely predictable: open-ended requirements met arbitrary budget ceilings, and something had to give. Again, predictably, it was military requirements. The idea became accepted that the budget would meet less than the full stated requirement in any given year, with whatever remained being an unanalyzed "risk" to be accepted by the administration. Thus, the administration had its budget, the military its requirements. This approach was bound to produce imbalances and inconsistencies. Half of a $100-billion defense program chosen unsystematically is very different from a balanced, carefully chosen $50-billion program.

Moreover, this method of determining the defense budget focused the attention of civilian leaders almost exclusively on the total budget level, to the exclusion of direct and serious concern with related military effectiveness and need. The main concern of the Secretary of Defense and his staff was with cutting the Service requests to fit predetermined budget limits. Although many individual members of the Office of the Secretary of Defense (OSD) felt personally concerned about the effectiveness of the military forces, there was no organized effort on the part of OSD to assure adequate but economical forces. As General Taylor put it at the time: "It is not an exaggeration to say that nobody knows what we are actually buying with any specific budget."[8]

Another result of this approach was that when the Secretary of Defense was forced to make a cut, he had no adequate way of relating individual Service priorities to the over-all national strategy and force structure. In 1958, for example, the Senate Armed Services Committee told Secretary McElroy to select either the Army's Nike-Hercules or the Air Force's Bomarc as the continental air defense missile, but not both. The next year, McElroy told the committee that his office had not been able to decide on a division of funds for Hercules and Bomarc. He suggested that the Congress "hold our feet to the fire." The Armed Services Committees of both the Senate and the House examined identical sets of facts and arrived at opposite conclusions. The Services' opinions were as follows:

- Army: interceptors and Nike-Hercules but no Bomarc.
- Air Force: interceptors and Bomarc but no Nike-Hercules.
- Navy: no more forces needed for continental air defense.

Since no agreement could be reached among the Services, an arbitrary cut was made across all forces involved.

The unchanging budget fractions did not reflect the changing relative needs of the Services. For example, the Army's need for new procurement money was low in the mid-1950's because it had inherited excess equipment from Korean war production and a large unspent backlog of funds from Korean war appropriations. By the late 1950's, however, the Army badly needed funds for modernization of its equipment; yet its share of the total defense budget during this period remained almost constant. Similarly, in the early 1960's, if the Nike-Zeus antiballistic missile (ABM) defense system had been approved, the Army would have had to take the funds for it out of something else—doubtless from land forces, although there is little logic in the proposition that an increase in ABM defense spending must be accompanied by an equal and offsetting decrease in spending on land forces. Similarly, during the 1950's the Navy was building aircraft carriers at the rate of almost one per year. Obviously, this was something that would not have to go on indefinitely. The Navy could surely have found alternative uses for that shipbuilding money, but it is not obvious that the best national use was more shipbuilding. It might have made sense, for example, to take advantage of the reduction in Navy procurement needs when the carrier fleet was nearly complete by transferring the remaining funds to the Army for its equipment procurement or to the Air Force for its ballistic missile program.

The use of arbitrary budget ceilings and inflexible Service fractions also encouraged the idea that each Service was "entitled" to that much money and could count on its percentage, regardless of the effectiveness of its programs in meeting the nation's needs. This approach fostered, in addition, the idea that if the Secretary of Defense or someone on his staff favored a particular program, they would have to find the means to pay for it. Perhaps the most spectacular illustration of this was the Navy's reluctance to include much for the Polaris program in its budget at a time of very great national need. The development of the ICBM by the Soviet Union in the late 1950's and early 1960's made U.S. strategic retaliatory forces, then mostly bombers, extremely vulnerable to surprise attack. (While it subsequently became clear that the missile gap was not real—only that development had not yet become production— the prospective vulnerability of the bombers was real and serious.) The Minuteman program of ICBM's based underground in dispersed concrete and steel blast-resistant silos, and the Polaris program of intermediate-range ballistic missiles based in submarines, were both solutions to this problem and matters of vital national necessity. Nevertheless, in its budget requests for fiscal years 1961 and 1962, the Navy budgeted for only three Polaris submarines in each year. One of the first things that President Kennedy and

Secretary McNamara did when they came into office was to speed up the Polaris program and to authorize the building of ten Polaris submarines in each of these fiscal years. Nobody, to our knowledge, has since questioned the necessity or the wisdom of that action. But at the time, senior Navy officers, when confronted with arguments for increasing the Polaris program based on urgent national need, replied: "Polaris is a *national* program, not a Navy program." By this was meant: the Polaris mission is not a traditional Navy mission and therefore should not be financed out of the Navy's share of the defense budget. That was a rather disappointing thought for those who liked to think of the whole Navy as a national program.

The Navy's point, that a reduction in other Navy programs was not necessarily the logical source of funds for Polaris, was a good one; a cutback in Air Force bomber procurement would have been a more logical choice. But the fact that Polaris was a more urgent national need than other Navy programs, and that the Navy did not recognize this in its proposed budget, does illustrate the fallacy of budgeting by Service rather than by mission.

Arbitrary budget ceilings and the extrapolation of existing Service fractions year after year led the Services to develop an extensive arsenal of tactics for attempts to increase their share of the total defense budget. One such Service tactic was to hold on to its force structure, even if it could not be supported with available manpower and matériel. Thus, for years the Army held on to a force structure of fourteen divisions on paper even when it did not have the funds to support ten. The chief result of spreading resources so thin was that while the Army had its fourteen divisions, the nation had few divisions that were fully ready and usable. But using the fourteen paper divisions as a point of departure, however, greatly strengthened the Army's hand in the negotiations over budgets. By having a force structure larger than could be adequately supported, the Army was able to point to unmet needs ("shortages") as a basis for claiming a larger budget. (As some cynics have remarked: "The worst thing you can do to a Service is take away its shortages.")

Another such tactic was the "foot in the door," or the "thin edge of the budget wedge." A Service would buy into a new weapon system by understating its cost or purchasing only the major items of capital equipment now, without asking for all the necessary personnel and support items. Again, it would later point to these deficiencies and try to get money to correct them. The consequences of this tactic can be seen in General Curtis LeMay's testimony in 1956 before the Senate Subcommittee on the Air Force:

Next, let's look at the expansion that has taken place in SAC. For the period January 1953 through January 1956 we see the expansion in bases, units and personnel. We have had 123 percent increase in our air refueling squadrons, a 77 percent increase in bases and a 35 percent increase in wings, with only a 20 percent increase in personnel. This means that we have had to spread our trained resources very thin. In fact, we have had to spread it too thin. This had its impact on our combat capability. . . .

In general terms, the plan for expansion of the Air Force has developed ahead of the base structure to support it. The building of the bases has lagged behind the production of airplanes to form the wings; this has resulted in a shortage of bases and a crowding up of units and aircraft on bases.[9]

The trouble with this budget tactic is clear: it can lead to imbalances that deprive the United States of needed military capability. The strategic bombers for which the United States was paying so much money were not yielding the military power they should have, because they did not have all the supporting elements needed to make them a fully effective weapon system. Bombers without personnel or bases are useless; the nation would be better off with fewer bombers and more support.

McNamara had a name for another technique used by the Services: "slashing the gold watches." Once while at Ford, after reducing a department's budget, he got a howl of protest because the department's manager, instead of working toward cutting waste and improving efficiency, sought to meet his new budget by cutting out the customary presentation of gold watches to men who retired after forty years or more of service. The annual battle between the Congress and the Post Office with threats to cut back on home mail deliveries is an example of the same tactic. The pre-1961 defense program contained many distortions caused by such bargaining tactics.

The fact that financial planning for the Defense Department looked only a year ahead also led to a number of serious consequences. Because total systems costs (operations as well as procurement, support as well as direct costs) were not known and therefore not used in making procurement decisions, program decisions were, in effect, made in ignorance of their future cost implications. Programs were approved without corresponding changes in budget limits. Thus, when budget time came, all the real program decision making had to be redone.

This one-year-at-a-time financial planning in the context of separate financial and force planning laid undue emphasis on *this* year's costs to the neglect of effectiveness and future costs. The Services were quite willing to cut this year's budget for a new weapon system in order to get the program started, and the budget examiners were glad to make the same cut in order to reduce this year's budget.

A good example of overemphasizing current costs was the rejection of the 1957 Cordiner Commission's recommendations for military pay increases in skill areas that were in short supply. The Commission justified its recommendations with detailed calculations showing that in a few years, because fewer highly skilled servicemen would be hired away by lucrative civilian jobs, the pay increases would more than pay for themselves by reductions in training costs. However, lacking a multiyear financial plan, the Eisenhower administration had no way of seeing the probable future savings and therefore turned down the proposal on the basis of increased present costs. But genuine economies often require the expenditure of more money now to save proportionately greater amounts of money in the future.

Another consequence of one-year financial planning was that (when combined with expenditure limits and the many incentives for the Services to start new weapon systems) it led to overcommitment, which led in turn to costly cancellations and stretch-outs that could have been foreseen with a longer-range financial planning system. The House Appropriations Committee in its report in 1960 described the problem this way:

Piecemeal financing resulting from conformity to fixed expenditure ceilings, coupled with the attempt to keep going as many as possible of the promising programs, has all too often resulted in weapon systems being advanced to the readiness-for-production stage much too late to be of maximum effectiveness for the purpose intended. In too many instances these programs were delayed, cut back, or stretched out, because of the expenditure limitations. As a result valuable time was lost and the weapon systems became obsolete before they could be developed. It is the sad story of "too little, too late."

Simply stated, the problem is merely one of taking into account the full implications of the entire financial burden over the life, involving a period of years, of each and every military development project at the earliest possible date. This has not been done in the past, and particularly at the highest levels in the Executive Branch where control has tended in recent years to evolve to that of the single expenditure limitation. The expenditure limitation is such an easy method of establishing a control it can be exercised by a single person in a key decisionmaking position. This method of control, however, tends to ignore the detailed project evaluation of expert staff at lower levels, procedures for which have evolved over a period of many years.[10]

In defense planning, a year is arbitrary and short. By 1968, defense officials often found it necessary to look at forces and costs both as far in the future as 1977 and as far in the past as 1961 for an adequate perspective on trends and changes. A single year's look is bound to lead to a faulty perspective. As the Senate Subcommittee on National Policy Machinery put it:

Particularly in the area of national security, our Government needs to extend its budgetary time horizons farther in the future. We need to know where the cost of present plans and activities may take us, not simply through the next fiscal year, but for several years ahead.

A 12-month budget reveals only the tip of the fiscal iceberg. The initial outlays for the man to the moon program will result in billions of dollars being spent during the remainder of this decade. The development of major weapon systems and foreign aid programs are other obvious cases in point. Cost estimates, to be meaningful, must be based on the full expected lifetime of programs.[11]

Among the attempts at fixing the pre-1961 budgeting system was a "priority" budgeting scheme. Under this system, the Services were asked to prepare three or sometimes four budgets (called A, B, C, and D budgets) at different funding levels set by OSD. The priority aspect of the budget was that, in theory, successively higher budgets contained items with a lower relative priority or value to the overall defense posture. The main problem with this scheme was that the *Services,* not the Secretary of Defense, chose the priorities. The Services could put the carriers and bombers in the low budget and most of the Polaris and Minuteman missile programs in the higher budget, thereby using gamesmanship to get money for pet programs, items which they wanted but which the Secretary of Defense was unenthusiastic about. Moreover, even if the Services had played fair, they, not the Secretary of Defense, had the initiative in putting the budget together, since individual Service plans, not Department-wide plans, were the basis for their priorities.

Lack of a Central Plan

One reason for the lack of strong central leadership and integrated force and financial planning was the complete absence of a central plan to give balance and coherence to the whole effort. For example, Navy briefings to the Secretary of Defense in 1961 on the number of Polaris missile submarines required never mentioned the existence of the U.S. Air Force, although most of the strategic retaliatory forces were in the Air Force. When the Air Force made analyses of how many Minuteman missiles were required, it assumed that no more Polaris submarines would be authorized than whatever the existing number happened to be. Neither Service had recourse to any authoritative statement of the approved force structure plan of the other Services. The Army did not have an authoritative statement of how much airlift was being planned for it, against which to plan its own forces; and the Air Force did not have an authoritative statement of how many Army divisions were being planned or what their readiness was intended to be. There was great and unnecessary duplication in some areas, combined with shortages and imbalances in other areas. The lack of a unified plan approved by the Secretary of Defense meant that there was no firm base for planning or for the evaluation of individual Service proposals.

Likewise, individual Service planning was deficient and lacked integration of forces and finances. Indeed, as late as 1966 the Army still had no single, authoritative force plan. It had one plan for personnel, another for procurement, another for strategic planning with the JCS, and so on; but none was centrally controlled and

integrated by the Army. Field commanders had the authority to
change their units' tables of organization and equipment (TO&E's)
and to do so in such a manner that requirements grew without limit
and without adequate management control. The lack of central
control and integration meant, for example, that the logistic, manpower, and financial planners had no systematic way of knowing
when requirements had increased, and they were not consulted
about the feasibility of the increases. Thus, this "TO&E creep" was
a continuing source of paper shortages.

Duplication in R&D

During the 1950's, there was a great deal of concern about unnecessary duplication and overlap in research and development
programs. Although there is room for differing opinion on what was
unnecessary duplication and what was necessary insurance, several
programs—the full development and deployment of both the Air
Force's Thor and the Army's Jupiter intermediate-range ballistic
missiles, for example—represented clear-cut cases of unnecessary
duplication. In many ways, the management system encouraged
duplication. The Services had every incentive to start up as many
promising new systems as they could in an effort to strengthen their
claims to larger shares of future budgets. Thus, in 1960, more than
a dozen systems were either in procurement or in engineering
development for the intercontinental delivery of nuclear weapons.
Later analysis indicated that about half of those systems were
unnecessary and that some should never have been started in the
first place. We are referring, for example, to the Snark subsonic
cruise missile and the Skybolt air-launched ballistic missile, both of
which combined the disadvantages of the bomber (vulnerability on
the ground and slow time to target) with the disadvantages of the
missile (small pay load and relatively low accuracy and reliability);
and to the B-70 and the B-58 bombers, both of which were based on
the incorrect premise that high speed and high altitude were the
most effective way to penetrate enemy defenses.

In May 1957, the House Appropriations Committee indicated its
displeasure with this costly duplication. According to the Committee: "Each service, it would seem, is striving to acquire an arsenal of

weapons complete in itself to carry out any and all possible missions. It is the firm belief of the committee that this matter of rivalry is getting completely out of control. It is expensive and undesirable, and points up the need for more effective direction and control."[12] Three years later the same Committee, in its report accompanying the 1961 Department of Defense appropriations bill, said:

What is happening . . . is that the military services are allowed to proceed with a multiplicity of development projects up to the point where further development or production bumps against a rigid expenditure ceiling. It is often only at this point that a decision is made as to whether or not to proceed further with a particular project. Consequently, many projects are canceled at this point in time not because they are not successful or desirable developments, but only because to proceed further would involve the expenditure of funds in excess of a preconceived expenditure limitation.[13]

The Committee then recommended the following:

The present system should be revised to permit the orderly development of alternative approaches to weapons systems on a development basis only. The system should recognize the necessity to eliminate alternatives at the time a decision is made for quantity production. It is this decision that is all important. At this point there should be a full evaluation of: (1) the military potential of the system in terms of need and time in relation to other developments, by all the military services, and (2) its follow-on expenditure impact if approved for quantity production.[14]

Lack of Quantitative Standards of Adequacy

The almost complete lack of quantitative standards of adequacy for U.S. forces provided another major piece of unfinished business. More importantly, no major participant in the force planning and budgeting process was seriously trying to develop them. The intense battle over budgets drew top-level attention away from military needs and effectiveness. There were no Department-wide readiness standards or reports. The Secretary of Defense was not regularly informed on the readiness of the combat forces; indeed, readiness was apparently not defined in a measurable way. There were no criteria, however crude, for how much strategic retaliatory power, or how much tactical air power, was enough. Indeed, it is doubtful that anyone even knew exactly how much tactical air power the United States had, judging by the difficulties the Systems Analysis staff faced, in the early 1960's, in trying to take a precise Department-wide inventory of tactical aircraft. This lack of quantitative standards of adequacy meant that, in many cases, "minimum" military requirements were 30 percent more than what we had, whatever we had. More seriously, the main product of the Defense Department—combat-ready forces able to support the foreign policy of the United States—seemed to be a rather incidental by-product of the management and budgetary system.

These are rather remarkable facts that have been little understood. Many people seem to think our military leaders have always had precise standards for military requirements that enabled them to derive the forces needed to support national strategy. But as General Taylor has reminded us: ". . . the Joint Chiefs of Staff have all the faults of a committee in settling controversial matters. They must consider and accommodate many divergent views before action can be taken. In seeking unanimity, they spend much time trying to overcome dissent."[15] Thus the Chiefs were kept busy negotiating individual Service proposals based largely on institutional interests and estimates of what the traffic would bear. No systematic attempt was made to analyze and develop criteria for answering the question, "How much is enough?" Again, in General Taylor's words: "A thorny matter, such as the determination of 'how much is enough' for the size of the Strategic Air Command and the other atomic deterrent forces, can be and has been sidestepped for years."[16]

The Senate Subcommittee on National Policy Machinery, chaired by Senator Henry M. Jackson, put it this way:

Business has a yardstick for judging its effectiveness—profit and loss statements. Efficiently run private enterprises also hold their managers strictly accountable for results.

It is necessarily more difficult for our Government to determine how well its national security programs are faring. By what criteria do we measure the success or failure of some assistance programs? How do we judge whether we are getting the most for our money?

Granted the difficulties, our Government pays insufficient attention to this problem of performance measurement. The whole field is almost unexplored.[17]

Cost Estimates

The lack of reliable information on the costs of weapon systems provided yet another area of unfinished business. While the Air Force was well along in developing total-weapon-system cost estimates, the other Services were hardly aware of the concept. Similarly, information was lacking on the costs of major military missions. No one really knew, because there was no way of knowing, how much the United States was spending on strategic offensive forces, continental air defense, tactical air, and the like. Nor did any responsible OSD official have a reliable estimate of the total impact on defense spending of adding, say, another wing of B-52 bombers. Only the procurement costs and a few other bits and pieces were identified with the B-52's.

Without good cost estimates, the management of R&D programs presented serious problems. We have already alluded to the understatement of the costs of new weapons as a way of "buying in" to new programs and to OSD acceptance of these understatements because they provided a way of holding down this year's budget. Studies done at The Rand Corporation and the Harvard Business School in the late 1950's and early 1960's indicated that new weapon systems generally ended up costing two to three times as much as they were estimated to cost when the program was originally approved, even after allowing for changes in the over-all price level and changes in the quantity produced.[18]

Slippages in schedules and considerable shortfalls in effectiveness and performance were also the rule. These deficiencies, when coupled with the primitive state of the art in weapon-system cost estimating, contributed to gross underestimates of the costs of new weapon systems. Such underestimates biased decisions against improving U.S. military effectiveness *now* and in favor of developing new systems, which in fact rarely materialized when and as promised. Current effectiveness was sacrificed in favor of a future effectiveness that was often never realized. To make matters worse, the bias was unsystematic. In some cases, the underestimation in cost was threefold; in other cases, it was six-, eight-, or even tenfold. Any comparisons of effectiveness in relation to cost were bound to be unreliable. The result was an R&D effort which too often seemed to operate on the principle, "None of the present systems work as well as they should, but all future systems will work perfectly!"

Part of the reason for the continued slippage and increased costs can be attributed to the R&D philosophy being followed in the 1950's. According to this philosophy, to take advantage of the latest technology, each new weapon system should incorporate the latest advances in every aspect of the state of the art. If a new airplane was to be built, for example, the theory called for developing a new engine, a new airframe, and a new fire-control or electronic system —all on such a schedule that they would be brought together for assembly at the same time. Supposedly, this would save money by weeding out projects unrelated to a new weapon system. The trouble with this philosophy was its implicit assumption that one can schedule inventions and that new technology is predictable. Experience showed that new airplanes rarely ended up with the engine or fire-control system originally intended for them. In the real world, one or two of the components might appear on time, but others would fail to progress as projected. As a result, development costs would come out much higher, and the total system would be completed much later than had been originally planned.

In most cases during the 1950's and early 1960's, the escalation in project costs not only reflected the near impossibility of successfully estimating and executing the many interacting innovations typically called for at the time projects were started; it also reflected innumerable changes along the way—not just changes to solve unexpected problems but changes approved to take advantage of the latest technologies. Thus, a self-propelling tendency toward cost escalation, schedule slippages, and performance inadequacies was built into the system. Projects were approved on the basis of a given technology. Then new technologies evolved. These were swiftly perceived as new opportunities for greater "performance" and as making the preexisting techniques obsolete. Changes were approved, and with them higher costs, delays, and unforeseen technical problems as the new techniques were merged with the rest of the system.

A typical result of this process was the splintering of an initial project into several projects. For example, the F-102 airplane became the F-102 and the F-106. The Atlas ICBM became Atlas A, Atlas B, Atlas C, and Atlas D. Titan became Titan I and Titan II.

In fact, so many weapon systems were started for precisely the same basic purpose that, once begun, changes were not only permitted but encouraged. The dictum seemed to be, "I can, therefore I must." Thus, new technological possibilities became new military requirements. In some cases, such as the development of nuclear fission and later, nuclear fusion, this sequence was necessary and correct. The trouble is that not every qualitative change in technique is the military equivalent of the hydrogen bomb.

The growth of this pattern during more than a decade, starting about 1950, had enormously inflated the cost of weapons development, choked the system with too many projects that could not be properly supported, and led to the creation of technologically impressive but militarily useless weapon systems. As was often said in the late 1950's and early 1960's, the better had become the enemy of the good.

Lack of OSD Staff Assistance in Requirements Planning

Finally, the Secretary of Defense had no full-time staff help, responsive to him and independent of Service interests, on the main product of the Department of Defense: military strategy and force requirements. All the Secretary's Presidentially appointed civilian assistants had areas of responsibility corresponding to traditional civilian skills, such as finance, science and technology, personnel management, and production. Strategy and force requirements were assumed to be a military preserve, despite the many nonmilitary factors obviously involved. What is wrong with this idea will be discussed in detail in Chapter 3. But let us make clear now that the issue is not whether the military's voice should be the main source of advice on questions concerning strategy and force requirements; it is and it should be. The issue is whether it should be the *only* voice—whether the Secretary of Defense also needs *independent* staff assistance on these questions. We believe that he does. Civilians with an independent and more objective point of view who can

bring their own planning, analytical, and management skills to
bear on these questions can make an important and necessary contribution.

In outlining these areas of unfinished business in defense management in 1961, we do not want to suggest that they were all
solved in the next eight years. They weren't. Many are still with us.
Some are perhaps insoluble. But between 1961 and 1969, some were
solved, others were greatly ameliorated, and some were perhaps
made worse. One purpose of this book is to record the development
of some of the concepts and tools, newly fashioned or borrowed,
that were used to deal with these problems. We believe that it is
vital to the security of our country that the efforts to solve them be
continued.

The state of DoD management of strategy, forces, and budgets in
1961 is aptly summarized in two memorandums that were handed
to one of the authors when he joined the Comptroller's office in
January of that year. The first is a letter to Secretary of Defense
Neil McElroy dated August 18, 1959, from Congressman George
Mahon, then Chairman of the House Defense Appropriations Subcommittee. The second is a note concerning Mahon's letter written
to Deputy Secretary of Defense Thomas S. Gates on November 17,
1959, by one of Mr. Gates's military assistants. The two are reprinted below:

HOUSE OF REPRESENTATIVES
COMMITTEE ON APPROPRIATIONS
August 18, 1959

Honorable Neil McElroy
Secretary of Defense
Washington 25, D.C.

My Dear Mr. Secretary:

Now that the Congress has completed work on the 1960 Defense
Appropriation Bill, I would like to suggest some revisions in Departmental justifications that may be helpful to both the Department and the
Congress during review of the 1961 estimates. The revised budget structure adopted for the 1960 estimates has proven somewhat helpful,

however, certain revisions in the manner of presenting justification detail could be of greater benefit.

It would be most desirable if, in consideration of the 1961 military personnel and operation and maintenance estimates, the Committee were provided with budget back-up material on a major command basis. That is, all activities in each Service budget for these appropriations should be identified under the Command title from which each received military direction. The service of primary dominance in each unified Command should be responsible for bringing together all parts of a Command budget for special presentation requirements.

In addition to the Command breakout within appropriations, it is requested that an overall military forces presentation be prepared in considerable detail showing the manpower, major equipment and money, as reflected in the 1961 defense budget, to be assigned in the following suggested major areas:

1. Atomic retaliatory forces (identified with target assignments):
   a. Strategic Air Command forces.
   b. Tactical Air Command forces—which may be assigned to this mission (even though duplicated in other assignments).
   c. Navy attack carrier forces—which may be assigned to this mission (even though duplicated in other assignments).
   d. Navy POLARIS missile submarine forces.
   e. Army missile forces—which may be assigned to this mission (even though duplicated in other assignments).
2. Continental air defense forces:
   (Air Force, Army and Navy forces which may be assigned to this mission including warning and communications systems).
3. Strategic reserve forces:
   (Army, Marine Corps, Air Force and Navy forces which may be assigned to this mission [even though duplicated in other assignments], including air and sealift forces).
4. Forces deployed overseas as a part of our national commitments:
   (Army, Navy and Air Force [even though duplicated in other assignments], showing the where and why of such deployment).
5. Forces which may be assigned to maintaining sea and air lines of communication: (Navy anti-submarine warfare and patrol—others).
6. Reserve forces:
   (Manpower, equipment and mobilization reserves in supplies, equipment, facilities and production capability).

It is believed that such presentations in connection with the 1961 budget will be very helpful to both the Committee and the Department. Members of the Defense Subcommittee staff will be available to discuss with your people the details of this request.

Sincerely yours,
/ s/ George H. Mahon

OFFICE OF THE SECRETARY OF DEFENSE

November 17, 1959

MEMO FOR: Mr. Gates

SUBJECT: Functional Breakdown for the Budget

Mr. Sprague's [a Deputy Assistant Secretary of Defense] office has made an effort, working with the Services, to break down the '61 Defense budget into the major areas suggested by Congressman Mahon. The results within the building were that the Navy did not think it could be done, the Air Force doubted that it could be done, and the Army thought it could be done and submitted the best figures.

After studying the Service submissions, the Comptroller's office feels that: (1) it is extremely difficult to get figures (on the major areas Mahon has suggested) that DoD can stand behind in its testimony to Congress; and (2) even if the Comptroller were able to assemble such figures, there does not appear to be any agreed strategy against which the adequacy of the figures could be measured. (In other words, everyone has his own individual strategy, including Mr. Stans [the Director of the Bureau of the Budget], Dr. York [the Director of Defense Research and Engineering], the three Services, etc.)

Mr. Mahon is seeing Secretary McElroy next Monday and it is understood that the Secretary will discuss this problem with him at that time.

/ s/ E. F. Black

2

New Concepts and New Tools to Shape the Defense Program

By January 1961, there was widespread recognition of the need for improvement in defense management. Through studies done at The Rand Corporation, the Harvard Business School, and elsewhere, many of the weaknesses in the current approach to defense management had been identified. Congressional leaders had expressed a desire for reforms. The 1958 Act had provided the Secretary of Defense with the legal authority he needed if he was to play an active part in shaping the defense program, but it had not yet been fully used. Because of the enormous size and complexity of the defense program and the strong commitments of many to things as they were, the necessary reforms could not be made without strong leadership from the Secretary of Defense.

Secretary McNamara brought not only extraordinary managerial ability and drive but also a new concept of management to the Department of Defense. He made it clear at the outset that he intended to exercise fully his statutory authority, that he wanted all defense problems approached in a rational and analytical way, and that he wanted them resolved on the basis of the national interest. He insisted on integrating and balancing the nation's foreign policy, military strategy, force requirements, and defense budget. In

March 1961, he shocked the Department by assigning ninety-six separate projects (complete with specific questions and deadlines) to its various components for analysis and review. Many of the projects concerned items that had long been considered sacrosanct. He made clear his belief in active management from the top. As he described it:

In many aspects the role of a public manager is similar to that of a private manager. In each case he may follow one of two alternative courses. He can act rather as a judge or as a leader. As the former he waits until subordinates bring him problems for solution, or alternatives for choice. In the latter case, he immerses himself in his operation, leads and stimulates an examination of the objectives, the problems and the alternatives. In my own case, and specifically with regard to the Department of Defense, the responsible choice seemed clear.[1]

The role that McNamara chose was not an inevitable one. As noted previously, the accepted role of the Secretary of Defense before 1961 was that of a referee. And there were compelling reasons for McNamara to have accepted that role: refereeing the Services' struggles over limited funds is less demanding personally and less risky politically. It is also less threatening to vested Service interests and more satisfactory to some members of the Congress. It takes courage for the Secretary of Defense to be a leader, to become personally involved in shaping strategy and forces.

The Planning-Programming-Budgeting System: The Fundamental Ideas

While McNamara was determined to lead, the available management information and control systems for him to do so were inadequate. He found that the Secretary of Defense had the legal authority and responsibility for defense decisions, but lacked adequate ways to exercise his authority and meet his responsibility. As McNamara described the situation:

From the beginning in January 1961, it seemed to me that the principal problem in efficient management of the Department's resources was not the lack of management authority. The problem was rather the absence of the essential management tools needed to make sound decisions on the really crucial issues of national security.[2]

To obtain the needed information and control systems, McNamara turned to his Comptroller, Charles J. Hitch. Hitch, formerly Head of the Economics Division at Rand, was one of the nation's leading authorities on program budgeting and the application of economic analysis to defense problems. McNamara charged him with the responsibility for making a systematic analysis of all requirements and incorporating these into a five-year, program-oriented defense budget, the first of which was to be completed in nine months. Hitch met his goal. He led the establishment in DoD of what, years later, came to be known as the Planning-Programming-Budgeting System, or simply "PPBS." In recent years, PPBS has been discussed at great length. It is not our purpose here to repeat all the arguments for and against it.[3] It is our purpose, however, to identify the basic ideas that served as the intellectual foundation for PPBS as it operated in DoD until January 1969.

Decision Making on the Basis of the National Interest

The fundamental idea behind PPBS was decision making based on explicit criteria of the national interest in defense programs, as opposed to decision making by compromise among various institutional, parochial, or other vested interests in the Defense Department. The main purpose of PPBS was to develop explicit criteria, openly and thoroughly debated by all interested parties, that could be used by the Secretary of Defense, the President, and the Congress as measures of the need for and adequacy of defense programs. In developing the defense program, it is the Secretary of Defense who is charged with ensuring that the interests of the nation take precedence over the special institutional interests of the military departments, the defense contractors, the scientists, the localities, and other groups that make up or depend on the Defense Department. To do so, he must examine proposals from a broader perspective than that of the organization proposing them, choose among real alternatives, and ascertain at what point further spending on a given military program results in incremental gains so small that it is no longer justified. Thus, PPBS starts with a search for plain statements of the openly defensible national purposes that each program is meant to serve, for alternative ways of achieving these purposes, and for criteria by which to judge competing alternatives. This idea provides both the goal and the rationale for PPBS.

The implementation of this idea led to a greater centralization of major-program decision making in the Office of the Secretary of Defense (OSD). This led in turn to charges of overcentralization. But we are convinced that there is no viable alternative to centralization of major policy decisions regarding strategy, force, and financial planning. (This is not true of all policy decisions or execution, however.) The revolution in military technology alone makes this almost imperative. The great technical complexity of modern weapons, their enormous cost, and their lengthy period of development place an extraordinary premium on sound choices for major weapon systems. For the top management of DoD, these choices have become the key decisions around which much of the defense program revolves. They cannot be made piecemeal by several separate and perhaps competing subordinate echelons. They must be directly related to national security objectives rather than to the tasks of any one of the Services. A centralized decision-making authority is needed at the top to attain and exercise the over-all perspective necessary to integrate the contributing parts into a coherent whole. Finally, decentralized decision making in strategy and force planning simply has not worked.

The success of the effort to develop criteria of the national interest in defense programs has varied widely. In some areas, good measures were developed. For example, study and reflection over the years made it clear that the overriding national interest in strategic retaliatory forces was to provide "assured destruction"— the unmistakable ability to strike back after an attack on the United States and destroy the society of the aggressor. Hopefully, if we have that power, no aggressor will choose to attack us. But that criterion was not without its controversial implications. It demanded, for example, that U.S. strategic retaliatory forces be able to survive even a surprise enemy missile attack and then retaliate by penetrating the enemy's defenses. As discussed later, the B-70 bomber and the Skybolt missile failed to meet those tests; and despite loud and long objections from their advocates at the time, it is now generally agreed that to buy them would not have been in the national interest.

In the field of strategic mobility, it was possible to define a timetable for the rapid deployment of U.S. land and tactical air forces to reinforce allies in various theaters around the world. It was then possible to determine, under various assumptions, the best ways to provide that capability. In other areas only the first steps were taken toward defining the national interest served by major defense programs. In land forces, for example, only very crude indicators of capability were developed. No satisfactory criteria were evolved to help determine how many or what kinds of divisions were needed to support national objectives. Much the same can be said for tactical air forces. But, whether the measures were good or poor, the attempt to put defense program issues into a broader context and to search for explicit measures of national need and adequacy was a basic goal of PPBS.

Considering Needs and Costs Simultaneously

A second basic idea underlying PPBS was the consideration of military needs and costs together. Put another way, decisions on forces and budgets should be made together, because they cannot sensibly be made apart. Ends and means interact. What is worth trying to do depends in large part on how much it costs. If an administration is not willing or able to meet the costs implied by its foreign policy and strategic objectives, it should revise its objectives to bring them into line with the budget it is willing and able to provide. Otherwise, the consequence will be an imbalance between objectives and forces and in all probability an imbalance between planned forces and the actual budgets and programs provided to support them. As McNamara once explained it: "I do not mean to suggest that we can measure national security in terms of dollars—you cannot price what is inherently priceless. But if we are to avoid talking in generalities, we must talk about dollars: for policy decisions must sooner or later be expressed in the form of budget decisions on where to spend and how much."[4]

The explicit acceptance of the relevance of cost in defense

programs was (and still is) deeply resented by some. While the situation has changed radically now, we frequently heard charges of overemphasis on cost: "Where national security is concerned, money is no object"; "We must buy system X—we can't afford to compromise on national defense"; "Nothing is too good for our fighting men." The cries are still familiar, if somewhat less frequent. But the fact is that our total resources are always limited and must be allocated among many competing needs in our society; and the nation has always compromised on national defense, even in wartime. Benefits and costs are associated with every defense program. One cannot get effectiveness without paying a cost. The way to get the most effective total defense program is to try to put each dollar where it will add the most to total effectiveness. The emphasis is not on cost, but on cost *and* effectiveness together.

Still, the idea persists among some that the United States can and should establish military requirements without serious regard for cost and then each year should meet as many of them as possible with the inevitably limited budget that the real world will dictate. All that is required is for the military experts to say what is needed. This "need only" approach to military requirements was summarized by Senator Barry Goldwater in its pure form in the hearings on air power held in 1956. "If I have any criticism of the Air Force since the Second War," he said, "it has been their seeming timidity to put down on paper what they want and then let those of us who believe in them fight for that amount, and let the money take care of itself."[5]

One trouble with this theory as the basis for a management system—and it was prevalent before 1961—is that it produced unbalanced programs. When the defense budget had to be cut, inevitably the prestige items (carriers, divisions, air wings) were retained and the unglamorous but essential support items (ammunition, spare parts, fuel) were cut. As noted earlier, for example, in 1961 the Army had managed to hold on to fourteen divisions in its force structure, but had only a few weeks' supply of ammunition and logistic support for these divisions, and that in unbalanced amounts. Indeed, at the time, the Army's stated matériel requirement exceeded the budgeted inventory and procurement level by $24 billion.

Allocating resources among competing programs is one of the most important jobs of the Secretary of Defense. He is constantly making decisions on whether to assign more or fewer resources to this or that program. This responsibility presses even more heavily on the President. No President wishes to shortchange the defense effort. Yet he sees other priority needs and recognizes that the nation's future also depends on solving the critical problems of the cities and meeting our growing educational, health, welfare, environmental, and transportation needs. The unavoidable fact is that our society has other needs besides military power. A main job of the Secretary of Defense is to assist the President in making judgments as to how much should be spent on military power relative to other wants. Thus, he and the President must consider cost when they consider defense needs. They may choose to delay considering it or to consider it only implicitly, but they cannot choose to ignore it.

With a defense budget as large as the one the United States now has, choices have become more and more difficult. If our national leaders were faced with a clear-cut choice between social programs and the safety of the country, there is little doubt how they would decide. But, in fact, U.S. defenses are strong, and all-or-nothing defense decisions rarely exist. The type of choices that the President, the Secretary of Defense, and the Congress constantly face is not between a capability to strike back in the event of a Soviet attack, and no such capability; rather, they must decide whether to spend an extra $2 billion for the ability to strike back with the goal of killing 120 million rather than 100 million Russians with retaliatory forces, or of destroying 60 percent rather than 50 percent of the Soviet attack submarines with antisubmarine warfare forces, or of moving ten divisions rather than eight to Europe in ninety days. Moreover, an extra $2 billion spent on one of these purposes might yield less in long-run security than the same amount spent on one of the others or in some totally different way.

The notion, then, that in some meaningful sense the nation's military requirements can be determined without considering costs is false. Military requirements, like all other requirements, have to be decided by judgments as to what resources will be devoted to what purposes and what sacrifices of other purposes will be made.

The nation's leaders are likely to do a much better job by explicitly recognizing this fact than by pretending that costs are not relevant. PPBS, through its emphasis on the total cost of a defense program in relationship to need, and its search for alternatives that yield the greatest military effectiveness from the resources available, has worked to enhance an awareness of the relevance of cost.

It has been suggested that PPBS has worked too well in this respect and has led to overemphasis on cost. Has this, in fact, happened? It is very hard to make a convincing case that it has, in light of the sharp increases in defense budget requests during 1961–1964. Even the corollary charge that the system leads to a preference for the cheapest weapon is disproved by the record. The Minuteman II and III ICBM's, the Poseidon submarine-launched ballistic missile, the F-4 and the A-7 fighter/attack aircraft—to name only a few—were all justified on the basis of cost-effectiveness analyses done under the PPB system. Each costs more per plane or missile, but less per unit of effectiveness, than its predecessor. In each case, however, the Secretary of Defense judged that the margin of extra effectiveness per unit was worth the extra cost, and the more expensive alternative was approved.

Explicit Consideration of Alternatives

A third basic idea of PPBS was the explicit consideration of alternatives at the top decision level. By an alternative, we mean a balanced, feasible solution to the problem, not a straw man chosen to make a course of action preferred by the originating staff look better by comparison. It could be argued that the Secretary of Defense has always considered alternatives. For example, because the JCS regularly recommend forces costing roughly 25 to 35 percent more than the final budget the President believes the nation should provide, a set of alternatives is offered: the JCS's force levels with their implied budget and the administration's budget and implied force levels. But these were not even attempts at solution of the problem of balancing military needs and other needs. Each looked at only one side of the coin. A basic goal of PPBS was to ensure that the Secretary of Defense could consider several alternatives in which costs, forces, and strategies had been considered together.

This search for alternatives, and their explicit consideration by top management in DoD, was a vital part of the defense decision-making process. Because of the many conflicting values involved, the huge costs, and the complexity and uncertainties inherent in any defense program decision, it is not enough for the Secretary of Defense to consider only a single staff solution, no matter how well reasoned it may be. Most decisions regarding the size and mix of forces require judgments about the objectives being sought and the circumstances in which the forces are to be used. These are matters of broad national security policy. The only way the Secretary of Defense can effectively translate these judgments into meaningful action is by choosing from among alternative programs. Through organized adversary proceedings, PPBS helped to identify and clarify the key issues and assumptions in these programs and to lay out the alternatives in such a way that the Secretary and other politically responsible leaders could better understand the essentials and make a reasoned choice.

Indeed, organizing information along the lines that would be useful to political leaders was a main purpose of PPBS in the Pentagon. For example, PPBS translated the defense budget from *inputs,* such as procurement and personnel, into *forces,* such as strategic retaliatory forces and airlift and sealift forces, and from forces into *outputs,* such as targets destroyed or troops deployed. It translated the detailed technical criteria produced by experts into broader criteria that would be of more significance to political leaders—weapon yield, reliability, and accuracy into target destruction, and target destruction into lives lost and lives saved in a nuclear exchange, for example.

In this way, PPBS helped correct the inherent bias in DoD toward the expert's viewpoint. We have often heard men who were running successful programs say they were unable to understand why the Secretary of Defense was not buying more of their particular system. Why stop with 41 Polaris submarines, with 14 B-52 wings, with 1,000 Minuteman missiles, with 14 C-141 squadrons—to name only a few such programs? The answer is not because they were not well-managed programs; they were. Rather, it was because the best available evidence indicated that the value to the nation would be small in relation to the cost.

Proponents of a new weapon system, particularly project managers, tend to grow enamored of their creation and sometimes lose perspective. The fact that it works or that knotty technical problems were overcome in its development becomes, in their view, sufficient reason to buy the weapon in quantity. They often lose sight of the over-all objective the weapon is supposed to help reach, and they fail to examine closely enough whether their system contributes more toward that objective than some competing system.

For example, proponents of air defense are naturally eager to buy more and better missiles, radars, and interceptors in order to shoot down more enemy bombers. Indeed, their jobs properly are based on finding ways (all of them costing money) to shoot down a larger and larger proportion of hostile aircraft. But viewed nationally from the desk of the Secretary of Defense (or the President), the air defense task looks quite different. To him, the objective of air defense is not merely to shoot down enemy aircraft, but rather to limit the damage these aircraft can inflict on U.S. population, industry, and military facilities. Shooting down aircraft is merely one of several ways to achieve that objective. The secretary may, for example, decide that he will get more effectiveness (in terms of limiting damage) by building shelters or dispersing key military facilities or buying intercontinental missiles that can strike an enemy's air bases and destroy his bombers before they can be launched. Or he may decide that it is best to rely on deterrence and not buy an active defense. PPBS aided in this decision process by organizing information into broad mission-oriented categories and by translating the technical jargon of the expert into terms that had more meaning for the generalist. Surely, the number of lives saved by the expenditure of $10 or $20 billion on an ABM system under each of various assumed circumstances is of greater significance to the generalist than the "single-shot kill probability" of a Sprint missile against a re-entering Soviet warhead. Similarly, the number of division forces that can be deployed to Europe within thirty or sixty days should be of more significance to him than the number of ton-miles logged by the ships or aircraft. Such broad measures, which took considerable analytical effort to develop, were presented each year between 1961 and 1969 to the President in special memorandums for that purpose and to the Congress in the Secretary of Defense's statement on the program and budget.

Indeed, under the PPB system more and better information about the *broad basis* for defense decisions was made available to Congressional committees than ever before. One indication of the increased volume of information being provided to the Congress by the Secretary of Defense can be seen by comparing the Secretary's annual statement to the Congress before and after 1961. Secretary Gates's last presentation ran 33 pages double-spaced and ended with the apology: "Mr. Chairman and members of the Committee, I appreciate your patience and courtesy in listening to this rather lengthy statement. I felt that it was important to describe the 1961 Defense budget in some detail and show how our policies and programs related to our total national strategy." Secretary McNamara's first presentation ran 122 single-spaced pages plus 44 pages of detailed tables; his last ran 256 single-spaced pages plus 24 pages of detailed tables.

This increased volume of information was matched by an increase in quality. Carl Vinson, then Chairman of the House Armed Services Committee, told McNamara after the presentation of the first of his seven posture statements before the Committee:

I want to say this. I say it from the very bottom of my heart. I have been here dealing with these problems since 1919. I want to state that this is the most comprehensive, most factual statement that it has ever been my privilege to have an opportunity to receive from any of the departments of Government.

There is more information in here than any committee in Congress has ever received along the line that it is dealing with. It is so full of information all one has to do is just study it. You dealt with both sides of the problem. When you reach a decision, you set out the reasons why you reached that decision. You point out why—it probably could have been done the other way.[6]

These sentiments were strongly echoed by Senator Richard Russell, Chairman of the Senate Armed Services Committee.

If, then, as one Senate subcommittee has recently concluded, "Members of Congress clearly have not welcomed all the implications of PPB," it can surely not be because PPBS reduced the amount of useful information available to its members.[7] In fact, one of the problems with the PPB system from the point of view of some members was that it was providing too much information of certain kinds. By forcing open debate on explicit alternatives, PPBS was breaking up the façade of DoD internal agreement. Both sides of difficult decisions were being presented with greater frequency and in greater detail than before. As Senator Karl Mundt expressed it in hearings on PPBS conducted in 1967:

We used to face the question, "How much should we spend for a weapons system?" Defense had a united front and asked for a certain amount of money. Now we have to make decisions . . . on which defense system and techniques we should have. . . . It is in the wrong arena at our end of the Avenue, because we are not the experts in defense, and we are not the economists and the engineers. We are here trying to make overall policy and to do what we can to keep the budget relatively sound. It is very difficult if part of [the] team says you need B-52 bombers, otherwise in the early 70s you will have no bombers at all, and other officials say, "Don't worry about that, just let the B-52 bombers go, and don't put any money in." That shouldn't be the kind of decision we have to make.[8]

If the Congress shouldn't have to make such multibillion-dollar decisions, who should? Senator Mundt's attitude is representative of a serious problem faced by the civilian leaders of the Defense Department during the years 1961–1968. PPBS was making available more useful information to Congress, but ironically some members often didn't seem to want it.

Active Use of an Analytical Staff

Few of the decisions that the Secretary of Defense must make are either simple or noncontroversial. He is constantly given conflicting views on matters of great importance. There is conflict not only in the opinions of his advisers and experts but frequently in the evidence and "facts" they present. It is imperative that the Secretary have independent staff assistance to look at problems from his point of view and double-check the facts for him. Thus, a fourth basic idea of PPBS, at least as it was practiced in the Pentagon between 1961 and 1969, was the active use of an analytical staff at the top policy-making levels. Most large organizations, governmental or otherwise, have some kind of analytical or planning group somewhere in the organizational structure. However, these staff groups are often little more than window dressing—passive contributors to the decision-making process. They neither report to, nor receive guidance from, the top on what studies to undertake and for what reasons. Their continued existence depends on remaining noncontroversial, and many of them excel in this respect.

But in the Defense Department, the active use of an analytical staff at the top levels was a key element of PPBS from the beginning. The staff we are referring to is the Systems Analysis office. Established by Secretary McNamara early in his administration, this office was charged with the responsibility for analyzing force requirements and weapon systems. It undertook studies directly at his request. These studies were then reviewed by all interested parties and formed a major input to the decision-making process. The controversy surrounding the Systems Analysis office since its inception attests to its important and active role in providing information and analysis for the Secretary of Defense.

The analytical effort of the Systems Analysis office was conducted mainly by broad mission areas such as tactical air forces, antisubmarine warfare forces, and land forces, rather than by Service. The office thus integrated the weapons, data, and ideas of the Services into force packages arranged so that the Secretary could see what types of capability were proposed, what he was buying, and how the package related to over-all needs. Understandably, an office with the responsibility of looking at the entire defense program, independently of Service interests, was disliked by those who felt threatened. Equally understandably, an office whose job was to question, to probe, and to challenge Service proposals would be a center of controversy. At the same time, the activities of such a staff at the top levels of DoD unquestionably stimulated the development of better analytic staffs in the Services and the JCS and resulted, consequently, in better staff work.

The Systems Analysis office was frequently criticized for slowing down the decision-making process unnecessarily, delaying decisions to buy badly needed weapons and equipment, and stifling innovation. As one critic put it, "the systems analysis business is being used to kill ideas and to delay them. . . . I know of no study that has been made . . . by the Department of Defense which has not caused delay, or which has added one iota to our national defense, not one."[9] This criticism rests on the false premise that all delay is bad. Some delays are inherent in defense management. When the Secretary of Defense is faced with a difficult decision on a program costing the taxpayers millions or even billions of dollars, he must take the time to examine the issues, weighing the costs and the expected returns in effectiveness, before making a decision. The alternatives would be either to accept blindly all the recommendations that are made, or to make quick decisions on some arbitrary basis. Either approach is clearly inadequate. The American people—who ultimately receive the benefits, but also must pay the bills—have the right to expect decisions to be made on the basis of as thorough and objective an analysis as possible.

More to the point, however, the active use of analytical staff at the top policy-making level in any organization is likely to result in more time being spent on thinking through the strategic basis of a new proposal. Much of the "delay" attributed to the Systems Analysis office was caused by the fact that new weapon systems were often proposed without adequate strategic justification. As a general rule, where the strategic basis for a new system had been thought through, decisions were relatively fast and frequently favorable. The Poseidon submarine-launched ballistic missile system, the C-5A transport, the A-7 fighter bomber, and the Multiple, Independently Targetable Reentry Vehicle (MIRV) are all examples of such prompt and favorable decisions. On the other hand, where the strategic basis had not been carefully thought through, decisions, as a rule, were slower and sometimes unfavorable. The B-70 bomber, nuclear-powered frigates, and the Nike-X ABM system are examples. In short, the major cause of delay of a proposed system was more often inadequate strategic justification than any particular action or inaction on the part of the Systems Analysis office. Further, rather than acting as a roadblock, the office, by helping innovators do the necessary strategic thinking, provided them with criteria they could use to defend their projects, thus aiding innovation.

A Multiyear Force and Financial Plan

A fifth basic idea of PPBS was a plan combining both forces and costs which projected into the future the foreseeable implications of current decisions. Such a plan was not meant to be an inflexible blueprint for the future, or a set of goals that must be achieved.

Rather, it was a projection of the implications of past decisions, a set of official planning assumptions, and a point of departure in the continuing search for improvements. Having such a plan forces a decision maker to look ahead to the time when today's decisions will have their most important effects and to judge programs versus needs in the light of their consequences over time. If a decision maker insists on seeing costs over a period of years, proponents of new programs find it harder to conceal the future cost implications of decisions made today.

Without such a plan, it is impossible to bring together at one time and place all the relevant information needed by the Secretary of Defense and his principal advisers for making sound program decisions and seeing that they are carried out. A multiyear plan that deals with forces and costs in a comprehensive manner is necessary if the Secretary of Defense is to play an active role in shaping national security policy; indeed, it is essential if there is to be a comprehensive and consistent policy.

Open and Explicit Analysis

A final basic idea underlying PPBS was that of open and explicit analysis; that is, each analysis should be made available to all interested parties, so that they can examine the calculations, data, and assumptions and retrace the steps leading to the conclusions. Indeed, all calculations, data, and assumptions *should* be described in an analysis in such a way that they can be checked, tested, criticized, debated, discussed, and possibly refuted by interested parties. The results of an analysis should not be blindly accepted simply because they appear at the end of an impressive-looking document called a study, accompanied by a sheaf of endorsements signed by high-ranking officials. The validity of a proposition should be established on the basis of some other criterion than an appeal to authority. The important element is the quality of the proof, and not the reputation or age or experience of the author. The esteem in which the originator of an analysis is held is not sufficient reason for believing the finding of the analysis.

By the end of 1968, the need for open and explicit analysis was generally accepted in DoD. But the concept was a radical and controversial departure when McNamara introduced it in 1961. In fact, there was much debate at the time over the wisdom of requiring that all studies be made available to the Secretary of Defense and his staff. The fear was that this would lead to additional pressures for biasing studies to support predetermined conclusions. As it turned out, however, the open and explicit approach made it difficult for any group to get away with manipulating an analysis (though the attempts didn't stop). The Services and the JCS could check OSD studies to see if assumptions were biased to make a point; and, of course, OSD could do the same for their studies. The result was that, in most important cases, the Secretary of Defense heard all sides. In reviewing a joint analysis he got a much more precise statement of the issues, the assumptions, and the uncertainties than would otherwise have been the case.

The open and explicit approach has many important advantages. It helps protect a large organization against persisting in error over the long run. Of course, all parties might agree on an analysis containing biased or erroneous assumptions, but the chances of this happening are reduced if each party is given an opportunity to comment independently. Such an approach is also the best way of handling the uncertainties that pervade defense issues. It makes better sense to recognize explicitly that the future is uncertain and design a strategy based on uncertainty—one that includes options and gathering additional information to resolve uncertainties—than to pick a particular assumption and treat it as if it were a certainty. In addition, open and explicit analysis helps build confidence in the soundness of a study's conclusions. All sorts of mistakes can be made under the guise of analysis, just as they can under the guise of judgment and experience. There may be cases in which some people overemphasize the cost, and other cases in which they overstate the potential gains in effectiveness. But this is less likely to occur if the analyst is required to lay the whole study out, showing the estimated benefits and costs, the evidence for them, and the calculations. When this is done, others, including critics, can review and judge the analysis for themselves.

Finally, the concept of open and explicit analysis is particularly important to groups outside DoD such as the Congress, the Bureau of the Budget, and the interested public. By giving these groups a better handle on defense issues, such analyses promote more effective interrogation and debate. And by bringing outside groups into the decision-making process, the chances are reduced that only parties with a pro-defense bias—a bias that is almost impossible not to have if one works in the Pentagon—will participate in the decision.

The concept of open and explicit analysis was generally accepted in the Pentagon by the end of 1968. While some studies were still being sent to the Secretary of Defense with only their conclusions and recommendations, making it difficult to ascertain why the results came out that way and how the conclusions related to the initial statement of the problem, such events were becoming less frequent. In large part this was because the military staffs knew that their studies would be reviewed by the Systems Analysis office.

Ironically, it was this process of open and explicit analysis that provoked much of the controversy over "downgrading military judgment." Far from being ignored, professional military judgments were subjected to thorough and rigorous review from all angles. In the debates accompanying this process, many military experts felt that their judgments should not be subjected to searching scrutiny by what they considered to be amateurs and outsiders. But the fact is that most military judgments implicitly include economic and political components as well, and it is important that the Secretary of Defense and the President be able to distinguish these.

In sum, the fundamental idea behind PPBS was decision making based on explicit criteria related to the national interest in defense programs as opposed to decision making by compromise among various institutional and parochial interests. PPBS also emphasized the consideration of real alternatives, the importance of evaluating needs and costs together, the need for a multiyear force and financial plan, the regular use of an analytical staff as an aid to decision makers at the top levels, and the importance of making analyses open and explicit. These were the basic ideas underlying PPBS and the management tools that made the system work.

PPBS never became a closed, rigid, or perfected management system. Indeed, in its broadest sense it was less a management system than a philosophy of management—a philosophy that, we believe, helped to channel the initiative, imagination, dedication, hard work, and judgment of the military and civilian leaders in DoD along more rational and objective lines than previously.

The Planning-Programming-Budgeting System: The Major Tools

To implement these basic ideas, a number of new management tools were needed. The most important of these, originally, were the Five-Year Defense Plan (FYDP), the Draft Presidential Memorandum (DPM), the Systems Analysis office, and the active use of the technique of systems analysis. Additional tools, added later, were the readiness, information, and control tables and the Development Concept Paper (DCP). By 1968 these formed the principal means by which the Secretary of Defense obtained information and perspective on proposals to shape the over-all U.S. defense program. How each worked is outlined briefly below.

The Five-Year Defense Plan

A decision by the Secretary of Defense to develop, procure, or operate a weapon system affects not only the current defense budget but future budgets as well, the latter far more than the former as a rule. When he decides to begin the engineering development of a new system, with procurement presumably to follow, he initiates a stream of expenditures which can eventually include development, procurement, and operating and maintenance costs of the completed system. He needs not only a record of current costs and manpower but also projections of this information far enough ahead to enable him to estimate the main consequences of today's decisions. The Five-Year Defense Plan, or FYDP, was developed to provide this record.

Physically, the FYDP was a series of force tables giving an eight-year projection of forces and a five-year projection of costs and manpower, displayed in mission-oriented programs. Because the Department had had such a master plan since 1961, by 1968 the basic FYDP tables carried force, cost, and manpower information from previous years, providing defense programs with a recorded past as well as a projected future.

By 1968, the FYDP, at its broadest level of aggregation, covered ten major military programs: strategic forces, general-purpose forces, intelligence and communications, airlift and sealift, guard and reserve forces, research and development, central supply and maintenance, training and medical services, administration and associated activities, and support of other nations. These major military programs were aggregates of "program elements," which comprised the basic building blocks. Each program element was an integrated force or activity—a combination of men, equipment, and facilities whose military capability could be directly related to national security objectives. For instance, the B-52 bomber force, together with all the supplies, bases, weapons, and manpower needed to make it militarily effective, is such a program element. Other examples would be attack carriers, infantry divisions, or tactical air wings. Groupings of program elements were based on a common mission or set of purposes, with elements either complementing each other or serving as close substitutes to be considered together in making major program decisions. There were in all about a thousand program elements. These were continuously updated, new ones being added and older ones combined or deleted.

The key point about a program element is that it combines both costs and benefits. The benefits were the ways in which it helped to achieve broad national security objectives. The costs were primarily the total appropriations associated with the program, not just in the current fiscal year but over the lifetime of the program.

What did the FYDP do? Most importantly, it tied together force and financial planning. As we have argued, sound decisions on forces cannot be made without carefully reviewing their total cost and manpower implications. For example, when deciding how many tactical aircraft to buy and operate, defense planners should consider not only the costs of the aircraft but the costs of the personnel required to operate and maintain them, the costs of training the pilots, and the costs of the housing, runways, depot stocks, hospitals, equipment, and other resources needed to support the force. With the aid of such tools as the FYDP, for example, defense planners found that every dollar spent directly to buy and operate a tactical aircraft leads to at least another dollar in support costs.

The FYDP also provided an official set of planning assumptions for use throughout the Department. It was an authoritative record of what the Secretary of Defense had approved for purposes of force and financial planning, and a common reference point for subsequent changes. With the FYDP, a common base existed for planning in hundreds of separate DoD agencies and offices. The left hand could know what the right hand was doing and even what it was planning to do. Logistics planners could see how many and what kinds of divisions and squadrons were projected and budget for ammunition accordingly. Each military Service could see what was planned for the others and thus better determine what forces were needed for common missions. Air Force planners, for example, could see how large an Army was planned and design their airlift capability to match. Furthermore, with a common set of planning assumptions, the wastefulness associated with starting or continuing a great many individual Service projects, all of them designed to do the same job, could be and was significantly reduced. By providing a common base, the FYDP led to the acquisition of better-balanced and better-supported forces. By clearly relating forces to their costs and to the defense budget, the FYDP gave financial planning the same output orientation as force planning.

While the FYDP provided a road map for the defense program over the next five years, it did not represent an inflexible official program of the U.S. government. The President was not unalterably committed to the FYDP even over all, much less in detail; and the Congress, which authorizes and appropriates funds on a one-year basis, quite frequently showed that it was not so committed. Both the President and the Congress retained the freedom to shift plans and respond flexibly to new situations. Arguments that a long-range plan such as the FYDP ties a President's hands by committing him in advance for five years of expenditures are simply wrong. On the contrary, an organization's flexibility to move in a new direction is greatly reduced if it lacks a clear picture of the direction in which it has been heading.

Another major function of the FYDP was to provide a vehicle for assuring orderly program changes and making certain that these changes were accurately recorded. In the Defense Department, decisions on forces and programs were made in a variety of ways and in many separate documents. Eventually, however, the affected military service had to submit a "program change request." A document called a "program change decision," signed by the Secretary or the Deputy Secretary of Defense, was then issued for each decision. The program change requests had to be based on reproducible calculations leading to specific cost and manpower estimates. OSD staff members could question the originating Service about reasons for the change, methods of estimation, and assumptions used in the calculations, so that a mutually understood position could be reached.

The program change decision recorded exactly how the forces, manpower, and costs in the current FYDP were changed by the decision. Periodically, an updated FYDP was issued which summarized all changes that had been approved. The former confusion caused by the necessity of maintaining a thick and ever-growing sheaf of memorandums and other documents, rather than a single compact volume, for an up-to-date record of decisions was thus eliminated.

The FYDP, and the backup data that supported it, also permitted better estimates of the total cost of existing and proposed new programs. These estimates included all procurement, construction, personnel, and operating costs, in current and future years, related to a given program. Development of these kinds of output-oriented costs, which are essential for rational decision making, was one of the original purposes of PPBS, and by 1968 a good deal of progress had been made in this regard. The system provided a framework for giving top DoD decision makers an understanding of the long-term financial implications of program decisions.

Obtaining relevant cost information, however, turned out to be a very difficult task, and there is still considerable room for improvement. The difficulty of estimating the cost of new equipment, and the tendency for gross underestimates, persists and is well known. Equally important is the old problem of "tip of the iceberg" cost estimates. To deploy one squadron of aircraft, for example, a long tail of training base support, logistics, communications, and so on is required. The cost of these support elements often exceeds the investment and direct operating cost for a system or program. Only recently has the relationship of these indirect and support costs to major programs been well enough understood to be considered explicitly. The point is that obtaining comprehensive and relevant costs—which was, of course, a fundamental objective of PPBS—proved to be a difficult analytical job, not just a simple accounting problem. Doing it right requires a clear understanding of the operations and characteristics of the programs themselves. The Defense Department made impressive strides in this direction in the 1960's under the PPBS framework, but considerable work remains to be done.

In addition to ensuring that the Secretary's program decisions were known and carried out, the FYDP provided the main basis for the Service's budget submissions each fall. The major program and force issues were thrashed out in an annual force review cycle, which began in the spring. In the fall, the Services submitted a budget that priced out the latest update of the FYDP (although they could, and did, submit supplementary requests). This meant that the budget review, which was a highly demanding task in itself, could focus on the financial requirements for an approved program without addressing all the major program issues of DoD. One important contribution of the FYDP was that the central functions of a budget review—deciding how much money was really needed for an approved program, identifying funds that could be deferred because of slippages in production schedules, and so on—could be accomplished more effectively.

The FYDP thus provided a vehicle by which the Secretary of Defense could make program decisions and tie them into the preparation of the annual budget. By the end of 1968, both the FYDP and the programming system that supported it were well-established, functioning systems. Yet nobody pretended that they were final or perfect. A major piece of unfinished business, for example, concerned the development of a way of learning how authorized resources were actually being used to accomplish defense missions. For budget planning purposes, estimates were made of resources needed for operating and maintaining the forces, and funds were apportioned accordingly. However, until 1968, there was no mechanism for systematic feedback on how these resources were actually being used, or whether the apportionments were accurate. As discussed further in Chapter 9, Project PRIME (Priority Management Effort), set up in the spring of that year by the Comptroller of the Defense Department, was an important and necessary step in this direction.

The very characteristics of the FYDP that made it an effective management tool also led to much of the criticism directed against it. Since the FYDP did constitute an official, explicit record of program decisions and tentative planning assumptions, it required the Secretary to make controversial decisions explicitly. This is quite a different procedure from simply setting a one-year budget ceiling without nailing down choices between competing claims for resources. Unfortunately, setting a one-year ceiling, as we have seen, can lead to starting and continuing more and larger programs than the budget can adequately finance, since the long-term financial implications of decisions are not explicitly considered, and the pressure for approval of competing programs does not have to be met head on. In the short run, however, a simple budget ceiling generates less political heat than a system that requires explicit, long-range program decisions. It also generates less animosity among the military. It is easier to accept "I'm sorry, but there just isn't enough money in the budget for your worth-while program" than "In my judgment your proposal isn't worth the extra money."

The Draft Presidential Memorandums

Because debate over issues in DoD is vital to the decision-making process, most Secretaries of Defense have searched for ways to structure this process so that it keeps to the basic issues, gives every interested party his day in court, and reduces the emotionalism inherent in major defense issues. The key vehicle for performing this function between 1961 and 1969 was the Draft Presidential Memorandum, or DPM.

The DPM's originated in 1961. In the process of preparing for President Kennedy a "white paper" on U.S. nuclear strategy and forces, members of the new administration team in the Pentagon questioned many of the assumptions behind the strategy of massive retaliation, the relationship between that strategy and the programmed nuclear forces, and the balance and mix of U.S. nuclear forces, and they explored the implications of using different assumptions. As questions were raised and debated, the desirability of undertaking such a basic review of other areas became apparent. What was needed was an appropriate vehicle. The prestige and importance of a memorandum for the President seemed to fit the bill perfectly. As Secretary McNamara has recalled:

I wanted a vehicle—and President Kennedy was very interested in a vehicle—to acquaint him with the background of military decisions. But the more I thought about it, the more it seemed like a good device to get the views of appropriate departments for my own review. By passing [the DPM's] back and forth [between me, the Services, and the JCS] we were able to force the divergent views to the surface. I insisted that each party of interest comment.[10]

The growth in the number of DPM's reflected McNamara's desire to have all major defense programs considered and analyzed as a whole. This is a good illustration of what we like to call "Mc-Namara's First Law of Analysis": always start by looking at the grand totals. Whatever problem you are studying, back off and look at it in the large. Don't start with a small piece and work up; look at the total first and then break it down into its parts. For example, if cost is the issue, look at total system cost over the useful life of the system, not just at this year's operating or procurement costs or last year's costs. If you are analyzing a particular strategic offensive weapon system, start by looking at the total strategic offensive forces. If you are considering nuclear attack submarines, look at the total antisubmarine warfare force, which includes land- and sea-based patrol aircraft, destroyers, sonars, and the like. One simply cannot make sense out of costs, or missiles, or submarines without looking at totals. The DPM's were a practical result of this principle.

From two DPM's in 1961 (one on strategic nuclear forces and one on general-purpose forces), the number grew to sixteen by 1968.[11] Listed in the sequence in which they were prepared, these were:

1. Logistic Guidance for General-Purpose Forces
2. Asia Strategy and Force Structure
3. NATO Strategy and Force Structure
4. General-Purpose Forces
5. Land Forces
6. Tactical Air Forces
7. Escort Ship Forces
8. Antisubmarine Warfare Forces
9. Amphibious Forces
10. Naval Replenishment and Support Forces
11. Mobility Forces
12. Strategic Offensive and Defensive Forces
13. Theater Nuclear Forces
14. Nuclear Weapons and Materials Requirements
15. Research and Development
16. Military Assistance Program

All of these were drafted originally in OSD, and all but two (Research and Development and Military Assistance Program) were prepared by the Systems Analysis office. This procedure reflected McNamara's desire to have these documents prepared initially under the supervision of officials directly responsible to him and to have the first drafts written without compromise or bargaining with other interested parties. Then they were sent to the Services and the JCS for comment. In this way, the DPM's forced a clearer statement of opposing positions for him to consider. Each DPM covered the rationale for the Secretary's recommendations and explained how his position related to proposals made by the JCS and the Services. Each DPM also showed explicitly the force and budget implications of the different views.

By 1965, the DPM's had become the principal program decision-making documents in the Defense Department. As the DPM's evolved, a workable system for processing the various drafts in DoD was developed and formalized. The resulting DPM system became a unique and highly effective management tool for dealing with controversial issues of military strategy and force planning.

Perhaps the best way to illustrate how this system worked is by outlining some of the key functions of the DPM's. First, and most important, they served as vehicles for orderly interrogation and debate. The DPM's gave the Secretary of Defense the initiative in reviewing defense policy and forces. Thus, he was not constrained to consider only those questions and alternatives raised by the Services and the JCS, nor did he have to accept debate on the terms favored by organizations advocating their own positions. Rather, he would, via the DPM's, encourage a full debate on every issue that concerned him. This is an important defense against the Secretary's being pressured at the last minute for a quick decision on an important subject of which he knows little or nothing and about which very scanty information is presented. It also gives him the advantage of making full use of a staff that can independently review Service force and weapons requests for him.

During the spring and summer months of each year, preliminary drafts of the DPM's (called "For Comment" drafts) were circulated to the Services, the JCS, and other interested parties. These drafts were prepared under the personal guidance of the Secretary of Defense, using the latest available analyses and intelligence information and the known positions of the Services and the JCS. They spelled out concisely the assumptions, rationale, and supporting analysis for the Secretary's tentative recommendations in the area covered by the DPM. Because of preliminary work at the staff level, even at this early stage of processing, the DPM incorporated a great deal of the analysis and judgments of the Services and the JCS. After publication of the preliminary drafts, the Services and the JCS were given a month in which to comment formally on the drafts. This began a process of debate and interaction which lasted most of the year, generated special studies and additional memorandums, and culminated in a summary memo to the President, which gave a concise statement of the position of the Secretary, the JCS, and the Services on each major force issue in the budget. The process ensured that every interested party not only had his say but had an opportunity to say it several times, not only to the Secretary but to the President as well. This situation is in sharp contrast to the one the Senate Preparedness Investigating Subcommittee reported in 1959:

Furthermore, the Joint Chiefs as a group were given only 2 days to consider the total program and never considered such important aspects as the size of the Army, whether to include an aircraft carrier or—most fundamental of all—what deterrent forces are needed.[12]

Moreover, since the DPM's combined strategy, force requirements, and financial considerations, the Services and the JCS were brought directly into the process of putting together the defense budget. Again, this is in sharp contrast to the situation prior to 1961. According to General Taylor:

The Joint Chiefs of Staff as a body took no part in the formulation of the 1960 budget—nor had they in previous years. This fact has often surprised the Congress, which always expects the Chief of Staff to give them competent advice on the budget. But thus far, the Secretary of Defense has never given the Chiefs as a body a clearly defined role in budget-making.[13]

In essence, the DPM review process was structured so that all interested parties were asked—indeed forced—to criticize the Secretary's tentative recommendations. Their comments went directly to the Secretary. Often this process was repeated several times as points were clarified, errors uncovered, and analyses refined in light of the comments received. The DPM's thus became a means of orderly communication between the Secretary, the military departments, and the JCS. A common language emerged; no longer could the various parties speak different dialects. All were forced to expose their reasoning to analysis and debate. As this process of orderly debate through open and explicit analysis took hold, it served to identify areas of agreement and disagreement, to isolate key assumptions, and to focus attention on areas of uncertainty where judgment must be applied. It did not, of course, relieve the Secretary of Defense of the burden of making the final decisions. No management tool can do that. But it did ensure that all interested parties received "due process," that the relevant factors were thoroughly and explicitly considered, and that differing views and the reasons for them were clearly stated.

Another important function of the DPM's was to give top management in DoD an overview of forces having a common mission and to present this overview in such a way that busy officials could personally read and react to it. Each DPM assessed, in twenty pages or fewer, a total functional area for the proper integration of strategy and forces, the best mix of forces, and the effect of proposed changes on the total picture. For example, the DPM on strategic offensive and defensive forces dealt with the totals of Army, Navy, and Air Force strategic systems. It laid out the possible objectives of these forces, assessed their capabilities to meet these objectives, compared the overall capability of U.S. forces to that of potential enemies, and analyzed proposed changes in or additions to these forces. In this way, the Secretary and other top officials could better judge the over-all adequacy of U.S. forces and evaluate the need for change. This way of looking at problems is simply not possible without an overview, however rough, and a common point of reference for differing views.

The DPM's also functioned as an agenda of future issues and studies that the Secretary was interested in. Frequently the DPM's were used to outline new problems or threats that were foreseeable and to request studies by the Services and the JCS of these matters. The DPM's were also used to summarize in layman's language for the nonspecialist the results of any new or ongoing studies in DoD. Thus, in a direct way, the DPM's served as a report on as well as a stimulus to the Department's ongoing analytical effort.

Finally, the DPM's functioned as decision documents. They became the means by which the Secretary of Defense submitted his
recommendations to the President and, subject to the President's
approval, the means by which he made his decisions and policies
known throughout the Defense Department. Taken together, they
were a central source of policy guidance and an authoritative historical record of what the Secretary had done and his reasons for doing
it. As McNamara said, when asked if he were planning to write his
memoirs: "They're [the DPM's] a far better source than any personal memoirs."[14]

The Development Concept Paper

Another management tool for structuring debate in the Pentagon
was the Development Concept Paper (DCP). The DCP's, which
were not made a regular procedure until 1968, represented an
attempt to bring the advantages of the DPM system to the research
and development area. They were introduced because of McNamara's
belief that, all too frequently, development of new weapon systems
(the TFX was a case in point) had been initiated without careful
study of the costs, operational advantages, and technical risks. The
purposes of the DCP were to examine the performance, cost, and
schedule estimates, as well as the technical risks, on the basis of
which a decision could be made to start or continue an R&D program
and to document the reasons for going ahead with a development
program so that the program could be reconsidered if the reasons for
its existence changed. Each interested party was required either to
concur in the estimates or to state his objections explicitly. The goal
was not to insist on completely accurate cost and schedule estimates;
this is impossible in an area of inherently large uncertainties. Nor was
the goal to plan inventions; advances in technology are not susceptible to orderly prediction. Rather, it was to combat the strong
tendencies toward gross overstatement of expected performance, and
gross understatement of costs and risks, merely to get a new project
under way.

The DCP's also set thresholds for these estimates which, if exceeded, would call for reconsideration of the project by the Secretary
of Defense. Estimates in a DCP were periodically updated, and the

new estimates compared with the original ones, so that the Secretary could see whether expectations were being realized and the reasons for continuing the project were still valid. The DCP's helped bring into the open for debate, before time and money had been spent and perhaps wasted, any conflicting ideas about the potential usefulness of a proposed new weapon system.

Readiness, Information, and Control Tables

Frequently, to meet a specific management problem, force tables, displays, and controls were needed in more detail than those in the FYDP. One example of such specialized tables was those developed to record by month and quarter the approved plan for the deployment of U.S. forces to Southeast Asia, their consumption rates, and projections of these figures over time. Known as the Southeast Asia Deployment Plan, this set of tables provided a single, authoritative base for the various DoD components to use in their manpower, logistic, financial, and procurement planning so that all would properly mesh together. They were developed and kept up to date, and progress against the approved plan was monitored by the Systems Analysis office.

Another example was the tables contained in the Land Forces Planning and Control Memorandum. By organizing the literally thousands of individual Army and Marine Corps units (ranging in size from a combat division of 17,000 to a two-man well-digging detachment) into meaningful functional categories, these tables not only helped to improve knowledge of the functions and capabilities of U.S. land forces; they also gave the Secretary of Defense and the leaders of the Army and Marine Corps a means of effectively controlling manpower and equipment totals.

The Strategic Force and Effectiveness Tables provide another example of such specialized tables. They contained official projections of U.S. and Soviet forces, options available to each side to increase its forces, operational factors describing the performance of each weapon system, and calculations showing the effectiveness of U.S. and Soviet forces under various assumed conditions. The tables, which were updated whenever new intelligence estimates became available, provided an agreed-upon basis for evaluating U.S. and

Soviet strategic forces. Basic contributions to the development of these tables were made by all components of DoD: by military planners in the Service staffs and in the Joint Staff, and by civilian planners in OSD. As a result of this effort, the experts were in agreement on how one got from any single set of assumptions to the results they produced. Differences in results remained, but they were due largely to differences in assumptions; and each party knew what these differences were. This made it possible for top-level DoD officials, who were not themselves technical experts in nuclear planning, to distinguish the important assumptions and concentrate their attention on those areas. They did not have to waste time on controversies over the basic facts or in worrying about whether the complex calculations had been done correctly. This led to much more informed management decisions than were possible before.

To meet the need for readiness standards and controls—a need dramatically emphasized by the Berlin crisis of 1961—a system of readiness tables, updated on a monthly basis, was established. These tables served as an authoritative statement of what and how many U.S. forces were available for deployment at any given time to particular overseas areas. The basic data for these tables came from the Services. The data were then reviewed and assembled for the Secretary of Defense by the Systems Analysis office. (An important byproduct of the fact that the Service submissions on readiness and on requirements were reviewed by the same OSD office was the enforcement of a previously lacking consistency between the two.) These tables proved invaluable in uncovering areas requiring more high-level management attention. McNamara once called them "the most important documents in the building."

Systems Analysis: The Office and the Technique

A final component of PPBS was the establishment of a strong Systems Analysis office with an explicit charter to review questions of military strategy, requirements, and force structure, using modern techniques of analysis. Both the office and the use of the analytical technique that gave it its name have been subjects of continuing controversy. What follows is a discussion of the technique of systems analysis, or more specifically the technique as it was used in analyzing problems of program choice in the Office of the Secretary of Defense during the years 1961–1968. In the next chapter, we shall discuss the role and functions of the Systems Analysis office and why the Secretary of Defense needs such an office. Suffice it to say here, the office was established to give the Secretary independent staff assistance in reviewing JCS and Service proposals regarding force and weapon system requirements, in developing alternatives to these proposals, and in integrating data regarding requirements, costs, and effectiveness.

What is systems analysis? Like sin and virtue, systems analysis means different things to different people. In the world of industry, it is used to describe many different kinds of jobs. Many universities offer courses in systems analysis, but few courses are alike. There are several books on systems analysis, but they discuss largely different things.[15] Moreover, few if any of these jobs or courses or books bear much resemblance to systems analysis as it was developed and used in the Department of Defense.

The term itself emphasizes two basic aspects of thinking about defense problems. First, the word "systems" indicates that every decision should be considered in as broad a context as necessary. In most cases, decisions deal with elements that are parts of a larger universe, or system. Good decisions grow out of a recognition that each element is but one of a number of components working together to serve a larger purpose. The strategic bomber, the airfield, the pilot, the fuel, and the bombs are all parts of one weapon "system." One cannot make sense out of requirements for any one part without looking at the whole system and at the objectives it is intended to achieve. Similarly, the bomber system is but one element of a larger system of interrelated parts: the strategic offensive forces. One cannot make sense out of bomber requirements without looking at the whole strategic force. Systems analysis emphasizes the explicit consideration of all factors that bear on a particular decision in terms of the system these factors together constitute.

The word "analysis" emphasizes the need to reduce a complex problem to its component parts for better understanding. Systems analysis takes a complex problem and sorts out the tangle of significant factors so that each can be studied by the method most appropriate to it. Questions of fact can be tested against the available factual evidence; logical propositions can be tested logically; matters of value and uncertainty can be exposed and clarified so that decision makers can know exactly where to apply their judgment.

Doubtless a better term should have been found. "Systematic analysis" or "quantitative common sense" would have been more accurate and meaningful. But the label used is really beside the point. It isn't what it is called that is important, but what it is—and what it isn't.

Systems analysis is a reasoned approach to highly complicated problems of choice in a context characterized by much uncertainty; it provides a way to deal with differing values and judgments; it looks for alternative ways of doing a job; and it seeks, by estimating in quantitative terms where possible, to identify the most effective alternative. It is at once eclectic and unique. It is not physics, engineering, mathematics, economics, political science, statistics, or military science; yet it involves elements of all these disciplines. It is much more a frame of mind than a specific body of knowledge, which explains why economists, physicists, military officers, and liberal arts graduates can all be good systems analysts—or bad ones, for that matter. A good systems analyst is a relentless inquirer, asking fundamental questions about the problem at hand. In short, just as PPBS is more a management philosophy than a specific set of management tools, so systems analysis is more a philosophy than a specific set of analytical techniques.

Let us also make clear some things that systems analysis is not. It is not entirely new. Its roots go back to whenever man started comparing costs and gains. In many ways, it is merely a new name for an approach to decision making which good management has always practiced. As Colonel G. A. "Abe" Lincoln, the distinguished Head of the Department of Social Sciences at West Point from 1953 to 1969, remarked to one of the authors after a lecture to the cadets on systems analysis in the early 1960's: "You know, you aren't doing anything new. You're just applying the techniques of rational decision making we've been teaching for years. The only difference is that you're *doing* it."

According to some accounts, systems analysis means the use of high-speed computers and complicated mathematics to reduce all problems to complex formulas, with much attention to costs and numbers and none to effectiveness and judgment, military or otherwise. "Decision making by computer" is the way this view is often summarized in the press. Such descriptions show a lack of knowledge not only about systems analysis and about the force planning process in DoD but also about the ways Service leaders and the Joint Chiefs of Staff make their views known and about the willingness of Secretaries of Defense to have their judgment replaced by computers.

Systems analysis is not synonymous with computers. There is no essential connection between the two. Development of the former in no way depends on the latter. Computers are useful in the analysis of problems requiring large-scale data handling or many repetitive calculations; for example, in calculating fallout patterns or the damage to population and industry caused by nuclear weapons. What computers are doing here, however, is calculating, a task that except for the volume of data involved can be (and was in DoD for a long time) done by hand. Whether it is desirable to use a computer for a particular problem depends on the amount and character of the data and the calculations. Computers cannot replace analysts and decision makers, however, because they are not a substitute for good, clear thinking. (Unfortunately, many attempts at clear thought that have nothing to do with computers are often called "computer thinking.") Just as analysis is the servant of judgment, computers are a servant of analysis.

Systems analysis is not a panacea for the problems of defense. Most defense issues are highly complex, with variables of unknown or uncertain magnitude. Even the best studies leave much to be desired. And no study can account for all the variables or quantify all the factors involved. But analysis can be an aid to judgment by defining issues and alternatives clearly: by providing responsible officials with a full, accurate, and meaningful summary of as many of the relevant facts as possible, an agreed-upon list of *dis*agreements and their underlying assumptions, and the probable cost of hedging against major uncertainties.

Finally, systems analysis is not "scientific" in the same way as physics or engineering. In important ways, systems analysis draws upon the scientific method, using that term in its broadest sense; however, this fact does not make it scientific. Openness, explicitness, objectivity, the use of empirical data, quantification, and a self-correcting character—the basic characteristics of the scientific method—are desirable and feasible goals for systems analysis. But analysis in a policy environment calls for more than simply applying the scientific method. Too many of the underlying assumptions of policy decisions are *not* rigorously verifiable, or cannot be verified at all. Many of them involve value judgments by policy makers as to what an uncertain future is likely to be, or should be. The point of analysis is not to give the answer, but rather to show how the answer depends on various assumptions and judgments.

In any analysis, the assumptions drive the conclusions. There can be no doubt about that, nor about the fact that there is no single "right" set of assumptions, but only a variety of sets of relevant assumptions, each more or less equally defensible. Some people suggest, however, that many analyses of force requirements, since they are based in each case on someone's assumptions, should not be believed. If by that they mean that a piece of analysis should not be taken as an authority simply because it *is* an analysis, we would agree. In fact, one of the main jobs of the Systems Analysis office was to examine the assumptions used in analyses done by the Services and, where desirable, to suggest alternative assumptions to the Secretary of Defense. And, as we have noted, analyses done in OSD were subject to similar counteranalyses by the Service staffs. In doing an analysis to persuade the Secretary that he ought to approve the development and procurement of a new aircraft, a Service might include the assumption that the cost per pound is half that of all preceding aircraft. The plausibility of such an assumption can be checked and tested and called to the attention of the Secretary. He can choose to believe if it is supported by good evidence, or he might well require detailed analysis and explanation. All assumptions, regardless of origin, can be put to the test of debate and common sense.

In this important sense, systems analysis becomes a method of interrogation and debate suited to complex issues. It is not a substitute for debate, but rather a set of ground rules for a constructive and convergent debate. It gives the participants useful guidelines for clarifying and resolving disagreements. It requires that methods of calculation and assumptions be made explicit so that they can be double-checked; it helps in identifying uncertainties and evaluating their importance. It encourages the use of a consistent set of assumptions for evaluating competing weapon systems, so that a weapon system is not bought or rejected on the basis of a set of assumptions most favorable or prejudicial to it. In short, in a very meaningful sense, systems analysis as actually used in DoD was a way to focus debate on specifics rather than generalities. And to the extent that it succeeded, the debate became more concerned with *what* was right than with *who* was right.

Systems analysis usually includes numerical calculations. Where appropriate, it applies modern analytical methods, including economic theory, mathematical statistics, operations research, game theory, and various techniques known as "decision theory." To some practitioners, unfortunately, the application of these fancy mathematical techniques has become synonymous with systems analysis itself. The fact is, however, that most of the systems analysis work in the Department of Defense between 1961 and 1969 used nothing more complex than simple arithmetic and a pragmatic approach to problems that emphasized certain fundamental ideas or "working" premises. Understanding these premises—which stood the test of use and helped systems analysis contribute significantly to the management of the Defense Department—is more important than understanding the whole bagful of fancy techniques.

The main working premise of systems analysis as it was used in the Pentagon was to remember that analysis is the servant of judgment. Systems analysts tried to distinguish which factors and assumptions were important to the decision, why they were important, and how they affected the outcome, so that the decision maker could focus his judgment on the really crucial issues. In all cases, the aim was to illuminate and inform judgment, not to replace it. Indeed, systems analysis *cannot* replace judgment, because no important defense policy issue will ever be wholly susceptible to precise analysis.

The fact that systems analysis was used in the Pentagon as the servant of judgment and not as a substitute for it needs to be emphasized, because there has been much misunderstanding of this point both by critics of the use of systems analysis in defense policy making and by some systems analysts themselves. The critics point out that there are always important uncertainties in any policy issue and that for this reason judgment must play the decisive role in making sensible choices. To a large extent, they are right. But they are wrong in making an indiscriminate attack. Systems analysis can solve some parts of a problem and in this way remove some elements of uncertainty from the decision process. As McNamara once said:

I am sure that no significant military problem will ever be *wholly* susceptible to purely quantitative analysis. But every piece of the total problem that can be quantitatively analyzed removes one more piece of uncertainty from our process of making a choice. There are many factors which cannot be adequately quantified and which therefore must be supplemented with judgment seasoned by experience. Furthermore, experience is necessary to determine the relevant questions with which to proceed with any analysis.

I would not, if I could, attempt to substitute analytical techniques for judgment based upon experience. The very development and use of those techniques have placed an even greater premium on that experience and judgment, as issues have been clarified and basic problems exposed to dispassionate examination. The better the factual basis for reflective judgment, the better the judgment is likely to be. The need to provide that factual basis is the reason for emphasizing the analytical technique.[16]

The reasons for the critics' concern over the role of judgment is understandable. Much of the formal literature on analytical methods —particularly that on operations research—seems to suggest that formulating the problem, gathering data, and making assumptions are uninteresting preliminaries and that the action really starts when the mathematical model begins to calculate the optimum solution. But in most analyses of policy issues, the vast majority of the important effort is devoted to seeking and then asking the right questions, formulating the problem, gathering relevant data and determining their validity, and deciding on good assumptions. Rather than preliminaries, these items are in fact the heart of good systems analysis.

In the world of operations research and computers, the name of the game is to calculate the best solution, given certain assumptions. But in the world of policy analysis, there is no best solution to most questions, because there is no single universally valid set of assumptions and no agreement on values. There are only better solutions and worse solutions. Avoiding bad solutions is a sufficiently ambitious goal for most policy analyses.

For example, in evaluating the decision to deploy a full-scale, antiballistic missile (ABM) defense, the important thing was not to design a mix of ABM and air defense systems that was optimum for some single set of assumptions. It was, instead, with the help of systems analysis, to identify such key facts as that (1) a full-scale ABM would be ineffective in saving U.S. cities if the Soviets reacted by deploying penetration aids, multiple warheads, and more offensive forces and (2) a full-scale ABM system would be ineffective in saving many lives after a full Soviet attack if the system were deployed without a large-scale civil defense program.

Or to take another example, in evaluating alternative levels of strategic offensive forces, the Systems Analysis office, working with the Services and the JCS, developed a graph depicting theoretically how the number of Soviets killed or Americans saved related to various numbers of U.S. offensive missiles. As one would expect, the curve rose steeply at first and gradually flattened out after the destruction of the most vital targets was assured and the United States could attack only less and less worth-while targets, or as targets probably already destroyed were reattacked. While there was no single "best" point at which the United States should stop acquiring offensive missiles (Minuteman and Polaris) to use in a retaliatory attack, it is clear that over 1,500 the additional returns became very low. A judgment had to be made. What analysis did was to help the Secretary of Defense avoid committing many billions of dollars for substantially larger numbers of additional offensive missiles, whose effect would be to raise the probable number of Russians killed by an amount insignificant either to deterrence or actual war—assuming that the Soviets did not react to our increased deployment—and perhaps to achieve virtually no net gain if the Soviets did react. This particular curve could not tell the Secretary of Defense the best answer, but it did help identify a lot of bad ones.

In brief, the suggestion of a conflict between judgment and analysis is false. Ultimately, all defense policies are made and all weapon systems chosen on the basis of judgment. There is no other way. The real issue is whether judgments have to be made in a fog of inadequate and inaccurate data, unclear and undefined issues, conflicting personal opinions, and "seat of the pants" hunches, or whether they can be made in the clearer air of relevant analysis and experience, accurate information, and well-defined issues. The point is to render unto analysis the things that are analysis's and unto judgment the things that are judgment's.[17]

Another working premise of systems analysis was summarized by one of the mottos of the Systems Analysis office: "It is better to be roughly right than precisely wrong." The motto was a reminder to analysts to concentrate, not on pinpoint accuracy on a part of a problem, but on approximate accuracy over the total problem. The ability to recognize, make judgments about, and be comfortable with *roughly right* information and analysis is a most valuable but scarce talent. It is the opposite of suspending judgment until calculations are precise and "all the facts are in." All the facts will never be in, and in the meantime decisions have to be made on the best information available.

A third such premise was to fit the analytical tools to the problem at hand. Emphasis was placed, not on the tools themselves, but rather on defining and solving problems by whatever tools seemed most appropriate. In other words, the choice of methods used was based on the problem and the availability of data, not vice versa. Again, this contradicts the impression one gets from reading much of the academic literature on systems analysis. Many authors appear to be mesmerized by the analytical tools and more concerned with fancy techniques than with finding workable solutions to real problems, using whatever tools may fit. They emphasize methodology as if the only choice were between a rigorous analytic solution and nothing.

Complex mathematical and computerized methods certainly have their place, especially when many quantifiable factors and numerous calculations are involved. They proved to be highly useful in analyzing U.S. strategic nuclear forces and strategic mobility forces. It would have been wrong not to use them on these problems. Nevertheless, it is impressive how much can be, and was, done with the simplest tools of analysis. In fact, most of the really important contributions made by the Systems Analysis office between 1961 and 1969 were based on simple analytical tools, often being worked out by hand with no more sophisticated equipment than pencil and paper.

For example, as discussed further in Chapter 4, the tool that finally cut through the maze of conventional force ratios based on counts of divisions in Europe was a simple cost analysis. For years, civilian leaders in DoD had been told that NATO forces in the critical center region of Europe, numbering around 25 divisions, were hopelessly outnumbered by those of the Warsaw Pact, numbering about 175 divisions. Put simply, the problem was finally resolved by counting soldiers, equipment, weapons, and supplies, instead of divisions. At one point the debate centered on the development of "equivalent effectiveness" ratios for a U.S. and a Soviet division. None of the complex methods tried—war games, simulations, and the like— proved to be helpful in making this assessment. Finally, the Army staff was asked to estimate what it would cost to buy a complete Soviet division force, if its equipment were made in American factories and its soldiers were paid American wages and supported at the American standard of living. The answer came back that the United States could buy three Soviet-type division forces for the cost of one of ours at U.S. prices. Now, of course, cost does not equal effectiveness; *but additional cost plus good judgment ought to yield additional effectiveness.* In other words, if a U.S. division force costs as much to buy as three Soviet-type division forces, it ought to be at least as effective as three of theirs, or else we should redesign our divisions along Soviet lines. And if this was true, simple division counts alone were inadequate as a means of comparing forces.

A final working premise of systems analysis as used in DoD was the substitution of numbers for adjectives where possible. Rather than carry the analysis only to the point where he can say that system A is "better" than system B because it will cost "less" or last "longer," a good systems analyst will attempt to determine how much better in terms of, say, targets destroyed, how much less in terms of total systems cost over a five- or ten-year period, and how much longer in terms of operationally useful life. But while systems analysis stressed treating quantitative aspects quantitatively, this was not to say that all matters could be reduced to numbers, or even that most could be, or that the most important could be. It was merely to say that the appropriate method for dealing with some aspects of problems of choice requires numbers.

The issue here is not numbers versus adjectives, but clarity of understanding and expression. Numbers are an important part of our language. Where a quantitative matter is being discussed, the greatest clarity of thought is achieved by using numbers, even if only expressed as a range. To say that nuclear power for surface ships offers something between X and Y percent more capability per ship to carry out a given mission is much more useful than to say that nuclear power provides a "major increase" in effectiveness. This is not to rule out judgment and insight. Rather, it is to say that judgments and insights, like everything else, need to be expressed with clarity if they are to be useful.

Even when uncertainties are present, it is better to use numbers than to avoid them. Quantitative analysis is possible even if there are uncertainties. There is a substantial literature on the logic of decision making under uncertainty going back at least as far as Pascal, Bernoulli, and Bayes in the seventeenth and eighteenth centuries. Moreover, there are simple techniques for dealing with uncertainties which make it possible to point out the major ones for the decision maker and indicate their significance. In fact, rather than conceal uncertainties, a good analysis will bring them out and clarify them. A best guess, of course, is not the same as certain knowledge. It is desirable to examine the available evidence and determine the bounds of uncertainty. In many analyses done for the Secretary of Defense, the Systems Analysis office carried three estimates through the calculations: a "best" or most likely estimate, an "optimistic" estimate, and a "pessimistic" estimate. This procedure was dubbed "bop (for *best, optimistic, pessimistic*) estimates." Of course, there may be differences of opinion in defining the three categories, but generally a meaningful range can be found to satisfy all parties.

"Bop" estimates, for all their difficulties, produced some unexpected benefits. For one thing, they led to valuable clarity of thought on the matter of comparing our forces with those of our opponents. There is a common philosophy that, in all cases of doubt, the safe thing to do is pick from the high end of the range of uncertainty in estimating the enemy's capabilities and from the low end in estimating one's own. If the question is missile reliability, for example, safety lies in overestimating theirs and underestimating ours. This might be the best approach if we had unlimited resources. But, in fact, it can be just as dangerous to overestimate the enemy's capabilities, relative to our own, as to underestimate them. Overestimates do not necessarily lead to insurance and safety; they may lead to the pricing of important capabil..ies out of the market and to strategies of despair. For instance, if the Warsaw Pact really outnumbered NATO 175 divisions to 25, a logical inference would be that we could not hope to stop a Pact attack with nonnuclear means, and therefore we must rely on the immediate use of nuclear weapons, in which case U.S. conventional forces in Europe serve no useful purpose and should be cut back to save money.

Some have criticized systems analysis on the grounds that it tends to overemphasize factors that can be reduced to numbers and under-emphasize factors that cannot. As one Senate subcommittee has cautioned: "An analysis which emphasizes cost-effectiveness and gives special attention to quantification runs the risk of shortchanging or ignoring non-quantifiable costs and benefits."[18] There is a poten-tial danger here. It is possible for an analyst to become so intrigued with the measurable aspects of the problem that he gives inadequate attention to important nonquantitative factors. However, the ten-dency to ignore important factors, quantitative or nonquantitative, is a failing that is less likely to occur under the systems analysis ap-proach than under alternative approaches. For it is a vital part of systems analysis to bring to bear the best of relevant, modern analytical techniques for organizing data and summarizing important aspects. If an individual must lay out clearly all his assumptions, objectives, and calculations, both his critics and the decision maker can see what was done and whether the analysis overemphasized quantitative factors, if indeed it did. But if he is allowed to keep it all in his head, in an appeal to experience and judgment, others have no way of knowing what factors were emphasized. Our own experience suggests that the intuitive judgment of the experienced professional in any complex field often rests on at least as great an oversimplification of important aspects as that of the most quantitative-prone systems analyst.

A Final Point

No large organization—military or civilian, public or private—is likely to pursue automatically the broader national interest, as dis-tinct from its own institutional and parochial interests, without external forces and leadership in that direction. The main job of the Secretary of Defense, we believe (and McNamara believed), is to lead the Department in the pursuit of the national interest. He cannot do this job by passively administering a predetermined budget ceiling, rubber-stamping his approval on agreed JCS recommendations, and adjudicating Service disagreements. He has to take the initiative, raise issues, provoke debate, demand studies, stimulate the development of alternatives, and then decide on the basis of fact and merit. PPBS has proved to be a valuable instrument for helping the Secretary of Defense be an effective participant in the strategy, force, and financial planning process in DoD.

While we think the potential value of PPBS is high, there are obvious limits to what any management system can do. It can't turn poor judgments—or judgments one happens to disagree with—into good, agreeable decisions. It can't prevent poor or haphazard analysis. It can't provide an instant data base. It can't guarantee leadership, initiative, imagination, or wisdom.

The future role of PPBS in the Department of Defense depends greatly on the attitude of the Secretary of Defense. The *sine qua non* for PPBS is to have a Secretary who wants it, understands it, and is prepared to use it. If the Secretary of Defense does not want or understand PPBS and the management tools that make it work, they cannot be forced upon him. As one observer has said: "PPBS can be a splendid tool to help top management make decisions; but there has to be a top management that wants to make decisions."[19]

Much of the controversy over PPBS, particularly the use of systems analysis, is really an attack on the increased use of the legal authority of the Secretary of Defense and an expression of a view about his proper role. The individual Secretary's concept of management is the critical element in determining the kind of management system that will be used in the Defense Department in the future.

CHAPTER

3

Why Independent Analysts?

Controversy over the Systems Analysis Office

Very few people, with the possible exception of a few economists, believe that national economic policies should be decided mainly by economists. Very few people, except for a few welfare workers, believe that national welfare policies and programs should be determined primarily by welfare workers. Even fewer people believe that our nation's educational programs and policies should be determined mainly by teachers and professors. These matters are all considered too important to be left to the experts. Indeed, what we need in these fields is more "civilian control." And yet, ironically, many people believe that national military policies and programs should, in effect, be the exclusive preserve of the military. Of course, they pay lip service to the principle of civilian control. But let the Secretary of Defense overrule the Joint Chiefs of Staff (JCS) on a recommendation about weapons or force requirements, and watch the charges of "downgrading the military" fly. As the House Armed Services Committee expressed it (after noting McNamara's refusal to go ahead with a new manned bomber, a new interceptor, and a few other JCS-sponsored items) in their report authorizing defense appropriations for fiscal 1969:

. . . the committee feels that too much emphasis has been placed upon the recommendations of persons who lack actual military experience and a frame of reference which can best be gained by long immersion in military matters over a period of years. Not enough emphasis, it is felt, is placed upon the recommendations of those who have attained their knowledge through years of doing and being exposed to the actual threat of extinction by a determined enemy. There are, unfortunately, some policymaking civilians in the Department of Defense who seem to know the cost of everything, but the value of nothing.

The committee is acutely aware that morale among the officers of the armed services has been steadily eroding. One way to reverse this trend is to substantially curtail the authority and number of those who make their decisions which affect the future survival of America with a slide rule, and to seek instead the advice of those who have been trained throughout their adult lives to the task of preserving America and our way of life.[1]

This chapter sketches the role played by independent civilian analysts in the Systems Analysis office between 1961 and 1969 and explains why we believe such analysts should continue to play a substantial role in planning military strategies and forces. We use the terms "independent civilian analysts" and "career military officers"— or civilian analysts and military for short—in a special sense. Not all civilians are independent of the military bureaucracies. Not all military officers lack intellectual independence. But a successful career in a military Service does demand a very full commitment of a man's allegiance and an apparent acceptance of shared beliefs. The important distinction, however, is not military versus civilian, but degree of career and intellectual independence.

Before proceeding, we want to note clearly two fundamental points. First, civilian advice on questions of military strategy and force planning was never intended to replace—nor can it ever replace—military advice. The Systems Analysis office in no sense supplanted the JCS. To argue that it did is really to insult the JCS, whose members have a statutory obligation to present such advice to the President and are quite capable of making their views known in any case. The main source of advice to the President and the Secretary of Defense on strategy and force planning has been and remains the JCS, and nobody we know challenges that arrangement. But many people question whether the Secretary of Defense should also have *substantial* (as opposed to token) civilian help on these matters. That is the real issue: not civilian participation per se, but civilian participation that is effective and meaningful. To have such an impact, the degree of participation must at least be sufficient to enable the Secretary, if he chooses, to modify substantially the military strategies and forces put forward by the JCS. Essentially this means having alternative proposals available in the same degree of detail as those offered by the JCS.

Second, every group has its limitations, including the civilian analysts. Among the limitations of civilians are a lack of detailed knowledge of military operations, an essentially intellectual—rather than a life—commitment to military matters, a tendency to concentrate on the quantifiable aspects of a problem and to treat numbers as immutable truths, and, often, a lack of appreciation for the practical problems involved. There is also the danger that a conceptual solution will be mistaken for a practical solution, that victory in debate will be mistaken for victory in war (though the civilian analysts aren't alone in either of these).

But the question at issue here is the need for substantial participation by independent civilian analysts, and part of the answer comes from a frank recognition of the institutional limitations on the career military officer. In speaking of the limitations of career military officers as strategists and force planners, however, we want it to be absolutely clear that we are discussing group and not individual behavior. The U.S. officer corps is highly professional; it is well educated. These men dedicate their lives often at great personal sacrifice for the benefit of their country. They take their responsibilities seriously and bear them with fortitude. Individual by individual, few professions can compare with the American officer corps for high standards of training, ability, and commitment to public service. We know from personal experience officers who are in training and intellect the peers of any civilian analysts and better than most. Hence, we do not want our discussion of military institutional limitations and group behavior to be taken to suggest anything less than the greatest respect for the dedication, honor, and ability of military men as individuals. But every group has its limitations and its blind spots—including the civilian analysts.

Prior to 1961, strategy formulation and force planning within civilian-set budget limits were dominated by the military. While many civilians had held senior positions in the military departments and in the Office of the Secretary of Defense (OSD) before this time, these positions represented traditional civilian skills such as finance, administration, production, personnel, law, science, and engineering. Except for what he could get from others on a strictly *ad hoc* basis, all of the Secretary's advice on military strategy and force planning came from the JCS and the Services. No organization in OSD had a charter to deal with these important issues. The Secretary was almost completely dependent on military advice, and he had no effective way to challenge it. In other words, force requirements, estimates of the cost and effectiveness of new weapon systems, the best mix of forces and the like, by and large were what the military said they were.

As we have seen, one of McNamara's major innovations was to establish a predominantly—but not exclusively—civilian group to work full time to advise him on such questions. Operating initially under the Comptroller, this group gradually expanded in numbers and responsibilities and in 1965 was established as a separate entity under an Assistant Secretary of Defense. The charter that established the Office of the Assistant Secretary of Defense for Systems Analysis read, in part:

The responsibilities of the Assistant Secretary of Defense (Systems Analysis) are

1. To review, for the Secretary of Defense, quantitative requirements including forces, weapons systems, equipment, personnel, and nuclear weapons.

2. To assist the Secretary in the initiation, monitoring, guiding, and reviewing of requirement studies and cost-effectiveness studies. . . .

Under the direction, authority and control of the Secretary of Defense, the Assistant Secretary of Defense (Systems Analysis) shall perform the following functions:

1. Develop measures of cost and effectiveness in order to make quickly and accurately analyses of a variety of alternative programs of force structure, weapons systems, and other military capabilities projected over a period of several years.

2. Assemble, consolidate, summarize, and present data in various forms so as to show the total implications of alternative programs in terms

of relative costs, feasibility and effectiveness and the problems of choice involved.

3. Analyze and review quantitative requirements in the following functional fields:

   a. Force Structures
   b. Total Manpower
   c. Weapons Systems, and Major End Items of Matériel; e.g., bombs, torpedoes, ships, vehicles, ammunition
   d. Nuclear Weapons
   e. Transportation, including mobility and deployment
   f. Information and communication systems closely related with the above requirements.

4. Analyze and review quantitative military requirements of allied and other foreign countries.

5. Assist the Secretary of Defense in initiating, monitoring, guiding, reviewing and summarizing of requirements studies. . . .[2]

This charter clearly put the civilian-led Systems Analysis office into an area that had been the exclusive preserve of the military professionals on the Service and JCS staffs. Yet there was no requirement, written or unwritten, that members of the Systems Analysis office have any formal military training, or, indeed, even any prior military experience. Nor was there any requirement that a certain percentage of the office's personnel be career military officers. (In fact, the number of such officers averaged about one-third, and they made a significant contribution.)

Many students of national security affairs would not find this anomalous. The Eberstadt task force on National Security Organization reported to the first Hoover Commission in 1949:

Much has been written and said about the incapability of civilians to deal with military matters. Military science, it is said, can be the province only of the military. That may be true on the battlefield: it is not true in the realm of grand strategy. Modern war cannot be left solely to the generals.[3]

The task force then recommended, among other things, a greater centralization of authority in the Secretary of Defense and improved coordination between civilian and military officials throughout the national security organization.

Others, particularly military men, have seriously questioned such civilian participation, however. General Thomas D. White, former Chief of Staff of the Air Force, clearly reflected the deep resentment of the military when he wrote in 1963:

In common with many other military men, active and retired, I am profoundly apprehensive of the pipe-smoking, tree-full-of-owls type of so-called professional "defense intellectuals" who have been brought into this nation's capitol. I don't believe a lot of these often over-confident, sometimes arrogant young professors, mathematicians and other theorists have sufficient worldliness or motivation to stand up to the kind of enemy we face.[4]

Another Air Force Chief of Staff, General Curtis E. LeMay, echoed these sentiments five years later. In the preface to his book entitled *America Is in Danger,* he noted:

. . . the military profession has been invaded by pundits who set themselves up as popular oracles on military strategy. These "defense intellectuals" go unchallenged simply because the experienced professional active duty officers are officially prohibited from entering into public debate. The end result is that the military is often saddled with unprofessional strategies. . . . Today's armchair strategists, glibly writing about military matters to a public avid for military news, can do incalculable harm. "Experts" in a field where they have no experience, they propose strategies based upon hopes and fears rather than upon facts and seasoned judgments.[5]

Nor has this kind of criticism been limited to Air Force generals. Vice-Admiral Hyman G. Rickover has been one of the most outspoken critics of civilian force planners. In May 1968, testifying before a House subcommittee, he compared them to "spiritualists" and "sociologists" and accused them of "playing at God while neglecting the responsibility of being human." He went on to say:

The social scientists who have been making the so-called cost effectiveness studies have little or no scientific training or technical expertise; they know little about naval operations. . . . Their studies are, in general, abstractions. They read more like the rules of a game of classroom logic than like a prognosis of real events in the real world. . . .

In my opinion we are unwise to put the fate of the United States into their inexperienced hands. If we keep on this way, we may find ourselves in the midst of one of their cost effectiveness studies when all of a sudden we learn that our opponents have ships that are faster or better than ours.[6]

Some Congressional supporters of this point of view have been equally outspoken. As noted earlier, during 1968 and 1969 the Chairman of the House Armed Services Committee repeatedly called for abolishing the Systems Analysis office. (Fortunately, these attempts were blocked by the Senate Armed Services Committee.) Further, he made it clear in his correspondence with Secretaries Clifford and Laird that it was the function itself he objected to, not just how it was carried out.

Thus, there is little doubt that the direct and effective participation of civilian analysts in force and weapon system decisions has been, and remains, highly controversial. Whether the practice will continue appears uncertain. Civilian analysts in the Pentagon came in for their share of criticism by Republican leaders during the 1968 Presidential campaign. And the Nixon administration waited a full year before submitting the name of a new Assistant Secretary of Defense for Systems Analysis to the Senate for confirmation.

What, if anything, would be lost if strategy and force planning again became virtually an exclusively military preserve? We believe a great deal. These issues lie at the heart of the Secretary of Defense's responsibilities. If he is to carry out these responsibilities, he must exercise independent judgment; he must be able to take the initiative when the national interest demands it. To do so, he needs a staff of competent analysts directly responsible to him who are dedicated to looking at questions of strategy and forces—and especially their interrelationships—from his and the President's viewpoint. A Secretary cannot be a strong and active leader in the critical area of planning national security policy without staff assistance that is independent of vested Service interests.

There are risks in this role for both the Secretary and the staff. A Secretary of Defense who actively seeks the best solutions to problems, rather than simply engineering compromises among competing interests, will inevitably offend some powerful advocates whose views are not accepted. Nevertheless the Secretary has the responsibility to advise the President and the Congress on how much of this country's resources ought to go into defense and how those resources should be used. To make judgments on the merits of proposals presented to him, the Secretary needs to see the case *against* each proposal as well as the case for it. An essential part of the job of the Systems Analysis office was to see to it that the case against proposed programs was properly developed. For example, the office developed much of the case against deploying the Army-proposed full-scale antiballistic missile system when it was debated in DoD between 1964 and 1968. Similarly, it developed much of the case against the Air Force's new manned bomber and the Navy's nuclear-powered frigates. Thus, much of the criticism directed against the civilian analysts was really related to specific decisions; people who, for one reason or another, disliked a particular decision attempted to fault the process that led to it. Also, a Secretary who seeks control over defense policy and programs will at times offend the powerful heads of Congressional committees. The staff that has advised him or provided information on controversial matters will also come under fire.

Notwithstanding the controversy that surrounded it, the Systems Analysis office was the only predominantly civilian staff organization in the Defense Department whose primary and full-time responsibility was to investigate and provide information, ideas, and advice on questions of strategies, force requirements, and costs from the perspective of the Secretary of Defense. The institutionalization of the office was a direct outgrowth of the centralizing and integrating forces reflected in the defense reorganizations of 1947, 1949, 1953, and 1958. The office was led by a Presidentially appointed civilian because it was established to give the Secretary of Defense a point of view that was independent of the military authority structure and individual Service interests. In matters of strategy and force planning, the Secretary already had as much military advice as he could possibly use. What McNamara saw in the Systems Analysis office was a group of men who worked for him and him alone, with his problems and the national interest seen with a perspective similar to his own uppermost in their minds. The existence of such an analytical staff freed him from total dependence on the military staffs. It enabled him to lead—to challenge, question, propose, and resolve disputes—instead of merely serving as a referee or a helpless bystander.

Of course, other OSD staff offices also look at problems from the

Secretary's viewpoint, but they are not primarily concerned with strategy and force requirements. The Director of Defense Research and Engineering is concerned with science, technology, and weapons design and engineering; the Assistant Secretary for Installations and Logistics specializes in logistics management—transportation and warehousing policies, procurement, real property, and inventory management; the Assistant Secretary for Manpower and Reserve Affairs specializes in manpower management problems—pay and allowances, medical care, education and training, and reserve affairs; the Comptroller is a financial manager, chief budget officer, and auditor; the Assistant Secretary for International Security Affairs is a political adviser, diplomat, and coordinator with the State Department; the Assistant Secretary for Administration is concerned with Department-wide organizational problems and with OSD administration; the Assistant Secretary for Public Affairs advises the Secretary of Defense and other DoD officials on public affairs, handles or controls all press releases, public briefings, speeches, and press queries; the General Counsel is a legal adviser and often a general trouble shooter.

That the Secretary needs full-time staff help in planning forces and strategy might be clear enough, but can civilians give him that help? For the reasons discussed below we believe they not only can, but must.

The Nature of Military Requirements

The main reason for civilian participation in the strategy and force planning process is the nature of military requirements. Put simply, the JCS and the Services, acting independently, cannot possibly determine the nation's military requirements, because except in the most local and immediate situation, there is no such thing as a "pure" military requirement. Our military needs depend on the objectives that our national leaders decide to pursue and on the intensity with which they want to pursue them. What is worth trying to do depends, among other things, on what is possible, on how effective the means for doing it are, and on what it costs. No amount of patriotic oratory can overcome the fact that our national resources are limited. Money spent for defense cannot be spent elsewhere, as any politician knows and as dissatisfied voters do not forget. Therefore, choices have to be made. If we buy more nuclear deterrence, we have fewer resources for meeting other national needs, whether military or nonmilitary. Each choice of a major military objective and the forces to go with it involves judgments about the relative priorities of various military and nonmilitary needs. A decision on the number of divisions that should be maintained to defend Europe depends on a large number of factors, only a few of which are military. The list includes, among other things: costs, as they relate both to budgets and to the balance of payments; judgments about sharing the defense burden between ourselves and our allies; political and psychological judgments about the effects of various military force deployments on the political behavior of our friends and enemies; estimates of the threat, and judgments about the deterrent value of our strategic nuclear forces.

Put another way, at the national policy level, ends and means interact. What are ends from one point of view are means from another. A given objective is likely to be only one of a number of alternative ways of achieving a still broader objective. For example, in arriving at a posture for antisubmarine warfare (ASW) the military officers responsible might take as their objective the achievement of, say, 90 percent attrition against the enemy's submarine fleet within the first ninety days of a war. This might or might not be a reasonable objective, depending on the cost of achieving it and on alternative paths to the broader objectives of limiting damage to U.S. military and commercial shipping and moving the necessary men and supplies overseas. It might be the case that the ability to inflict 90 percent attrition within the first ninety days would be inordinately costly, or it might be that a lesser amount of ASW forces combined with a commercial shipping stand-down and an effective airlift might do the job less expensively. The important point is that there is nothing absolute about achieving 90 percent attrition within ninety days. To the officers in charge of antisubmarine warfare, such a rate may appear to be a "requirement," but to the Secretary of Defense, or the President, destroying the enemy's submarine fleet is only one means of achieving the broader objectives of limiting damage to our ships and getting men and material where they are needed. If they should decide, after comparing more ASW forces with other programs, to divert some resources to alternative means and thus achieve only 80 percent (or lower) attrition in the ninety-day period, this decision in no way implies a failure to meet one of the nation's military requirements. In choosing defense policies, national officials are faced, not with rigid, immutable requirements, but with a range of possible objectives that depend on factors other than military ones. At one end of this range lies a set of modest military objectives coupled with the most austere forces that could possibly achieve them. This end is characterized by little military security, but it involves correspondingly low costs. At the other end of the range lie ambitious military objectives coupled with forces large enough to assure a high confidence of being able to achieve them even under most unfavorable circumstances. This end is characterized by great military strength, but heavy costs. Somewhere between these extremes lies a host of intermediate objectives.

As a hypothetical example of this broad range of possible objectives, the United States might elect, on the one hand, to (1) abandon all commitments to defend Pacific areas beyond Hawaii; (2) maintain no more than a token capability to assist our NATO allies in case of a European war; and (3) maintain a strategic nuclear force which, if the Soviet Union should attack the United States with a force no larger than predicted by intelligence, would be able to destroy 10 percent of the Soviet population in retaliation. On the other hand, the United States might elect to (1) maintain enough forces to overwhelmingly defeat attacks on friendly nations in Europe, the Middle East, Southeast Asia, and Korea, (a) without having to use nuclear weapons, (b) even if the attacks were made in all areas simultaneously, and (c) even if we had no advance warning; and at the same time (2) maintain a strategic nuclear force which, if the Soviet Union should attack the United States with a far larger force than estimated by intelligence, would nevertheless be able to destroy 75 percent of the Soviet population and virtually all of her industry in retaliation.

While these alternatives are perhaps extreme, they are not beyond reasonable consideration. The modest objective approximates a "Fortress America" posture. The ambitious objective permits the United States to respond to a conceivable, if unlikely, threat. But the point is that, faced with this wide range of possible objectives, not to mention the more reasonable ones between these extremes, military experts cannot possibly determine a pure and simple military requirement for the country. There can be no single "right" answer to the question, "What are U.S. military requirements?" It depends on how ambitious the objectives are. These objectives, in turn, depend on a balance between the benefits to the nation and the costs and risks involved. This means that our elected national leaders must exercise choice among desirable objectives. It also means that to set the military budget, they must look realistically at the outputs of different military programs. Thus, defense policy issues involve much more than questions of military operations or cause-and-effect relationships between military forces. These are *national* policy issues involving political, economic, and technical factors as well as military ones. At the highest level of government, these various aspects of national security policy must be taken into account simultaneously, and the defense decision-making process must be designed to contribute to that endeavor.

Balancing military objectives with other national objectives is an immensely difficult job. Responsibility ultimately rests with the President, as head of the Executive Branch of the government, and with the Congress. (The division of responsibilities between the President and the Congress is, of course, complex. That we refer in this chapter to the President and the Secretary of Defense as the principal decision makers should not be interpreted as downgrading the equally important role of the Congress in these matters.) The particular balance between military and nonmilitary objectives which the President presents to the Congress each year in his legislative and budgetary programs is made by him in the light of recommendations solicited from his senior advisers, both military and civilian, and his estimate of what he can persuade the Congress and the public to support.

In emphasizing the many factors entering into a defense issue and the many backgrounds and skills that need to be applied, we do not mean to suggest that military men should exclude themselves from nonmilitary aspects of a problem; that would be neither realistic nor desirable. Nonmilitary factors interact with military ones in an intimate way, so that they are difficult to separate. Moreover, some military officers are well qualified in other areas, such as the physical sciences, economics, diplomacy, and so on. But we do want to emphasize two points. First, because force planning intimately involves nonmilitary factors, there is a definite need for representation from other backgrounds, disciplines, and points of view in the planning of forces and strategies. Because military officers have such powerful career interests in military solutions to national security problems, it is especially important that they not be allowed exclusively to judge the relevant nonmilitary factors. Much of the job of the Systems Analysis staff was to help the Secretary reach more balanced decisions by drawing on these additional backgrounds and viewpoints. Second, it is wrong to drape all defense planning with the mantle of "military judgment" or "operational experience." Military judgment, if by that is meant specifically the experience and knowledge gained by military men in combat, comes at a very high price. But this valuable currency is cheapened when exaggerated claims are made for it. Nor is it fair to suggest that military advice and experience are being ignored, or that military judgment is being downgraded, when the Secretary of Defense makes a decision contrary to that of his military advisers. He has to balance many factors in a decision. Most people will agree to this in theory, but it is a fact often forgotten when concrete examples arise.

A Supposititious Alternative

The fact that the JCS cannot establish a military requirement before the nation's military and nonmilitary objectives have been brought into balance by our national leaders does not, in itself, justify the need for substantial participation by civilian analysts. As an alternative to having the Joint Chiefs state a single and absolute military requirement for the country, one might suggest that they instead develop a list of priorities of possible military objectives which would cover the spectrum from modest to ambitious. With each set of objectives, the JCS could define the military forces required to achieve the various objectives with various degrees of confidence and risk. And for each level of military force, the JCS could tabulate the estimated cost. This would allow the Secretary of Defense and the President to weigh the cost of various degrees of military security against possible risks and against the nation's other needs before making a choice. Having done that, the military forces would be defined by military men, all without the help of civilians.

While this procedure might sound attractive in theory, its premises are completely unrealistic. It would limit the Secretary of Defense to the role of judge rather than leader. Though he could select one of the alternatives presented in the JCS list, he would be unable to challenge the particular objectives and alternatives which the JCS chose to present. He would be unable to get independent evaluation of the JCS estimate of the amount of military force required to attain a particular objective with a given degree of confidence. He would be unable to probe for and suggest an alternative mix of forces which might achieve a given objective at a lower cost. And he would have to take it on faith that the cost estimates listed in the menu next to a given set of objectives would be accurate when the time came to pay the bill. In short, though such an arrangement is possible in theory, the Secretary of Defense could not stand up for the national interest in the area of his principal responsibility: determining fundamental national security policy.

The reason he could not is simple. Challenging, testing, probing, checking, and suggesting alternatives in an informed and responsible way are more than any one man can do by himself. He would have to have a staff to help him, and that staff would have to become deeply involved in matters in the province of the military professionals. This is the only way the Secretary of Defense can exercise initiative and avoid becoming a captive of the information generated by the military staffs. In the most direct sense, it is the only way the country can be assured of achieving a significant degree of civilian control.

The need for such independent staff assistance in the Defense Department is far from a new idea. Samuel Huntington expressed the issue quite clearly in 1957 in his book *The Soldier and the State:*

The greatest single deficiency in the organization of the Department of Defense was the absence of the proper staff assistance for the Secretary. Legal authority was meaningless without the organizational means to exercise it. "The creation of the staff facilities," Forrestal said in 1949, "is paramount even to the increase in power." The Secretary was surrounded by antagonists. In front were the State Department and the NSC, presumably pointing out the path of national policy; behind him the Treasury and the Budget Bureau, always acting as a drag; on either side, the Joint Chiefs and the Comptroller pushing him off the road in one direction or another. The Secretary, however, was institutionally naked and defenseless. It was not surprising that his functions were encroached upon by other agencies or that he himself found it necessary to identify his interests and role with that of some other agency. He had no support with which to maintain an independent stand.

One argument raised against this need for more staff assistance for the Secretary was the already great size of the Office of the Secretary of Defense. The OSD was intended, it was said, to be a small policy-oriented unit but it had expanded to gigantic proportions with a staff of over two thousand. What use could the Secretary possibly have for any more staff assistance? He was surfeited with staff. *The reply to this, of course, was that the important issue was not how much staff the Secretary had but rather what kind of staff he had, and to what extent the staff was actually his.* A staff is only a real aid to an executive when its outlook is his outlook and its interest is his interest. No one of the Secretary's principal staff organs had a scope or an interest as broad as that of the Secretary. The Joint Chiefs gave him military advice; the Comptroller gave him budgetary advice and represented the needs of the economy; his other eight assistant secretaries all had limited functional responsibilities and interests; the service secretaries defended their own service needs. The Secretary's office, as formally defined, was not really his office. It contained agencies and officials representing forces independent of him and whom it was his job to balance and control. The Secretary had assistance to help him accomplish everything except the discharge of the one responsibility which was his and his alone: the formulation and enforcement of overall defense policy. What was needed was the institutionalization of the secretarial viewpoint: a small, competent, corporate body to aid the Secretary in developing the interests and advice surrounding him into a comprehensive military program. This absence of staff agencies with a secretarial perspective made the Secretary unable to play an independent role and to formulate his own viewpoint. Instead of rising above this subordinate interest within his department, the Secretary was forced to lower himself and identify his interest with that of one of his subordinate agencies.[7]

Similarly, writing of his experience in the Admiralty in the early days of World War II, Winston Churchill said:

One of the first steps I took in taking charge of the Admiralty and becoming a member of the War Cabinet, was to form a statistical department of my own. For this purpose I relied on Professor Lindemann, my friend and confidant of so many years. Together we formed our views and estimates about the whole story. I now installed him at the Admiralty with half a dozen statisticians and economists whom we could trust to pay no attention to anything but realities. This group of capable men, with access to all official information, was able, under Lindemann's guidance, to present me continuously with tables and diagrams. . . . They examined and analyzed with relentless pertinacity all the departmental papers which were circulated to the War Cabinet, and also pursued all the inquiries which I wanted to make myself.

At this time there was no general governmental statistical organization. Each department presented its tale on its own figures and data. The Air Ministry counted one way, the War Office another. The Ministry of Supply and the Board of Trade though meaning the same thing, talked different dialects. This led sometimes to misunderstandings and waste of time when some point or other came to a crunch in the Cabinet. I had, however, from the beginning my own sure, steady source of information, every part of which was integrally related to all the rest. . . . It was most helpful to me in forming a just and comprehensible view of the innumerable facts and figures which flowed out upon us.[8]

Effective leaders reserve the right to challenge preferred solutions, to be skeptical, to suggest alternatives, and to demand analysis rather than assertions. McNamara, the strongest leader the Defense Department has known, operated under the theory that information is power. To help him get that information in the area of military objectives, force requirements, and costs, he created the Systems Analysis office. This office did for McNamara what the statistical department did for Winston Churchill in World War II; it filled the void in the Office of the Secretary of Defense of which Huntington spoke in 1957.

Military Expertise

Even granting that an effective Secretary of Defense needs a staff that works for him alone, one cannot escape the further question of whether civilians are qualified to discuss military matters on equal terms with professionals whose lives have been devoted to the study, and risked in the application, of military science. The answer to this hinges on which part of the spectrum of military affairs one considers. Without question, the civilian members of the Systems Analysis office (except for a few with prior military service) were unqualified to lead men in combat. They pretended to no ability to command an attack carrier, to launch an ICBM, to lead an infantry squad, or to determine the best tactics for a particular military operation. At the same time, however, it is hard to see how knowledge of these matters is sufficient to determine national security objectives, the total forces required to achieve those objectives, and their costs. One doesn't have to have been an infantryman to study how big an Army the United States should have or a pilot to study how big an Air Force. Indeed, there is evidence to suggest that such knowledge can be a disadvantage, because it discourages seeing the larger picture.

One of the main traits of career military officers is a preoccupation with means rather than ends—with performance rather than effectiveness. This is because careers are largely built around particular military means, not around the identification and solution of broad military problems by whatever means seem most apppropriate. Retired General Curtis LeMay spent his career in long-range bombers and, throughout his career, remained an unabashed advocate of strategic bombing as the solution to most of the military problems facing the United States. Vice-Admiral Hyman Rickover is a naval nuclear power-plant expert who would solve U.S. antisubmarine warfare problems by buying more nuclear-powered ships. All this is not to say that there are no military experts capable of solving broad military problems; but they are the exception, not the rule. The normal military career is built around the mastery of a particular means of waging war, and when an individual reaches the top levels of his Service, he is likely to continue to look to that means to solve the problems that arise.

Equally important is the mistaken popular view of what "military science" is all about, at least in its strategy and force planning aspects. Some believe that military strategy and force planning is an insider's business and that civilians cannot possibly design military forces any more successfully than a layman could design bridges. This view will not stand up to close scrutiny. What is commonly called "military science" is not scientific in the same sense as law or medicine or engineering. It encompasses no agreed-upon body of knowledge, no prescribed curriculum, no universally recognized principles that one must master to qualify as a military professional. (The so-called "principles of war" are really a set of platitudes that can be twisted to suit almost any situation.) Graduates of the military academies and war colleges cannot state with any precision what strategy and force posture may be needed to support certain foreign policy objectives, because there are no great immutable military laws to determine these requirements, and few military men would claim that there are.

While there has been some recent improvement in this regard, even our most highly trained officers, the graduates of the four-year military academies, still receive very little instruction in planning or analyzing strategy and force requirements. And, interestingly enough, what instruction they do receive along these lines is based largely on the works of civilians. Military professionals are among the most infrequent contributors to the basic literature on military strategy and defense policy. Most such contributors are civilians: Bernard Brodie, Paul Hammond, Malcolm Hoag, Samuel Huntington, Herman Kahn, Henry Kissinger, Thomas Schelling, Albert Wohlstetter, to name only a few. Generally speaking, military academy students pursue a curriculum not unlike that of most undergraduates in a civilian university. They study engineering, government, economics, history, languages, and the like. Their initial vocational training has characteristically been centered either on small-unit tactics or on historical accounts of battlefield maneuvers, contests between fleets, or bombing campaigns. It has not centered on the choice of military objectives as one of many competing national objectives. It has not concentrated on the design and analysis of broad, alternative strategies and forces. It has not focused on applying modern analytical techniques to problems of strategy and force planning. Nor does later Service-oriented instruction substantially alter the picture. Military officers have a great deal to learn just to master the technical demands of their profession, and much of this later instruction concentrates on that. At branch and career schools, officers are taught largely how to plan and conduct low-level tactical operations in the particular branch of their particular Service, using current equipment. They are not trained in tactics and operations with future equipment which is the concern of the force planner. Later, at staff and war colleges, they are taught much the same thing, but on a larger scale and on a combined arms basis. They are only inferentially taught how to analyze and evaluate over-all strategy and force structures. In short, military officers cannot—simply on the grounds of formal training—speak with any more authority than well-informed civilians when it comes to discussing, understanding, and contributing to problems concerning total force requirements and design. Indeed, given the rapid turnover on the military planning staffs in DoD, as opposed to that on the civilian side, there is some question, so far as direct and continuing experience with force planning problems in a particular functional area is concerned, as to who the more experienced really are.

But what about what might be called career experience? Again, there is little in the typical officer's early career experience that qualifies him to be a better *strategic* planner than, say, a graduate of the Harvard Business School. The first two decades of a typical military career are focused largely on command and staff jobs concerned primarily with the management and administration of small field units, either in garrison or in combat. Such experience is too local and immediate to have much bearing on projected grand strategy or long-term force levels and major weapons procurement. Furthermore, the deliberate policy of giving career primacy to developing generalists leads the ambitious officer into a wide variety of disparate command, staff, and administrative positions at various echelons, creating a broad background of brief and discrete experiences, none of which are much preparation for contributing to high-level *national* defense policy and strategies. Indeed, even the most senior military staff work is mainly a continuum of service management and administration on a larger scale. There is little that is specifically military in a typical background of career development experiences which can be identified as preparation for participating in the decision-making dialogue involving strategy, forces, and weapon mixes at the national level. (However, many military officers do obtain advanced degrees from leading civilian universities, which enhances their knowledge and their analytical skills.)

Thus, while the Harvard Business School may not be the best training for rendering advice on over-all strategy and forces, neither necessarily is battalion or brigade command experience and graduation from a service staff school. Whatever the optimum is, no single institutional group has a monopoly on it. The point is that military professionalism is largely in the conduct of military operations, not in the analysis and design of broad strategies. And while many of our most distinguished strategists are military men, not all strategists are military men, and most military men are not strategists. Both civilians and military men can bring to discussions of strategy and force planning elements that the other can bring only with great difficulty, if at all. Because of the limitations and strengths of *both* civilians and military men, there is a need for both in such discussions.

Some Factors Limiting Military-Sponsored Alternatives

A second reason why the Secretary of Defense must look beyond the military for information, advice, and staff support on questions of strategy and force planning is that, more often than not, JCS- and Service-supported alternatives are unrealistic and unresponsive to the needs of the Secretary of Defense. We have already touched on one of the reasons for this: the protection of institutional interests. There are other institutional factors. One is inter-Service competition.

The Services actively compete with each other in fulfilling many of the major missions of the Department of Defense. Both the Air Force, with Minuteman missiles and manned bombers, and the Navy, with Polaris and Poseidon submarines, provide strategic offensive systems; the Army, Navy, and Air Force all compete for mobility missions; Air Force and Marine Corps land-based aircraft, Navy carrier-based aircraft, the Army's armed helicopters, all compete for tactical air missions. There are certain advantages to this competition; but there are also disadvantages. Like any bureaucracy, each Service naturally advocates reliance on its own chosen instruments. Moreover, each Service speaks its own dialect; it may be impossible, without detailed probing, to determine the bases for differences on key issues or key assumptions in their arguments. The Services should not be expected to produce balanced and objective viewpoints on issues for which they are competing for funds or prestige. Nor, as discussed further below, can the JCS, who are the same people, representing the same institutions, temporarily serving in another capacity.

In addition, a Service tends bureaucratically to neglect or undervalue programs that support the missions of other Services or new or unconventional missions that the Service feels will draw funds away from traditional missions. The Navy was cool toward the Polaris program in the late 1950's and early 1960's because it drew funds away from other Navy programs; similarly, it has recently been cool toward Fast Deployment Logistics Ships, because they would be used mainly for Army missions. As a result, many issues of national policy significance may not even be raised by the Services.

Even more importantly, if the military want to approach a problem in a particular way, they will be reluctant to expose the Secretary of Defense to alternatives that might take him in another direction. In other words, the Secretary cannot depend on the Services and the JCS to develop for his consideration alternatives that are responsive to his interests, if his interests are perceived to be contrary to those of the military. For example, several times during the Vietnam build-up, the JCS wanted to call up the reserves and involuntarily extend terms of service. The President preferred—for many reasons—not to do so. Yet, no plan ever came from the JCS showing *how* the build-up could be done without reserve call-ups or involuntary extensions of tours. It was the Systems Analysis office that finally had to develop such alternatives.

Or take the balance-of-payments problem caused by maintaining over 300,000 American troops in Europe. Whenever this problem forced consideration of a troop reduction, the JCS approach was to propose withdrawal of visible combat units, because they are politically and psychologically and militarily the most important units ("slashing the gold watches")—and, therefore, the most difficult to withdraw. The JCS did not favor any reductions and therefore never produced a plan that would realistically get at the problem by first reducing headquarters and support personnel or identifying and cutting back marginal activities, before withdrawing major combat units. Again, such plans had to be initiated in the Systems Analysis office.

The controversy over deactivating the 6th Infantry Division provides yet another example. During the spring of 1968 it became apparent that some cutbacks in defense programs were unavoidable. The main reasons were the increasing costs of the Vietnam conflict and Congressional insistence on a cut in federal spending as the price of agreeing to President Johnson's proposed 10 percent tax surcharge. As a result, the Department of Defense had to cut fiscal 1969 expenditures by $3 billion and the approved Five-Year Defense Program by almost twice that amount. Fortunately, the Secretary of Defense did not have to levy quotas on the Services and let them cut at will. Instead, he was able to identify and eliminate programs of relatively low priority from the point of view of total defense needs, or, if you will, the national interest.

One of the programs that the Systems Analysis office suggested be cut was the 6th Infantry Division, a recently authorized unit that had only just begun to form. Since a cut in total Army manpower and some reductions in equipment for units in the United States were inevitable, it made sense to us to take all the cuts at one time in one place, the 6th Division, enabling the Army to concentrate the available resources in the other four active divisions in the Army's Strategic Reserve and upgrade their readiness. This seemed particularly appropriate in view of the fact that Congressional leaders were concerned over the readiness of the four divisions and Army leaders had been complaining of their inability to get them ready because of personnel shortages. Nevertheless, the Chief of Staff of the Army objected strongly to this recommendation and proposed instead to spread the cuts over all five divisions in the Strategic Reserve and other Army units in the United States. Secretary Clifford agreed with Systems Analysis that it was better to have four combat-ready divisions, fully manned and equipped for quick deployment, rather than five understrength, underequipped divisions that could not be ready for combat much faster than National Guard divisions. Whatever the reasons for the Army's position—and institutional considerations were obviously one—the important point is that if the Secretary had been forced to rely exclusively on the Army for alternatives to meet the problem, a proposal to drop the 6th Infantry Division from the force structure would certainly not have been one of them.

Perhaps the best example of the unrealistic alternatives provided by the military, however, can be found in the Joint Strategic Objectives Plan (JSOP). The JSOP is a document in several volumes prepared annually by the JCS staff (called the Joint Staff) with help from the military departments. It contains the forces that the JCS believe are required to carry out national strategy and military objectives. Before 1969, the JSOP consistently recommended forces costing 25 to 35 percent more than those finally approved by the

President and the Congress. For example, during the seven years of McNamara's leadership, total defense spending would have been over $120 billion higher if he had approved all the JSOP-recommended forces. The JSOP in itself was ample evidence of the lack of realistic alternatives presented by the military experts to the Secretary of Defense. One result is that no Secretary of Defense has ever approved all the forces recommended in the JSOP.

Another reason why JCS- and Service-supported alternatives sent to the Secretary of Defense are unrealistic and unresponsive is *intra-*Service competition. Each Service is itself a coalition of strong and competing viewpoints. For example, the Navy is really three navies—the surface Navy, the air Navy, and the submarine Navy, not to mention the Marine Corps—and each group competes vigorously for money and missions. To a lesser degree, the same can be said of the Tactical Air Command and the Strategic Air Command in the Air Force, and air defense and ground combat elements in the Army. As a result, a Service position will already be a negotiated compromise by the time it gets to the Secretary of Defense (or the JCS), with many strongly held views or ideas suppressed.

Although there are exceptions, most military officers are forced for career reasons into the traditions and ways of thinking not only of one Service but of one particular area within that Service. For example, in the Navy comparatively few officers get an overview of antisubmarine warfare. That field is composed of officers who are expert in submarine-versus-submarine warfare, in destroyer-versus-submarine warfare, or in land-based or sea-based aircraft-versus-submarine warfare. Few have a really wide range of experience during their early years when their attitudes are being formed. While senior officers attempt to rise above the narrow parochialisms of their particular areas within a Service, and indeed above their Service itself, it is a psychologically difficult thing for any man to do. We are all most at ease in familiar surroundings, and the military man has the greatest confidence in the forces he understands and knows best. This tendency is reflected in recommendations as to the priority of military objectives as well as to the best kinds of forces for achieving them.

The degree to which such channelized thinking affects the military professional's recommendations depends, of course, on the individual himself. But even those whose thinking is utterly unparochial face yet another barrier. Picture, if you will, the difficulty that an admiral in the 1930's, somehow foreknowing that aircraft carriers were to be the capital ships of the future, would have faced in recommending against further battleship construction. The system would have allowed him to recommend *for* new carriers, but it would hardly have tolerated, much less have provided incentives for, recommendations *against* the battleships cherished by his less farsighted fellow officers. Similarly, a senior officer in the Strategic Air Command, even if he felt that ballistic missiles were preferable in every way, would find it most awkward to propose that the United States should reduce its bomber force. It would be acceptable for him to propose more missiles, but unacceptable to propose no more bombers. Even more unthinkable would be a proposal from that officer to eliminate some Air Force Minuteman missiles to pay for a larger number of Navy Polaris missiles, even if he was convinced that the trade would be a good one.

The military Services, working individually, are not in a good position to make recommendations on over-all defense programs. Admirals parceling out part of a Navy budget to pay for sea-based ballistic missiles (as opposed to carriers), Air Force generals parceling out part of an Air Force budget to pay for land-based ballistic missiles (as opposed to bombers), and Army generals parceling out part of their budget to pay for an antiballistic-missile defense system (as opposed to more divisions) cannot, except by the most improbable accident, generate a well-balanced and integrated strategic force. The Joint Chiefs of Staff try to overcome such problems, and to some extent they do. But even that organization falls far short of the mark, for a number of reasons.

Except for the Chairman, each of the Chiefs of Staff has two jobs. He is at once the senior officer of his particular Service and a member of the joint body. Such an arrangement, while preferable to having no joint organization at all, limits the role that the Chiefs can play in resolving differences between Services and in making recommendations that, though necessary to a balanced and economical program, are distasteful to individual Services. A Chief's primary responsibility and therefore his organizational loyalty is, both understandably and indeed necessarily, to his own Service, not to an abstract concept of unity which the JCS organization is supposed to represent, and certainly not to the Office of the Secretary of Defense. The Chief of Naval Operations is unlikely to recommend shifting the nation's land/sea-based tactical-air mix in favor of additional land-based Air Force squadrons. The Army Chief of Staff is unlikely to recommend expanding the Marine Corps at the expense of the Army. The Chief of Staff of the Air Force is unlikely to recommend buying armed helicopters for the Army rather than tactical fighters for the Air Force. Nor is any man of integrity who has spent the morning as a Service Chief arguing the case *for* a program likely to spend the afternoon arguing *against* it in his role as a Joint Chief simply because he is then supposed to have a wider viewpoint. The Chiefs cannot be both advocates and judges.

The problem, if it can be called that, arises not because these men are less than dedicated to their nation's best interests, but precisely because they are so dedicated. Their first duty is to see that their own Service is first-rate. This is greatly reinforced by having its origin in the completely honest but nonetheless ingrained attitudes and loyalty to a particular Service and its traditions which are the product of a lifetime's dedication. As General LeMay puts it: "I make no claim to objectivity. It is well known that I am partial to air power as a defensive arm of our country. However, I have been and shall continue to be as fair to the other services *as my experience will permit.*"[9]

This problem is even greater in the case of the Joint Staff on whom the Chiefs themselves depend (to the extent that they don't use their own Service staffs). The Joint Staff is composed of officers borrowed from the individual Services. Unlike the Chiefs themselves, who face retirement at the end of their assignment to these most senior of all military positions, the Joint Staff officers face a return to their parent Service and continuation of their careers. These men's activities during their tour in the Joint Staff are far from secret. Taking a strong position in opposition to the one held by a parent Service can have a fatal effect on chances for promotion. The Joint Staff officer cannot casually adopt a position independent of his Service. For this reason, the Joint Staff is and must be more of a negotiating organization than an analytical one.

Inter-Service disputes in the JCS are usually resolved in a compromise position recommending at least part, sometimes all, of each Service Chief's position. Aside from avoiding distasteful splits in the

JCS, this also satisfies the Chief's inherent conservatism in estimating force requirements. Thus, the JCS is really a committee of hostile and competing interests, and its positions are generally compromises arrived at through hard bargaining. The Chiefs can always agree on more for everybody; and since this is the path of least resistance, it is the one most frequently taken. One little-known and unfortunate by-product of this course is that the Secretary of Defense and the other Presidentially appointed civilian leaders in DoD find it very difficult to get meaningful professional advice—uncontaminated by bargaining twists and political slants—on force level aspects of national security problems from senior military officers. What they are more likely to get is high-quality advice on the political and legislative repercussions. Our senior military officers are politically very sophisticated and their headquarters responsibilities require them to spend considerable time keeping abreast of political affairs. Although there are distinguished exceptions, and the urgent pressures of daily work make it quite understandable, the fact is that few senior military officers in the Pentagon give sustained personal study to the complex strategic issues underlying force requirements or to the analyses of force and weapon requirements prepared by their staffs.

Innovation and Change

A third major reason the substantial participation of civilian analysts is needed is the independent point of view they can bring to the force planning process. Military officers as a group (and some civilians as well) are in a position to have very limited intellectual and career independence. While many individuals succeed in standing up to the system, there are numerous institutional factors working to limit the officer's intellectual independence. The whole military ethos, conditioned by rank, hierarchy, and discipline, conflicts with the ideas of intellectual independence and objectivity. The military man lives in an atmosphere in which many assumptions, attitudes, and beliefs—generally unspoken—are shared. Some of these, which directly affect strategy and force planning, are well known. For example, most military officers naturally emphasize the military aspects of problems. At one time or another over the past five years, practically every four-star military officer directly involved has described Vietnam as *mainly* a military problem. Similarly, there is an unspoken but widespread assumption that only military (rather than diplomatic or economic) means can assure national security. The Soviets build more ICBM's; the Army proposes an ABM. Those who would deal with the problem by negotiating arms-limitation agreements are viewed by many military men with suspicion. Moreover, most military officers, understandably, have great confidence in the effectiveness of military force in general, and their own preferred arms in particular, as solutions to the nation's security problems. As a result, more military capability is always considered better, and more is usually deemed necessary.

Officers who do not share these beliefs are liable to reprisal on their annual fitness reports. These reports, which serve as the basis for promotion, offer ample opportunities for punishing anything less than wholehearted cooperation. This lack of career independence further helps to ensure conformity to the Service point of view.[10]

By way of contrast, intellectual and career independence were the chief characteristics of civilian analysts in the Systems Analysis office. Relatively unhampered by tradition or institutional restraints, free from the need to build consensus, without a predetermined position to sell, and without the need to be good soldiers, these analysts could more easily ask the hard questions and pose genuine alternatives, arriving at a recommendation via a more rational and objective process. They were not constrained to defer to rank, age, experience, or chain of command. They had the time to think about important long-range policy problems and the room for imagination, initiative, and fresh thinking. They were comparatively free to gore sacred cows. Such liberties are institutionally very difficult to exercise in a military organization, joint or single Service.

There have been loud complaints about civilians "muzzling the military"; but anyone who is familiar with the system knows that most of the muzzling is done by the military themselves. It would be very unusual, for example, for a Chief of Staff to put forward a position on some subject by saying: "Colonel Smith has had a good idea, which I think merits top-level consideration but with which I personally have certain reservations" (something that is not unusual for Assistant Secretaries of Defense to do). In fact, it is very difficult for an individually promoted idea to reach the Chief of Staff level through normal Service channels. Before this can happen, a proposal must have the agreement of all interested parties. Extensive lateral and vertical coordination is a common feature in both the Service staffs and the Joint Staff, with each different agency exercising its "chop" as the price of its concurrence. As a result, the original idea is likely to be bargained and negotiated until a bland compromise is reached that is acceptable to everyone.

For these reasons, excellent ideas generated by very capable military officers are often suppressed in the Services because they run counter to powerful bureaucratic interests. One of the most important contributions of civilian analysts in the Systems Analysis office has been to identify such ideas, bring them to the attention of the Secretary of Defense, and get a hearing on their merits. One such example is the concept of airmobile warfare.

Originally this concept was worked out by imaginative and progressive officers in the Army such as then Lieutenant General Hamilton Howze, Brigadier Generals H. W. O. Kinnard, Delk Oden, and Walter Richardson, and Colonels John Norton, A. J. Rankin, and Robert Williams. However, the Systems Analysis office made a useful contribution to its development and implementation. Furthermore, the testing, evaluation, and speedy introduction of an airmobile division into the force structure received the strong and energetic support of the Secretary of Defense. Without the active, positive interest of the Secretary and of civilians in the Systems Analysis office, it is highly doubtful that the United States would have had an airmobile division or a large and growing Army helicopter force ready to deploy to Vietnam in 1965.

In the spring of 1962, Secretary McNamara sent the Secretary of the Army two memorandums directing him to re-examine in detail the Army's qualitative and quantitative requirements for aviation. The Secretary felt that the Army had failed to exploit opportunities to improve tactical mobility through the greater, more imaginative use of aviation. Before these memorandums were sent, Army officers who supported the airmobile concept were having a very difficult time getting their ideas heard. These memorandums gave them the charter they needed to bring their ideas to the attention of top officials in the Defense Department, where they got the prompt action they deserved. In response to the Secretary's directive, the Secretary of the Army established the "Howze Board" (named after General Hamilton Howze, the director of the study effort). The Board's findings led to the formation of several experimental units, including the 11th Air Assault Division, the predecessor of the 1st Cavalry Division (Airmobile) which has been used so extensively in South Vietnam. The two memorandums, which are reprinted below, were drafted for the Secretary of Defense's signature by the Systems Analysis office.

Airmobile Concept Memorandums[11]

THE SECRETARY OF DEFENSE
Washington, D.C.
April 19, 1962

MEMORANDUM FOR THE SECRETARY OF THE ARMY
SUBJECT: Army Aviation (U)

This is in response to your two November 1, 1961 memoranda which discussed Army aviation and presented the Army's proposed procurement program.

These studies greatly enhanced my understanding of what the Army is seeking to achieve through its organic aviation. However, the quantitative procurement programs fall considerably short of providing, in the near future, modern aircraft to fill the stated requirements. While it appears to me that the Army can and should turn increasingly to aviation to improve its tactical mobility, your memoranda do not give a clear picture regarding either the optimum mix of aircraft types or the absolute total numbers that will be required.

Attached is an analysis of your studies made by my office. I would like your comments on this analysis with particular emphasis on the proposed increased buy of Army aircraft for 1964 and on the position that your predicted requirements in this area through 1970 are too low. These comments should be submitted by 15 May 1962.

Furthermore, I would like the Army to completely re-examine its quantitative and qualitative requirements for aviation. This re-examination should consist of an extensive program of analyses, exercises and field tests to evaluate revolutionary new concepts of tactical mobility and to recommend action to give the Army the maximum attainable mobility in the combat area. It appears to me that air vehicles, operating in the environment of the ground soldier but freed from the restrictions imposed by the earth's surface, may offer the opportunity to acquire quantum increases in mobility, provided technology, doctrine, and organization potentials are fully exploited. I believe further that these mobility increases can be acquired without increased funding by reducing less effective surface transportation systems concurrently. The Army's re-examination should therefore give special attention to the following:

(1) To what extent can aviation be substituted for conventional military surface systems of vehicles, roads, bridging, engineer troops, theater supply and hospital complexes, etc.?

(2) Should newer concepts of VTOL or STOL fixed-wing aircraft be substituted for helicopters, as a means of avoiding some of the high procurement and operating costs of helicopters?

(3) May we use heavy tactical airlift, combined with new techniques in air dropping and possibly better airfield construction and repair capability, to provide part of the logistic support for ground operations? There should be considered the possibility that Air Force lift may be available, after the first thirty or so days of a strategic lift, to augment Army tactical lift capabilities.

(4) What qualitative requirements can be defined for immediately developable V/STOL air vehicles optimized for such purposes as surveillance, target acquisition, weapons platforms, command posts, communications centers, or troop and cargo carriers of significantly heavier loads?

(5) What organizations and operational concepts are required to exploit the potential increases in mobility? Consideration should be given to completely air-mobile infantry, anti-tank, reconnaissance, and artillery units.

(6) What other concepts and ideas, as well as major limitations, bear on this subject? We should seriously consider fresh, new concepts, and give unorthodox ideas a hearing.

The results of the study should be presented in terms of cost-effectiveness and transport-effectiveness factors. The study should involve the full use of field tests and exercises to test new concepts of mobility.

In addition, the use of operations analysts in planning, observing, recording data, and analyzing results for the field test program appears to me to be essential to the effective accomplishment of the entire re-examination.

As a first step in your re-examination of Army aviation requirements, I would like by 15 May 1962 an outline of how you plan to conduct the program. The actual re-examination should be completed and your recommendations submitted by 1 September 1962.

(Signed) ROBERT S. MCNAMARA

THE SECRETARY OF DEFENSE
Washington, D.C.
April 19, 1962

MEMORANDUM FOR MR. STAHR

I have not been satisfied with Army program submissions for tactical mobility. I do not believe that the Army has fully explored the opportunities offered by aeronautical technology for making a revolutionary break with traditional surface mobility means. Air vehicles operating close to, but above, the ground appear to me to offer the possibility of a quantum increase in effectiveness. I think that every possibility in this area should be exploited.

We have found that air transportation is cheaper than rail or ship transportation even in peacetime. The urgency of wartime operation makes air transportation even more important. By exploiting aeronautical potential, we should be able to achieve a major increase in effectiveness while spending on air mobility systems no more than we have been spending on systems oriented for ground transportation.

I therefore believe that the Army's re-examination of its aviation requirements should be a bold "new look" at land warfare mobility. It should be conducted in an atmosphere divorced from traditional viewpoints and past policies. The only objective the actual task force should be given is that of acquiring the maximum attainable mobility within alternative funding levels and technology. This necessitates a readiness to substitute air mobility systems for traditional ground systems wherever analysis shows the subtitution to improve our capabilities or effectiveness. It also requires that bold, new ideas which the task force may recommend be protected from veto or dilution by conservative staff review.

In order to ensure the success of the re-examination I am requesting in my official memorandum, I urge you to give its implementation your close personal attention. More specifically, I suggest that you establish a managing group of selected individuals to direct the review and keep you advised of its progress. If you choose to appoint such a committee, I suggest the following individuals be considered as appropriate for service thereon: Lt. Gen. Hamilton H. Howze, Brig. Gen. Delk M. Oden, Brig. Gen. Walter B. Richardson, Col. Robert R. Williams, Col. John Norton,

Col. A. J. Rankin, Mr. Frank A. Parker, Dr. Edwin W. Paxson, and Mr. Edward H. Heinemann.

Existing Army activities such as Fort Rucker, RAC, STAG (Strategic and Tactics Analysis Group, Washington, D.C.), CDEC (Combat Development Experimental Center, Ft. Ord) and CORG (Combat Operations Research Group, Ft. Monroe), combined with the troop units and military study headquarters of CONARC, and in cooperation with Air Force troop carrier elements, appear to provide the required capabilities to conduct the analyses, field tests and exercises, provided their efforts are properly directed.

The studies already made by the Army of air mobile divisions and their subordinate air mobile units, of air mobile reconnaissance regiments, and of aerial artillery indicate the type of doctrinal concepts which could be evolved, although there has been no action to carry these concepts into effect. Parallel studies are also needed to provide air vehicles of improved capabilities and to eliminate ground-surface equipment and forces whose duplicate but less effective capabilities can no longer be justified economically. Improved V/STOL air vehicles may also be required as optimized weapons platforms, command and communications vehicles, and as short range prime movers of heavy loads up to 40 or 50 tons.

I shall be disappointed if the Army's re-examination merely produces logistics-oriented recommendations to procure more of the same, rather than a plan for implementing fresh and perhaps unorthodox concepts which will give us a significant increase in mobility.

(Signed) ROBERT S. MCNAMARA

The Increasingly Analytical Basis of Force Planning

The changing environment of military strategy and force planning provides a fourth main reason for the participation of civilian analysts. The problems of selecting strategies and weapon systems today are quite unlike those that existed before World War II. Then, military technology changed relatively slowly in relation to the average length of a military or political career. Soldiers and statesmen could learn most of what they needed to know about military power and the relationship of weapon systems and forces to national security from books and their own direct experience. The personal experience of military and civilian leaders, combined with the collective experience of centuries of warfare, was immediately relevant to contemporary affairs; there was no strongly felt need to interpret their experience by the careful rules of scientific method.

But something new has been happening since World War II. Science and technology have "taken off" and are now in a period of rapid, accelerating growth. Nuclear weapons, electronic devices, computers, large-scale rockets, and space vehicles are only a few products of the revolution in military technology. Before World War II, we did not plan on technological change; we merely adjusted to it. Now we are forced to plan on it. We are debating the extent to which inventions can be scheduled, and we have weapon systems that are obsolete while still in development.

This development has important implications for the strategy, force, and financial planning process. Rampant technological change is producing not only better weapons of familiar kinds but many new kinds of weapons as well. The progression from the B-17 to the B-52 was straightforward and apparently obvious. But now we face the possibility of developing any of literally dozens of distinctly different strategic nuclear delivery systems, not to mention other kinds of weapon systems and forces. And the number of possibilities is expanding. A similar expansion is taking place in almost every kind of warfare. We have not escaped, however, the ancient necessity for choice arising from the scarcity of available resources. Technology today provides more options for military hardware than we can possibly buy. We cannot afford to develop and procure a dozen different strategic nuclear delivery systems at the same time. If we tried, we would doubtless end up squandering our resources and not doing a good job on any of them. We have to choose.

Not only has the revolution in military technology changed the character of our military program; it has also, to a significant degree, blurred the lines separating the various Services. Is a missile an unmanned aircraft, as the Air Force likes to think, or a piece of long-range artillery, which is the Army view? Most major military missions today require the participation of more than one of the Services. Our principal concern must therefore be centered on what is required by the Defense establishment as a whole for a particular military mission —not on what is required by a particular Service for a part of that mission. This is equally true for the development of major new weapon systems. In this environment, the limitations of the individual Services, discussed earlier, take on even greater significance.

Another implication of the rapid pace of technological change is that many of today's weapons differ markedly from the weapons used in World War II and in Korea. Although it is difficult to know exactly how and to what extent, this means that some aspects of earlier combat experience are probably out of date; and peacetime experience with military operations, however valuable, does not completely make up for this. The wars of the future will differ in important ways from the wars of the past. If we are to prepare for the future, we must address these changes in a systematic way and try to understand their implications for the choice of weapon systems and strategy. This problem is not unprecedented. The machine gun reduced to irrelevance much of the tactical planning preceding World War I. Armored warfare made a mockery of the assumptions on which the Maginot Line was based. The development of naval aviation dealt battleships such a blow that their defenders became a symbol of adherence to outmoded thinking. But the problem is of greater proportions today than ever before. To deal with it, both the Secretary of Defense and the military leaders are being forced to rely increasingly on analysis to buttress their experience and judgment.

Modern-day strategy and force planning has become largely an analytical process. The increasing role of analysis is reflected in the fact that each Service has now developed its own "systems analysis office" in the Pentagon in addition to contracting with predominantly civilian "think tanks" to support its planning effort. The main reason for the military's large and increasing use of civilian analysts is that civilians are often better trained in modern analytical techniques (although the number of trained officers is increasing). Moreover, freed from the frequent diversions to other tasks that the career military officer must face, the civilian has more time to concentrate on developing his analytical skills and more opportunities to use them. In any event, as the force planning process becomes more analytical, the argument for excluding civilians from this process on the grounds that they lack relevant operational experience becomes less and less convincing.

Another important implication of the increasingly analytical nature of the force planning process is the need for an "analytic policeman."

Each Service and each important group within a Service is constantly seeking ways to expand its mission and its size and is not immune from using biased assumptions to make its case. Inter-Service rivalry is a poor substitute for independent civilian analysts in OSD, because the Services, like the JCS, agree on more for everybody. Nor can one realistically expect the analytical groups working for each of the Services—such as The Rand Corporation, the Center for Naval Analyses, and the Research Analysis Corporation—to be completely objective in their studies. Valuable as they are, these groups tend to take on the philosophical coloration of their sponsoring organization, if for no other reason than they are exposed to the same environment and the same influences and get most of their information from the sponsoring organization. Thus, a need remains for an analytic policeman for studies done both within and outside the Defense Department.

Most of the analytical effort in the Department of Defense, by necessity and by preference, is made by the Services and the JCS, either in their own organizations or through the nonprofit think tanks they maintain. One of the functions of the Systems Analysis office was to suggest to the Secretary of Defense potentially useful study projects. When he accepted a suggestion, he would direct the Services or the JCS to begin the project and would ask the Systems Analysis office to monitor the work to assure that details were taken care of, that the assumptions used were satisfactory, and that the final product was in fact responsive to the Secretary's needs.

From time to time the Systems Analysis office did its own analyses. Many times, this was the result of sheer frustration—of not being able to get the Services to do the kind of analysis the Secretary wanted.[12] Mostly, however, these independent analyses were made as straw men—starting points for debate and discussion. This proved to be a highly effective technique for turning the discussion from generalizations to specifics.

No Secretary of Defense has the time personally to conduct discussions of all the complex issues that eventually come to him for decision. He must have a staff to do that for him—a staff that, it is hoped, will ask the questions he would like to have asked himself. The problem lies in sifting through the complexities of each decision in enough detail to discover the key issues. The goal of the Systems

Analysis office was to explore each problem in advance and present the Secretary with a clear understanding of which parts were matters of fact, which matters of differing assumptions, which matters of differing interpretations, and which matters of differing opinion. This process is time-consuming. The Secretary has neither the time to do it in the detail it deserves nor the ability to make good decisions in its absence.

In its role as an analytic policeman, the Systems Analysis office tried to make sure that the methods of analysis used in various studies, and the assumptions that went into them, were both explicit and consistent. It is difficult to overestimate the importance of the latter. Much of the office's work involved enforcing the use of a consistent set of assumptions for evaluating competing weapon systems, so that DoD would not buy one weapon system on the basis of a set of assumptions particularly favorable to it, and another on the basis of a different set of assumptions particularly favorable to it.

In checking assumptions over the years, two things became quite clear: (1) it is always possible to invent assumptions that make any proposed weapon system look good; and (2) generally speaking, there is no single "right" set of assumptions, but a variety of sets, each more or less equally defensible. It is unfortunate that these important points are not widely understood. Far too many people believe that the assumptions offered by the Service sponsoring a new system are the only ones that should be considered. Others keep looking for the "right" set of assumptions, in the way ancient alchemists looked for the philosopher's stone. As a result, they identify a set of assumptions that leads to the conclusion they hoped would emerge and then put forward this conclusion as soundly established, not realizing that quite another conclusion could have been derived from equally defensible but different assumptions.

A good example of the policing function occurred in the establishment of a method of calculating strategic nuclear force requirements. Unlike conventional wars, with their ebbs and flows, their countless decision points, and their tendency toward long durations, strategic nuclear war would probably be short-lived. There is no relevant experience and hence no choice but to rely on analysis. Given a set of forces on either side and a set of assumptions (the list, though long, is not intractable), probable outcomes can be calculated, at least roughly. The problem was that in the Defense Department in the early 1960's there were so many ways of making the calculations that it was almost impossible to determine whether differences in the results were due to differences in method or in assumptions. Over the years, the Systems Analysis office worked with the Services and the JCS to develop a mutually agreed-upon method of calculation. As a result of this work, the Secretary of Defense and other top officials could stop worrying about whether the complex calculations had been done correctly; each advocate could reproduce and verify the results for himself. Differences in results remained, but they were due to differences in assumptions; and each party knew what these differences were. The Secretary could consider each in turn and make his own assumptions as well. This led to more informed decisions than were possible before.

Making assumptions explicit is often the key to understanding why analyses show what they do. (As the saying goes, "Tell me your assumptions and I'll tell you your results.") For example, in the early 1960's, an Air Force analysis showed that the RS-70 (the reconnaissance-strike version of the supersonic B-70 bomber project) was the least expensive weapon for destroying Soviet missile sites to reduce the damage they could cause us. However, one key assumption of the analysis was left implicit. One reason for the apparently fine performance of the RS-70 turned out to be the assumption that the Soviets would not fire their intercontinental ballistic missiles (ICBM's) for several hours after we had had warning that a strike against us was imminent. With that assumption, the Soviet ICBM's might have been easy targets for the RS-70. But if the Soviets chose to fire their ICBM's at the outset, such RS-70's as escaped destruction on the ground would reach the USSR only to find empty ICBM launchers.

Keeping assumptions consistent is also important. In 1963, one of the major reasons for buying the Navy's new light attack aircraft, the A-7, was that it had a much longer range than the then current A-4. The justification was that this longer range would allow aircraft carriers to remain at sea far beyond the range of most Soviet aircraft. However, in 1967, a Navy analysis of the number of missile ships needed to defend our carriers against Soviet aircraft assumed initially that they would be subject to raids by short-range Soviet aircraft, thus increasing the requirement for missile ships. We suggested that unless there was some reason for such a drastic change in tactical doctrine, the analysis should be conducted with the same assumptions used in the A-7 project. They were, and the "required" number of missile ships was reduced accordingly.

An even more striking example of the importance of consistency in assumptions concerns scenarios for antisubmarine warfare (ASW) with the Soviets. In 1967, when the Navy was arguing for the new VSX carrier-borne antisubmarine aircraft, it produced a study which assumed that all Soviet submarines would be predeployed on the high seas before we could trap them in or near their ports with barriers of mines and our own submarines. Under such circumstances the United States would be heavily dependent on sea-based patrol aircraft for offensive ASW action; thus the case for going ahead with the VSX was convincing. A year later, with the VSX project approved, the Navy argued for more submarines to increase the number of patrol zones near Soviet submarine bases. Again, they produced a massive study to support their proposal. But *this* study assumed that Soviet submarines would not be predeployed, thus making the case for more submarines appear convincing. In fact, both sets of assumptions are possible and deserve consideration. Our point is simply that the requirements for both weapon systems should be considered under both assumptions in a balanced way.

In addition to ferreting out hidden assumptions and enforcing the use of consistent and reasonable assumptions for evaluating competing weapon systems, the Systems Analysis office acted as the Secretary of Defense's interrogator. On the theory that cross-examination is the best way to reach the truth, the office stimulated debate to ensure that all points of view were considered.

A case in point is the debate over the full-scale deployment of an antiballistic missile system (ABM) for defending U.S. cities against Soviet attack, an important debate in the Defense Department between 1965 and 1968. In 1966 the Secretary of the Army and the JCS recommended to the Secretary of Defense that he approve the full-scale deployment of the Nike-Zeus ABM system to defend U.S. cities against a Soviet nuclear attack. While initial estimates of the cost of the system were between $10 and $20 billion, McNamara believed that the eventual costs of such a system would reach $40 billion. But the costs were not the most important question. The decisive issue was whether a full-scale ABM defense system at any cost, deployed together with complementary fallout shelters and air defense, would in fact save many millions of lives in a nuclear war.

As the time neared for a decision, Secretary McNamara noticed that the Army's estimates of the number of American lives saved by a full-scale ABM system in a Soviet attack gave a very different and much more optimistic picture than the estimates produced by the Systems Analysis office. In a way, this was not surprising, since the Army was the main proponent of the system, and the Systems Analysis office, as the Secretary's chief interrogator, was charged with the responsibility to make the case against the system. So McNamara asked the Secretary of the Army and the Assistant Secretary of Defense for Systems Analysis to sit down together, with their respective experts, and prepare for him a memorandum of points of agreement and stated known disagreement. In other words, if they disagreed in any estimates, it had to be for reasons that could be stated precisely and explained in laymen's language; it could not be because one side or the other added differently or used different computers. He wanted to know what those reasons were, so that he could judge them himself.

The Army staff and the Systems Analysis staff were briefed on the exercise. The experts on each staff were to lay out all the calculations, step by step, compare them, identify differences, and bring these differences to the attention of their respective leaders. The staffs did just that. In the process, some errors were discovered on both sides. That is not surprising, given such a complex problem involving so many computations. Nor was it surprising how much more zealous and effective each staff could be in discovering mistakes in the other's calculations than in its own.

As the staffs worked, they ironed out the errors and minor technical points and prepared a list of about a dozen significant differences in assumptions and methods. These points were then discussed and debated by the leaders of the two sides. In most cases, it was clear which staff's approach was better, so each side conceded a few points to the other. In a few cases, differences were debated at length. In these cases, calculations showing the probable outcome each way, holding everything else unchanged, proved to be helpful in judging whether the difference was crucial enough for a decision by the Secretary of Defense. Sometimes the calculations showed that an assumption that one side or the other had thought important really was not.

By this process, the most decisive factor in the whole problem—the probable Soviet reaction—was finally identified. The Army's analysis had assumed, implicitly, that the Soviets would continue to deploy the same number and kind of offensive forces projected for them by the national intelligence estimates, even in the face of a major U.S. ABM deployment. Given that assumption, a full-scale ABM system in the United States could be very effective. But if one assumed that the Soviet Union, like the United States, would react to enemy deployment of an ABM system by deploying more missiles and multiple warheads and other devices to overcome opposing defenses, the proposed ABM system would not be effective in protecting our cities from attack. The calculations done by the Systems Analysis office had assumed that the Soviets would so react.

Finally, the Army and the Systems Analysis office prepared an agreed table showing ABM effectiveness with and without Soviet reaction. Those calculations allowed the Secretary of Defense, the President, and other officials to focus on the key issue of the probable extent and character of the Soviet reaction to our ABM deployment. Once the Secretary of Defense and the President had made the judgment that the Soviets almost certainly would react to offset the effectiveness of a U.S. ABM system, the calculations done by the Systems Analysis office became the foundation of the Secretary's case against deployment of a full-scale ABM defense of our cities.

Through this adversary proceeding between opponents with a serious interest in proving their points—a procedure as old as Anglo-Saxon law—the Secretary of Defense got his answer to the question of why the estimates of effectiveness differed. If the experts on both sides agreed, the calculations were likely to be as reliable as human minds could make them. This, of course, did not guarantee that they were right. Both sides may have accepted—indeed, probably did accept—assumptions that would later turn out to be incorrect. Nobody can predict the future accurately. But insofar as possible, human minds were on top of the calculations. And the Secretary wasn't forced to depend on biased or one-sided calculations.

Much of the controversy surrounding the Systems Analysis office resulted from this role. In other words, the office was controversial because it was supposed to be controversial. Its job was to probe, to question Service proposals, to suggest alternatives, to be the Secretary's interrogator. Much of the support for the continued existence of the Systems Analysis office by the Senate Armed Services Committee has been based on the Committee's understanding of the need for an office in OSD to perform this role. For example, Senator Henry M. Jackson made the point quite clearly in the following exchange between himself and one of the authors before the Senate Preparedness Subcommittee on June 3, 1968:

Senator Jackson: I think it is important . . . that we have a good debate and discussion on these fundamental issues. . . . My understanding of Dr. Enthoven's role is that he is there as the devil's advocate raising questions that should be raised, and he makes his recommendations, but he is not the final authority on what the decision is going to be.

Dr. Enthoven: That is correct, sir.

Senator Jackson: And this adds to the debate and discussion. Now, we do not have to agree with Dr. Enthoven, but as in the legal process, the greatest art known to man in getting the truth is the art of cross-examination. I think it is important that these questions be asked, and if an advocate has a good proposal, you will know that it is a good proposal if it can withstand the ruthless interrogation that takes place to try to get the truth. I think it is important that the committee understand the proper context of this whole dialog and discussion that is going on today.
Have I stated your role?

Dr. Enthoven: Yes.

Senator Jackson: Is that essentially correct?

Dr. Enthoven: Yes sir.

Senator Jackson: You are not acting as the Secretary of Defense, or the Secretary of the Air Force, or the Secretary of the Navy. You are in the decisionmaking process from the standpoint of making recommendations based on the techniques that people in your profession have developed to raise questions and seek answers, so that the final authority can reach the kind of decision that hopefully will be a better one than it would be without this kind of dialog.

Dr. Enthoven: Yes, sir; that is correct.[13]

The Case for Independent Analysts in Summary

The Secretary of Defense, if he is effectively to carry out his responsibilities as an executive officer of the government and a politically responsible Cabinet official, must be a leader rather than a judge. He cannot provide leadership in the area of his most critical responsibility—planning national defense policy and the forces to support that policy—if he is the prisoner of a single staff solution or if his alternatives are limited to those negotiated by the military staffs. He needs staff assistance that is independent of the military authority structure and of institutional interests. He needs to be able to choose from among realistic alternatives. This is the heart of the matter and explains why the Systems Analysis office was created.

Military men, no matter how well trained in military science or how experienced in military operations, cannot bring to the councils of government all that is necessary in the formulation of national security policy. Such policy involves much more than military considerations, and because nonmilitary factors are involved, individuals with different backgrounds, attitudes, and perspectives should participate. Civilian analysts are not necessarily smarter nor do they work harder than military officers. But they do have different backgrounds and are generally better trained in modern analytical techniques. More important, because their futures are not hostage to Service retaliation, they are freer to ask hard questions, pose genuine alternatives, and arrive at a recommendation by an objective process.

Arguments against civilian participation in the strategy and force planning process on the grounds of a lack of training and experience will not stand up to close scrutiny. (Indeed, our experience has been that it is often the civilian analysts who have studied in detail and mastered the military aspects of problems under consideration.) Military science cannot furnish unambiguous answers to the question of what our military objectives should be and what they will cost; nor has military instruction really concentrated on answering such questions. Certainly, the belief that our nation's military leaders can derive the forces we need from broad statements on our national goals is not true. In this regard, the scope of military expertise tends to be greatly exaggerated, to the detriment of public understanding and, in the long run, of the military profession. Exaggerated claims of competence can only lead to disappointment and disillusionment as the facts become known.

For a host of reasons, including inter-Service and intra-Service competition, Service and JCS staffing procedures, the strong desire of each Service to expand its size and usefulness, the preoccupation of most officers with military means rather than ends, and the lack of career independence among members of the military profession, the range of alternatives presented to the Secretary of Defense by his military advisers will be constrained by institutional factors. With rare exceptions, they are likely to call only for varying degrees of "more" since this is the only position that can be agreed to by all parties and since it satisfies the military planners' inherent conservatism. If the Secretary wants a wider range of alternatives—alternatives that include "less" as well as possible nonmilitary solutions—he will need civilian analysts possessing the necessary analytical skills and with the charter to cut across Service institutional jurisdictions and integrate force and mission contributions from all the Services. This does not mean that alternatives offered by civilian analysts are necessarily "better" than those of the military. But they are likely to be more broadly based, balanced, and concerned with getting the most from available resources. In any event, some kind of countervailing power is clearly needed if the Secretary of Defense is to sort out the desirable and the undesirable changes.

For many of the same above-mentioned reasons, civilian analysts are needed to pick up good *military* ideas squelched by the Service bureaucracies. Indeed, contrary to the charges of stifling innovation, civilian analysts often enhance the chances of meaningful innovation and change.

Finally, technology has reduced the value of past military experience and increased the inherent uncertainty of planning for the future. "Truths" about defense are now tentative hypotheses at best. In many important respects, all participants in the business of planning our future strategy and forces are beginners. The importance of this task and the huge costs associated with it make force planning on the basis of experience and intuition alone an increasingly unacceptable alternative. We must inform our judgment by good analysis wherever possible in order to reduce as far as possible the levels of uncertainty.

While a logically rigorous analytical process is far from perfect in dealing with complex matters such as national defense, good approximations—objectively and rationally devised—are both necessary and valuable. The analyst can free the decision maker from questions that can best be resolved through analysis, leaving to him the more difficult questions that can be resolved only by judgment.

For these reasons, civilians, despite their own shortcomings, can bring to the discussion of military strategy and force planning valuable elements that would otherwise be absent. We do not pretend that civilians are somehow superior to military planners in ability, character, or dedication. They aren't. And that is not really what we have been arguing here. Rather, we believe that both the military planner and the civilian planner suffer from their own limitations and benefit from their own strengths. We are convinced that arbitrarily excluding either from substantial and effective participation in the formulation of the nation's defense policy would be folly. Clemenceau put it that "war is too important to be left to the generals." Eisenhower countered with "What do politicians know about fighting a war?" Viewed in perspective, both views are legitimate. In the process of determining how much defense is enough, the nation needs the benefit of both.

4

NATO Strategy and Forces

Background

One of the first major policy changes sought by the Kennedy administration in 1961 was to reduce the reliance on nuclear weapons for deterrence and defense and increase the reliance on conventional forces, especially in NATO. This change in strategy was not officially adopted by NATO until May 1967. During the interval, millions of words were written and spoken, both in this country and in Europe, regarding the merits and implications of this change. Much of the discussion in Europe sharply questioned American intentions in proposing it, causing persistent strains in the alliance. Why didn't the Americans simply admit that they wanted to back away from their nuclear guarantee? How could reasonable men fail to see that emphasizing nuclear weapons increased their deterrent value? How would the Russians react to such a change in policy? How could NATO possibly hope to defend conventionally against 175 Soviet divisions? What about the costs? In the United States, the discussion was equally sharp. Why were our intentions being questioned? How could reasonable men oppose any effort to de-emphasize nuclear weapons? How would the Soviets react to such a change? How could NATO possibly hope to defend conventionally against 175 Soviet divisions? What about the costs? On both sides of the Atlantic, the key "fact" was the overwhelming Soviet conventional superiority. Any discussion of conventional defenses soon became stuck on this "fact" and the enormous expense and effort that would be required to offset it.

The roots of the persistent belief that NATO's conventional forces are hopelessly outnumbered run deep and date back to the beginning of the alliance. At the time the treaty was signed, intelligence estimates indicated that the dozen or so scattered, understrength Western divisions in Europe faced 25 fully armed Soviet divisions in Central Europe and, over all, at least 140 to 175 Soviet divisions at full battle strength. (With such a disparity, the estimates did not even bother to include the numerous divisions of the Soviet satellite countries.) Certainly, such gross inferiority suggested that a huge build-up in allied forces would be needed to permit NATO to defend itself without the use of nuclear weapons—that is, to have a "conventional option." Yet, neither the United States nor the Europeans were willing to try to match the Soviet conventional capability. The allies felt strongly that any choice between economic reconstruction and increasing military forces should be made in favor of the former. The United States was unwilling to undertake such an expensive task by itself. Besides, given U.S. nuclear superiority and the lack of an imminent Soviet invasion, neither side felt there was a pressing need for such a build-up. Furthermore, the NATO treaty was not conceived—at least by many of its civilian architects—as a vehicle for actually redressing NATO's military inferiority. Rather, its purpose was to clarify American intentions regarding any Soviet attempt to change further the European balance of power.[1] Such a visible United States commitment to Europe, the first such "entangling" alliance in U.S. history, backed by U.S. nuclear might would be sufficient to stop Soviet expansion. The treaty's power lay in the American military potential: "It is the potential which counts," Senator Vandenberg told his colleagues, "and any armed aggressor knows that he forthwith faces this potential from the moment he attacks."[2] On the other side of the Atlantic a similar note was being sounded. As British Foreign Minister Ernest Bevin put it: "I would emphasize . . . that the real purpose of this pact is to act as a deterrent. . . ."[3]

Despite such statements, the Congress still sought explicit assurances that the treaty would not require the United States to contribute sizable land forces. Indeed, it even questioned the need for the proposed military assistance program to help our allies build up their own forces. The military assistance program (Mutual Defense Assistance Act of 1949) that was finally approved by the Congress was seen as a short-term effort consisting largely of supplying weapons from our surplus World War II stocks.

NATO was thus born with a psychological "complex" about conventional forces. The allies could never hope to match the Soviet hordes. Any attempt would be enormously expensive. Given U.S. nuclear power, such an attempt was unnecessary. The nuclear superiority of the United States was considered clearly adequate to deter any Soviet aggression. This initial concept of the alliance—a clear statement of American intentions, backed by actual nuclear forces and potential conventional forces, the whole constituting a credible deterrent—was to survive with minor revisions as the official NATO policy until 1967.

Challenges to this concept came quickly. By August 1949, the U.S. nuclear monopoly had disappeared in the fallout from the first Soviet nuclear test. The obvious rapid increase in Soviet nuclear capabilities afterward surprised even the most pessimistic. The once clear U.S. nuclear superiority became less and less clear. In June 1950 the deterrent value of nuclear forces was seriously challenged by the invasion of South Korea. Potential conventional forces proved to be a poor substitute in Korea for existing forces.

Largely as a result of these events, the NATO Council meeting in Lisbon in 1952 approved force goals calling for 96 NATO divisions by 1954. It was the last time that NATO was seriously to consider a conventional option until U.S. insistence almost ten years later.

The Lisbon force goals were so far above the existing or even the likely allied force levels that they were met with considerable skepticism. The London *Times* noted that since they would undoubtedly not be met, announcing them simply combined "the maximum amount of provocation with the minimum deterrent effect."[1] The Lisbon goals did accomplish one thing, however. They firmly established the concept of the immense cost required for NATO to meet the postulated Soviet conventional threat. (The equipment and supplies for the requested divisions and aircraft alone would have cost $40 to $50 billion, even then.)

The new Eisenhower administration looked at the costs involved and quickly abandoned any notion of matching Communist forces locally in any theater. The administration proclaimed instead the strategy of "massive retaliation." On January 12, 1954, Secretary of State John Foster Dulles announced that in order to get a "maximum deterrent at a bearable cost" the government had decided to "depend primarily upon a great capacity to retaliate, instantly, by means and at places of our own choosing." "We need allies and collective security," he said, "[but] our purpose is to make these relations more effective, less costly. This can be done by placing more reliance on deterrent power and less dependence on local defensive power."[5] At the same time, the first tactical nuclear weapons were deployed with U.S. forces in Europe, and the Atomic Energy Act of 1954 was passed, permitting information on these weapons to be shared with our allies.

The policy of "massive retaliation" had its immediate effects on NATO planning. In late 1954, the North Atlantic Council formally authorized the NATO commanders to base their plans on the prompt use of nuclear weapons, whether the aggressor had used them or not. Field Marshal Montgomery stated this policy quite clearly:

I want to make it absolutely clear that we at SHAPE are basing all our operational planning on using atomic and thermonuclear weapons in our own defense. With us it is no longer: "they may possibly be used." It is very definitely: "They will be used if we are attacked." In fact we have reached the point of no return as regards the use of atomic and thermo-nuclear weapons in a hot war.[6]

As a result of increased emphasis on the immediate use of nuclear weapons, NATO abandoned efforts toward reaching the original Lisbon goal of 96 divisions and in 1957 adopted a more modest set of goals calling for 30 combat-ready divisions in the center region and deemphasizing the need for reserve forces. At the same time it was made clear that these 30 divisions were "nuclear" forces. This new set of goals was adopted at a time when the Soviet threat was still officially estimated at 175 divisions, of which 140 were said to be active. Furthermore, it was assumed that a total force of 400 Soviet divisions could be mobilized in thirty days. Compared with the NATO *goal* of 30 divisions, the Soviet threat was so huge that any significant NATO resistance without nuclear weapons did indeed seem impossible. This notion was further reinforced by a steady stream of "we can't possibly defend conventionally" statements from NATO's military leaders. The assessment of General Matthew Ridgway, Supreme Allied Commander in Europe (SACEUR) and successor to General Eisenhower, was typical: "Within the strictly military field, I find the disparity between our available forces and those which the Soviet rulers could bring against us so great as to warrant no other conclusion than [that] a full-scale attack within the near future would find Allied Command Europe critically weak to accomplish its present mission."[7]

Thus, as the Kennedy administration prepared to take office in 1961, despair and hopelessness over the massive Soviet conventional threat had made nuclear response the essence of NATO strategy. Whether strategic or tactical nuclear weapons were better and how Europeans would participate in their control were still open issues (as discussed below), but almost all parties agreed that nuclear weapons were the only solution. They were supposedly a cheap, "modern," and efficient solution to a difficult problem. The conventional forces available to NATO were largely unready, unequipped, poorly positioned, and poorly trained. The perceived Soviet conventional superiority had in many ways become a self-fulfilling prophecy. Since the Soviet conventional forces were assumed to be so superior, little effort was made to improve the NATO forces; since little effort was made to improve them, the NATO forces were indeed inferior. As one NATO official replied when asked by a member of the new administration why his nation's conventional forces were given only a three days' supply of ammunition: "We do not expect to be able to hold for more than three days." To which his questioner is reported to have responded: "If you only have three days of ammunition, you can be damn sure you won't be able to hold any longer!"

The Limited Role of Nuclear Weapons

The view that nuclear weapons alone were an adequate deterrent in Europe had not gone entirely unchallenged. Even before taking office,

President Kennedy, for one, had recognized the dangers of overreliance on strategic nuclear weapons. As a Senator, he had said:

Under every military budget submitted by this Administration, we have been preparing primarily to fight the one kind of war we least want to fight and are least likely to fight. We have been driving ourselves into a corner where the only choice is all or nothing at all, world devastation or submission—a choice that necessarily causes us to hesitate on the brink and leaves the initiative in the hands of our enemies.[8]

The arguments against overreliance on strategic nuclear weapons, however, did not originate with the Kennedy administration; their intellectual roots go back much further. During the Truman administration, the policy planning staff in the State Department, under the direction of Paul Nitze, had prepared an unusually perceptive document, NSC-68, which foresaw the danger of piecemeal aggression unless the conventional military forces of the United States and its allies were substantially strengthened. Along the same lines, Dean Acheson had argued in 1951 that one reason why we could not continue to rely on retaliatory air power as a sufficient deterrent was the eroding effect of time. While we had a substantial lead in air power and nuclear weapons then, the value of our lead would diminish with the passage of time. And this would take place despite our continued advances in nuclear technology. "The best use we can make of our present advantage in retaliatory air power," he argued, "is to move ahead under this protective shield to build a balanced collective force in Western Europe that will continue to deter aggression after our atomic advantage has diminished."[9]

In 1954, William W. Kaufmann's criticism of the doctrine of massive retaliation, contained in a monograph entitled *The Requirements of Deterrence,* published by the Center for International Studies at Princeton University, attracted widespread attention in the government and press. His closely reasoned, thorough, and scholarly critique of the doctrine raised serious questions about its desirability or feasibility. Similar conclusions were being reached by a number of strategists at The Rand Corporation. Some leading military men, most notably General Maxwell Taylor, were also becoming aware of the limitations of the massive-retaliation strategy.

In Europe, also, the limitations of strategic nuclear weapons for deterrence and defense were being emphasized by a few public figures. B. H. Liddell Hart, a well-known military historian and theorist, in an article published in 1954, roundly criticized the American strategy of massive retaliation. "That argument," he said, "was evidence of very confused thinking on the top levels—clearly contradictory to the experience of the years when America possessed a monopoly of atomic bombing capacity."[10]

By the time the Kennedy administration took office, it had become increasingly clear to many that strategic nuclear forces, aimed at the Soviet homeland, were an ineffective or at least unusable form of power in a local conflict, even in the critical area of Europe. Further, these weapons simply did not deter local wars. They had not deterred Communist guerrilla action in Europe or in Asia; they had not prevented the Communists from openly using force in Korea and Southeast Asia. In crisis after crisis, it became apparent that the United States was not willing to invoke massive retaliation. The threat to use these weapons when the Soviets could strike a devastating blow in return was not a credible response except in the most extreme circumstances.

The main reason for the impotence of strategic nuclear weapons lies in their enormous power. Because they are so destructive, their use must be reserved for the most desperate circumstances. But if nuclear weapons have to be reserved for the most vital issues—and both sides have them—the side with strong conventional forces is in a position to have its way on all issues less than vital. The side without adequate conventional forces will have no means for effective resistance in such confrontations. The side with strong conventional forces could use "salami-slice" tactics, or piecemeal aggression, in the belief that it would be unchallenged on all but national life-and-death matters.

To point out the limited role of U.S. strategic nuclear forces is not to say that they did not have an important relationship to NATO. They obviously did. In view of our visible political and military commitment to NATO, the Soviets could never be sure that the United States would not use strategic nuclear forces in the event of an attack on Europe, even at the risk of a Soviet attack on the United States. In this sense, nuclear weapons were obviously important in helping to deter aggression—even aggression limited to the European theater. But what if deterrence failed? If the war began with an all-out Soviet attack on targets that included our cities, the answer was simple. We would reply in kind. But what if the war started with less than an all-out attack? What if the Soviets used only conventional forces? Would we still respond with a nuclear spasm? As McNamara repeatedly noted: "One cannot fashion a credible deterrent out of an incredible action." Strategic nuclear weapons had a role, but it was intrinsically a limited one.

Even had the arguments concerning the limitations of strategic nuclear forces been widely accepted by 1961, however, there still remained tactical nuclear weapons whose use would be limited to the battlefield. The possibility of using tactical nuclear weapons as an alternative to the holocaust-or-humiliation dilemma of strategic nuclear weapons had become more attractive, particularly to the NATO military commanders, as the shortcomings of massive retaliation became more apparent. The main arguments here were that these weapons provided a viable option short of general nuclear war, that they averted the huge costs of a major build-up of conventional forces, and that they were a more effective deterrent than conventional weapons. By 1961, several thousand tactical nuclear weapons had been deployed in Europe for delivery by aircraft, artillery, and missiles. These weapons were designed to hit nearly the same kinds of targets as conventional weapons, such as tank and infantry units, field headquarters, airfields, and logistic installations. Furthermore, they were operated by the traditional kinds of military units—artillery battalions, aircraft squadrons, and the like—and were organizationally integrated with conventional forces. For these reasons, tactical nuclear weapons seemed in many ways very much like conventional weapons, only with a bigger punch that would enable the West to offset the manpower advantage of the other side. The distinction between small tactical nuclear weapons and modern conventional weapons became blurred in the minds of many. As one writer put it: "Even the little Davey Crockett makes *large* conventional artillery forces not merely unnecessary but rather a joke and it is difficult to live for a long time with an expensive joke."[11] Admiral Arthur Radford's remark in 1953 that as a result of adopting the massive-retaliation doctrine "atomic weapons have virtually achieved conventional status within our Armed Forces" had become all too true. In

SACEUR's Emergency Defense Plan (EDP), at the first alert his forces went into their general nuclear war posture.

The major argument for using tactical nuclear weapons was, of course, that a conventional option was infeasible. Quite aside from this, however, the tactical nuclear case rested on several implicit assumptions which later analysis was to show to be wrong or at least highly doubtful. The first of these assumptions was that tactical nuclear weapons could substitute for manpower imbalances. Careful studies later suggested the opposite. More manpower probably would be needed to fight a tactical nuclear war than a nonnuclear war.[12] The reason was quite simple. When both sides have tactical nuclear weapons and when these weapons are used in large enough numbers or large enough yields, the engaged front-line divisions are rapidly destroyed. Since NATO had only meager reserves (the 1957 force goals cut mainly the reserve forces, because it was reasoned they would be useless in a nuclear war), it would be unable to form a new front against Soviet reserve forces. Without a front to make the Soviets concentrate, they would not present—and NATO could not acquire—good nuclear targets. In short, while the advocates of the tactical nuclear option argued that we must resort to nuclear weapons because of the weight of Soviet manpower, the chief result seemed to be that the battlefield was dominated by Soviet reserve, rather than front-line, divisions.

Another doubtful assumption underlying the limited nuclear war concept was the feasibility of adequate limitations on yields, targets, and numbers of weapons to keep collateral damage and civilian casualties down and thus to prevent the war from escalating to a general strategic level. Although theoretically the controlled use of small-yield nuclear weapons against strictly military targets could keep collateral damage low, the prospects for these limitations working out in an actual war appear to be very low because it would be extremely difficult for either side to determine whether restraints were being maintained—and the first side to violate them has an overwhelming, if not decisive, advantage.

One reason that the prospects for limiting collateral-damage escalation are so poor is that no weapons of any kind, nuclear or conventional, can consistently be delivered precisely and accurately on military targets and only on military targets. On the battlefield, targets usually cannot be located accurately, especially if they are behind the front line, as most nuclear targets would be. In fact, one of the key elements of tactics taught in all armies is to avoid being detected by the enemy. Artillerymen and bomber pilots compensate for this by firing at "suspected targets," or by blanketing likely areas of terrain with large barrages, thus using far larger numbers of rounds or bombs than would theoretically be needed to kill all the available targets. This explains why the actual number of casualties caused per shell or per bomb in all past wars has been only a tiny fraction of the number that would have been caused if most of the weapons had been fired at known, located targets.

In a tactical nuclear war, the problems of target acquisition and location are particularly difficult because of the probable damage to friendly target-acquisition and communication systems and the need to maintain safe distances from friendly troops. Most of the major systems used in tactical nuclear warfare are highly vulnerable, particularly ground forces, aircraft, short-range nuclear delivery systems, target-acquisition capabilities, command and control facilities, lines of communication, and logistic support systems. Moreover, these systems tend to be highly interdependent. If one major component of the over-all complex collapses, other components are in danger of becoming inoperative.

One implication of these vulnerabilities and interdependencies is that the duration of any kind of controlled tactical nuclear battle is likely to be, at most, a few days. Another is that this vulnerability produces immense pressures for further escalation. The tendency toward area or terrain—rather than discrete—fire, higher yields, and deeper strikes would be reinforced by the desire to take out the enemy's delivery systems before he could use them. Where both sides have soft and concentrated forces, as is the case in Europe, enormous advantages accrue to the side that strikes first. The side that is losing at one level of conflict may thus be tempted to preempt to a higher level in order to improve his prospects, especially if he fears a sudden escalation on the part of the opponent. Even under the best circumstances, the potential for escalation and large-scale collateral damage is enormous.

Soviet planners seem to have recognized these problems in the design of their tactical nuclear weapons and delivery systems. Rather than building large numbers of short-range, low-yield systems that would be very vulnerable and useful only for killing discrete, well-located targets, the Soviets have emphasized higher-yield, mobile tactical missiles primarily useful for terrain or blanketing fires, or for strikes against fixed logistics installations and airfields. Indeed, the Soviet force structure raises serious doubts about their *capability* to fight a limited tactical nuclear war, much less one in which collateral damage and civilian casualties are to be kept to low levels. Limited nuclear wars with one side using discrete-fire techniques and the other using terrain-fire are likely to be notoriously one-sided in favor of the latter. Equally important, most of the Soviet's nuclear delivery capability in Europe is based inside the Soviet Union. In short, the Soviets have neither the organization nor the force structure for a limited nuclear war fought exclusively against military targets in an engaged battle zone.

The risks of escalation to general war during a tactical nuclear conflict are high for still another reason. A well-defined "firebreak" exists between conventional and nuclear war. Because of differences in the effects of conventional and nuclear explosives, violations of the firebreak are readily detectable; thus there is no ambiguity about the kind of war being fought. This firebreak is the most obvious discontinuity in the spectrum of modern warfare. The concept is widely recognized and has been observed for twenty-five years.

The possibility of establishing a similar firebreak for an engaged tactical nuclear battle abounds with uncertainties. Even the distinctions suggested for differing levels of tactical nuclear war are filled with ambiguities. Distinctions between yields of weapons would be difficult if not impossible to establish; even the number of weapons used would be hard to determine. Limitations on targets and geographical areas would be subject to misinterpretation. The temptation to exploit these ambiguities would be great and the chance for a critical mistake, enormous. The rules of a limited nuclear war would be complex and unclear, even assuming that all parties involved tried to abide by the rules.

In conventional war the rules are comparatively simple and clear. The upper limit of escalation is not shrouded in uncertainty. Conventional war can still be a test of strength; tactical nuclear war, because of the ambiguities mentioned, is more likely to be a test of will. It is vital to preserve the recognizable firebreak existing between conventional and nuclear war. Fortunately, world leaders on all sides have seemed to sense the importance of maintaining this firebreak and have refrained in all crises to date—Korea, Cuba, Berlin, and Vietnam, for example—from entering the uncertain area of nuclear warfare even in the most tense situations.

Studies and war games which attempted to account for these difficulties showed that high casualty rates and a great amount of collateral damage were likely to result from a tactical nuclear war in Europe. Even under the most favorable assumptions, it appeared that between 2 and 20 million Europeans would be killed, with widespread damage to the economy of the affected area and a high risk of 100 million dead if the war escalated to attacks on cities. In the light of this, it was difficult to see how initiating a tactical nuclear war would satisfy the United States' basic goal of defending the people and territories of NATO Europe. When the defense of Europe is seen to entail its nuclear destruction, the European incentive to permit the use of nuclear weapons on its soil diminishes rapidly.

To point out the deficiencies of the tactical nuclear case was not to make a positive case for a major conventional option or to imply that we needed no tactical nuclear capability or that tactical nuclear weapons did not have an important, if limited, role in our defense posture. While such capabilities were not a substitute for conventional capabilities, they were a desirable complement. In fact, OSD studies at the time suggested at least four reasons for retaining such an option.

The first reason, quite simply, was that several thousand tactical nuclear weapons, including bombs, missiles, artillery shells, and atomic demolitions, were already in Europe. Not only had the United States increased its own tactical forces in the area; it had also encouraged the European allies to buy nuclear delivery systems and had committed itself to stockpiling nuclear warheads in Europe for these systems. This was not a situation that defense officials could, or wanted to, change drastically at the time. To attempt to do so would have raised the specter of an imminent U.S. withdrawal from Europe.

Many Europeans regarded a repetition of World War II as the worst catastrophe that could befall them. Indeed, despite U.S. assurances, they feared the implications of a conventional option for deterrence, for actual war, and, most particularly, for their defense budgets. They recalled vividly that the United States had taken the lead only a few years earlier in advocating a nuclear strategy for NATO and insisting that nuclear weapons were a cheap solution to the problem of defending NATO. It would take time to dissipate these fears and get the facts straight. While U.S. officials worked to do so, maintaining the presence of tactical nuclear capabilities helped to reassure the allies of U.S. will to use whatever weapons were necessary for their defense.

A second reason for maintaining tactical nuclear forces in Europe was that they made some limited contribution to the deterrence of conventional as well as nuclear aggression. The presence of nuclear forces in Europe placed inhibitions on the enemy. It forced him to face the prospect that initiation of a conventional conflict might prompt a nuclear response. And if he had massed his forces for a conventional attack, as probable, he would be in exactly the wrong deployment to take a nuclear strike. In short, nuclear forces provided an option, albeit a low-confidence option, to help accomplish our objectives.

The third reason was that tactical nuclear capabilities were required to deter a first use of tactical nuclear weapons by the Soviets. Without such a capability, the Soviets might be tempted to launch nuclear strikes against allied ground and tactical air forces in Europe. With such a capability, the United States could credibly threaten extensive damage to Soviet ground and tactical air forces in retaliation.

Finally, tactical nuclear capabilities represented a worth-while hedge against the possibility of failure in other parts of the NATO force posture. Despite growing confidence in the feasibility and desirability of a major conventional option, the possibility could not be excluded that, under certain circumstances, NATO's conventional defenses might fail. To meet such a contingency, the United States needed the intermediate option provided by tactical nuclear forces.

Thus, theater nuclear forces did have a role to play in the defense of NATO. But like the role of strategic nuclear forces, it was intrinsically a limited one. Theater nuclear weapons contributed to deterring an all-out Soviet conventional attack or a tactical nuclear attack; they permitted the United States to respond in kind if tactical nuclear weapons were used. But they were not a substitute for conventional forces. They were not a guarantee of successfully stopping a Soviet attack. They were cheap only if one neglected risks. They did not solve the suicide-or-surrender dilemma. They provided options, but only after forcing us to initiate a nuclear war. And as William Kaufmann has aptly pointed out, "one lesson learned by all high American policymakers, whatever their Administration or political affiliation . . . is that the decision to use nuclear weapons is so awesome that most other alternatives look better at the time—if they exist; and they usually do."[13]

The positive case for needing a major conventional option was quite straightforward. Conventional forces could be used to counter Soviet aggression without the strain on the unity of the alliance that using nuclear weapons would entail. A strong conventional capability offers a major alternative to suicide-or-surrender. It would underpin diplomatic action in peacetime and support firm resistance in crisis. Possible measures of arms control, including actions to halt the spread of nuclear weapons, would be facilitated by the kind of military diversification that includes a major conventional option.

Moreover, conventional forces, once used, are far less destructive and would kill far fewer civilians than their nuclear counterparts. Conceivably, favorable and meaningful military results could be achieved with conventional forces; using tactical nuclear forces, by contrast, represented entry into an area in which we had had no prior combat experience and which involved such major uncertainty concerning the behavior of troops, civilians, and governments as to offer only low confidence of a favorable outcome. Of equal importance, the risks of escalation to general nuclear war appeared substantially smaller in conventional than in tactical nuclear conflict.

Finally, a conventional option would help relieve another source of serious strain on the alliance: the question of who controlled the nuclear button. Whatever else it meant, having no effective conventional option placed an additional premium on the American nuclear guarantee. Put bluntly, it meant that the allies were largely at the mercy of this guarantee. During the period when the United States had a clear nuclear superiority, this had been an unpleasant but tolerable situation; but now that the Soviets had a significant nuclear capability as well, would the United States really risk sacrificing its

cities to punish the Soviets for invading Europe? The possibility that
the United States might not was causing major strains in the alliance.
The problem, however, lay not so much in personal mistrust of the
Americans as in the basic shortcomings of the official NATO strategy. For the same reasons that dynamite is not a good substitute for a
fly swatter, nuclear weapons are not a good substitute for conventional forces against a wide range of likely military threats. If the
United States didn't use its nuclear forces, Europe could be overrun
by the massive Soviet conventional forces. If the United States did
use its nuclear forces, Europe (and the United States) could be
devastated. The questioning of the "credibility of guarantees" was
really a questioning of the credibility of NATO's options.

The initial response to this questioning, however, was not to
reassess the role of nuclear weapons, but to search for a device that
would reduce allied fears over dependence on the Americans. The
British and the French decided that the solution lay in having their
own independent nuclear forces. Military theorists in both countries
recognized that these small, independent forces would be highly
vulnerable to Soviet forces, both offensive and defensive. But they
reasoned that these forces could deter a Soviet attack in Europe
because they could "trigger the American response." This involved a
curious piece of logic: the Americans can't be trusted to retaliate
against the Soviets for attacking France (or Great Britain); therefore,
we will have our own independent nuclear force to cause the Americans to retaliate against the Soviet Union for a French (or British)
attack on the Soviet Union. Whatever else this decision may have
implied, it meant that fewer resources would go into British and
French conventional forces.

One U.S. response to the problem was to seek ways to give the
allies a larger share in the control of an American or a collective
nuclear capability, the so-called Multilateral Force, or MLF. At first
glance this looked like a good way to relieve allied fears over exclusive U.S. control. Later, however, in attempting to work out the
detailed arrangements, it became clear that such proposals raised
impossible problems regarding political sovereignty and military command.

All these considerations, in varying degrees, led to the conclusion
early in 1961 that a strong conventional capability in Europe was

highly desirable. But the strategic worth of a conventional option was, of course, only half the issue. Even those who could not accept the need for the build-up of conventional forces did not favor reducing the existing level. In fact, during the Korean war and the Berlin crisis of 1961, most NATO allies strengthened their conventional forces to some degree. The other half of the argument, therefore, was the cost of attaining a meaningful conventional option, over and above the existing level. Even the most "optimistic" estimates called for at least a 20 percent increase in U.S. and allied defense budgets. Studies of NATO land-forces requirements in the late 1950's and early 1960's estimated that 50 to 60 NATO divisions would be required for the defense of Germany alone, of which more than 40 would have to be active, high-readiness divisions. (Over 100 divisions were said to be required for NATO as a whole.) These estimates of requirements called for nearly double the number of divisions then available in Europe and only served to reinforce the general impression that a conventional defense was too expensive to be considered seriously. And costs aside, why should the United States or its allies go to great expense to enlarge NATO's ground forces when, according to the official strategy, their main function was only to offer enough resistance to trigger a nuclear war? The "fact" of the massive Soviet superiority in conventional forces, and the suicide-or-surrender option it posed, were still the dominant elements in the NATO strategy debate. The measure of progress was to be the official NATO strategy. It was against this background that the process of analyzing the 175 Soviet divisions was to proceed.

How Big Is the Soviet Army?

As defense officials first approached the problem of defending NATO in 1961, there appeared to be no satisfactory way out of the suicide-or-surrender dilemma posed by the alleged massive Soviet superiority in conventional forces. Tactical nuclear weapons clearly weren't the answer. There was no viable concept for fighting a limited nuclear war then, and today after eight years of effort one still has not been developed. In the initial struggle with this problem, there was a lot of talk about "the pause." The idea was that while NATO could not possibly hope to match Soviet conventional forces, it might be able to maintain enough conventional forces to put up a resistance for a few days and therefore delay, for at least a short while, the need to use nuclear weapons. However, it was quickly pointed out that this concept was merely a short-term postponement of the suicide-or-surrender dilemma, and not an escape from it. The only satisfactory escape from the dilemma lay in NATO's having adequate conventional forces—which in the U.S. view meant forces approximately equal in military power to those opposing them on M-Day (the day mobilization starts) and each day thereafter. Once this point was made, the first task was to determine what it would take to achieve such a capability. This depended on the size of the Soviet Army.

In the 1950's and early 1960's (and to some extent even today) the standard military briefings given at NATO headquarters and by the Joint Chiefs of Staff compared the NATO and Warsaw Pact forces solely in terms of divisions. In 1961, the usual comparison was 175 well-equipped, well-trained, fully ready Soviet divisions facing about 25 ill-equipped, ill-trained, unready NATO divisions in the center region. The conclusion of the briefings was always the same: NATO could hold for only a few days before it would be forced to use nuclear weapons.

The "fact" of these 175 Soviet divisions had been questioned before. For example, in *The Uncertain Trumpet* General Maxwell Taylor had examined relevant demographic factors and noted the following: the population of the United States and that of the USSR were roughly equal; the population of our NATO allies exceeded that of the Warsaw Pact allies; and the NATO countries as a whole were considerably wealthier than the Warsaw Pact countries as a whole. Therefore, General Taylor argued, it was surprising to expect that the Soviets would be able to support an army so much larger than that of the NATO countries.[14] In 1961, the Systems Analysis office, working closely with the Office of the Assistant Secretary of Defense for International Security Affairs (ISA), began to use this argument and push it a bit farther. For example, we found that about half of the Soviet population was involved in agriculture, presumably producing the food necessary to feed the whole population, whereas only some 10 percent of the U.S. population was involved in agriculture at the time. These figures suggested that, in terms of readily available manpower, NATO should have had a substantial advantage. In similar fashion, Systems Analysis and ISA made a complete review of aggregate population data, gross-national-product data, basic resources bearing especially on conventional strength, technical skills, and composition of the economies of the NATO allies and the Warsaw Pact countries. This review posed a basic dilemma. If anything, it appeared that it would be much harder for the Soviets than for NATO to support a large army. In short, the picture of 175 Soviet divisions facing 25 NATO divisions did not seem consistent with aggregate economic data.

The next step was to add up the total number of men under arms in the NATO and Warsaw Pact countries. Intelligence estimates showed that, in terms of total numbers of men under arms, in 1961 NATO had over six million men on active duty compared with about four and one-half million for the Warsaw Pact. Even in land forces alone, the NATO allies had more men on active duty. Obviously these gross manpower figures gave little indication of effective strength on the battlefield; some NATO countries had extensive commitments outside Europe, and not even all the forces in Europe could be used to meet a massed Pact attack in the center region. Nevertheless, these basic strength figures raised the question of what specifically could cause NATO to be so badly outnumbered on the battlefield while it had one-third more men under arms.

The next step involved finding explanations for two paradoxes which continuously reappeared in the studies. As early as 1962 it became apparent that there was something badly wrong with merely counting divisions. At that time, the United States was planning to spend an average of $2.2 billion a year to equip the Army's 22 division forces (16 active divisions and 6 priority National Guard divisions). At that rate, if the Russians were equipping 175 divisions (the official NATO estimate) at anything like U.S. standards, they would have to be spending the equivalent of $17.5 billion a year. Even if they were equipping only half that number they would still have to be spending almost $9 billion a year—roughly four times what we were spending. This seemed highly improbable in view of the fact that $17.5 billion was more than the United States was spending at the time for *all* military procurement, not only for the Army but for the Air Force, the Navy, and the Marine Corps as well. Moreover, it did not square with other demands being placed on the Soviet economy, including programs they were known to be emphasizing. This did not prove that the Soviets couldn't be doing it, but it made the 175 division figure highly suspect. This accounting puzzle became known in OSD as the "PEMA paradox" (after *P*rocurement of *E*quipment and *M*issiles, *A*rmy, pronounced "peema"—the budget account for procuring equipment for the Army—see Table 1).

Table 1. PEMA Paradox

	U.S.	USSR
Divisions	22[a]	175
Army Equipment Expenditures	$2.2 billion	?

[a] Active Army plus National Guard and Reserves.

A similar paradox emerged on the side of personnel strengths. In 1961, the United States had nearly a million men on active duty in the Army, organized into 16 combat divisions plus support. The Soviet Army numbered roughly two million men, only enough, by our standards, to support an army of about 40 divisions. Yet the Soviets were supposed to be supporting an army of 175 divisions. This disparity of a factor of four was christened the "people paradox" (Table 2).

Table 2. People Paradox

	U.S.	USSR
Divisions	16[a]	175
Active Duty Strength	960,000	2,000,000

[a] Active Army.

In view of the aggregate economic data and the "PEMA-people paradoxes," it seemed probable either that the intelligence estimates of Soviet divisions were wrong or that what the Soviets called a "division" was far different from what we called a "division," or that we were making terribly inefficient use of our manpower and equipment, or a combination of these. Moreover, it appeared that, while the concept of a division might be useful for other purposes, perhaps it was not a meaningful indicator of units of military strength. Perhaps, also, part of the explanation had to be found elsewhere.

As the Systems Analysis and ISA staffs dug into the problems of the readiness of U.S. active, reserve, and National Guard divisions, we became much more aware of the importance of distinguishing between combat-ready units and unready units—units that might be merely paper aggregations of men and equipment. Similar questions were raised about the Soviet Army. A more detailed review of the 175 divisions indicated that at least half of them were cadre divisions (that is, essentially paper units) with perhaps 10 percent of their manpower on board and far from 100 percent of their equipment. If these divisions were to be counted for the Soviets in the total comparison of military strength, our low-priority National Guard and reserve divisions, numbering somewhere between 40 and 50, ought also to be counted, together with similar units for our NATO allies. Part of the problem, it appeared, was that the grand total of the Soviet force structure, including many paper units that had little real military power, was being compared with the total of combat-ready units for the NATO allies. Under rules like these, NATO was lucky to be doing as well as it was in the comparisons!

Establishing the difference between combat-ready and cadre divisions solved only half the problem. Even with this distinction, there were still some 80 combat-ready Soviet divisions. How did these remaining divisions compare with ours? The JCS and the United States Commander-in-Chief in Europe (CINCEUR) counted these Soviet divisions and ours on a 1 for 1 basis in their briefings. No weights were given to reflect differences in manpower, firepower, or other capabilities. Again, this did not seem right. For example, the firepower scores—a weighted index of the firepower of different Army weapons, a way of adding up the total division firepower— were not constructed for the purpose of comparing military forces, but for evaluating hypothetical outcomes in war games. The weights used were largely arbitrary, with little basis in theory or combat experience. Even with all these qualifications, however, the firepower scores still indicated that a U.S. division had much more firepower than a Soviet division. On this basis, Systems Analysis and ISA challenged the Army staff as to why U.S. and Soviet divisions were being

treated as equal. Gradually the Army was forced to concede that a
U.S. division should count for more than a Soviet division. In 1962
and 1963, the Army's official ratio rose from 1.1 to 1 to 1.3 to 1;
between 1963 and 1967 it rose farther to 1.7 to 1. The 1.7 to 1 figure
was about the ratio of manpower in the U.S. and Soviet divisions
themselves, not counting the nondivisional support units.

In 1962 another big step was taken in the analysis of this problem.
With assistance from the Systems Analysis office, the Army was
asked to do a cost analysis of two different U.S. divisions: one organized the way the U.S. Army was then organized and equipped, the
other organized according to Soviet doctrine and concepts of organization and equipment. The idea behind this exercise was very simple:
if the Soviets had devised a better way to design a division, we ought
to benefit from their ideas and get more for our money. (This had
little to do with "standard of living" items such as food, medical care,
and the like. These were removed from the problem by pricing the
Soviet forces in terms of American prices.)

When the joint Systems Analysis–Army study was completed,
several interesting results emerged. First, it appeared that if we
organized along Soviet lines we could buy at least 2.2 Soviet divisions
for the cost of one of ours. This suggested the question: If we could
buy 2.2 of theirs for one of ours, shouldn't ours be about 2.2 times as
effective as one of theirs? If it wasn't, perhaps we were making a
mistake and ought to reorganize along Soviet lines. To some military
planners this appeared to be largely a debating point, but it was not
so intended. If the Soviet Union really could buy combat power much
more cheaply than the United States through a superior form of
organization, perhaps we should take a leaf from their book. In fact,
back in 1961 when McNamara had commissioned his 96 studies, one
of them was a request for a comparison of the Tables of Organization
and Equipment (TO&E's) of the various allied and enemy countries
with our own and an evaluation of the effectiveness they produced.

The JCS answered the "reorganization" question with the argument that "cost does not equal effectiveness." The Secretary of
Defense countered by explaining that he fully agreed, but that additional cost *plus good judgment* ought to equal additional effectiveness. That is, if we were spending our money wisely and if one of our
divisions cost twice as much as one of theirs, it ought to be about

twice as effective; otherwise, we ought to buy two divisions like theirs.

No reorganization of the Army was needed. The problem was not one of organizational concepts, but of counting unequals as equals. Later studies were to show that if we organized along Soviet lines, we could have about 3 divisions for the cost of one of our present divisions (without reducing the American soldier's standard of living); but it was not at all clear that such a reorganization would produce a more effective U.S. Army. We would simply be changing the size of our nominal units (what unit size carries the name "division" is, after all, arbitrary) and changing the mix of certain elements of the force. For example, we would be giving up a lot of combat-engineer, artillery, antitank, and communication support in favor of a bigger tank force. To some degree we would also be sacrificing staying power for initial capability. While the best blend of these various parts of an army is, of course, a matter of considerable uncertainty, one conclusion was quite clear: the name "division" in no way described an equivalent unit of combat power in the Soviet and U.S. Armies (not even as adjusted by applying small multiples, such as 1.1 or 1.7, of Soviet divisions for one U.S. division).

The initial reaction of the Services and the NATO commanders to these studies was not to reexamine their estimates, but to explain away the differences on other grounds. A whole new set of arguments was raised to account for the overwhelming Soviet conventional superiority. The arguments came in various forms, but they all made essentially the same point: these differences could be accounted for by the higher standard of living and better treatment of the individual soldier in a Western army. Many of our soldiers, it seemed, had to man typewriters and post exchanges and medical facilities, while most Russian soldiers were out in the field with their rifles. At one briefing it was explained at great length that the Army had to have a fancy mobile field kitchen to give each of our soldiers a hot meal every day, while the Russian soldiers were accustomed to eating soup out of one huge kettle. Apparently, we were going to lose a war in Europe because U.S. soldiers didn't eat soup. A large part of 1962 and 1963 was spent dealing with arguments of this kind.

Part of the reason for these arguments was that in the early 1960's the Defense Department lacked a clearly articulated concept of a "division force" (the combat division—16,000 men—plus the combat support and service support units—32,000 men—required to support it in a theater) as a tool for planning U.S. forces and analyzing those of the enemy. The division force concept was being developed and the term was being used, but it wasn't until 1966 that the U.S. Army had its force structure worked out in these terms. Thus, in the early 1960's there was much confusion about the role and significance of nondivisional military personnel. For example, there was a tendency to think of the combat division as representing the only combat "teeth"; the units (artillery, aviation, engineering, reconnaissance, signal, transportation, supply, maintenance, medical and administration) required to sustain the division in a theater—the tail—were counted as support and overhead, not combat capability. In fact, as more analysis was to show, there was a great deal of division force combat power outside the combat division itself; for example, in artillery and reconnaissance units. Furthermore, without the combat support and service support units, the actual combat capability and staying power of the combatants diminishes significantly. The U.S. concept of organization assigns a much higher percentage of the division force to the nondivisional units than does the Soviet. But this doesn't necessarily mean that the U.S. ratio of combat power per man is lower.

In response to the standard-of-living argument, the Army was asked to identify components of U.S. division force structure that were standard-of-living items yielding military power less than proportional to their cost, so that they could be eliminated during the budget review. It turned out that they were unable to do so.

In each case, the Systems Analysis office tried to check out the details of the arguments. One of the striking things about this operation was the extent to which the experts fell back on hearsay and how little factual information was available to prove or disprove their contentions. One such contention, for example, was that a much higher percentage of our people were medical personnel than was the case for the Soviets. We checked this out carefully and found to our surprise that, though we had more doctors, we had fewer total medical personnel per soldier than the Soviets. And, because our medical personnel were more highly trained and better equipped, we should have been able to give better treatment with fewer of them. Careful evaluation was never able to substantiate any major difference in the combat power of the two armies based on differences in standard of living. The arguments that "we have more medical personnel who don't fight," "half our people are behind typewriters," "the Russians all eat soup but we have to have a lot of cooks," and so on appeared to be nothing more than myth—myth that says the Soviets are poor, tough, and accustomed to hardship while we are wealthy, soft, and pampered. (If one were to believe this, one would be driven to the conclusion that the United States is too handicapped by luxury to produce an effective army.) The differences could not be explained away by standard-of-living arguments, nor by shorter supply lines, staying power, cultural needs, or the myriad of arguments based largely on unsupported opinion. Indeed, during these debates it became clear in OSD that measures of effectiveness based largely on "judgment," and not reproducible and directly relatable to fact, were highly unsatisfactory, because they could be manipulated to prove almost any point. This conclusion was to be borne out in many other areas, particularly in the field of readiness evaluation, with painful frequency.

Further analysis indicated that a *fully mobilized* U.S. division force had about three times as many people as a *fully mobilized* Soviet division force and cost about three times as much (in U.S. prices). In addition, the analysis showed that the equipment cost per man (again in U.S. prices) was, roughly speaking, the same for the U.S. Army and the Soviet Army. And since most of the peacetime cost (about 80 percent of a Western army) is in manpower, the measurable aspects of military effectiveness, if we were managing our resources well, ought to be roughly proportional to manpower. Thus, by 1965, we knew that a Soviet division force cost only about a third that of a U.S. division force, had only about a third as many men, and (we had strong reason to believe) was only about one-third as effective. Moreover, in terms of men per division deployed in the center region of NATO at the time, the U.S. division forces had about 40,000 soldiers per division in Germany compared with about 13,000 for the Soviets. In short, eliminating paper divisions, using cost and fire-power indexes, counts of combat personnel in available divisions, and numbers of artillery pieces, trucks, tanks, and the like, we ended up with the same conclusion: NATO and the Warsaw Pact had approximate equality on the ground. Where four years earlier it had appeared that a conventional option was impossible, it now began to appear that perhaps NATO could have had one all along.

By 1968 the continuing debate over the comparative strength and effectiveness of the Warsaw Pact and NATO armies had produced some useful clarifications. Many people had thought that the Systems Analysis office was trying to measure the real effectiveness of the two armies, all factors considered, and that somehow this real-effectiveness measure could be used as a reliable indicator of who would win in the event of a war. In fact, our statements were not sufficiently precise on this point. Critics correctly argued that larger armies have been defeated by smaller armies and that there are many other important factors besides numbers of soldiers and vehicles and guns. In short, spending more on your army than your enemy does on his doesn't necessarily guarantee that you will win the war. These points are quite valid, and they forced greater clarification of exactly what we were saying. Morale, generalship, judgment on the choice of weapons, terrain, luck, training—all have a great deal to do with the outcome of a particular war. But sensible policy formation requires that these factors be carefully sorted out. It makes a big difference in the planning of U.S. strategy and peacetime military posture whether our land forces are outnumbered 5 to 1 or not. If we are outnumbered 5 to 1, it is unlikely that any amount of brilliant generalship or high morale or good luck is going to produce military victory or a successful defense. Readiness and training and proper plans and deployments won't help much either.

In a perverse sense it is rather comforting to be outnumbered 5 to 1 by your enemy, because then there is no point in making the effort to deploy your forces in the right place, or to ensure that your forces are ready, or to insist on proper training standards. If, however, the opposing force numbers are approximately equal, these factors become more important. We then have more incentive for making sure that our forces are ready, well trained, and well equipped. This was the reason for the analyses: not to attempt to predict the likely outcome of a war, but to determine what the real balance of military forces and capability was. If we really were outnumbered 5 to 1 or if it really did take the United States three times as many men as the Soviet Union to create a given unit of fighting force, there was little need to discuss broader strategic questions, such as a conventional option, or worry about deployments, readiness, training, and equipment. As it was, by 1967 it had become clear (in OSD but unfortunately not to the Services or the general public) that NATO and the Warsaw Pact were roughly equal in terms of soldiers, guns, vehicles, infantrymen, and the like. In many respects, we were "superior"; in some respects, they were.

Tactical Air Forces

Like the development of fair standards of comparison for land forces, a similar process was required for NATO and Warsaw Pact tactical air forces. In the early 1960's, estimates of the balance of air power in NATO and the Pact stressed an alleged superiority in numbers of aircraft in the Soviet force compared with the NATO force. The same studies that earlier had called for 50 to 60 divisions to defend Europe also called for about 7,000 tactical aircraft. When one considers that, in the 1960's, a modern tactical aircraft cost more than $2 million to buy and one-fifth that much to operate per year, the financial implications of this requirement are staggering: a $14-billion investment and about $3 billion per year in direct operating costs for tactical air forces in Europe alone. In addition to their massive ground force and their build-up in strategic weapons, could the Soviets really have acquired a tactical air force that required an investment this large to counter?

The first step in dealing with this problem was again to get an accurate count of the *total* forces available to each side. Peeling off the layers of overstatement and getting agreement on the basic numerical facts proved immensely difficult. As late as 1966, an Air Force briefing to a group of NATO Defense Ministers indicated that NATO was outnumbered 3 to 1 in deployed combat aircraft. Needless to say, the briefing concluded that NATO would lose the air battle in a few days. Given the huge U.S. increases in spending on tactical air forces since 1961, how could this be? Part of the problem was that the briefing was comparing nearly the total Soviet inventory with only part of the U.S. inventory: the number of U.S. aircraft in combat units. This made a substantial difference, since only about two-thirds of our aircraft are in combat units. The reason again is that we organize differently. In the United States, we have advanced flying training units as well as combat units. The function of these units is to give pilots combat training in the type of aircraft they will actually fly in combat. The Soviets perform this training function in the combat unit. Incidentally, when OSD suggested to our own Services that they adopt this procedure, the suggestion was met with a number of arguments as to why it was not a viable way of doing the job. If it is not viable for us, one would conclude that it is not viable for the Soviets. In any event, comparisons of aircraft assigned to line units do not indicate the total assets available to each side.

Another part of the problem involved the way U.S. and other NATO aircraft are assigned to various commands, such as the European Command, Pacific Command, Atlantic Command, Aerospace Defense Command, and Tactical Air Command. Naturally, only a small percentage of the whole U.S. or allied force is assigned to any one of these commands in peacetime, although in war a large percentage would be deployed to the area of greatest priority. In particular, if it were necessary to do so to save Western Europe, the United States would surely redeploy most of its aircraft from the Pacific to the European theater. Nevertheless, the tendency, understandably, is for each commander to compare his own assigned forces with practically all the forces available to the other side. This creates serious problems because the Congress and the JCS give so much credence to the theater commanders' requirements as a standard of military need. This tendency, coupled with basic differences in organizational structure and assignment policies, further compounded the problem of getting fair comparisons.

The issue of inventory counts was finally settled in 1966. The event that forced a resolution of this issue was a joint U.S.–German Air Force study which concluded that NATO air forces could not "handle" the Warsaw Pact longer than three days in the event of a war, because the Pact had more and better aircraft. Seemingly, the large, costly build-up in U.S. tactical air forces since 1961 had had no impact on our relative military position. Secretary McNamara expressed disbelief and asked the Systems Analysis office to look into the matter. Our review of the study showed that, given the study's assumptions, NATO would be lucky to last three days. Only aircraft formally committed to NATO were considered to be available for the war, large numbers were withheld for nuclear missions, and the Pact was permitted a full reinforcement capability, while U.S. reinforcement was assumed to be severely limited. As a result of such assumptions, the Pact started the war with an overwhelming local numerical superiority in the center region of Europe. The study ignored the fact that at the end of three days NATO's total remaining world-wide aircraft inventory was still much larger than that of the Pact; that even under the assumptions used in the study, the engaged NATO aircraft were far more successful in proportion to their numbers than Pact aircraft; and that during the three-day period, the greatly outnumbered NATO air forces still destroyed about the same number of close-support ground targets as did the Pact. In a slightly broader context, therefore, the opposite conclusion from that drawn by the study could be reached; namely, that at the end of three days the Pact was in a considerably worse numerical position than NATO and that during the three-day war NATO aircraft had proven their qualitative superiority.

As a result of these findings, Secretary McNamara asked the Systems Analysis office and the Joint Staff to prepare a joint memorandum comparing Free World and Communist tactical air inventories. This memorandum was to describe the points of agreement on facts and their interpretation, and the points of disagreement on interpretation. It was to be prepared on the basis of consistent assumptions and the latest intelligence estimates, and it was to serve as the authoritative source for future questions regarding numerical comparisons. It was also to serve as the basis for a letter to the German Defense Minister explaining Secretary McNamara's understanding of the basic facts regarding NATO and Pact tactical air forces.

The final memorandum, agreed to by all parties, concluded that there was no aircraft gap. Indeed, at that time the United States and its allies had substantially more tactical aircraft world-wide than the Soviet Union and its satellites. In Europe, not only was the total aircraft inventory of all the NATO allies (center region and flanks) numerically larger but, as discussed below, the aircraft were better designed for conventional operations.[15]

This exercise proved to be highly useful for a number of reasons. First, it ended the argument about comparative inventories and established clearly that the NATO allies had more tactical fighter and attack aircraft than the Warsaw Pact. Second, it was a great step forward in classifying these aircraft according to combat capability and bringing out the fact that the Warsaw Pact tactical air forces were primarily defensive and that the NATO allies were much stronger in offensive capability than the Warsaw Pact. Third, in their eagerness to point out NATO's inadequacies, the Joint Staff built an impressive case showing that U.S. aircraft were vulnerable, concentrated on too few bases, lacking in conventional ordnance, and the like. Systems Analysis agreed these were important deficiencies badly in need of correction. Indeed, the exercise clearly demonstrated a point we had been trying to make for some time: far too much time and effort had been spent arguing for more aircraft, and far too little spent making sure that the aircraft we already had were properly based, sheltered, maintained, and supplied with ammunition.

The second major step in the tactical air debate involved accounting for differences in the quality, design, training, and support of the NATO and Pact air forces. A modern air force is a highly technical, complicated operation which is poorly described by simply comparing numbers of aircraft. Some of the factors that must be considered are the number of missions that can be flown per day with available maintenance resources, the pay load that can be carried, the type of bombs, missiles, and guns available, the kinds of electronic equipment on board, and, above all, the level and quality of pilot training. Generally speaking, U.S. tactical aircraft cost more than twice as much to produce as the types used by the Warsaw Pact (if we were to produce them), and we had strong reason to believe that U.S. aircraft are more than twice as effective. When these qualitative factors are considered, the Pact force turns out to be a very specialized one, designed mainly for intercepting bombers over its own territory. Their capability for offensive action is extremely limited. The U.S. and part of the NATO force, in contrast, consists primarily of multipurpose aircraft with far greater levels of maintenance support and far higher training standards. In fact, on the average, NATO aircraft can carry two or three times the pay load of Pact aircraft, can loiter several times as long on air patrol, and are flown by pilots with twice the annual training. Combining these factors with NATO's superiority in total inventory, it was not difficult to see why NATO should have a considerable advantage over the Pact in tactical air power.

Having established these points, the Systems Analysis office then attempted to develop indicators of effectiveness. The first step was an index of range and pay load: how much pay load each of the aircraft could deliver on a typical combat mission. This indicator brought out the fact that the U.S. and NATO total pay load was much larger than that of the Warsaw Pact and that it was growing at a much faster rate. These numbers began to appear in the Secretary of Defense's annual program and budget statements starting in 1966.

In addition, Systems Analysis tried to develop an index of target effectiveness; that is, to calculate the ability of our tactical air force and the enemy's to destroy a representative array of targets, such as tanks, bunkers, and personnel. At first this effort was stymied by the unwillingness of the Air Force to work toward an agreed position. We pressed on with the study independently and finally concluded that, even after allowing for major improvements in Pact forces, the NATO advantage over the Pact in potential offensive power from tactical air forces in 1968 should be at least 4 to 1. When this conclusion became known, the Air Force insisted that a joint review take place. The review lasted for more than a year. Every calculation, every assumption, every detail, was subjected to the closest scrutiny. The Air Force's final position, based on the most conservative assumptions, was that while the NATO force was about twice as effective per aircraft as the Pact, the over-all offensive effectiveness of the NATO tactical air force was only equal to that of the Pact. The Secretary of the Air Force personally took the position that NATO's offensive capability was twice that of the Pact. This represented an enormous step forward from their official position of two or three years earlier. As in the land-forces debate, the myth of overwhelming Pact tactical air superiority could not stand up to close scrutiny.

Having established the apparent fact of a rough balance in conventional forces in Europe, what did it mean? Approximate parity cannot guarantee that our side could *win* a conventional war in Europe or hold every inch of allied territory under every conceivable condition. With modern battlefield mobility an attacker can achieve local superiority, break through, and cause a great deal of damage even if his forces across the entire front are no more than equal to those of his opponent. On the other hand, the advantages of approximate equality of conventional power are substantial. First, if NATO's strength approximately matched the Warsaw Pact's, the Soviets should be strongly deterred from conventional aggression, because they could have little confidence of success unless they planned an attack so massive that NATO's most vital interests would clearly be threatened and the probability of escalation to nuclear war high. Under these circumstances, such a deliberate conventional attack would be no more rational than a deliberate nuclear attack. Second, if it is generally recognized that the opposing forces are roughly equal, the enemy does not have a firm base for political aggression based on one kind of military superiority. There would be little profit in attempting to exert military pressure for political purposes. If the Warsaw Pact began to move units up to the Iron Curtain, so could NATO. Third, such a posture would give NATO high confidence of dealing successfully with the many possible conflicts involving forces appreciably smaller than the enemy's total. Finally, approximate equality is a condition that both sides can accept politically. If the forces on the two sides are equal and generally known to be so, neither side need feel threatened; the relationship can be stable, minimizing the likelihood of an arms race. For these reasons, the matching forces criterion appeared (and still appears) to be a realistic and useful peacetime planning goal.

The Situation in the European Center Region in 1968

Table 3 outlines the military balance in the critical center region of Europe in mid-1968 in terms of land forces immediately available to either side.[16] The data describe the situation prior to the invasion of Czechoslovakia in August 1968.[17] Although there have been some changes in the deployment of Soviet forces since then, these changes do not invalidate the basic point of the comparison.

As the table shows, if one counts only divisions, NATO is obviously outnumbered in immediately available forces. However, if one counts the number of men in those divisions, or in the division forces, NATO actually has slightly more men immediately available. This is true even at the rifle-platoon level: NATO has as many men available as the Pact. The reason for the disparity between division counts and manpower counts is that the term "division" by itself has very little significance; what size of unit carries the name "division" is, after all, quite arbitrary. Russian divisions at full strength have only 8,000 to

Table 3. M-Day Land Forces in the European Center Region^a **in Mid-1968**

Force	NATO		Warsaw Pact
Divisions	28–2/3^b		46^c
Manpower in Divisions	389,000		368,000
Manpower in Division Forces	677,000		619,000
Riflemen (NATO as percent of Pact)		100%	
Equipment (NATO as percent of Pact):			
Tanks		55%	
Antitank Weapons		150%	
Armored Personnel Carriers (APC's)		130%	
Artillery and Mortars (number of tubes)		100%	
Divisional Logistic Lift		150%	
Total Vehicles		135%	
Engineers		137%	

Notes:
   ^{a} Center region includes West Germany, Belgium, The Netherlands, and France for NATO; East Germany, Poland, and Czechoslovakia for the Pact.
   ^{b} Includes five French divisions.
   ^{c} Twenty-two of which are Soviet, and twenty-four of which are East European, including eight Czech.

10,000 men, while a West German division has 20,000 men. The average NATO division force in the center region has about 23,600 men (actual peacetime strength), compared with about 13,500 for the average Pact division force. The average U.S. division force has about 40,000 men. In the face of such enormous differences in size, discussions of the number of divisions on either side can only lead to gross misunderstanding of the situation and, more seriously, to strategies of despair.

The fact of roughly equal manpower is particularly significant. A soldier, unlike a division, is a relatively equivalent unit, if he is similarly trained and equipped by either NATO or the Pact. Also, as noted before, manpower is by far the largest cost item—about 80 percent—of maintaining a Western army. Therefore, since the number of soldiers in the center region is about equal, we are in fact already paying most of the cost of maintaining an equal military capability in NATO in terms of conventional forces.

Because of the considerable differences in the structure of NATO and Warsaw Pact divisions, it is not very helpful to use the traditional method of calculating division "equivalents." There is no satisfactory way of adding up the very different capabilities provided by tank firepower, infantry firepower, artillery firepower, engineer support, logistic support, and so forth. A better approach is to compare each major element of the force separately; that is, armor, artillery, engineers, and the like.

As Table 3 shows, the Pact's largest potential advantage is in tanks; NATO has only about 55 percent as many in central Europe. But it is not clear that this numerical superiority is a decisive advantage. It reflects Soviet tradition, which stresses tanks heavily. NATO armies have deliberately chosen to place less emphasis on tanks than do the Soviets. We could increase the emphasis on tanks if we thought that the total effectiveness of our forces would be enhanced thereby. In any case, NATO tanks are qualitatively better (and cost more); the M-60, the Leopard, and the Chieftain are more accurate at long range than the main Warsaw Pact tanks, the T-54 and the T-55. Also, since NATO would be on the defensive along most of the front, its 50 percent advantage in infantry antitank weapons would be important. Historically, such advantages have enabled the defender to exact an exchange ratio of 3 to 1. Studies show that NATO tanks and antitank weapons have a high kill potential against Pact tank forces; and to this must be added the additional kill potential of NATO's tactical aircraft and armed helicopters. Although we cannot draw the conclusion from these studies that NATO would necessarily defeat the Pact tank force, neither can we necessarily conclude that NATO would not. In any event, clearly we are not in a hopeless situation.

In nearly every other area of land-forces capability, NATO holds the advantage in *immediately available* forces. As shown in Table 3, NATO has 30 percent more armored personnel carriers than the Pact. The number of artillery and mortar tubes is about the same on both sides. However, because of better ammunition, better accuracy of certain weapons, and greater ammunition-expenditure rates because of more logistic capability, NATO's firepower is greater than that of the Pact. Since NATO forces have considerably more men engaged in logistic tasks in and behind the division, and more transport vehicles per combat vehicle, NATO's ability to supply ammunition and fuel and to keep tanks operating should also be greater. The Soviets apparently plan on lower ammunition-expenditure rates, particularly for artillery weapons, than NATO does.

Thus, in most measures of size, the forces facing each other in central Europe are roughly equal. The Pact forces are structured differently, but this is more a question of force mix than of force size. We could change our mix of weapons within the same budget level if we thought it would be more effective. Indeed, as we have said, if we really felt that the Soviet superiority in numbers of tanks gave them a net military advantage, we could replace some of our other weapons with tanks. The point is that the NATO armies have preferred to put their money into a mix that includes more communications, more helicopters and light planes, and more of other things. In addition, the fact that the U.S. Army has not proposed any major change in its armor-infantry mix is strong evidence of the fact that Army force planners believe the current mix is about right. Indeed, most such planners agree that armor is not effective except in proper balance with infantry and the other combat arms. In sum, there are reasons for the choice that has been made. But it should be recognized that this is a deliberate choice. And when U.S. military leaders point to the larger number of Soviet tanks as an indicator of superiority, they should be challenged to explain the weapon-systems mix they have chosen for their own armies. All too frequently in the past they have had it both ways.

Rough equality in force size does not, of course, necessarily mean that NATO has enough land forces, or perhaps more than it needs. Before drawing any conclusions on the adequacy of NATO's conventional forces, one must carefully consider other important factors such as readiness, state of training, geography, force deployment, and reinforcement capability. In addition, we are well aware that intangibles such as morale and generalship can be more decisive than force ratios. Numerically inferior forces have defeated or held numerically superior forces many times in the past. But we doubt that the remedy in such a case, when forces are found to be qualitatively defective in some way, is to add more qualitatively defective forces. Furthermore, there can be no justification for accepting qualitative deficiencies in our forces.

Reinforcement capability is particularly critical. Ideally, NATO should have some margin of superiority in its land forces on M-Day to offset certain Pact advantages in reinforcement capability and to allow for the possibility that the Pact might begin to mobilize before NATO does. Reinforcement and mobilization capabilities are extremely difficult to evaluate accurately. The Soviets are often credited with the ability to put many more men and equipment into the center region than NATO can in the first few weeks of a mobilization. It is important, however, to understand what lies behind this estimate. It is clear, for example, that the estimated greater Pact capability does not stem simply from having more men under arms in peacetime. As shown in Table 4, the NATO countries have 30 percent more men under arms than the Warsaw Pact, *excluding* U.S. increases for the Vietnam war. (Or, what amounts to the same thing, excluding U.S. forces in the Pacific and Asia.)

Table 4. **World-wide NATO and Warsaw Pact Manpower in Mid-1968 (excluding U.S. increases for Vietnam)**

	NATO	Warsaw Pact
Army/Marines	3,000,000	2,850,000
Navy	1,070,000	470,000
Air Force	1,400,000	880,000
Total Men	5,470,000	4,200,000

Nor does the greater Pact capability stem from having a greater reserve of trained military manpower. Because of their short terms of service, the NATO countries train more men per year than does the Pact. Even geographical deployment does not explain much of the difference; while the United States has several hundred thousand men in or committed to the Pacific theater (besides the personnel added for the Vietnam war, not included in the table), the Soviet Union has deployed several hundred thousand men along its long border with China. (That the Soviet relationship to China is a key consideration in the NATO-Pact balance is a fact not yet widely enough recognized.)

Finally, the assumed greater Pact capabilities do not stem from a larger investments of resources in its forces. NATO consistently has a larger defense budget than the Warsaw Pact. In 1968, for example, NATO's total defense budget was about 50 percent greater than the Pact's, measuring both in terms of U.S. prices and excluding U.S. expenditures for Vietnam. In other words, NATO could have "bought" the Pact forces in 1968—paid their soldiers at U.S. pay scales and procured their equipment from U.S. factories at U.S. prices—with one-third less budget than was available to NATO.

The explanation for these seemingly contradictory facts is twofold. First, the ability of the Soviets to mobilize and deploy large numbers of understrength divisions *as adequately supported combat-ready units* has been overstated, while our mobilization ability has been understated. The Soviets are often credited with the ability to mobilize cadre divisions and deploy them to the center region in less than two weeks. At the same time, even though our reservists are organized into units and trained on a regular basis, while the Soviet reservists are not, our ability to mobilize and deploy reserve divisions is measured in months. Put simply, with respect to mobilization, the Soviets are often assumed to be able to do many things that we cannot.[18]

The highly unsatisfactory nature of U.S. Army appraisals of its own readiness is a continuing problem. Our National Guard personnel get almost as much annual training as an Israeli reservist. Yet, while our National Guard divisions are judged by the Army to require months to get ready for deployment, Israeli reservists have in fact been able to go on offensive operations with twenty-four hours' notice. Either our methods are very inefficient, or our standards are much too conservative, or we are crediting the Soviets with things they cannot do—or some combination of all these. What is evidently needed is a detailed analysis of what we do and what the Soviets do to prepare forces for deployment; if their method is better, we should adopt it.

A second part of the explanation lies in the fact that the European countries, especially the Germans, have not provided the relatively inexpensive unit training and equipment needed to turn their large reserves of trained men into effective combat units. Improved mobilization capability is only one of the important, and relatively inexpensive, measures that NATO countries can, and should, take to realize the full effectiveness of existing manpower. Balancing of ammunition stocks, improvement of unit training, and better deployability to wartime locations are other examples of such measures.

Both sides still face important problems in the area of reinforcements; but again the Soviets have traditionally been credited with advantages in this area. Upon close inspection, however, these advantages turn out to be primarily differences in reinforcement concepts—differences which result in the Pact initially getting more—but far less trained—men to the front than NATO in a given period of time. Again, in part, this is a result, not of being overwhelmingly outnumbered, but of a deliberate choice by our military experts regarding the value of trained versus untrained manpower at the front. If we thought the Pact would gain a major advantage with its temporarily larger force, we could change our predeployment training times.

When realistic mobilization factors are applied to the forces available, and the smaller size of Soviet divisions is properly taken into account, the differences in reinforcement capability are not large. Of course, about 20 percent of the initial NATO force is supplied by France, whose support some think is uncertain. At the same time, over half the initial Warsaw Pact force is East European.

In light of recent events, it should be obvious that we can rely on French cooperation in the defense of Western Europe with at least as much confidence as the Soviets can rely on satellite cooperation in an attack on Western Europe. This factor in itself is an interesting side light in the history of the NATO strategy debate. Until the early 1960's, not much attention was given to the role of the East European forces; the Soviets alone seemed so overwhelming that the East European forces seemed peripheral at best. When these forces were considered at all, they were thought of as a marginal asset at best and possibly a liability. As the *Economist* reported in 1963: "One of the calls on Russian military manpower, which does not affect the Americans to anything like the same extent, is the need to keep an avuncular eye on the markedly reluctant heroes manning the East European armies." United States intelligence estimates as late as 1967 stated roughly this same conclusion. Certainly, events leading to the Soviet invasion of Czechoslovakia raised doubts as to the loyalty of the Czech Army in a European war.

As the perceived size of the Soviet force began to shrink under closer analysis, it became apparent that the Soviet forces alone were substantially outnumbered by the NATO forces, even after mobilization. Suddenly, despite the increasing independence of the East European countries from the Soviet Union, intelligence reports and Service staff estimates began to count the satellite divisions as nearly

·equivalent to Soviet divisions. (The Soviets themselves seem to have begun to put more emphasis on their East European allies in the early 1960's by building up their readiness and strength.) Indeed, it appeared that whatever headway the Systems Analysis office made in reducing the number of Soviet divisions was offset by an equivalent number of newly found satellite divisions. One way or another, the number of well-equipped, well-trained, combat-ready Pact divisions stayed at 175 in military threat estimates.

In reality, the situation that existed in mid-1968 was a combat-ready Warsaw Pact land force in Eastern Europe half of which was made up of Soviet forces, about equal in size to the NATO force in Western Europe. In addition, the Soviets maintain a mobilization and reinforcement potential in the western USSR consisting mainly of fairly low-readiness divisions. This is a reasonable posture to *defend* against a NATO attack or to exert conventional military power in a crisis; but it is hardly the posture of a giant with such overwhelming conventional superiority that it could crush NATO in a few days.

With respect to tactical air power, the situation is different: NATO has a significant advantage. This advantage adds to the confidence that NATO's land forces could be made effective enough to contain the Pact forces in a conventional conflict. A comparison of tactical air forces in the center region is shown in Table 5.

While NATO has about 28 percent fewer aircraft immediately available in the center region than the Pact, it has considerably more aircraft in its world-wide inventory and thus a much greater reinforcement capability. Equally important, NATO aircraft are far better qualitatively by almost every measure of relative capability— range, pay load, ordnance effectiveness, pilot training, loiter time— and far better suited to conventional operations. NATO has a much higher proportion of multipurpose aircraft with a greater bomb-carrying capacity, while the Pact has a much higher proportion of interceptors not well suited to offensive action. NATO aircraft have about 2.4 times as much pay-load capability per aircraft as Pact aircraft on typical combat missions. NATO air forces also have a much greater capability for front-line defense.

Calculation of the numbers of tanks or personnel the NATO and Pact air forces could kill per day under varying tactical assumptions shows that NATO forces have two and one-half to five times the kill potential of the Pact force when both sides use ordinary bombs and

Table 5. NATO and Warsaw Pact Tactical Air Forces in the European Center Region in Mid-1968

	NATO	Warsaw Pact
Number of Deployed Aircraft	2,100	2,900
Total World-wide Inventories of		
NATO Center Region and Pact Countries	10,500	7,200
Percentage of Force by Mission Capability (Center Region):		
Primarily Interceptors	10%	42%
Multipurpose Fighter/Attack	48%	15%
Primarily Attack	9%	6%
Reconnaissance	13%	8%
Low-Performance	20%	29%
Total	100%	100%
Effectiveness Indicators (NATO as percent of Pact)		
Average Pay Load	240%	
Typical Loiter Time	250–500%	
Crew Training	200%	

rockets, and an even greater advantage if the best available U.S. munitions are used. These estimates take into account sortie rates, aircrew proficiency, and pay loads for each air force. NATO air forces also have at least two and one-half to five times the loiter time capability of Pact first-line fighters. (Loiter time is a good measure of the ability of either side to patrol its front lines, protect its bombers, or attack the other side's bombers.) A key question is how effective the Soviet interceptors would be in stopping NATO fighter bombers. While this cannot be determined precisely, one thing is clear: with its high percentage of multipurpose aircraft, NATO has more flexibility than the Pact. NATO can use its aircraft partly for offensive attacks and partly for protection against Pact interceptors, as the situation requires. Considering the limitations on the Pact's ability to patrol the front lines, NATO aircraft should be able to penetrate Pact defenses and attack Pact troops. Finally, the average NATO pilot gets twice as many flying hours per month as the average Pact pilot. The average Pact aircraft spends more time out of commission per flying hour than the average NATO aircraft. Pilot training and aircraft maintenance are expensive, but they give us a more effective air force.

All these factors change the conclusions derived from a simple counting of aircraft. NATO air forces have much greater offensive power than the Pact. However, as with land forces, many of NATO's air advantages are only potential. They are in danger of being wasted because relatively inexpensive but critically important matters are being neglected. For example, the present vulnerability of our air bases could be reduced inexpensively. We badly need to build aircraft shelters. It makes little sense to refuse to invest $100,000 for a shelter to protect an aircraft costing between $2 and $8 million. We also need to establish better runway repair capabilities and to take other measures oriented toward providing more active and passive defense for our air bases. Otherwise, we are in danger of losing many aircraft in the first few days or hours of a war, as the Arabs did in 1967.

In summary, based on years of study, we believe that NATO's conventional forces are not smaller than those of the Pact and, therefore, that a strong conventional capability is feasible. This is not to say that NATO could defeat the Soviets or could unilaterally reduce its forces in safety. The balance is close—so close that even moderate changes can have a significant effect on the balance of military power. In addition, as we have pointed out repeatedly, there are a number of serious qualitative problems. We are not getting what we are paying for because we are not providing all the "horseshoe nails" needed to realize the full potential of NATO's existing conventional forces. The major missing nails include aircraft shelters, modern air ordnance, ground ammunition, and a larger allied mobilization capability. There is also considerable room for improvement in troop deployments, allied pilot training, manning levels, and training levels (resulting from short terms of service). By correcting these deficiencies, NATO could greatly increase the effectiveness of its conventional forces without big increases in costs. But to do so requires concentrating our efforts on solving the real problems of military readiness and effectiveness against realistic threats rather than spending so much time and effort devising ways of meeting an exaggerated threat.

The Lessons Learned

What lessons can be drawn from this discussion of the debate over the conventional military balance in Europe? First and most important, the discussion shows that the "facts"—the givens of a major strategic or political problem—need careful and continuous reexamination. These givens can so circumscribe the options that no desirable solution seems possible. Instead of debate over viable alternatives, years of unproductive and irrelevant argument on how to reconcile the irreconcilable can take place. More importantly, strategic alternatives can be arbitrarily narrowed, or fundamentally different alternatives never considered. Most of the nuclear strategies proposed for NATO were based on the fundamental assumption that we did not have a chance using conventional forces.

In the case of NATO, many of the "facts" that politicians and strategists had to work with were estimates, supplied by military and intelligence staffs, of the relative strengths of NATO and Warsaw Pact conventional forces. From the earliest days of NATO to the present, these estimates have generally indicated the gross inferiority of NATO to the Pact. Not only were the Soviets given seven times as many divisions, but the quality of the divisions was supposedly being constantly upgraded. Alastair Buchan's argument in 1960 could as easily have been written in 1968: ". . . the fact that the official NATO calculations of Soviet Army strength—175 divisions (of which about 140 are operational)—have not changed in ten years, should not obscure the fact that within this traditional framework there has been scope for great tactical and technical innovations. . . . For it is the improved quality of these forces that is of importance."[19] Only recently has this perceived gap in numbers and quality begun to narrow. Progress in this direction has been extremely slow, and there is still a long way to go. Unfortunately, many would still agree with the assessment made by the *Economist* in 1968: "The NATO and Warsaw Pact countries are locked in a nuclear stalemate. But so far, come fair political weather or foul, Russia has maintained its superiority in conventional forces."[20]

Other "facts" concerned the value of tactical nuclear weapons to offset NATO's supposed inferiority in manpower and conventional forces and the ability to fight a controlled nuclear war. These "facts" provided an easy escape from the difficult problem of maintaining strong conventional forces in NATO.

The acceptance of these "facts" as the starting point for strategic debate severely limited any serious consideration of the merits of the proposed strategy of flexible response. A conventional option was automatically assumed to require major increases in defense budgets, which politicians on both sides of the Atlantic were unwilling to make, particularly since nuclear weapons were assumed to be a substitute for manpower and therefore a viable alternative. Furthermore, the mere debate over the new strategy, in the context of forces thought to be grossly inferior to the other side's, was said to be dangerous, because any admission of possible restraint in the use of nuclear weapons would invite military aggression by the superior conventional forces on the other side. Even discussion of a conventional option, it seems, would weaken the nuclear resolve.

Even the simple, inexpensive step of making adequate plans and logistic provision for existing forces was largely ignored because of the presumed hopeless inadequacy of the forces. (The inadequate plans then became part of the "facts" demonstrating the inferiority of the NATO forces.) Ironically, the kicker in this vicious train of logic is that the same "facts" have more recently been used by some members of the Congress as a justification for drastically reducing even the existing level of forces, which, being so obviously inadequate, are presumed to have little more than token value anyway.

Understandably, they feel that if we are outnumbered 7 to 1 we might as well make it 10 to 1 and save the money. Yet thorough investigation with simple analytical tools convinced two Secretaries of Defense that the alleged "facts" of the conventional balance in Europe were not facts at all. Rather they were a series of assumptions, often made low in the bureaucratic hierarchy and carried up to the highest policy levels with all the adverse consequences discussed above. In nearly all cases, different assumptions were equally or more justifiable and would have vastly changed the givens of the strategic and political debate. What was needed was someone to challenge these assumptions.

A similar situation exists today with respect to reducing the balance-of-payments cost of our European deployments. Because our divisions in Germany are the biggest, most visible, and best-known element of our deployments, many people assume that most of the balance-of-payments cost must be associated with these divisions. But actually the four and one-third divisions we maintain in Germany (including combat and service support) account for less than 40 percent of our expenditures in Europe. This is true in part because the average rank of these combat personnel is relatively low and because proportionately more of them live in government quarters. Many of our expenditures abroad relate to less important functions, such as the operation of overlapping and expensive higher headquarters, the operation of air bases no longer needed, the operation of redundant communications, and the operation and maintenance of peacetime facilities. Reductions in these activities would be significant, since over-all manpower ceilings would also be reduced and operating and maintenance costs cut. The alternative of redeploying divisions and squadrons from Europe to the United States would save very little and could create major military and political problems. We can and should continue to reduce peripheral support activities in Europe in order to minimize the need to remove combat units.

Such reduction will require careful, detailed research. For while it seems clear that the guiding principle should be to cut fat before muscle—to withdraw noncombat support and administrative personnel from Europe before combat forces—our experience with such exercises in the Department of Defense has shown this to be a difficult principle to follow, primarily because of the opposition and bargaining tactics of the Services. As a general proposition, asking the Services to come up with proposals for reducing balance-of-payments expenditures results in proposals that yield minimum savings per unit of capability lost. Almost invariably the Services recommended cutting combat forces first.

A second conclusion that can be drawn from the NATO strategy debate is that it shows the direct relevance of cost even to such highly political issues as national and international strategy. Although it is not usually stated that way, much of the argument over NATO strategy has, in fact, concerned the question of the cost and actual worth of different levels of conventional capability. The worth of conventional versus nuclear forces is obviously a highly subjective issue and one difficult to analyze. It depends on judgments as to the intentions of the enemy, his perceptions of the credibility of our nuclear deterrent, how these perceptions would be strengthened or weakened by declaratory policy on the use of nuclear weapons and the like. It also depends on judgments as to the reactions of allies when put to the test of actually using nuclear weapons and on calculations of the effects of different kinds of nuclear weapons on both sides. With questions of this difficulty at the center of the NATO debate, it is no wonder that no consensus could be reached and that the debate was at times so frustrating and divisive. Yet, if a conventional capability had been viewed as a viable alternative—that is, financially feasible instead of prohibitive—most of the debate would simply not have taken place. And many of the tough questions of intentions, psychology, and deterrence could have been avoided or minimized as bars to action.

Those who claimed that possession of conventional capabilities weakened the nuclear deterrent were thinking of the costs of fixing the "inadequate" conventional force in being. No one proposed reducing NATO's conventional forces during the Berlin crisis in 1961 in order to show unmistakably that alternatives to the use of nuclear forces would be closed. No one suggested that the Soviet conventional build-up weakened the Soviet nuclear deterrent. Rather, the NATO debate centered on how much the existing forces would have to be increased—presumably a great deal—to meet the conventional capabilities required by the flexible-response strategy. Had more high-level attention been focused from the beginning on requirements for the conventional option in the new strategy and how much it would cost, much of the argument over whether the options were worth the cost would have been clearer and perhaps unnecessary.

A frequently stated but mistaken view of setting strategy and force requirements is that the process is one of starting at the top with broad national objectives and then successively deriving a strategy, force requirements, and a budget. It is mistaken because costs must be considered from the very outset in choosing strategies and objectives. If nothing else, the NATO strategy debate shows that costs *are* considered, either implicitly or explicitly. When this consideration is implicit, there is less chance of checking its accuracy. Recognizing that cost is relevant and considering it explicitly in a decision reduces the likelihood of this kind of problem.

A third conclusion is that the NATO strategy debate revealed the persistent bias of the military and intelligence bureaucracies toward overestimating one's enemy by making "conservative assumptions." It also showed the unintended reverse effects of this bias. These "conservative" assumptions did not have the anticipated effect of eliciting more forces and higher budgets in NATO. Instead, they convinced many political leaders that the effort required would be so great as to be infeasible. They created a feeling that even the existing level of military forces was militarily irrelevant, since if a war were to start, the estimates implied that NATO would lose very rapidly anyway. Therefore, the reasoning went, if we were forced to live dangerously, we might as well live cheaply. As a legacy of this reasoning, NATO's large investment in forces is still not producing its full potential military capability, because of a failure to bother with inexpensive but essential requirements such as supplies, deployment plans, and passive defenses for air bases. Furthermore, the feeling of military irrelevance is adding to the pressure for indiscriminate force reductions.

It can be just as dangerous to overstate as to understate the enemy threat. In the case of NATO, overstatement has led to strategies of desperation, particularly with respect to the threatened prompt use of nuclear weapons. The effect of overstating the strength of the Soviet Army has been not only to get a smaller NATO force but also to reduce the incentives for the NATO countries to make the NATO armies fully combat-ready. Overstatement also undermines public credibility, encouraging the feeling that we are getting nothing useful for our military spending. (As one critic has put it: "The United States is constantly spending more [for defense] and enjoying it less.") The Warsaw Pact's land and tactical air forces do present a serious threat to NATO; but it is a manageable one, and within our present budgets we should be able to oppose those forces effectively—if we will recognize the threat realistically and concentrate our attention on meeting it.

To do this, the civilian leaders of all the NATO governments need to learn the true facts of the military balance for themselves, in detail; they should not stop at a count of divisions and aircraft. They should consider more meaningful indicators of military power, such as soldiers, guns, vehicles, training activity rates, and sorties. They should give particular care to assuring that the same rules and definitions are used to evaluate both Pact and NATO forces. And they should be careful to review the arguments used by the NATO military establishments to justify expensive items of equipment in view of the estimates of Pact capability from simpler, cheaper items. It is wrong to assume that we are stuck forever with inefficient equipment or organization. If the Pact really does get equivalent strength with fewer men or cheaper equipment, we should find out why and perhaps adopt some of their concepts for the future design of our own forces.

A wider appreciation of the rough equality of force size on both sides should yield several important benefits. It suggests that a satisfactory NATO conventional capability is feasible, at planned or moderately increased budget levels, provided that NATO supplies, protects, and uses its existing forces more effectively. It also suggests that an effective military strategy of flexible response is feasible. This is vitally important to our security; without effective nonnuclear forces, NATO would be politically weak in a crisis. Nuclear weapons, when both sides have them, are not an adequate substitute for conventional forces. They are too dangerous and destructive to form part of a credible response except in the most extreme circumstances. In a conflict involving strategic nuclear forces, there is a grave risk of escalation to attacks on cities and unacceptable damage to the West. Similarly, in a conflict involving tactical nuclear forces we could lose as many men as the Pact and kill millions of civilians whom we were trying to defend. It is for these reasons that we must maintain enough conventional force to deter conventional aggression and to avoid being forced to initiate the use of nuclear weapons. An approximate balance of NATO and Pact conventional capabilities, both before and after mobilization, should enable us to meet this objective.

In addition, an appreciation of the rough balance of forces should divert attention from large increases in the number of divisions and troops and toward better training, ammunition supplies, deployments and mobilization plans, aircraft shelters, and so on—the unglamorous essentials necessary for an effective fighting force—which are all too often slighted in NATO forces.

An appreciation of the existing rough balance of forces in Europe would also help the American people to understand the important military purpose served by the U.S. forces there. They *do* help maintain the conventional balance. They are *not* irrelevant. If NATO were really outnumbered 175 to 25 divisions, it wouldn't make much difference if we reduced the U.S. forces there. As it is, U.S. forces are needed to maintain the balance and should not be reduced without replacement by those of other NATO allies or without corresponding reductions by the Pact.[21]

A final conclusion to be drawn from the NATO strategy debate is that simple tools of analysis have considerable power. The tool that cut through the maze of conventional force ratios was a simple cost analysis; on the tactical air side, it was simple "bean counting" on the basis of comparable assumptions. In neither case was it necessary to go beyond logic, common sense, and elementary arithmetic. No fancy mathematics or complex simulation models or computer programs were used, or needed, to establish the fact of rough equality. The Army's cost analysis showed that while keeping our standard of living and pay scales we could, in fact, buy three Soviet division forces with the resources with which we were buying one U.S. division force. If we chose to continue to buy division forces of the U.S. type in preference to three times as many division forces of the Soviet type for the same cost, it must be because we believed our divisions were at least three times as effective; otherwise, we were not getting the most effectiveness out of our resources. Alternatively, to say that our division forces were less than three times as effective was to imply that the organization and equipment of our Army were less efficient than those of the Soviets. If this was the case, reorganization was needed, perhaps along Soviet lines. This was a matter of simple and fairly compelling logic. It was understood, if not accepted, by all parties. After this, the myth of Soviet superiority in land forces was to continue, but on other grounds than equipment or manpower, and thus less convincingly.

The myth of Pact superiority in tactical air power could not withstand the test of addition, once the addition was done on the basis of comparable assumptions. While the Pact had nearly 40 percent more aircraft actually deployed in the center region, NATO had 50 percent more tactical aircraft available for employment in Europe than the Warsaw Pact, and NATO aircraft had important qualitative advantages. If NATO could not handle the Warsaw Pact air force for more than a few days, as the studies were showing, surely it was for reasons other than number and quality of aircraft. Again, the logic was compelling and easily understood.

The results of these simple analyses challenged the thinking and conclusions of a decade. One wonders why they were not done earlier, or whether they would ever have been done without the insistence of the Secretary of Defense and the availability of an independent analytical staff such as the Systems Analysis office to challenge "facts," raise questions, point up basic assumptions, and suggest possible alternative assumptions. These challenges constitute a key reason for the existence of such a group as the Systems Analysis staff in the Pentagon. One cannot reasonably expect the military or allies to challenge assumptions that are congenial to a position they favor. Nor can one expect traditional views to overturn themselves. It takes searching analysis and proof. And, as the following suggests, even this does not always guarantee success. In December 1969, after conceding that the Warsaw Pact had only a slight advantage in total manpower (990,000 to 826,000), *Time* magazine still reported: "Because NATO forces are outnumbered 2 to 1 on the crucial central front and would be quickly overrun in the event of an all-out ground attack, the NATO defense ministers also agreed to new guidelines that provide for quicker use of tactical nuclear weapons."[22] Comforting old myths do, indeed, die hard.

5

Nuclear Strategy and Forces

The Early Decisions

In the Presidential campaign of 1960, John F. Kennedy made it clear that one of the priority items for review in his administration would be the doctrine of "massive retaliation." Long before the campaign and its "missile-gap" oratory, Kennedy had aggressively attacked the basic assumption that strategic nuclear forces could be relied on as a universal deterrent to war. He called for recognition of the limited role of nuclear weapons and, in light of this, for major improvements in the U.S. nonnuclear forces. His reasons were clear and fundamental. The U.S. nuclear monopoly was gone. The Soviets had strong nuclear and nonnuclear forces. Under these circumstances, in Kennedy's words:

[Soviet] missile power will be the shield from behind which they will slowly, but surely advance through Sputnik diplomacy, limited brush-fire wars, indirect non-overt aggression, intimidation and subversion, internal revolution, increased prestige or influence, and the vicious blackmail of our allies. The periphery of the Free World will slowly be nibbled away. . . . Each such Soviet move will weaken the West; but none will seem sufficiently significant by itself to justify our initiating a nuclear war which might destroy us.[1]

Immediately after his inauguration, President Kennedy directed the Secretary of Defense to undertake a thorough review of U.S. military strategies and programs. This review was another step in the shift away from massive retaliation and toward a new defense strategy to become known as "flexible response."

A series of studies at The Rand Corporation in the 1950's[2] had pointed out the dangers inherent in the growing vulnerability of U.S. strategic retaliatory forces.[3] Studies in OSD in 1961 confirmed this appraisal. As the Soviets acquired more and more intercontinental ballistic missiles (ICBM's), U.S. strategic retaliatory forces, which at the time consisted almost entirely of some 1,500 intercontinental bombers concentrated on about 60 bases, were becoming more and more vulnerable to a surprise attack. Indeed, if allowed to continue, the vulnerability could reach a point where these forces might invite, rather than deter, a surprise attack. Clearly, a large force of protected nuclear firepower that could not be knocked out in a surprise Soviet missile attack was an absolute prerequisite for a deterrent posture.

The vulnerability problem was not widely or well understood. At best, people thought of it only as a matter of the survival of U.S. offensive weapons rather than the survival of a whole posture, including vital decision-making elements and their communications. Moreover, while overestimating Soviet forces, most people also attributed to them very unsophisticated strategies that failed to take advantage of their real capabilities or our known weaknesses. For example, in 1960 few people thought in terms of mixed bomber and missile attacks, in which Soviet missiles would be used to destroy U.S. bomber bases, soft missile sites, and the control centers of the air defense system, leaving their bombers free to "mop up" against these and less urgent targets. In the event of even a poorly planned attack, it appeared likely that most of our very costly strategic defensive posture would be destroyed before it could be used.

Perhaps the most critical vulnerability problem, however, lay in the U.S. high-level command structure, which was located in a comparatively small number of points on or near Strategic Air Command (SAC) bases or major cities, all of which were themselves prime targets for enemy attacks. Most of the facilities were soft, and most of the communication links were vulnerable. A well-designed Soviet attack would probably have begun by destroying all these points in a closely coordinated missile volley. A successful attack would have deprived our forces of their authorized commands to proceed to targets. In all likelihood, if all U.S. forces obeyed their orders, our ICBM's would have remained on the ground to be destroyed by follow-up Soviet bombers, and our air-borne bombers and our Polaris submarines would have returned to bases already destroyed by Soviet ICBM's.

While the implications of the vulnerability problem were being assessed in DoD, the 1961 Berlin crisis took place. Whatever else this crisis may have showed, it further convinced the leaders of the Kennedy administration that strategic nuclear forces, no matter how powerful and protected, were not by themselves an effective deterrent to all forms of aggression. These two goals—reducing the vulnerability of our strategic posture and increasing the capability of our nonnuclear forces—provided the rationale for most of the early defense decisions.

The first steps taken to improve the nonnuclear forces are well known and need only be summarized here. The number of active combat-ready Army divisions was increased from 11 to 16, and the number of active Air Force tactical air wings from 16 to 21. The annual rate of procurement of conventional weapons and ammunition and equipment was almost doubled. Over one hundred thousand additional men were added to the Army. The size of the Special Forces was greatly increased. The Marine Corps's strength was increased and the Marine Corps Reserve expanded to a full fourth division/wing team. A major expansion of airlift capabilities was undertaken. The tempo of modernization of naval and tactical air forces was greatly speeded up. Research and development funds for work on nonnuclear weapons and ordnance were significantly increased. Important improvements were made in organization, training, readiness, and particularly the balance among elements of our general-purpose forces. By 1963, the United States was well on the way to having a meaningful alternative to the choice between responding to nonnuclear aggression with nuclear weapons and surrendering.

The capability of U.S. and allied nonnuclear forces, in relation to their probable opposition, is an important factor in the determination of U.S. strategic force requirements. A strategic posture that must deter, for example, a limited Soviet nonnuclear attack in Europe must be far more powerful than a posture whose purpose is limited to deterrence of a nuclear attack. One of the most important contributions to national security made between 1961 and 1969 was the move toward a more satisfactory balance between U.S. nuclear and non-nuclear objectives and capabilities.

In order to reduce the vulnerability of the strategic posture, several major and controversial steps were taken. A decision was made to shift from the liquid-fuel, first-generation ICBM's, Atlas and Titan, to the solid-fuel, second-generation missiles, Polaris and Minuteman. Minuteman was not only less costly than Atlas and Titan but much less difficult to deploy in hardened underground sites and to maintain on a high-alert status. While more costly than Minuteman, the submarine-carried Polaris missile, because of its mobility and concealment, promised an even greater assurance of being able to survive a surprise attack. Accordingly, both the Minuteman and Polaris programs were drastically speeded up, and procurement funds were concentrated on these weapon systems. An Air Force recommendation to buy more B-52 heavy bombers was turned down, and a decision was made to phase out the large B-47 force over a period of five years.

These decisions did not mean, as some interpreted it at the time, that the new administration was opposed to bombers in principle. The United States already had plenty of bombers, but it had too few ballistic missiles. The intent then and later was to achieve a balanced, mixed force of bombers and missiles. In 1961, that meant buying more missiles.

Until the Minuteman and Polaris forces could be deployed in large numbers, primary reliance had to be placed on the bomber forces. Again, since vulnerability to surprise attack was the key consideration, it was apparent that the number of bombers on alert status was far more important than the total number available. In a surprise attack, bombers not on alert status would probably be destroyed on the ground. Accordingly, as a temporary measure until the Minuteman and Polaris deployments could be completed, the number of B-52's being maintained on a constant 15-minute ground alert was increased from one-third to one-half of the force.

An extensive program was undertaken to improve and protect the command and control facilities of U.S. strategic nuclear forces against a surprise attack. Several alternative national command centers were established, including some maintained continuously in the air. New procedures, equipment, and safeguards were introduced to make certain that only authorized national authorities could release nuclear weapons. Steps were taken to improve the survivability and reliability of communications systems, and all such systems were merged into a new National Military Command System.

In early 1961, the decision was made to phase out the lone Snark Squadron at Presque Isle, Maine. The Snark was an air-breathing, subsonic intercontinental missile which, because it was unprotected, would have had to be launched at the first indication of an attack. The Snark combined some of the worst disadvantages of the bomber (soft, concentrated basing; slow time to target; vulnerability in the air to enemy defenses) with some of the worst disadvantages of the missile (no recall after launch; relatively small pay load and poor accuracy), and it should never have been developed in the first place. Decisions were made later to phase out the Thor, Jupiter, and Regulus missiles as well. The intermediate-range, liquid-fueled Thor and Jupiter were deployed aboveground: four squadrons of the former in England, three squadrons of the latter in Italy and Turkey. Phasing out these intermediate-range ballistic missiles (IRBM's) also meant moving away from the concept of an overseas theater-based strategic deterrent. The Regulus was an air-breathing subsonic cruise missile designed to be launched by surfaced submarines.

The slow-reacting, unprotected land-based missiles were obviously highly vulnerable to attack. The Regulus was vulnerable to attack by surface ships or aircraft during its launching phase. Inasmuch as the Minuteman and Polaris programs had been substantially increased, the potential contribution of these older missiles would have been negligible.

As discussed more fully later, the advisability of deploying a full-scale antiballistic-missile (ABM) defense system was carefully evaluated. Such a system, the Nike-Zeus, had been under development since 1955, when planners first foresaw the great changes in nuclear warfare that would accompany the development of ICBM's. It soon became clear that the monumental technical problems involved in detecting, tracking, intercepting, and destroying ICBM's had not been satisfactorily solved by the Nike-Zeus system. The system depended on identifying an enemy warhead and launching a relatively slow antimissile while the warhead was still far out in space; it was, therefore, highly vulnerable to even primitive decoys that could not reenter the atmosphere but which we could not wait to distinguish. Because of such limitations (and his belief that the Soviets would offset a U.S. ABM force with changes in their offensive forces), Secretary McNamara refused to approve deployment of the system.

These initial decisions regarding strategic nuclear forces were based more on early insights than on any satisfactory theory of "how much is enough." For example, however one measured deterrence, our forces had to be able to survive an attack; hence the switch to Minuteman and Polaris rather than Atlas or more bombers. Similarly, if deterrence failed and a war came, it would be useful to have alternatives to the "spasm" response envisioned in the then current war plan; hence the need to develop options in the war plan and secure the command and control facilities for their execution. While important, however, such insights could carry one only so far. What was badly needed was a theory of requirements—a conceptual framework for measuring the need and adequacy of our strategic forces.

The results of not having had such a framework before 1961 were evident on all sides. The strategy, the forces, the R&D program, and the military planning effort were out of balance. Despite the inevitability of the day when the Soviets would have a secure retaliatory or "second-strike" force, the United States was proceeding with large and costly programs that could be justified only if we were trying for a first-strike capability—that is, an ability to destroy in a first strike the Soviets' ability to retaliate. Indeed, in 1961 the Air Force's stated goal was to achieve a "credible first-strike capability." But because of Soviet progress in missile development and deployment, it should have been clear even in 1961 that such a first-strike capability for the middle and late 1960's would be unattainable, regardless of how much we were willing to spend.

Along the same lines, the Defense Department was spending billions on the early Minuteman, Polaris, and B-52 programs; it was also spending billions on the Atlas, Titan, Snark, Thor, Jupiter, Regulus, B-47, B-58, B-70, nuclear-powered airplane, Hound Dog, Skybolt, and Nike-Zeus programs. And there was no coherent pattern or plan for deciding how much of which system we should retain or buy.

The lack of an adequate conceptual framework was particularly evident in the force planning effort. Even the relatively simple idea of considering all strategic forces together was still very new and controversial. In the late 1950's, the Air Force and the Navy were individually developing strategic weapon systems and war plans as if the other Service did not exist. As late as 1960 there was no formal mechanism for coordinating strategic target plans. In that year Secretary Gates took the major forward step of establishing a Joint Strategic Target Planning Staff under the direction of the Commander-in-Chief of the Strategic Air Command. In 1961, the Navy presented a briefing to the Secretary of Defense on the requirement for Polaris submarines. The briefing began with a list of targets to be destroyed, a calculation as to how many missiles should be programmed per target, how many were needed on station, how many were needed in the total force to maintain that number on station, and thus why a force of 45 Polaris submarines was required. In the entire briefing, there was not one reference to the existence of the Air Force or its weapon systems, despite the fact that most of our nuclear firepower was then in Air Force bombers. Air Force briefings, at the time, acknowledged the existence of the Navy's contribution, but assumed that no more Navy systems would be deployed than those already approved by the Congress.

Without some measure of total needs and capabilities, there was no effective way of appraising our strategic posture. One of the most widely used arguments against repairing the growing vulnerability of the strategic forces (for example, the generally admitted fact that we would automatically lose two-thirds of our bombers—those not on alert—in the opening minutes of a war) was a "minimum-deterrent" position, an argument that the United States would always have *something* left, after absorbing an attack, with which to strike Soviet cities and that, regardless of how little, the Soviets would be unwilling to accept that risk. But those in DoD who used this argument were unwilling to acknowledge, much less accept, its implications. If the threat of a few bombs was really enough to deter the Soviets, and if we didn't care how we performed should deterrence fail, the strategic mission could have been done for about a third of what was being spent at the time. Without a theory of requirements, what we were getting was the worst of both worlds; we were paying for a first-strike posture, but settling for a minimum-deterrent capability.

This observation points up one of the most distressing aspects of the force planning process in those years. Everything was put in terms of simplistic arguments with at most two steps. The Air Force argued for the B-70 by saying that a new bomber was needed, or that bombers could do useful things that missiles could not, but they were not required to demonstrate that the B-70 was an important part of a coherent, total U.S. strategic posture that would really be able to accomplish the stated objectives. Moreover, the system did not require the participants to accept the unfavorable implications of their arguments. For example, the Air Force argued for the Skybolt air-to-surface missile on the grounds that the B-52 bombers could not penetrate enemy defenses without it. But when the Skybolt was canceled, no recommendation was made to phase out the B-52's. Arguments seemed to chase each other around in circles. People were not required to take responsibility for their previous positions. As a result, few seemed to see the difference between a new position because of previous error and a new position because of changed circumstances or a new position based on new error.

Developing a Theory of Requirements

Early in 1961, Secretary McNamara asked a group of military planners to take a look at strategic retaliatory force requirements over the next ten years. The group was very competent, and the resulting study (called the "Hickey Study") was by far the best available on the subject to that date. The study group developed a list of all strategic targets and, using the best available intelligence and their own judgment, projected the growth of these target lists over the next ten years. They then estimated the performance characteristics of the planned weapon systems of all the Services and calculated how many would be needed to destroy 75 percent and 90 percent, respectively, of the projected targets in each of the next ten years. These calculations were summarized and forwarded along with force recommendations to the Secretary of Defense.

The Hickey Study was a major advance, but like many good studies, it raised more questions than it answered. Why 90 percent or 75 percent? Why the same percentage for cities as for military targets? What were we really trying to do? What was the purpose of having the power to destroy these targets, not in terms of the narrow technical criteria of the force planner, but in terms of the broader criteria of interest to the Secretary of Defense, the President, and the Congress? The study had other limitations. For one thing, it treated only strategic offensive forces, giving no indication of their relationship to strategic defensive forces. Moreover, it assumed no Soviet reaction to major changes in U.S. forces. We do not point to these limitations to criticize those who did the study; one of the present authors participated in it. Our purpose is to indicate the state of the analytical art at that time.

Nor were such analytical shortcomings confined only to the military side of DoD planning. For example, when the DoD programming system was first designed in 1961, three major programs were established in support of our strategic nuclear posture: the Strategic Retaliatory Forces, the Continental Air and Missile Defense Forces, and Civil Defense. It was not until several years later, after we had gained experience in the analysis of these requirements, that we were able to take full account of the interaction of these three major programs by incorporating them all into a single analytical framework. Only then could we grasp the essentials of strategic nuclear war requirements and evaluate combined alternatives in the light of national security objectives.

As a result of early analyses of strategic force requirements, it became clear that some method was needed to integrate into the same analytical structure the estimates and projections of Soviet strategic offensive and defensive forces. That Soviet forces should be considered in determining our own requirements had, of course, long been recognized. What remained was to integrate these data into our own requirements calculations in a systematic and quantitative fashion. Even more important, as we shall see later, was the need to provide explicitly in the analyses for possible interactions between U.S. and Soviet strategic decisions.

Further analysis revealed yet another basic shortcoming: the need to recast in a more logical and up-to-date form the objectives, or purposes, of U.S. strategic nuclear forces. Traditionally, military strategy has been conceived of in terms of offense and defense; this pattern of thought was applied to strategic nuclear problems in the post–World War II period. For planning purposes, strategic forces were divided into two specialized groups, offensive and defensive, with civil defense as a third, independent component. But analysis and common sense convinced the leaders of the Department of Defense that the basic objectives of these forces were not offense and defense per se, but rather (1) to deter a deliberate nuclear attack upon the United States or its allies by maintaining at all times a clear and unmistakable ability to inflict an unacceptable degree of damage upon any aggressor, or combination of aggressors—even after absorbing a surprise first strike; and (2) should deterrence fail and a war occur, to limit damage to our population and industrial capacity. The first of these objectives became known as "assured destruction," the second as "damage limiting."

This reformulation of U.S. strategic objectives was much more than a matter of semantics. It was an attempt to find better criteria than "75 percent or 90 percent destruction across the board" for use in choosing which systems to emphasize and buy. It helped defense planners to focus directly on capabilities in relation to objectives, rather than merely categorize forces according to their offensive or defensive characteristics. When viewed in this light, it became apparent that the strategic offensive forces which one would normally associate with assured destruction—the ICBM's, the submarine-launched ballistic missiles, and the manned bombers—can also contribute to damage limiting. Under some circumstances, they can do so by attacking and destroying enemy delivery vehicles on their bases or launch sites before they are sent against our cities. Similarly, it became apparent that the strategic defensive forces which one would normally associate with damage limiting—the interceptors, the anti-bomber surface-to-air missiles (SAM's), and the antiballistic missiles (ABM's)—can also contribute to assured destruction by successfully intercepting and destroying the enemy's offensive weapons before they can reach our strategic offensive forces on their bases and launch sites.

It also became apparent that, since deterrence of a deliberate Soviet (or Chinese) nuclear attack upon the United States or its allies was the overriding objective of U.S. strategic forces, the capability for assured destruction must receive first call on our resources regardless of the costs and difficulties involved. The reason for this order of priorities is really quite simple. No matter how much is spent on them, damage-limiting programs can never substitute for an assured-destruction capability in the deterrent role. It is (and will remain) the ability to absorb a first strike and still destroy the attacker as a viable twentieth-century nation that provides the deterrent.

What kind and amount of destruction must we be able to inflict on an attacker to ensure maintaining our deterrent (or assured-destruction) capability? This vital question could not and cannot be answered precisely. Nor can it be answered solely by analysis; a judgment must be made. After careful study and debate, it was McNamara's judgment, accepted by Presidents Kennedy and Johnson, and not disputed by the Congress, that the ability to destroy in retaliation 20 to 25 percent of the Soviet population and 50 percent of its industrial capacity was sufficient. (As will be discussed in the next chapter, this judgment was influenced by the fact of strongly diminishing marginal returns at levels beyond these.) Such a level of destruction would certainly represent intolerable punishment to any modern industrialized nation and thus should serve as an effective deterrent to a deliberate nuclear attack on the United States or its allies. Significantly, few seriously challenged this judgment.

Next, it was observed that the United States anticipates and reacts to Soviet strategic moves, such as their deployment of an ABM defense system. So members of the Systems Analysis office, working with military planners in the Services and the Joint Staff, began exploring the implications of various assumptions about how the Soviets might react to similar moves on the part of the United States.

It is important to understand this interaction of opposing strategic forces and its relation to the strategic force planning process. If the overriding objective of our strategic nuclear forces is to deter a first strike against us, the United States must have a second-strike capability; that is, strategic forces of such size and character that they can survive a well-planned, large-scale surprise attack with sufficient strength remaining to penetrate the attacker's defenses and still destroy him. This capability to destroy him even after absorbing his surprise attack must be a virtual certainty, and clearly evident to the enemy. This is the foundation of U.S. deterrent strategy. Consequently, as long as deterrence remains the priority objective, the United States must be prepared to offset any Soviet effort to reduce the effectiveness of our assured-destruction capability below the level we consider necessary.

At the same time, however, if deterrence is also the Soviets' objec-

tive (as the available evidence has consistently and strongly suggested), we would expect them to react in much the same way to any
effort on our part to reduce the effectiveness of their deterrent (or
assured-destruction) capability against us. And we would also expect
them, in their planning, to view our strategic offensive forces as a
potential first-strike threat (just as we do theirs) and provide for a
second-strike capability. In other words, any attempt on our part to
reduce damage to our society would put pressure on the Soviets to
strive for an offsetting improvement in *their* assured-destruction
forces, and vice versa. Each step by either side, however sensible or
precautionary, would elicit a precautionary response from the other
side. This "action-reaction" phenomenon is central to all strategic
force planning issues as well as to any theory of an arms race.

Once the assured-destruction and damage-limiting objectives had
been formulated, and once the interaction of strategic offensive and
defensive forces contributing to these objectives—as well as the
reaction to such forces by the Soviets—had been understood, the
problem of calculating strategic force requirements was simplified.
Indeed, in sharp contrast to most other types of military requirements, those for strategic forces lend themselves to calculation. At
least the task presents a problem of finite dimensions, measurable in
terms of the number and type of weapon systems required to do the
job under various sets of conditions.

The first step in such a calculation is to determine the number,
type, and location of the enemy targets. The second step is to determine the number and explosive yield of the weapons that must be
delivered on each target to ensure a given probability of its destruction. The third step involves determining the size and character of the
forces best suited to attack each type of target, taking into account
such factors as (1) the number, weight, and yield of warheads that
each type of vehicle can deliver, (2) the ability of each type of
vehicle to penetrate possible enemy defenses, (3) the degree of
accuracy to be expected of each system, (4) the technical reliability
of the system (that is, the proportion of the ready operational
inventory that can be successfully launched within the prescribed
time), and (5) the cost of each system in relation to its effectiveness.

Since the most severe threat the United States must plan against is
a full-scale surprise attack, allowance must be made in the calcula-

tions for the losses that our forces would suffer before they could be launched. This exercise in turn introduces a number of additional factors, such as (1) the size, weight, and effectiveness of the enemy's strategic offensive forces, including warhead yields and the reliability and accuracy of his weapon systems, (2) the degree of survivability of each of our strategic offensive weapon systems under such an attack, and (3) the enemy's targeting options and likely choice among them.

Each of these factors involves uncertainties, but it is possible to introduce reasonable allowances for them in the calculations. For example, in dealing with estimates of the enemy's forces, studies done in the Systems Analysis office used a range of estimates covering not only numbers of weapon systems but also warhead yields, accuracy, and reliability. With respect to U.S. forces, we could reduce the range of uncertainty through extensive test programs, thus arriving at fairly accurate factors for the reliability, the accuracy, and even the vulnerability of each type of offensive weapon system.

Of course, the effectiveness of different combinations of systems will vary significantly with the assumptions about how the war starts, how it is fought, how each side responds to what the other side does, and the like. So, the analytical procedure must be developed in such a way that the assumptions can be varied and their implications explored systematically.

By the end of 1966, after six years of steady work on these problems, the Department of Defense had an agreed-upon set of numerical representations of the outcomes of nuclear wars under alternative assumptions. These numerical representations were incorporated in the Strategic Force and Effectiveness Tables described earlier.

The fact that an assured-destruction capability is so basic to U.S. national security dictated that requirements calculations be made on the basis of *extremely conservative* assumptions. This conservative bias produced two major results. First, it led to the buying of very large forces. In fact, between 1961 and 1969, U.S. assured-destruction capability in being remained consistently higher than the levels judged adequate by the Secretary of Defense and the President. For example, when the performance of the U.S. forces in 1968 was measured against actual Soviet forces, rather than the much greater potential threat envisioned in 1963, it was found that the United States had an assured capability to destroy nearly 50 percent of the Soviet population and nearly 80 percent of its industrial capacity in a retaliatory attack—much higher than the 20 percent and 50 percent levels, respectively, used for planning purposes.

Second, this conservatism led to the development of a systematic procedure for evaluating strategic forces against an even more severe threat than that shown at the high end of the predicted range in the National Intelligence Estimates. Such a "greater-than-expected" threat might include, for example, technological improvements like accurate Multiple, Independently Targetable Reentry Vehicles (MIRV's) on Soviet ICBM's, improved Soviet air defenses, and massive Soviet ABM deployments, which in combination could threaten the U.S. assured-destruction capability. Such costly threats were and are unlikely to appear, especially in view of the U.S. policy to respond. Nevertheless, because such threats were conceivable and within Soviet technical capacity, they were explicitly and systematically considered in the force planning process. Designing such a threat and using it in the requirements calculations provided yet another way to test the adequacy of programmed U.S. forces and the timeliness of planned options to meet such threats in the unlikely event that they actually arose.

Equally important, the concept of the greater-than-expected threat helped resolve the old dilemma of whether U.S. forces should be planned on the basis of the enemy's *capabilities* or his *intentions*. In 1960, Secretary Gates was sharply criticized for suggesting that the U.S. posture should be based on enemy intentions—on the actual forces he intended to deploy—rather than on the maximum he could deploy. Gates was reacting to the widespread tendency to compare the forces actually being planned for the United States with the maximum forces the Soviets could deploy, rather than comparing planned U.S. deployments with probable Soviet deployments and maximum U.S. capabilities with maximum Soviet capabilities. To counter the greater-than-expected threat, which was a generally agreed estimate of maximum Soviet capabilities, Systems Analysis helped develop the "U.S. force plus options"—a projection of what the United States could do, within realistic lead times, if the greater-than-expected threat emerged. Then, U.S. force and engineering development plans were based on the principle that the U.S. force plus options should be able to maintain a satisfactory level of assured-destruction capability in the face of the greater-than-expected threat. Meeting the maximum, but unlikely, Soviet capabilities with timely options is a prudent and far less expensive way than meeting them with actual forces.

In sum, as a planning tool, the greater-than-expected threat helped make the arguments about the adequacy of U.S. strategic forces more realistic and more precise. In addition, it helped focus attention on the more important considerations. It is the size and character of the assumed threats that determine the kinds and levels of U.S. forces.

Another important development on the road to building a work-able theory of strategic force requirements was educating ourselves and others to the shortcomings of what might be called the "comparison game." Some people believe that the way to measure the adequacy of U.S. forces is to compare them directly with those of the Soviets. If the Soviets outnumber us by some particular criterion—for example, megatons—this supposedly is prima-facie evidence that the Soviet forces are superior to ours and that ours are inadequate. Even though such direct comparisons are virtually meaningless, so many people insist on playing the comparison game that the Secretary of Defense is often compelled to participate, if only in self-defense.

Among the criteria available for use in comparing opposing forces are total megatonnage, pay load, weapons, and number of delivery systems. In our analyses, at first we used weapons and megatons; later, as emphasis on survivability grew, the number of launchers. But gradually it was realized that these are primarily measures of input: indicating what we have, not what we can do with it. To determine how well U.S. strategic offensive forces could achieve their objectives, one needed to know their ability to destroy particular kinds of targets. In short, in measuring effectiveness, we found it far better to concentrate on outputs, such as target destruction, than on inputs, such as megatonnage.

To appreciate this point, it is necessary to understand the relationships among weapon yield, blast effects, and accuracy and the impact of these factors in target-destruction capability. The important blast effects of nuclear weapons do not increase in direct proportion to increases in yield. As shown in Table 6, a 10-megaton weapon places a minimum of about thirty pounds per square inch (psi) of blast overpressure—enough to destroy large concrete and brick structures —everywhere within an area of about eighteen square miles. A 1-megaton weapon covers about four square miles with the same over-pressure. In other words, five 1-megaton weapons, if separately aimed to avoid overlap, would do more blast damage than one 10-megaton weapon.

Table 6. Relationship Between Weapon Yield and Blast Effect

Yield (megatons)	Distance from Ground Zero Covered by 30-psi Overpressure (feet)	Area Covered (square miles)
1	6,000	4
2	7,600	6
5	11,000	13
10	13,000	18

In addition, low-yield nuclear weapons are more flexible against large-area targets. The eighteen-square-mile area covered by a 10-megaton weapon would be roughly circular. However, very few area targets are shaped like circles. The twenty-square-mile area destroyed by five 1-megaton weapons could be more nearly shaped to match actual targets. Small targets, of course, are much more common than large targets; against these, the difference in effectiveness would be even greater. A single four-square-mile circular target, such as an air base, could be destroyed with a 10-megaton weapon, but much of the blast effect would be wasted on the surrounding countryside. Five such targets could be destroyed with five 1-megaton weapons. In sum, despite the reduction in total yield, five separately targeted 1-megaton weapons are generally more effective against both small- and large-area targets than one 10-megaton weapon. Thus, if the mix of weapons is well matched to the targets, the total number of deliver-able weapons is much better than total megatons as a measure of total force effectiveness.

It is important to note another relationship here. Suppose that we wanted to attack a target strengthened to withstand up to 100-psi blast overpressure—a missile silo, for example. The ability to do this can be measured in terms of "kill probability" (Pk), the standard military criterion for this purpose. The Pk of a missile depends on a number of factors, including weapon yield and accuracy. As shown in Table 7, assuming a desired Pk of 90 percent, increases in weapon accuracy permit a substantial reduction in weapon yield while still achieving the desired level of effectiveness. Thus, a 10-megaton weapon is needed to assure a Pk of 90 percent when the Circular Probable Error (CEP, the radius of a circle centered on the desired point of impact, where half the shots fall inside, half outside) is 4,000 feet. However, if accuracy is doubled, the weapon yield can be reduced to approximately one-tenth its original amount, while retaining the same Pk.

Table 7. Relationship Between Weapon Yield and Accuracy

Yield (megatons)	Accuracy (CEP in feet)[a]
10	4,000
4	3,000
1	2,000

[a] Required for a 90-percent Pk against a 100-psi target.

The lesson of the relationships among yield, lethal area, and accuracy should be clear. For attacks on relatively soft, area targets or on hardened, point targets, weapon yield or megatonnage by itself is a very inadequate measure of the effectiveness of U.S. forces. Depending on the accuracies achieved, it is the joint effect of yield and warhead numbers that is important. And as accuracies improve, clearly it is better to reduce the yield and weight of the individual warheads and to increase the number of separately armed warheads carried by U.S. delivery vehicles. Moving in this direction is also desirable in order to make room within a fixed pay load for penetration aids to counter possible ABM threats.

Recent developments in warhead technology, particularly the remarkable technology of the MIRV, permit the United States to build a force containing a high fraction of small, separately armed warheads. Thus, we have a basic choice between installing in our missiles one high-yield warhead or a number of lower-yield warheads. For example, on a hypothetical new missile it might be possible to carry either one 10-megaton warhead or ten 50-kiloton warheads. The effectiveness of these two possible systems is compared in Table 8.

**Table 8. Comparative Effectiveness of Two Hypothetical Missile Pay Loads[a]
(number of targets destroyed)**

Type of Target Destroyed	Ten 50-KT Warheads Totaling One-Half Megaton	One 10-Megaton Warhead
Airfields	10.0	1.0
Hard missile silos	1.2–1.7[b]	1.0
Cities of 100,000 population	3.5	1.0
Cities of 500,000 population	0.7	1.0
Cities of 2,000,000 population	0.5	0.6

[a] Both assumed to be reliably delivered.
[b] Variation depends on target hardness, delivery errors, and number of warheads allocated to each silo.

Note that the single 10-megaton warhead, to be sure, yields 20 times the megatonnage of the ten 50-kiloton, individually targetable warheads. Thus, if the United States had 500 missiles with this pay load, it could arm them with a total of either 5,000 megatons or only 250 megatons. Using megatonnage alone as the only criterion, the choice would obviously be the 5,000-megaton load. But if one were interested in effectiveness, one would select the 5,000 warheads and 250 megatons. For, as the table shows, the missile armed with the ten 50-kiloton warheads, compared with the single 10-megaton warhead, could destroy:

- 10 times as many airfields, soft missile sites, or other soft military point targets.
- Or 1.2 to 1.7 times as many hard silos.
- Or 3.5 times as many cities of 100,000 population.

While a force armed with the ten 50-kiloton warheads destroys only 70 percent as many undefended cities of 500,000 population, or 83 percent as many undefended cities of 2,000,000 population, as a force armed with the 10-megaton warhead, the United States already has more than enough warheads of larger yield in our forces to hit cities of these sizes if they are undefended. If the cities are defended (the more probable case), the ten-warhead pay load of the MIRV's would force the defense to shoot ten times as many interceptors as otherwise, again showing the superiority of using multiple small warheads. Thus, the reasons for the increased number of U.S. warheads and the accompanying sacrifice in total megatonnage should be clear. Arming U.S. missile boosters with small, multiple warheads (MIRV's) is much more effective than arming them with single, large-yield warheads by every relevant criterion of military effectiveness, even though they deliver much less total megatonnage. We say this in full awareness that total Soviet pay load is on the rise.

In sum, we should design forces and set levels of megatonnage, warheads, and missiles to match U.S. objectives—deterrence or target destruction—just as the Soviet Union designs its weapons and sets its force levels to match its own objectives. More importantly, however, U.S. weapons should be measured against U.S. objectives, not against Soviet objectives or Soviet weapon characteristics. What is good for us may not necessarily be good for them, and vice versa.

We can measure what we have and what we can do, and we can compare this information with estimates of Soviet capabilities. (If a single input index is needed, the number of separately targetable warheads is the least unsatisfactory one, because the number of targets destroyed increases almost in direct proportion to increases in the number of warheads.) Such comparisons are interesting, but they do not measure the U.S. ability to deter war or destroy targets, or the Soviet ability to accomplish its own objectives. The only useful index, we found, is the measurement of our ability to meet basic objectives.

In terms of numbers of separately targetable, survivable, accurate, reliable warheads, U.S. strategic forces have remained consistently superior to those of the Soviet Union. However, the relationship of this "superiority" to U.S. military and political objectives is unclear. In a conventional war, a numerical advantage in men and firepower can often defeat or force the retreat of enemy forces. Superior conventional forces can end a conventional war and are a source of political power in peacetime. However, once each side has enough nuclear forces virtually to eliminate the other's urban society in a second strike, the utility of extra nuclear forces is dubious at best. In this context, notions of nuclear "superiority" are devoid of significant meaning.

Strategic nuclear forces cannot seize territory, even when they are superior in numbers; they can only destroy it. As a result there is now no feasible way of ending a strategic nuclear war short of the total destruction of both sides, except through mutual control and restraint. Thus, such "nuclear superiority" as the United States maintains is of little significance, since we do not know how to use it to achieve our national security objectives. In other words, since the Soviet Union has an assured-destruction capability against the United States, "superior" U.S. nuclear forces are extremely difficult to convert into real political power. The blunt, unavoidable fact is that the Soviet Union could effectively destroy the United States even after absorbing the full weight of a U.S. first strike, and vice versa. Nor do we see that this is likely to change in the future.

Damage Limiting: The Full-Scale ABM Issue

Should the United States make a serious attempt to limit the damage to our society that would be caused by a full-scale Soviet nuclear attack on our cities? At one time, the answer must have seemed obvious to most people. How could one defend the proposition that we shouldn't even try? And, in fact, based on that answer, many billions of dollars were spent during the 1950's and early 1960's in an attempt to achieve such a capability. But the attempt was not successful. By the mid-1960's, a Soviet attack on our cities would have killed about as many people as if we had no defenses. Over the years, it became increasingly apparent that what was really protecting our society was our deterrent, not our damage-limiting posture.

In the mid-1960's, the opportunity to deploy a full-scale antiballistic missile (ABM) system for the defense of U.S. cities against a Soviet missile attack, as recommended by the Joint Chiefs of Staff, offered a new opportunity to reexamine the question of damage limiting. To understand the ABM issue, it is useful to review its history.

The Nike-Zeus ABM system, the predecessor of the Nike-X, Sentinel, and Safeguard systems, was first begun in 1955. Until the launching of the Soviet Sputnik in October 1957, the project was pursued at a leisurely pace. That dramatic example of Soviet technology, however, provided a new sense of urgency with regard to all aspects of advanced military technology, and the Nike-Zeus development was greatly accelerated. But when the Army proposed the production of initial sets of equipment in the spring of 1958, Secretary of Defense Neil McElroy argued, "We should not spend hundreds of millions on production of this weapon pending general confirmatory indications that we know what we are doing."[4] His view prevailed at the time.

In preparation of the fiscal 1960 budget, Nike-Zeus deployment again became an issue. The Army's initial budget request included $875 million for Nike-Zeus, mostly for the procurement of equipment and the construction of operational sites. President Eisenhower, however, sent to the Congress requests of only $300 million, for R&D and test facilities. After much debate, the Congress finally provided $375 million for Nike-Zeus and/or Army modernization.

In the fall of 1959, in connection with the development of the fiscal 1961 budget, the Army proposed a new Nike-Zeus deployment plan consisting of 35 local defense centers, 9 forward acquisition radars, and 120 missile batteries. An initial operational capability (IOC) was to be achieved by fiscal 1964 and the entire program completed by fiscal 1969, with a total investment cost estimated at $13 to $14 billion. This plan was rejected by President Eisenhower. With one dissenting vote, the JCS supported the President's position, and the Congress agreed to limit the program to research and development.

With regard to active ballistic missile defense, U.S. work on missile penetration aids and similar ABM countermeasures had made it increasingly clear that the Nike-Zeus system, as originally designed, would not be effective against the heavy ICBM attacks that the Soviets would be capable of launching in the late 1960's. Basically, this was because the system was designed around a relatively slow interceptor missile and mechanically steered radars. Because of the missile's slowness, it had to be fired long before the incoming targets reentered the atmosphere, thereby precluding the use of the atmosphere as a means of distinguishing real warheads from decoys and other objects. And because the radars were mechanically steered, the system's capabilities for handling many incoming objects simultaneously were low, leaving it highly vulnerable to saturation attacks.

These technical weaknesses in the Nike-Zeus system and its disapproval led, in 1961 and 1962, to the decision to develop a new and different system known as Nike-X.[5] To help solve the problem of reentry-body discrimination, the Sprint, a new high-acceleration, terminal-defense missile, was designed. Because of its fast reaction time, the defense could wait until the enemy attack had penetrated well into the atmosphere—where the warheads could be discriminated from other reentering objects—before firing, thus permitting more of its fire to be concentrated on the actual incoming weapons. To solve the problem of vulnerability to saturation attacks, development was started on a new family of radars that could scan the skies electronically instead of mechanically (which required rotation of the entire radar antenna) and thus could handle, simultaneously, many more incoming objects. This development was to eliminate one of the major limitations of the old Nike-Zeus system.

With the new radars and Sprint missiles, the defense missile battery should be able to bring firepower to bear on all targets entering the defended area. However, even if these batteries were deployed around all major U.S. cities, a large part of the nation would still be left undefended, and the attacker would have the option of ground-bursting his warheads outside defended areas, producing vast amounts of lethal fallout which could be carried over them by the wind. Moreover, a terminal (or local) defense compels the defender to allocate his resources in advance, leaving the attacker free to concentrate his resources against whatever targets he may choose at the moment of the attack.

To fill this gap and provide defense in depth, the development of a long-range interceptor missile was initiated in the spring of 1965. Called the Spartan, this missile would employ a much more effective warhead than any previously available—a warhead large enough to attack large numbers of objects out in space. The missile was designed to reach out to great distances and attack incoming objects at altitudes well above the atmosphere, thereby permitting a relatively small number of strategically located batteries to provide coverage for the entire United States. Thus, incoming objects would be attacked twice, once above the atmosphere and a second time as they (those that survived) entered the atmosphere. Moreover, by overlapping the coverage of the Spartan batteries, some of the attacker's inherent advantage against terminal defenses alone could be offset, since at the moment of the attack the defender would also have the choice of concentrating his resources over those targets he chose to protect.

In brief, it was clear that the Nike-Zeus system, as originally conceived, would not be an effective ABM system against the type of ICBM attack which the Soviets would be able to launch by the end of the decade. Accordingly, Secretary McNamara steadfastly maintained that although the development of the more effective ABM system (Nike-X) should be pursued, no production or deployment should be undertaken until much more was known about the system's technical capabilities and its probable effects on the strategic situation generally.

This view found substantial support in the Congress until 1967, when the Congress, opposing McNamara, appropriated some $168 million to prepare for the production of the Nike-X system. Congress' action was prompted in large part by the unanimous recommendation of the JCS that Nike-X be deployed for the defense of U.S. cities against a Soviet missile attack. On the other hand, Secretary Mc-Namara strongly believed that a full-scale deployment of Nike-X would be a vast waste of resources.

What is required for an understanding of his position is a careful analysis of the contribution that the Nike-X system might make to the defense of U.S. cities, under two different assumptions: (1) that the Soviets do not react to such a deployment, and (2) that the Soviets do react in an attempt to preserve their assured-destruction capability. McNamara deserves much credit for highlighting the fact that this is the crucial factor in any decision to pursue damage-limiting programs against the Soviets.

As shown below, analyses done by the Systems Analysis office indicated that if the Soviets chose to respond to U.S. deployment of the Nike-X—and they could do so in several different ways—they could offset the gains to the United States of such a deployment and could drive the probable number of U.S. dead after a nuclear exchange back up to the level where it would be *without* U.S. ABM deployment. In short, the Soviets have the technical and economic ability to offset any damage-limiting measures the United States might undertake, assuming that they are determined to maintain their deterrence against us. It was the virtual certainty that the Soviets would act to maintain their deterrence—even more than the continuing technical problems—which cast such grave doubts on the advisability of deploying the Nike-X system for the protection of U.S. cities against Soviet missile attacks. If the United States did deploy the system, all that would be accomplished, in all probability, would be to increase greatly the defense expenditures on both sides with no net gain in real security for either.

How could this be? Put simply, a defensive system to save U.S. cities from a Soviet nuclear attack must keep ahead of the Soviet threat, including their reaction to U.S. deployment of such a system. Such attempts are costly. Studies in the Systems Analysis office considered two stages in analyzing such a deployment. The first, called "Posture A," was an initial step recommended by the JCS. It represented an area defense of the continental United States and a local defense of 25 cities. It was estimated to cost about $13 billion in investment and $900 million a year to operate. The second step, called "Posture B," was an attempt to keep ahead of the Soviet threat. It included a higher-density local defense of some 52 cities. It was estimated to cost about $24 billion in investment and over $1.3 billion a year to operate. For Posture B, however, improved air and civil defense and antisubmarine warfare forces (at an estimated investment cost of between $4 and $5 billion) would also be needed. The pursuit of effective defenses would probably cost much more; the commitment appeared to be open-ended.

The United States probably could justify such costs if an ABM defense could effectively limit the ability of the Soviets to kill Americans. But any attempt to limit damage to ourselves, if we are attacked, also operates to remove the Soviets' confidence that they are deterring us from attacking them (that is, it takes away their assured-destruction capability). Table 9 gives one set of estimates of what would happen if the Nike-X defense worked and the Soviets did not react.

As the table shows, the Soviets would lose their deterrent if they did not respond. The Soviets have the technological and economic capability to respond in many ways, including adding MIRV's and penetration aids, adding sea-launched ballistic missiles (SLBM's) or a mobile ICBM, adding a higher pay-load missile, or some combination of these responses.

The Systems Analysis office then evaluated possible Soviet responses—responses that would restore their assured-destruction capability—and evaluated these responses in a variety of exchanges, including a Soviet first strike. Soviet responses, it will be recalled, which restore their assured-destruction capability also increase their

Table 9. Millions Killed in an All-out Strategic Exchange (1970's) Assuming No Soviet Reaction to a U.S. ABM System[a]

U.S. Programs	Soviets Strike First, U.S. Retaliates		U.S. Strikes First, Soviets Retaliate		Soviet Assured-Destruction Calculation
	U.S. Killed	Soviet Killed	U.S. Killed	Soviet Killed	
No ABM	110	120	120	80	100%
Posture A	60	120	50	80	10%
Posture B	20	120	30	80	Less than 10%

[a] The apparent paradox of striking first *and* still suffering more deaths results from different targeting strategies. The side that strikes first mainly hits military targets; the side that retaliates mainly hits cities.

ability to kill Americans in a first strike. Table 10, which was developed by Systems Analysis and presented to the Congress in the Secretary of Defense's 1968 posture statement, shows what would happen if the Soviets responded to Nike-X with MIRV's, penetration aids, and mobile ICBM's.

Such a Soviet response would, of course, threaten our own assured-destruction capability. We would then have to react. Viewing each other's build-up in forces as an increased threat, each side would undoubtedly take countermeasures, generating a costly arms race with no net gain in security to either side.

Many complicated assumptions had to be made to do the calculations underlying these tables. Other assumptions would have produced other numbers. Before making the decision, the Secretary of Defense reviewed many similar calculations. But, significantly, the basic conclusion shown by these tables—that the Soviets can offset the effect of a U.S. ABM defense of its cities—stood up under any reasonable set of assumptions.

In the light of these analyses of effectiveness, which were based on a carefully reviewed and agreed set of numerical representations of the outcome of nuclear exchanges under various assumptions, Secretary McNamara concluded that effective damage-limiting measures against the Soviets were not attainable, regardless of the amount we were willing to spend, so long as the Soviets were determined to maintain their deterrent against us. Thus, he recommended and the President decided against deploying Nike-X to defend our cities from Soviet attacks.

Table 10. Millions Killed in an All-out Strategic Exchange (1970's) Assuming Soviet Reaction to a U.S. ABM System

U.S. Programs	Soviet Response	Soviets Strike First, U.S. Retaliates		U.S. Strikes First, Soviets Retaliate		Soviet Assured-Destruction Calculation
		U.S. Killed	Soviet Killed	U.S. Killed	Soviet Killed	
No ABM		120	120	120	80	110
Posture A	MIRV, Pen-aids, + 100 mobile ICBM's	110	110	110	80	90
Posture B	MIRV, Pen-aids, + 500 mobile ICBM's	100	100	100	80	80

What is true for us is also true for the Soviets, however. The United States also has the technology, particularly with respect to missile forces, to make whatever adjustments may be required in its assured-destruction capability to counter any damage-limiting measures that the Soviet Union might undertake in the foreseeable future. From the beginning of the Nike-Zeus project in 1955 through the middle of 1968, over $4 billion has been invested on ABM research and development, including such projects as Nike-Zeus, Project Defender, Nike-X, and Sentinel. Moreover, between 1962 and 1968, more than $1 billion was spent on the development of penetration aids and other measures to help ensure that our missiles can penetrate Soviet ABM defenses. As a result of this enormous R&D effort on ICBM offense and defense, defense officials have acquired a comprehensive knowledge of the problems involved in a strategic war employing such systems. And we have sufficient resources in this country to acquire and maintain whatever forces may be needed to support a fully adequate assured-destruction capability, regardless of what our opponents may do.

Other Missions for ABM Systems

The decision to abandon damage-limiting programs against the Soviets as a feasible objective did not mean abandoning work on

ABM systems. Defending U.S. cities against a full-scale Soviet attack is only one of three distinct purposes that ABM systems have been proposed to serve. The other two are (1) to help protect our strategic retaliatory forces, particularly the Minuteman ICBM force, from a Soviet attack and (2) to defend against comparatively small and uncomplicated Chinese missile attacks and protect against accidents. To make sense out of the continuing debate over ABM deployments, it is essential that one keep these three distinct purposes clearly in mind. We welcome the broadly based debate on ABM that took place in the Senate in 1969 and that promised to resume in 1970.[6] Such debate can help defense officials to relate their programs more effectively to Congressionally supported objectives. The possibility of such effective challenges as the one made to Safeguard in the Senate in 1969 puts considerable pressure on defense officials to think through the justification for each program and to drop those that cannot be adequately defended. However, we very much regret that in the debate on Safeguard, the three purposes of an ABM system were frequently confused, and arguments against a system intended for the first purpose were incorrectly applied to a system essentially designed to serve the second.

The first of the three purposes has been described in the preceding section of this chapter. This section discusses the second and third.

The protection of the Minuteman missile force from Soviet attack was the main purpose of the Safeguard system recommended by President Nixon in 1969; it was a significant but secondary purpose of the Sentinel system recommended by President Johnson in 1967. The key issue involved in a system limited to the protection of the Minuteman force is how best to pursue the objective of maintaining U.S. retaliatory capability. If one accepts the necessity of a secure retaliatory capability, such a system need not raise the broader issue of what our strategic objectives should be.

The reason for an ABM defense of the Minuteman force is to protect it against accurately delivered Soviet ICBM warheads—a possible future threat. There are, of course, alternative ways of countering such a threat; the list includes "super-hard" silos and mobile ballistic missile systems such as the submarine-launched Poseidon, other underwater-based missiles, and Minuteman missiles mounted on trains or trailers. But the ABM defense of the Minuteman silos offers several advantages. It does not require the great expense of developing a whole new weapon system. The first several billion dollars spent are immediately productive of protected forces. In effect, since the components of the ABM system have already been developed, the United States can deploy them in the required amounts. If the Soviet threat does not become too great, ABM defense of Minuteman may prove to be the most economical solution. Moreover, the deployment of defenses for existing forces does not threaten the Soviet deterrent and puts little pressure on them to react; deployment of a new offensive system, if it adds to our total capability, would.

The main disadvantage of the ABM protection of Minuteman is that it can be overcome by the Soviets if they deploy a large force of accurate ICBM's with MIRV's. Thus, if the United States deploys a defense of Minuteman, and then the Soviets deploy a large force of accurate MIRV's, we will have bought only time, and we will have to replace our Minutemen with a less vulnerable system. (The amount of replacement would depend on the extent of the Soviet ABM deployment. If they have only a limited ABM system, Polaris and Poseidon alone would provide an adequate retaliatory force and no new system would be needed.)

The deployment of an ABM system to provide an area defense of the United States against Chinese ICBM attack does raise the broader issue of strategic objectives. The Sentinel system recommended by President Johnson in 1967 was designed primarily for this purpose; so was the 1970 increment of the Safeguard system recommended by President Nixon. (Indeed, with President Nixon's fiscal 1971 budget recommendations, Safeguard and Sentinel become virtually indistinguishable.)

Such a system would consist of several kinds of radars, long-range Spartan area-defense missiles, and some Sprint local-defense missiles. This system might limit the damage from a Chinese ICBM attack in the late 1970's to fewer than one million American dead. In addition, such a system might enhance the credibility of U.S. commitments to defend its Asian allies against Chinese nuclear attacks by making ourselves relatively invulnerable to Chinese nuclear attacks. Thus, our threat to retaliate against China, for example, if China attacked Japan, might be made more believable. Finally, such a system would offer some protection against some kinds of accidental missile firings.

But there is also a significant case against the anti-Chinese ABM system. First, the scenario in which it would be valuable is quite unclear. The United States already has an enormous retaliatory capability against China. It seems reasonable to argue that this will deter any premeditated attack. Moreover, for a very long time, U.S. offensive forces will be so large relative to those of the Chinese that, in all probability, we will have a very credible first-strike capability against them. It seems doubtful that Safeguard would substantially enhance that credibility. Thus, scenarios in which the anti-Chinese defense is necessary tend to center on those involving irrational behavior on the part of the Chinese. Several years of debate have failed to produce any very convincing evidence for the likelihood of this possibility.

Moreover, some Asians have argued that the fact that U.S. leaders believe a defense against Chinese ballistic missiles is needed—while we apparently can survive without an anti-Soviet defense—will greatly enhance the prestige of the Chinese nuclear program in Asian eyes. By drawing attention to the Chinese threat, it might increase pressures for development of national nuclear forces in India and Japan.

In 1967, the Joint Chiefs of Staff concurred in the decision to start the Sentinel program because, in their view, it was a first step toward a full-scale anti-Soviet defense of cities. If the distinction between an anti-Chinese system and the first step toward a full anti-Soviet system is so tenuous that our own experts can choose to ignore it, one should not be surprised if the Soviets also fail to see it and are thereby impelled to react by deploying more forces. A limited deployment of a primitive Soviet ABM system led the United States to decide to develop and deploy Poseidon and Minuteman III with MIRV warheads and to plan to add thousands of weapons to our potential forces. On the other hand, some officials have argued that the U.S. Sentinel-Safeguard deployment will put pressure on the Soviets to reach agreement with the United States on strategic arms limitations before we expand our ABM to an anti-Soviet system.

For these reasons, Sentinel was a very difficult decision in 1967—a truly marginal decision, as McNamara said at the time. While a very effective defense against Chinese ICBM's appeared feasible, it was only marginally clear that providing this capability was necessary or even desirable in view of the devastating retaliation China would suffer after an attack on the United States.

Since the fall of 1967, there have been several significant changes bearing on the case for an anti-Chinese ABM. In 1967, the U.S. military commitment in Vietnam was increasing, and the chances of a direct military confrontation between China and the United States appeared high. Since then, the policy of escalation has been replaced by "Vietnamization" and withdrawal of U.S. forces, by the Nixon Doctrine of "self-help" for Asians, and by a "low-profile" foreign policy for the United States. Given these new directions in U.S. foreign policy, the chances of a direct U.S.-Chinese military confrontation seem greatly reduced.

Another important change is the apparent cost of the program. In January 1968, the investment cost of the austere Chinese-oriented Sentinel ABM defense was estimated at $5 billion. Two years later, the cost estimates for Safeguard, a more ambitious system that includes defense of some Minuteman sites, exceed $11 billion. With the country facing inflation and urgent domestic priorities, the case for spending such a sum on an anti-Chinese ABM system now (April 1970) appears far from convincing.

Conclusion

With the decision not to try for a significant damage-limiting capability against the Soviet Union, the essential boundaries of a theory of requirements within which U.S. strategic forces should be designed had been set.[7] The foundation of this theory was deterrence of a deliberate nuclear attack against either the United States or its allies; and the foundation of deterrence was maintaining a powerful, well-protected, and well-hedged assured-destruction capability. Other strategic objectives—such as attaining the best possible outcome in the event that deterrence failed, avoiding further proliferation of nuclear weapons, and securing adequately safeguarded nuclear arms-control agreements—were important and desirable, but it was clear to all that deterrence was absolutely essential.

In a word, the first answer to the question "How much is enough?" had become "Enough to be sure that the United States can destroy one-fifth to one-fourth of the Soviet population and one-half of the Soviet industrial capacity, even after absorbing a full-scale surprise attack." This was the first test for judging the design and adequacy of U.S. forces against greater and greater Soviet threats. (The assured-destruction test did not, of course, indicate how these forces would actually be used in a nuclear war. United States strategic offensive forces have been designed with the additional system characteristics—accuracy, endurance, and good command and control—needed to perform missions other than assured destruction, such as limited and controlled retaliation.)

The evolution of a theory of requirements, from the pre-1961 notion of massive retaliation to deterrence based on assured destruction and damage limiting and finally to deterrence based on assured destruction only, rests on an enormous analytical effort with major contributions by both military and civilian analysts. It is an effort that became progressively more complex and refined after 1961. For example, most of the basic concepts—assured destruction, damage limiting, limited and controlled response—used in designing U.S. strategic forces were formulated before 1963. Rather than simplify later decisions, however, they made them more complex by raising important new questions. Assured-destruction needs suggested that Minuteman was clearly a desirable weapon system, but how many were needed? (General LeMay believed that at least 2,400 Minuteman missiles were required, and General Thomas Power, Commander-in-Chief of the Strategic Air Command, spoke of 10,000 to President Kennedy.) Should Poseidon be developed to replace Polaris? What types and what sizes of warheads should Minuteman and Poseidon carry? Should we buy the Air Force's proposed new bomber, the Advanced Manned Strategic Aircraft, or AMSA? Though one AMSA might be better than one B-52, how much better did it have to be? What should be done about air and missile defenses? What about civil defense? What would the Soviets be doing while we built up our defenses?

Such questions forced us to be more precise about the roles of our strategic forces, what we were buying them for, how well they would do their job, how their prospective performance might affect strategy, and finally what reactions were open to the Soviets. The development of a unified analysis of our total strategic offensive and defensive posture enabled us to find consistent answers to these questions; not only to the question of how much is enough in total, but also to how much of each available system is enough at the estimated prices. If we are to avoid gross waste and get the most for our defense dollars, we need to continue to seek answers to these questions.

CHAPTER

6

Yardsticks of Sufficiency

Approaches to the Question

In April 1963, Secretary McNamara spoke to the American Society of Newspaper Editors, assembled at the Statler-Hilton Hotel in Washington, D.C., about how the Department of Defense was answering the timeless question, "How much is enough?"

What I have been suggesting . . . is that the question of how to spend our defense dollars and how much to spend is a good deal more complicated than is often assumed. It cannot be assumed that a new weapon would really add to our national security, no matter how attractive the weapon can be made to seem, looked at by itself. Anyone who has been exposed to so-called "brochuremanship" knows that even the most outlandish notions can be dressed up to look superficially attractive. You have to consider a very wide range of issues—the missions our forces must be prepared to perform, the effects of a proposed system on the stability of the military situation in the world, the alternatives open to us for performing the missions required.

You cannot make decisions simply by asking yourself whether something might be nice to have. You have to make a judgment on how much is enough.

I emphasize judgment because you can't even be sure yourself, much less prove to others, that your decision was precisely right to the last dollar—even to the last billion dollars. But the decision has to be made.

There is an important difference between the way we make these tough decisions today, and the way they used to be made. Formerly, an arbitrary budget ceiling was fixed for national defense, and funds were then apportioned among the Services. Today we examine all our military needs, and then decide at what point our military strength is in balance with the requirements of our foreign policy.

There are, of course, sharp differences of opinion on where we should spend our marginal defense dollars. And here is where the responsibility most clearly falls on the Secretary of Defense, because here is where it must fall not only constitutionally but under any rational system. For these decisions can only be made from the point of view of the defense establishment as a whole, not from the point of view of the individual Services. Indeed the very biggest decisions—such as the basic kinds of forces we need, and the occasions on which we might want to commit those forces—must be made at an even higher level: for they involve basic questions of national policy which transcend the interest of the Defense Department, or the State Department, or indeed any part of the government, and must be made at the Presidential level. . . .[1]

The approach to determining military requirements as outlined by McNamara is in sharp contrast to that prevailing in DoD before 1961. One of General Maxwell D. Taylor's main complaints about the Defense Department in the late 1950's was the lack of quantitative standards of adequacy for measuring defense programs. No such standards existed because many of the Department's leaders believed that they could not be determined. As General Taylor described the situation:

Another set of basic issues which have to be decided concern the required size and composition of the so-called functional forces—the atomic retaliatory force, continental air defense, overseas deployments, limited-war forces, and the like. How much of these forces is enough? As early as 1956 I urged Mr. Wilson to require the Joint Chiefs of Staff to come up with practical yardsticks to tell us how much we should buy of these operational forces. Admiral Radford, Mr. Quarles, and others opposed such a procedure, arguing that these military matters cannot be submitted to scientific or engineering analysis. There are too many imponderables. These objections were accepted and to this day there are no approved goals for the size and composition of the functional forces. Thus the

Department of Defense builds the defense structure of the nation without blueprints, design models, or agreed factors of safety. It will never be possible for the JCS to produce an agreed tabulation of the forces needed for our security without first settling the basic question of how much is enough in the various operational categories. These yardsticks of sufficiency are the building blocks necessary to provide a solid foundation for defense planning.[2]

The belief that these matters cannot be analyzed—that "yardsticks of sufficiency" cannot be developed—has continued to plague the defense planning effort. It is this belief that underlies many of the charges of "downgrading military judgment" and "shortages" and "not meeting our military requirements." It persists despite the increasing evidence that military requirements not only can but must be analyzed, if we are to meet our national security needs and urgent domestic needs at the same time.

Why are questions of requirements so difficult to answer? Conceptually, the problem of determining requirements would appear to be straightforward:

- Get a clear statement of policy goals.
- Determine what military capabilities are needed, in what circumstances, to meet these goals.
- Figure out what forces are needed to provide these capabilities.

This seemingly simple process is beset with difficulties, however. It is not easy to get a statement of national policy that can be directly translated into military strategy. In some areas—strategic nuclear policy, for example—this has been done. Deterrence has been translated into assured destruction, and assured destruction into quantitative statements of adequacy. In other areas this has proven much more difficult. For instance, while nobody questions that the freedom of Western Europe is vital to U.S. interests, many alternative strategies have been proposed for defending that freedom, ranging all the way from the immediate use of nuclear weapons in the event of any aggression, however small, to massive nonnuclear defense at the border. Judgments as to which strategy is appropriate are not primarily military matters, but rather political and economic ones.

There is also the problem of translating a general strategy—for example, a forward nonnuclear defense of Western Europe against a major Warsaw Pact attack—into a sufficiently detailed set of specifications to be of use in estimating force needs. In this case, what do "forward" and "major" mean? What about giving up some territory temporarily? What if a nonnuclear defense fails? And so forth. Here again, fleshing out the details of a general strategy is a joint political-economic-military exercise; and here again there can be, and usually are, broad disagreements on how the major lines of strategy should be implemented in detail.

Even after these two problems are solved, the force planner is not out of the woods; far from it. Now he has to estimate exactly what U.S. forces will be needed to do the desired job, typically taking into account expected help from allies and the problem of burden sharing. This leads into another set of difficulties. We don't know with much precision what the enemy's forces and capabilities will be, no matter what we spend on intelligence. While the traditional military approach to this problem has been conservative, the resulting over-estimates of enemy forces have—as shown earlier—frequently done more harm than good. And the dangers of underestimating the enemy go without saying. What is needed is realistic estimates of enemy forces. Without them it is impossible to have a sensible strategy and force plan.

This problem aside, war still turns out to be a highly uncertain business, even if we know *exactly* what forces the enemy has and the precise state of equipment, training, and logistic support. Moreover, *proving* that a given amount of force is enough is an impossible task, especially in light of the wide range of war outcomes relative to force ratios. A well-led, smaller unit has been known to defeat a much larger, less well-led unit. The technological advance represented by the English longbow at the Battle of Crécy, during the Hundred Years' War, was far more important than the fact that the English were badly outnumbered. (Pitted against the longbow, over 1,500 French knights on horseback fell, compared with a few dozen English archers.) Tactical skill and surprise can also be decisive. World War II history shows, for example, that in tank-versus-tank engagements, the result is not much affected by the opposing forces' relative sizes; victory typically went to the side that shot first, because its tanks were usually well concealed and protected. Similarly, well-trained pilots in qualitatively inferior aircraft have repeatedly won dogfights against less well-trained pilots in superior aircraft. Supposedly, an offensive campaign requires a significant numerical superiority, but the Israelis conducted a very successful offensive campaign against the Arabs in 1967 with numerically inferior forces. The point is that force planning is not only a terribly uncertain and imprecise business, even with excellent intelligence, but also a business in which, because of the necessity for starting with national interests and goals, the military has no clear claim to special wisdom—although military expertise is one essential contribution.

Besides these inherent conceptual difficulties, many people—both critics of the military and some military leaders themselves—believe that military requirements are essentially open-ended anyway. Every year since the end of World War II, the original budget requests of the Services have been 25 to 35 percent greater than the budget judged to be adequate by the President and the Congress. This pattern has prompted some cynics to remark that "a military requirement is 30 percent more than what we've got now, whatever we have now." In fact, there is, in far too many cases, a sort of Parkinson's law of military requirements: they will always expand to use up the supply estimated to be available. As one of the authors once remarked to a four-star officer deeply involved in Vietnam requirements: "You know, your requirements always seem to grow until they have used up the available forces." "That's right," he answered, "I'll ask for all I think I can get."

Despite what often appears to be the case, real military requirements—that is, what it makes sense for the United States to buy—are not open-ended. It is not true that more is always better than less, or that the nation could always use more. The United States could have ten times as many strategic offensive forces as the Soviets and still not have enough, or one-tenth as many and have too much. Nor is it true that the nation is forever doomed to perpetual military "shortages"— a variation on the theory that requirements are open-ended. So long as the idea of open-ended requirements persists, however, there will be claims of "shortages."

Appeals to Authority

If military requirements are *not* open-ended, how can they be determined? Various approaches have been proposed, each with its vigorous and outspoken supporters. Many people believe that the only way to determine requirements is to ask the military experts. What is required is whatever the generals and admirals *say* is required, and that's that. While we agree that the recommendations of military experts must be considered seriously in reaching decisions on force levels, we emphatically reject the idea that their stated requirements should go unquestioned. To begin with, as we have pointed out in Chapter 3, it is impossible for military experts or anyone else to derive a purely military requirement except in the most limited of tactical situations; for example, capturing a particular hill. Even here the requirement is highly uncertain, because there is always a wide area for judgments on risk, enemy capabilities, leadership, and morale—to say nothing of the basic judgment on whether the hill must be taken. But it is a long way from specifying the number of troops to do a limited job to specifying the total U.S. force structure. In this larger context, many important factors must be considered, including strategic and political objectives, costs, possible enemy reactions, allied contributions, balance-of-payments effects, public support, and so on. In short, total U.S. force requirements are very far from being a purely military matter to be settled only by the military experts.

In addition, the military experts—the Joint Chiefs of Staff, in particular—are regularly subjected to massive institutional pressures for setting ever higher requirements. They have thousands of officers working for them whose very careers are bound up in getting more forces (and whose promotional possibilities vary directly with the expansion or contraction of their parent Service). These are men who have devoted their lives to military service and have associated mainly with other military officers. They are not intimately acquainted with the other needs of society or in a good position to balance them against military needs. And they have nothing to lose from calling for more forces and much to lose from accepting less.

In saying this, we intend no criticism of the JCS members personally, or the staff officers who serve them. Rather, we call for honest recognition of their conservative pragmatism in approaching the question of needs and of the institutional setting in which they operate. If anyone deserves to be criticized, it is those who would have us blindly accept the recommendations of the JCS as balanced, authoritative statements of the forces the United States must have.

Arbitrary Budget Ceilings

To get a better handle on requirements, some have advocated going to the other extreme of using arbitrary budget ceilings. This approach rests on the idea that the best policy is to allocate to defense some portion of the budget—usually some fixed percentage of the Gross National Product (GNP)—and then leave it to the military to decide how best to spend it. This is the view that operates in many European countries today, and the view that operated in the United States in the 1950's. For three basic reasons, we do not believe this to be a satisfactory approach for the United States. First, as explained at length elsewhere, need cannot be ignored in the force planning process any more than cost; the two must be considered together. The nation's force needs are far from being a purely financial question demanding only a financial answer. Neither a "requirements only" nor a "costs only" approach is a satisfactory way to plan for the nation's security. Second, in the past, leaving the allocation within the budget ceilings to the Services has resulted in serious imbalances in the total force structure, as the Services have fought to keep prestige items in their budgets at the expense of the "horseshoe nails" that make their existing forces effective and have kept existing forces and systems (battleships, horses, bombers) when new systems (carriers, tanks, missiles) should have replaced them.

Third, there is no discernible "optimum percentage of GNP" for defense spending. If it were really necessary, the United States could probably spend half of its GNP on defense for a sustained period of time. Under other circumstances, 5 percent might be wasteful. It depends on—to use an overworked phrase—national priorities. To see the fallacy of the theory that defense spending should be set at a fixed percentage of GNP, suppose that at a given level—say, 10 percent—the United States had forces considered to be adequate in every respect to meet its objectives. Then, if during the next year GNP grew—again, say, by 10 percent—this theory would dictate that we raise defense spending by 10 percent. Now, it is entirely possible that the higher GNP would make it reasonable for the nation to entertain more ambitious defense objectives, but that ought to be a reasoned choice, not a mechanical extrapolation from some fixed fraction of GNP.

Numerical Comparisons

Still another widely held approach to setting requirements would have the United States make a direct numerical comparison of its forces with those of potential enemies to ensure that it always has more of everything ("superiority") across the board. One major problem with such comparisons is that they often ignore crucial differences in quality. This was the case, as we have seen, with early comparisons of NATO and Warsaw Pact tactical aircraft. Quite apart from qualitative differences, however, a direct numerical comparison of U.S. forces with an enemy's forces may or may not even be relevant to our ability to accomplish national defense objectives. Often it is not. For example, in the field of strategic retaliatory forces, if the United States has enough forces to destroy completely the society of the Soviet Union in a retaliatory strike (after an attack on U.S. forces), it doesn't much matter how many forces the Soviets have.

Perhaps more than any other area, strategic forces show the irrelevance—in fact, the danger—of simply adding up the available forces on the two sides as a measure of adequacy. The danger of using such force comparisons is that we might mislead ourselves into thinking that our forces are adequate when they are not, or into thinking that our forces are not adequate when they are.

Suppose, for example, that the United States had 1,000 ICBM's, relatively inaccurate and all based above ground ("soft") on ten sites. Now suppose that the Soviets had only 100 ICBM's, but that they were all based underground in very "hard" silos, were widely dispersed, and were very reliable. In that case, even though U.S. missiles outnumbered Soviet missiles ten to one, we might very well not have enough forces. The Soviets could shoot several of their missiles at each of our ten sites and destroy virtually all of them, knocking out our retaliatory force. Our 10 to 1 numerical superiority, under these circumstances, would be meaningless, and we might indeed have an inadequate force. On the other hand, the Soviets, although badly outnumbered in this case, might have an entirely adequate force if the combination of their silo hardness and our missile inaccuracy meant that enough of their 100 ICBM's could survive an attack by our missiles to be able to strike back at our cities.

Yet even today, some members of the Congress continue to emphasize force comparisons as the best way of determining how well the nation is meeting its requirements. They compare the number of strategic nuclear warheads the United States can deliver with the number the Soviet Union can deliver, and they continue to assert the need for American supremacy—as if such totals had much to do with the realities of military power in the world. The more important fact is that either side has enough strategic retaliatory forces to destroy the other; and the more important problem is whether, in the face of changing technology, U.S. forces are appropriately designed to survive a Soviet attack. Thus, the annual counting exercise, where it is pointed out that the United States has three or four times as much of this or that as the Soviet Union, is not a very penetrating analysis of military needs or capabilities.

Or, to take another example of misleading numerical comparisons, in the field of naval forces and antisubmarine warfare, the relevant issue is not how many attack submarines the Soviets have relative to how many the United States has; their objectives are different from ours, and their force structure is correspondingly different. Rather, the issue is the adequacy of the total U.S. antisubmarine warfare posture—including not only attack submarines but land- and sea-based patrol aircraft, surveillance systems, and destroyers as well—to accomplish U.S. objectives.

The Services and their spokesmen in the Congress can be very vocal in pointing out cases where the Soviets outnumber us, and thus where we are not meeting our "requirements." We hear a lot about the number of Soviet attack submarines compared with ours, or the number of Soviet divisions compared with ours, or the number of Soviet megatons, but we hear little about the cases where we outnumber them. For example, we hear practically nothing about the comparative sizes of the U.S. and Soviet attack-carrier force (15 to 0); or about the fact that the U.S. amphibious-assault shipping fleet alone contains more tonnage than all combatant ships in the entire Soviet Navy; or that the United States has substantially more men under arms world-wide than the Soviet Union; or that its strategic forces can deliver three times as many separately targetable warheads.

Force comparisons have their uses, of course; but, by themselves, they are an inadequate basis for determining the nation's military needs. Even careful comparisons, accounting for qualitative differences, tell only what one has, not what one can do with it.

Another Alternative

If military requirements are not necessarily what the military say they are, if defense needs cannot be adequately set by arbitrary budget ceilings based on some fixed percentage of GNP, and if force comparisons alone are an unsatisfactory way to determine requirements, what approach *should* be taken? We would argue that military requirements ought to be determined by reasoned choice with the open participation of the responsible government officials, military and civilian. In other words, requirements should be set by a combination of analysis and judgment, with each issue being decided on its own merits. Such an approach explicitly recognizes that military requirements are a matter of choice, that there is no such thing as a "pure" military requirement in the abstract. Requirements depend on what we want to accomplish in the national security field, tempered by what we are willing to give up elsewhere. Analysis can help decision makers understand exactly what must be given up to reach a certain capability.

It was in the area of trying to develop yardsticks of sufficiency that the Systems Analysis office expended its greatest efforts and faced its greatest challenges; the results were mixed. In some areas the office was quite successful; in others, much less so. The most we would claim is that a good beginning has been made. The office has helped lay the foundation of a conceptual structure for determining military requirements; but the structure is a long way from being completed. Above all, our experience suggests that while there is no simple answer to the question of "how much is enough," the question is not unanswerable. The following sections describe, for strategic nuclear forces and for three components of general-purpose forces—tactical air forces, antisubmarine warfare forces, strategic mobility forces— how the problem of analyzing requirements was approached and with what degree of success.

Strategic Nuclear Forces

The approach to determining strategic force requirements has been covered in detail in Chapter 5. Basically, U.S. strategic offensive forces were sized according to their ability to destroy the Soviet Union as a viable nation in a retaliatory strike. The level of destruction required—20 to 25 percent of the Soviet population and 50 percent of Soviet industry, commonly called our "assured-destruction" capability—was based on a judgment reached by the Secretary of Defense and accepted by the President, by the Congress, and apparently by the general public as well. That judgment was influenced by the fact of strongly diminishing marginal returns, as illustrated in Table 11, showing the destruction potential of various levels of retaliatory attacks.

Table 11. Soviet Population and Industry Destroyed (Assumed 1972 total population of 247 million; urban population of 116 million)

1 Megaton-Equivalent, Delivered Warheads	Total Population Killed		Percent Industrial Capacity Destroyed
	Millions	Percent	
100	37	15	59
200	52	21	72
400	74	30	76
800	96	39	77
1,200	109	44	77
1,600	116	47	77

As the table shows, beyond the level of around 400 1-megaton-equivalent delivered warheads, delivering more warheads would not significantly change the amount of damage inflicted. Indeed, doubling the number of delivered 1-megaton-equivalents from 400 to 800 would increase the destruction of Soviet population and industry by only 9 percent and 1 percent, respectively. Such increases would have little if any additional deterrent effect. In other words, once U.S. programmed bomber and missile forces reached the level where we could, with high confidence, deliver 400 1-megaton weapons on the Soviet Union in a retaliatory strike, the gain from having more bombers or missiles to deliver still more warheads would be very small compared with the cost. Thus, the main reason for stopping at 1,000 Minuteman missiles, 41 Polaris submarines, and some 500 strategic bombers is that having more would not be worth the additional cost. These force levels are sufficiently high to put the United States on the "flat of the curve"—that is, at a point where small increases in target destruction capability would require enormous increases in forces, and therefore in cost. The answer to the question of how many strategic offensive forces are enough rests heavily on such flat-of-the-curve reasoning.

To ensure that U.S. assured-destruction capability remained at or above the level judged to be adequate, sensitivity calculations were made regularly, using various sets of assumptions to see how changing conditions would affect our capability. These calculations were instrumental in the decisions taken to enhance the capabilities of the strategic retaliatory forces, such as the production and deployment of penetration aids and MIRV's to overcome the Soviet ABM system, and Short-Range Attack Missiles (SRAM's) for the U.S. bomber force. Furthermore, as discussed in Chapter 5, U.S. forces were evaluated against a greater-than-expected Soviet threat (that is, greater than even the highest estimates shown in official intelligence projections) as a further test of the adequacy of U.S. programmed forces and the timeliness of available options. Such detailed analyses helped increase confidence in our ability to maintain an assured-destruction capability—"enough" retaliatory power—in spite of any Soviet efforts to take it away.

In the damage-limiting role, strategic offensive forces and strategic defensive forces also come up against diminishing marginal returns. Studies by the Systems Analysis office consistently showed, for example, that regardless of the amount we were willing to spend on an anti-Soviet ABM to protect U.S. cities we could not significantly reduce the number of American dead in an all-out nuclear exchange so long as the Soviets were determined to maintain their deterrent. And unless it was accompanied by an effective ABM and fallout-shelter system, antibomber defenses could not provide significant protection against large-scale attacks. Without an effective missile defense, even a perfect bomber defense would not save many lives, since the Soviets could simply strike U.S. cities with ICBM's. A Soviet first strike with missiles alone could kill over 100 million

Americans; their bombers could add less than 10 million, even if the United States had no air defense at all; and it would cost at least $10 billion to cut this latter figure in half. Is it worth $10 billion over the next five years to reduce the number of American dead, in the un-likely event of a nuclear war, from 110 million to 105 million?

Such calculations do not, of course, produce an optimum cutoff point for force levels. Someone has to judge where to stop. In the case of strategic offensive forces, these analyses helped the Secretary of Defense avoid committing many billions of dollars for additional weapons whose effect would be, at best, to raise the damage probabil-ity only a few percent. In the case of strategic defensive forces, they pinpointed the key facts: (1) that a full-scale ABM would be ineffec-tive in saving U.S. cities if the Soviets were to react to our deploy-ment by deploying penetration aids, multiple warheads, and more offensive missiles of their own; and (2) that an ABM system would be ineffective in saving lives after a full Soviet attack, if we were to deploy it without a large-scale civil defense program. Thus, while the analyses did not identify the best answer, they did help identify some bad ones.

The importance of looking realistically at enemy reactions in de-termining how much extra security the United States would get from adding more forces should be reemphasized. Answers to the question of how much is enough vary widely with assumptions about the nature of the enemy response. Identifying possible enemy reactions and giving them a numerical expression is more important (in avoid-ing bad decisions and gross waste) than calculating an "optimum" solution for some single set of assumptions. Summaries such as Tables 9 and 10 (see pages 189–190), which were developed by the Systems Analysis office during the debate over an anti-Soviet ABM and presented to the Congress in the Secretary of Defense's 1968 posture statement, show the importance of such analyses.

Another point illustrated by the analyses of strategic force require-ments concerns the futility of comparing forces on the basis of a single characteristic. It has been made public that the Soviets may soon have a greater megatonnage delivery capability than the United States, since they have apparently chosen to load their bombers and missiles with fewer weapons of larger yield. In 1967, the House Armed Services Committee published a report by the American

Security Council entitled *The Changing Strategic Military Balance, USA vs. USSR,* which warned of a mass "megatonnage gap" by the early 1970's and thus of Soviet strategic superiority. The report, whose signers included General Bernard Schriever, General Curtis LeMay, General Thomas Power, and Dr. Edward Teller (among others), was widely quoted in the press and cited by several Congressmen, including the Chairman of the House Armed Services Committee, as proof of the eroding U.S. strategic position. In fact, the report proved nothing: comparing forces by reference to a single weapon characteristic such as megatonnage is meaningless. As shown in Chapter 5, megatonnage delivery capability is not a good measure of force effectiveness or adequacy.

Rather than attempt to achieve a meaningless "superiority" in some simple comparative measure of strategic nuclear power, the United States must buy and maintain sufficient forces to meet its national objectives. The important question is not total megatons or numbers of delivery systems or any other single measure of strategic nuclear capability, but whether U.S. forces can effectively carry out their missions. Once we are sure that, in retaliation, we can destroy the Soviet Union and other potential attackers as modern societies, we cannot increase our security or power against them by threatening to destroy more.

General-Purpose Forces

General-purpose forces are forces maintained for all conflicts below the level of a general nuclear war. They include all Army and Marine Corps land forces, all tactical units of the Air Force, and most Naval forces except Polaris submarines. These forces protect U.S. national interests by deterring nonnuclear attacks on our allies and helping them defend themselves if they are attacked. Unlike strategic forces, general-purpose forces can both occupy and control territory.

The need for more general-purpose forces was one of the first major conclusions emerging from early OSD studies of the U.S. defense posture. The leaders of the Kennedy administration faced up to the fact that nuclear weapons, whether strategic or tactical, could not be a substitute for adequate conventional forces. They also recognized that existing conventional forces were inadequate to meet world-wide commitments without the use of nuclear weapons. Secretary McNamara began immediately to build up U.S. nonnuclear capabilities by expanding the number of divisions and air wings, adding to the strategic mobility forces, increasing the procurement of equipment and the amount of logistic support, and raising training levels. At the same time, a systematic study effort was launched to determine how many general-purpose forces would be needed.

The over-all level of U.S. general-purpose forces depends on what types of conflicts we anticipate, what countries we choose to assist, and to what degree these countries can defend themselves; in short, on what contingencies we prepare for. Thus, general-purpose forces cannot be determined by simply setting an over-all objective, such as the assured-destruction concept for strategic forces, and then designing these forces in light of the stated objective. The number of U.S. forces required is not discernible in any obvious way by direct comparison with total Soviet or Chinese forces. Rather, U.S. general-purpose force requirements depend on our interest in dealing militarily with particular contingencies around the world.

One way to highlight the problems associated with planning general-purpose forces is to compare it with strategic force planning. In the strategic area, it has made sense to most people to assume that the war is essentially over after the first massive nuclear exchange. The outcome of the war can be assessed in terms of the damage inflicted on the population and industry of each country involved. Since it is basically a "one-move" war for either side, a mathematical "model" can be constructed for calculating the amount of damage that either can inflict on the other as a function of the number and types of weapons they possess. One can then establish a criterion for the amount of retaliatory destruction U.S. national leaders want to be able to inflict on the Soviet Union or China, or both. Having done this, one can calculate the number and types of weapons needed to meet this criterion.

The situation is entirely different for general-purpose forces. Conventional wars generally last a long time. There are literally millions of moves or decision points, in contrast to the one-move strategic war. Even with high-speed computers, it is impossible to construct a model of a conventional war which realistically reflects all the possible alternatives available to each side. Then, too, one cannot predict with confidence the outcome of even small-unit engagements as a function of the opposing forces and arms. The reason is that the results of the engagement often depend critically on factors that are hard to measure or predict, such as tactics, surprise, terrain, training, leadership, and morale. The problem of estimating the outcome of a war in a sector or a theater is even more complicated, since that outcome depends on the outcome of many small-unit engagements plus the over-all tactics and strategy used by each side. Furthermore, conventional wars in the nuclear age are fought for limited objectives and are as characteristically political as military. In some cases, such as Vietnam, it is not possible to determine who is winning by calculating the number of casualties suffered by each side, or the amount of territory gained or held. Thus, realistically, it is extremely difficult to calculate how much better the United States might do if it placed another infantry division or tank division or wing of tactical aircraft in a particular theater.

Another distinguishing feature of general-purpose forces is that their aggregate firepower is not a direct measure of their ability to achieve an ultimate objective such as the defense or control of territory. While it is necessary to use firepower to destroy enemy targets in order to control territory, manpower is also required—proportioned to the size of the territory, the cooperativeness of the population, the size of the enemy land force, and the type of control desired. The Vietnam war, where the United States has practically unlimited firepower (in contrast to the enemy), is a case in point. This characteristic of general-purpose forces also explains why, beyond a certain point, air or artillery support, or even tactical nuclear weapons, cannot be substituted for Army and Marine maneuver units.

General-purpose force levels also depend on judgments about the areas of the world the United States wishes to defend and about where on the spectrum of aggression—from political subversion to overt full-scale invasion—one believes that more general deterrents, including the threat of nuclear war, come into play. Some people believe, for example, that an invasion of Central Europe would so clearly threaten U.S. vital interests, and so clearly risk all-out nuclear war, as to be outside the range of actions the Soviets would rationally consider. On the other hand, North Korean infiltration across the

Demilitarized Zone is apparently not deterred by anything but direct defense. This further emphasizes the dependence of general-purpose (and strategic) force requirements on basic political judgments about "scenarios"—about the visualized threats that are real enough to justify military expenditures in peacetime.

In making these judgments, a key factor is the evaluation of options. Suppose that an attack occurs which the United States cannot immediately halt with general-purpose forces. In such a situation, we could either try to stop the attack with nuclear weapons or give up allied territory until enough forces could be mobilized to regain it. Trying to stop an attack on another country by using nuclear weapons would involve many grave problems and uncertainties, in addition to the risk of escalation to nuclear attacks on the United States. If the enemy also has large numbers of nuclear weapons, as in Europe, the use of such weapons does not necessarily provide a net military advantage. Moreover, to destroy a large enemy land force requires many weapons or sizable yields; this requirement not only increases the danger of escalation but also causes great collateral damage and high civilian casualties, raising the question of whether such actions are consistent with our basic objective of saving the country from invasion. Finally, even if the enemy has no nuclear weapons, any gross inadequacy in the defending conventional forces would tend to vitiate the enormous firepower of nuclear weapons. By splitting up into small units and intermingling with the friendly population, the enemy can engage in close-in combat unsuited to the use of nuclear weapons. In sum, although the risk of escalation and high casualties inherent in the use of nuclear weapons may break the will of the enemy to continue, nuclear weapons will not necessarily guarantee actual control of territory against a determined enemy with superior conventional forces, particularly if both sides have nuclear weapons.

Mobilization and counterattack to regain territory are generally possible, but they normally involve large resources and high casualties. In other words, if a war starts which the nation is not prepared to fight with adequate general-purpose forces, the risk of escalation to nuclear war, the loss of life and destruction of property, and the military forces and casualties ultimately exacted would be much greater than would have been the case if the nation had been prepared. Of course, these risks are run—and costs exacted—only if war actually occurs; being prepared with general-purpose forces requires continuous and large expenditures in peacetime.

Further, to some extent U.S. general-purpose forces actually deployed overseas in peacetime take on a political significance beyond their purely military function because of the degree to which they symbolize U.S. commitment to the country involved. In addition, overseas deployments are an important cause of the persistent U.S. balance-of-payments deficit.

All these factors must be systematically considered in planning general-purpose forces. Basically, however, the requirements for these forces depend on the number and kinds of overseas conflicts the United States decides it must prepare for. This decision is based on broad judgments—primarily political and economic rather than military—as to what kinds of aggression are sufficiently likely and important to justify the peacetime costs of being prepared to meet them with general-purpose forces. We cannot, of course, plan to meet all the theoretically possible contingencies—"forty-odd Vietnams"—simultaneously. Nor do we really need to do so, for the risk that such a large number of contingencies will arise at the same time is very low. For these reasons, the policy of the Kennedy and Johnson administrations was to size U.S. general-purpose forces to meet the most demanding of the probable contingencies associated with our formal treaty commitments. For planning purposes, this meant meeting, simultaneously, a Warsaw Pact attack in Europe and a Chinese attack in Asia, while maintaining the ability to meet a minor contingency in the Western Hemisphere or elsewhere. Once enough general-purpose forces had been provided to meet minimum U.S. political objectives in these areas, a sizable strategic reserve was provided to serve as a hedge in either of these areas, or as a rotation base for a prolonged war.

Over the years, several important qualifications were made to this basic planning assumption of being able to fight "two and one-half" wars simultaneously. For example, in Asia, it was interpreted by the Secretary of Defense to exclude having enough active U.S. forces to fight a major conventional war in both Korea and Southeast Asia at the same time. Thus, the active U.S. land and tactical air forces were expanded by substantially less than the number deployed to Southeast

Asia. The assumption was that in the event of an attack on Korea while we were fighting in Vietnam, forces from Vietnam could be redeployed for holding actions in both theaters until reserve forces were mobilized. In Europe, the duration of a major conventional war was limited, for planning purposes, to a period of three months, thus reducing requirements for inventories, training, and logistic support to amounts far less than would be required for a capability to fight a war of indefinite duration. In addition, the NATO-oriented forces were not designed to meet a full-scale surprise Pact attack following a concealed mobilization. Rather, they were designed to provide an intermediate level of conventional capability—short of the capability to meet a "worst-case" conventional attack, but adequate for deterrence and for initial defense in the contingencies believed to be most likely. Similarly, in Asia no explicit provision was made in the peacetime force structure for enough forces to provide a sustained defense, or to mount a counteroffensive to restore territory initially lost, in the event of a massive Chinese attack.

Many of these qualifications to the basic planning assumption were not accepted by the JCS. On top of other differences in interpretation of strategy and much more conservative planning in certain areas, this accounts for why the JCS's estimates of force requirements often differed markedly from those of the Secretary of Defense. For example, the JCS assumed that Warsaw Pact aircraft were able to fly roughly twice as many sorties per day as NATO aircraft, that the United States had to preserve a large residual force after a high-intensity submarine war, and that base rights in allied countries could not be relied on. Even granting agreement regarding the "two and one-half" wars, there is room for considerable disagreement on the detailed planning assumptions. If the Secretary of Defense is to discharge his basic responsibility to decide on force levels, he must concern himself with such planning assumptions.

It is important to understand that by 1969 the approved program for general-purpose forces was the result of an evolution to adapt an existing force structure to a stated strategy. Many elements of the force structure were as much a product of individually justified changes in an existing force as they were a result of any integrated, over-all determination of strategic requirements. This effect was significant, for example, in the planning of tactical air forces, which accounted for almost one-fifth of the defense budget. These forces had been kept at about the same number of wings and total aircraft for seven years, but they had been increased very substantially in capability and cost by a nearly 1 for 1 replacement of older aircraft with much more expensive and more capable aircraft.

In the following sections, therefore, we shall not be describing a sophisticated and integrated theory for determining general-purpose force requirements. No such theory exists. Rather, we shall be describing only the analytical progress, some of it extremely meager, that had been made by January 1969 in the planning of tactical air forces, antisubmarine-warfare forces, and strategic mobility forces. We would be among the first to agree that, in these and in other areas, the development of satisfactory principles for planning general-purpose forces has further to go than it has come. At the same time, we believe that such planning came a long way between 1961 and 1969.

Tactical Air Forces

For years, the Systems Analysis office struggled with the question, "How much tactical air power is enough?" In the early 1960's, we reasoned that the effectiveness of the classic tactical air missions—air superiority, close air support, and interdiction—could be measured by their impact on the force ratio between opposing land forces, and thus that the land/air "trade-off" would be a decisive factor in sizing U.S. tactical air forces. Approaching the problem in the manner of an economist or operations analyst, we tried to develop trade-off curves for land and air forces yielding the same effectiveness.

Put another way, suppose that the United States were to spend an additional billion dollars to buy and operate tactical air forces that would destroy and disrupt enemy troop and supply movements deep behind his lines, thus limiting his ability to sustain operations at the war front. Suppose also that by this expenditure we were able to reduce by fifty thousand the number of personnel the enemy could support at the front. Then, would our land forces be better off, thanks to that enemy force reduction by our tactical air forces, than they would have been if we had spent the additional billion dollars to provide more land forces? Essentially, that is the question the Systems Analysis office spent years trying to define, document, and analyze in the hope of supporting a reasoned judgment. Unfortunately, we were unsuccessful. We simply could not find the relevant data with which to calculate how much better the United States would do if it had another wing of tactical air in a particular theater. Nor could we get a reasoned judgment from the military experts, based on the available data. Their conclusions were reached by inter-Service negotiation rather than by analysis. One major close-air-support study in the early 1960's, involving the Army and the Air Force, reached the informative conclusion that we needed more close air support and more land forces. Joint studies in which the Systems Analysis office participated became prolonged debates over basic assumptions and facts. Without agreement on the basic input factors, it was impossible to derive usable results about possible land-air trade-offs.

After blunting our lance for several years on the land/air trade-off problem, we realized that the actual decision making was being based on much simpler reasoning, such as a comparative count of enemy aircraft versus ours, and that this count was wrong. It was wrong, first, because it compared a number close to the total inventory of our potential enemies (the Air Order of Battle) with only a fraction of our own inventory (the Unit Equipment, or that portion of the forces nominally assigned to combat units). It was also wrong because it ignored qualitative differences between our aircraft and theirs. For example, a high percentage of Soviet aircraft are defensive interceptors, while a high percentage of ours are multipurpose fighter-bombers with good offensive capability. So, in 1964 the Systems Analysis office switched from trying to develop a sophisticated solution to the total tactical air problem to just getting the numerical counts straight and to developing effectiveness indicators that would take account of the expensive qualitative advantages being built into U.S. aircraft. In retrospect, it is clear that we should have made this switch sooner.

The question of inventory count was finally settled in 1966 by the Systems Analysis–Joint Staff "treaty" described in Chapter 4. The results of the work on this treaty of world-wide aircraft inventories were invaluable. For the first time there was agreement on the facts regarding inventories. For the first time comparisons were made on the basis of consistent assumptions. For the first time qualitative differences were explicitly recognized. The memorandum of agreement comparing available aircraft inventories became an annual exercise between the two staffs and the basis for the annual Secretary of Defense posture statement. It is an excellent example of how adversary proceedings between OSD and the Joint Staff can be used to get the facts straight for top-level decision makers.

Of even more importance than an agreed-upon, authoritative statement of total inventories was the explicit recognition that inventory comparisons alone are a poor measure of over-all capability. Our needs for tactical aircraft depend mainly on the number of contingencies we want to be prepared to fight simultaneously, on the sortie requirements for each contingency, and on the planning factors used in making the calculations. The sortie requirements for contingencies depend on the objectives of each side, their respective deployment capabilities, the bases available to them, and the quality of their aircraft. Matching—or exceeding—the Communists in capability in a given theater does not necessarily require that we match them on a 1 for 1 basis in aircraft.

To facilitate the integration of costly qualitative factors into numerical force comparisons, the Systems Analysis office began developing ways to give them numerical expression. (Our problem with the Services was not so much driving home the importance of qualitative differences as getting them to take credit for qualitative advantages, when comparing total forces.) We started by first devising a simple pay-load index that measured the number of tons of bombs that our forces (and our potential enemies) could deliver on a representative combat sortie. While our total inventory had increased only slightly, we found, as shown in Table 12, that the pay-load capability of our total force more than doubled between 1961 and 1967. By contrast, that of the Communists, which had started at a much lower level, increased only some 30 percent.

Table 12. Pay-load Capability of Tactical Aircraft (Free World, 1961 = 100)

End of Fiscal Year	U.S.	Total Free World	Total Communist
1961	55	100	53
1967	117	167	69

The use of the pay-load index was immediately met by the JCS and the Services with the argument that "pay load is not the same as force effectiveness." But McNamara responded along the following lines: "I agree. It's a very crude index. In fact, we ought to be ashamed of ourselves for using such a crude measure. But it's a lot better than just numbers or wings of aircraft, and it gives a much more accurate picture of the growth in our total capability. So I am going to go on using it until a better measure is available. Moreover, we are paying a lot for that increased pay load; if you don't believe it is yielding a proportionate increase in military power, then maybe we shouldn't be buying it. Perhaps we should be buying larger numbers of simpler, cheaper aircraft instead of the expensive ones you've been recommending."

From the pay-load index, we wanted to go on to develop an index of offensive target kill potential, which would show for a representative target array how many targets our tactical air forces could destroy per week or month, taking into account sortie rates, accuracy and lethality of ordnance, maintenance, and the like. Similarly, we wanted to develop an index of defensive target kill potential, showing how many enemy planes our forces would be able to shoot down in a representative engagement. However, partly because of analytic difficulty and partly because of opposition from the Services, we were not able to get very far down this road by the end of 1968. The Services could see clearly that with each step in the direction of quantifying U.S. qualitative advantages and developing appropriate indexes, we came closer to demonstrating that the United States had a tremendous advantage over its potential enemies in tactical air forces. For example, our own independent studies showed that against a representative set of target arrays, United States tactical air forces would have at least four or five times the capability to destroy these targets as would the enemy forces. In fact, while not agreeing to the factors and assumptions used in the Systems Analysis office's calculations, the Air Staff, which a few years earlier had been claiming that we were badly outnumbered, particularly in Europe, had, by 1968, shifted its official position to the point where it agreed that the tactical air relationship there was one of equality. The Secretary of the Air Force went even further, agreeing that NATO's offensive tactical air power was twice that of the Warsaw Pact.

In all these questions, the capability and quality of the opposing aircraft are very important. A table like Table 5 (see p. 155), which was developed by the Systems Analysis office in 1967, is very useful in displaying these characteristics and getting them explicitly considered in the planning process. As the table shows, by several significant measures NATO (especially U.S.) tactical air forces are superior to those of the Warsaw Pact. This is not surprising, since we have been spending far more on tactical air than the Communists. For example, the Soviet tactical air program would cost in U.S. prices (that is, if the aircraft were manufactured in the United States and the personnel were paid at U.S. rates) only about one-third of what the U.S. program costs.

While performance characteristics are important, they, like numbers of aircraft, must also be considered in context, however. Unfortunately, in judging current and planned tactical air forces, many people often equate one particular characteristic, such as range or speed or maneuverability or age, with notions of aggregate "superiority" or "inferiority." A supersonic aircraft is believed to be better than one that is subsonic. A new aircraft is automatically superior to an old one. Thus, each time the Soviets unveil a new aircraft that exceeds ours in some particular performance category, cries of our growing obsolescence are raised. But it is a mistake to equate superiority or inferiority with any single characteristic—even pay load. What is important is the effectiveness of the aircraft in relation to the job it must do.

For example, where in the past a small speed advantage might have been a decisive factor, today it may be of relatively little significance. Indeed, for close-air-support and interdiction operations such as those in Vietnam, the subsonic plane may have important advantages over a supersonic plane, even beyond the fact that it is cheaper and may be able to carry more pay load. It can dive at a higher glide angle and therefore bomb more accurately, and get away from the target faster by pulling up faster. Also, a subsonic aircraft is often considerably more maneuverable, and this can be an important advantage in a hostile environment. Over North Vietnam our pilots found that they could evade the enemy's surface-to-air missiles by outmaneuvering them.

Likewise, the effectiveness of an aircraft is not necessarily a function of age. In many cases we have found that an older aircraft fitted out with the best available missile, radar, fire-control, and other electronic equipment can be an effective system. This has been the case with the B-52. It was also the case with the F-106, where OSD and the Air Force found that an older and slower plane, if equipped with the latest weapon systems, would provide a lot more for the money in real air-defense effectiveness than the newest and fastest plane, the F-12.

The point is that it is not sufficient to use speed or age or some other arbitrary weapon system characteristic as a conclusive indicator of superiority or inferiority. One must look at the relationship of that characteristic to other characteristics and to the particular mission to be accomplished. The fact that we do or do not have the fastest or newest plane doesn't necessarily mean that we will win or lose; just as the fact that we do or do not have larger or smaller numbers of aircraft doesn't necessarily mean that we have enough or not enough. Balanced consideration must be given to the full range of factors: the objectives, the number and quality of the aircraft, the training and pilot skill, the ordnance, and so on. We are much more likely to get this balanced consideration through open and explicit analysis and debate than through emotional appeals based on a single aircraft characteristic.

Owing to the lack of a good conceptual basis for determining needs and the many uncertainties involving tactical air operations, it is not surprising that there was a wide diversity of views in DoD regarding how much of what type of tactical air support should be programmed. These differences concerned both the amount of tactical air support and the relative emphasis to be placed on the various missions. For example, there was strong support in the Air Force and the Navy for greater emphasis on deep interdiction, which requires large numbers of expensive aircraft, such as the Navy A-6 and the Air Force F-111. The objective of such attacks is to limit the enemy's ability to sustain operations at the front by destroying and disrupting his industry and transportation system. Systems Analysis studies suggested that there is reason to question the value of deep interdiction against industry and lines of communication, in both Europe and Asia. (Deep interdiction is to be distinguished from local battlefield interdiction, which is integrated with ground operations and thus aimed at temporarily halting enemy movements and resupply in a given area.) Historically speaking, the case for the deep-interdiction mission is poor. Neither in Germany, in Korea, nor in Vietnam were U.S. forces able to choke off, through bombing alone, the production of war matériel or its movement to the front. Since preparations for a conventional war in Europe are based on the assumption that it will not last more than a few months at high intensity, there would appear to be little value in programming forces to attack such facilities as steel mills, aircraft factories, and power plants. Capabilities contributing immediately to meeting the enemy's attack, such as close air support or combat troops, would appear to be more valuable than deep interdiction, which would make its main contribution later in the war.

In addition, the transportation network in Eastern Europe is large and redundant. It would be virtually impossible to disrupt the flow of essential war matériel from rear areas to the front by means of a conventional bombing campaign against railroad centers, bridges, and roads. Systems Analysis studies indicated that even if flow capacity could be reduced by as much as 90 percent, the remaining capacity would be enough to reinforce and resupply an 80-division Warsaw Pact force. Moreover, an interdiction effort of this magnitude would require forces far in excess of even those recommended by the Services. This point is important, because half an interdiction campaign is not worth much. Knocking out half the enemy's road and rail network does little good, if the remaining half is several times what he needs to move and supply his forces. Moreover, roads and railways have a way of not staying knocked out very long.

In the Asian theater as a whole, enemy logistic systems are characteristically hard to find and pinpoint; they have good repair capability and small supply requirements. Depriving them of something that they are not using at the moment seems to have little effect; they always have a "seeping resupply," at least. Their lines of communication are highly redundant, including small river craft, bicycles, trucks, trains, and human porters for transshipment around obstacles. Despite massive interdiction efforts during the Korean war, for example, the Communists were still able to support an army of over 600,000 at the front. United States experience in Korea and Vietnam has also shown the enemy to be very clever at developing countermeasures that make the interdiction effort relatively unremunerative, as well as costly to us.

Moreover, deep-interdiction missions are very expensive in terms of resource requirements. Since they go far into enemy territory and hit at well-defended targets, the attrition is usually much higher than on close-support missions. And since the attack aircraft must penetrate into heavily defended areas, they must be supported with expensive electronic countermeasures (ECM) aircraft and fighters, which raise the cost of the mission. For example, for the same amount of money to fly one interdiction mission per day against a power plant or a railroad yard in a war in Asia, the United States could fly some three to seven close-support sorties per day with fewer pilot losses.

All of this is not to say that there are no circumstances in which an interdiction campaign would be worth while. Such a decision would always depend on the particular situation in the theater. However, it does suggest that tactical air forces should not be *planned* on the assumption that we will be able to limit substantially the enemy's warmaking capability or limit forces he can support at the front by air interdiction. Since it appears that large force expenditures for deep-interdiction capability are not worth while—particularly when compared with the advantages of expenditures for direct combat capabilities such as close air support and maneuver forces—it would seem to make more sense to conduct only enough deep-interdiction attacks to harass the enemy, forcing him to devote a major effort to air defense, to disperse his aircraft, and to take other expensive precautionary measures; that is, to interdict only where the "leverage" or "cost exchange" is favorable. Adoption of such a policy would, of course, lead to major changes in the types of aircraft and ordnance now programmed and could lead to large reductions in the cost of U.S. tactical air forces.

In addition to our debate with the Services over the value of additional expenditures for interdiction, we also discussed the best way to increase over-all tactical air effectiveness. After the initial expansion of U.S. tactical air forces from 16 to 21 wings in 1961–1962, Systems Analysis held that the United States could realize large gains in actual tactical air capability by improving weapons effectiveness and delivery accuracy and by reducing vulnerability, at a fraction of the cost of buying more aircraft. This rationale was not accepted by the Services, who preferred to emphasize expanding the size of the force as the way to increase effectiveness.

The consequences of this basic difference in approach can be clearly seen in the debate over aircraft shelters. Every pertinent study and war game conducted since 1961 has led to the same conclusion: actions taken to reduce the vulnerability of U.S. tactical air forces on the ground—particularly the building of shelters—will greatly increase our ability to fight a conventional war. The potential pay-off in sustained combat capability far exceeds the shelter costs. (An $8 million plane can be sheltered for about $100,000.) Costs aside, it makes little sense to openly invite attacks on U.S. air bases. Yet, in 1963, 1964, and 1965 the Senate Armed Services Committee, prodded in part by the lack of enthusiasm of military witnesses, cut out of the defense budget the funds ($30 million, $20 million, and $22.4 million, respectively) proposed by the Secretary of Defense for aircraft shelters in Europe on the grounds of "grave doubts as to the practicality of this program." The willingness to spend billions for fancy new aircraft, coupled with the unwillingness to spend much smaller amounts for the unglamorous "horsehoe nails" needed to make them effective, is one of the most serious problems in the defense planning business.

In the absence of procedures for estimating force requirements, it was often difficult to determine what issues or assumptions people were disagreeing on, or what effect the disagreements had on the final answer. Nevertheless, the choice of how much of what type of tactical air power the United States should have was (and is) inescapable. By 1969, the magnitude of that choice involved annual spending of over $15 billion. The fact that there is no analytical basis for spending the $15 billion does not in itself necessarily mean we should not be doing it. One cannot prove that the amount should be $5 billion; but by the same token, there is no proof or convincing logic that it should not be $10 billion or $20 billion. If everyone would recognize this fact—and quit pretending that there is a decisive authoritative basis for the military's stated "requirements"—perhaps we would go slower about building in large increases in spending rates, take a harder look at costs per plane and at proposed cost increases, and insist on economic trade-offs where possible. The question to be asked at this point, we think, is not: "Can the United States use more tactical air?"

Rather, it is: "If we are going to spend another X billion dollars of the taxpayer's money, is there good evidence that it is needed in a more expensive tactical air force?"

How much tactical air is enough? Despite years of effort, we were unable to get enough agreement on the effectiveness factors to develop a satisfactory answer to this question. Our arguments regarding the adequacy of U.S. forces were thus based largely on comparisons of total inventory, pay load, costs, and the like—exactly the factors we've said *not* to look at. This approach cannot answer the question, "How much is enough?" At best, it can knock down a lot of bad arguments to the effect that we don't have enough. And the Systems Analysis office did accomplish that. Given the enormous costs of tactical air forces, the Defense Department badly needs to develop better criteria for sizing them.

Antisubmarine Warfare Forces

General-purpose naval forces are essential to the ability of the United States to meet contingencies overseas by enabling it to support its own and allied combat forces and to maintain the flow of merchant shipping to allies. The main threat to the U.S. ability to use the seas to the extent necessary to achieve national objectives is the large Soviet attack submarine fleet. As of 1968, the Institute for Strategic Studies in London reported that the USSR had some 380 attack submarines of all types which could be used against U.S. military and commercial shipping. However, many of these are obsolescent, short-range, diesel types. The most serious threat is posed by the Soviet fleet of 60 nuclear attack submarines.

The Soviet fleet, if unopposed, could exert strong coercive pressure on the United States in a peacetime crisis; or alternatively, inflict unacceptable losses on U.S. seaborne commerce and military shipping in wartime. Thus, we need an effective antisubmarine warfare (ASW) force to protect our naval attack and logistic forces and to prevent being cut off from allies in the event of a war.

Put simply, the Navy's basic approach to the Soviet submarine threat is to interpose a series of barriers between Soviet submarine bases and their targets. For example, a Soviet submarine moving from its home base to the principal shipping lanes in the Atlantic and the Pacific would have to pass through mine fields and through zones patrolled by U.S. attack submarines; it would then be subjected to intensive air patrols by land-based patrol aircraft and by patrol aircraft from ASW carriers. Finally, to attack a convoy, it would have to penetrate a destroyer-escort screen. If the submarine were successful in its mission, it would then have to pass through all these barriers again on its way home.

The barrier concept can be illustrated with a simplified, hypothetical example. Assume, first of all, that the Soviets have 200 submarines that can be used to attack our shipping in the Atlantic and the Pacific. Assume also that the United States deploys a total of five barriers in each ocean (mines, submarines, land-based patrol aircraft, carrier-based patrol aircraft, and destroyers, in that order) which their submarines must traverse to reach our convoys. Now assume that each Soviet submarine carries ten torpedoes, each with a 50 percent probability of killing one of our ships if fired at it. In other words, if a Soviet submarine should successfully penetrate the fifth barrier—the destroyer screen—it would, on the average, be able to kill five of our ships. Suppose, again hypothetically, that each of our barriers has a 20 percent probability of killing any submarine that passes through it. (In fact, of course, each type of barrier would have various kill probabilities against various types of Soviet submarines.) Thus, if the Soviets were to start out with 200 submarines, 160 would survive the first barrier, 128 the second, 102 the third, 82 the fourth, and 66 the fifth barrier. Those 66 would then be able to launch 660 torpedoes and sink 330 ships, all on the average. After their attacks, in trying to leave the defensive screen, 52 of the remaining submarines would get through the destroyer-escort barrier, 42 the carrier-based air barrier, 34 the land-based patrol aircraft barrier, 27 the submarine barrier, and 22 the mine barrier, getting home safely. These remaining 22 submarines would then refit and repeat the process: seven submarines would survive the second trip through the five barriers and sink 35 more ships. Thus, under this particular set of assumptions, the 200 Soviet submarines would sink some 365 of our ships in two trips; but the two trips would essentially eliminate the entire Soviet attack-submarine force. Again, this is a greatly simplified model with deliberately inaccurate factors, but the logic is basically the same as that used in the more complex and realistic Navy studies.

Now, suppose that the United States spends an additional $2 billion in ten-year systems cost (again a hypothetical number) to add another barrier of submarines. If all the other probabilities remain the same, 52 enemy submarines would survive the sixth barrier and sink 260 ships, 14 would get home safely, 4 would survive the second trip to attack the convoy again, and they would kill 20 ships. Thus, with a sixth barrier, 280 ships would be sunk as opposed to 365 with only five barriers. The judgment that must be made is this: Is the expectation of saving these additional 85 ships, in the uncertain event of a possible future war, worth $2 billion of certain expenditures in peacetime?

Obviously, this is a debatable question. We believe, however, that there are good and bad ways to conduct the debate. The worst way that we have heard goes like this: Certainly the expenditure must be made, because human life is involved—the lives of the seamen on the 85 ships that would be saved if another barrier of submarines were added. This is, unfortunately, the kind of emotional argument that so often frustrates defense planning. Surely, if the proponents of more ASW forces who use it were really concerned about human life, they would be looking for ways of spending that $2 billion on such things as improved health and medical facilities in the United States and overseas, or food for starving people, or even cheaper ways of saving these lives through naval forces, say, in non-ASW missions. It is hard to imagine an easier task than to find ways of spending $2 billion which would be more productive in saving human lives than in spending it on more antisubmarine warfare forces.

A better way to approach the question, we think, is to ask: How might the $2 billion otherwise be spent to achieve objectives similar to those being sought by deploying an additional barrier of submarines? Some obvious alternatives include more mine fields, land- or sea-based aircraft, destroyers, or cargo ships. Suppose, for example, that the money is spent on additional cargo ships. Assuming $20 million for each ship (including the value of the cargoes), that would be 100 ships. It might seem better to spend the money on these 100 additional ships. They would be useful in peacetime and would still put us 15 ships ahead of the 85 ships saved by the additional submarine barrier, in the event of a war. But that is not necessarily the case. The Soviet submarines might sink some Navy ships of great value, so that the extra barrier, instead of saving 85 average cargo ships, might in fact save a nuclear-powered aircraft carrier, which with its complement of aircraft costs over a billion dollars just to procure. Moreover, the 100 ships, even if all cargo vessels, might not be an adequate replacement for the ships that were sunk, if time of delivery or particular cargoes were critical. The 85 ships sunk by the enemy submarines that might have been saved by a sixth barrier might well be ships containing critical military supplies needed to stave off defeat in a theater until larger reinforcements arrived. However, if that is the problem, other ways of spending the $2 billion should be examined, including, for example, stock-piling military supplies in critical overseas locations.

The driving factor in all ASW calculations is the probability of kill (Pk). Variations in Pk dominate any differences in analytical methodology. (The seemingly mechanical operation of the simple "barrier" model cited above, for example, yields about the same results as the most complex model, if the same Pk's are used.) Pk values depend in large part on the quality of our surveillance and weapon systems—their range, speed, reliability, accuracy, and the like. Again speaking hypothetically, it is possible that with $2 billion, the average Pk of the barriers could be raised from, say, 20 to 25 percent. Would that be a better way to spend the money? Using the earlier model, an increase in Pk from 20 to 25 percent would mean that 48 enemy submarines would now survive the first five barriers and kill 240 ships. After returning home and being refitted, only three submarines would get back through the barriers for a second shot, killing 15 ships. In all, 255 ships would be sunk instead of 365. Thus, raising the Pk from 20 to 25 percent would theoretically save 110 ships. If this were the case, $2 billion spent on raising Pk's would be more productive than the same money spent on adding another barrier of submarines.

This particular conclusion has a basis in fact. We found that the return on a dollar spent raising the Pk's of existing U.S. forces—by introducing more effective weapon systems and better sensors—was far greater than the return from adding more forces. Indeed, any present or future advantages in ASW capabilities depend heavily on new sensors and weapon systems. Given this fact, increased force levels are not the best way to improve the ability of the United States to defeat the Soviets in an ASW campaign. If the sensors and weapon systems we are developing do not work, or if they work much less effectively than the Navy claimed when arguing for their approval, larger forces will be of little help.

Our effort to come up with a convincing analysis of ASW forces, one that everyone would accept and agree upon, failed. It failed, in part, because the U.S. Navy is made up of three competing branches, each proud of its own capabilities and traditions: a submarine Navy, a surface Navy, and an aircraft Navy. The Navy conducted its ASW studies by committee, with representatives from all three branches present. When it came time to gather assumptions on which to base the Pk's of the various Navy forces, each branch competed with the others in overstating performance claims for its own preferred weapon systems. Each feared that if it did not, future studies would show that all or most of the Soviet submarine force was being destroyed by one of the other branches, which might then get more of the total Navy budget. Also, each branch felt obliged, when stating the Pk's of its particular weapons, to use the numbers that it had earlier claimed would be achieved when it justified the R&D programs for those weapons. Since we were dealing with future wars and future forces, these assumed future Pk's were in fact the justification for very substantial current R&D programs. Thus, if a branch did not claim a high effectiveness for its proposed new weapons, it stood in danger of having its R&D budget cut back.

When all these inflated claims for Pk's were put together and run through a total-fleet war game, the results were, predictably, that our side won handsomely with the forces already approved by the Secretary of Defense; in fact, we won not only decisively but within a very few weeks. Indeed, it often appeared that we could have won the war quickly enough with even smaller forces. Given the high Pk's, it was apparent that the programmed forces were entirely adequate to do the job. In other words, the Navy's beliefs that more forces were needed could be decisively refuted with the factors used in their own studies. This put the Navy in a serious dilemma, one which it struggled with unsuccessfully for several years. As shown below, the dilemma was reflected in the fact that, for four years in a row, the Secretary of Defense asked the Navy to make an analysis of antisubmarine warfare which could be used as a basis for judgments on force levels and that, for four years in a row, the Navy made a study, got caught up in the same dilemma, and ended up disowning its own analysis as a basis for determining force levels.

Highlights from the Navy's ASW study chronology illustrate the point:

May 3, 1963: The Secretary of Defense requests a "broad quantitative analysis of requirements for ASW forces . . . ," and states that: "Among other things, this study should help us to determine whether the changes being made in U.S. national security policy (e.g., build-up of nonnuclear forces) and the changing capabilities of U.S. and Soviet weapon systems (e.g., the build-up of the Soviet nuclear powered submarine fleet) imply that there should be changes in the size and composition of ASW forces."

August 2, 1963: The Secretary of the Navy forwards the CYCLOPS ASW study to the Secretary of Defense. In his forwarding memo he states: "It is therefore a 'capabilities' rather than a 'requirements' study. Although, by extrapolation, certain broad inferences can be made as to future force requirements, such inferences can be dangerous because the capabilities and limitations of the opposing forces can, and probably will, change radically in a short time. Therefore, although I do not believe that this study is fully responsive to your request for force requirements, I do consider it an essential forerunner to a requirement study addressed to the period 1968–1972."

April 18, 1964: The Secretary of Defense requests the Navy to: "Analyze the Soviet submarine warfare threat, and the effectiveness of our anti-submarine forces in relation thereto. Based on such an analysis, recommend a long-range force structure for our anti-submarine forces."

August 13, 1964: The Chief of Naval Operations (CNO) forwards the preliminary report of the CYCLOPS II ASW study to the Secretary of the Navy, stating: "CYCLOPS II is a highly competent study of nonnuclear war at sea. . . . Even this preliminary report represents a forward step in measuring the effectiveness of ASW forces and will be of assistance to the Navy in analyzing ASW forces, weapons systems, and tactics. However, the study at this stage, although of great value, cannot be used as the basis for force level determinations in view of its recognized limitations."

He also states: "The study gives strong evidence that our R&D program, procurement planning, balance of ASW forces and war planning have been well balanced and are essentially correct."

August 13, 1964: The Secretary of the Navy forwards the CYCLOPS II ASW study to the Secretary of Defense stating: "CYCLOPS II indicates that with the dramatic improvements in our ASW capability which we expect to achieve within the next . . . [years] we will at least have the techniques to control the [nuclear attack submarine]. . . . I also realize . . . that there are serious questions which must be answered before we can use this study with complete confidence. . . . However, regardless of these questions and uncertainties, I believe the study does prove that we are generally on the right track in our drive to develop a combination of weapons systems capable of defeating the nuclear attack submarine."

He also states: "I agree with the Chief of Naval Operations that there are serious limitations on the use of this preliminary report of CYCLOPS II as a basis for long-range force decisions."

December 5, 1964: The Secretary of the Navy informs the Secretary of Defense that he proposes a Navy study project for 1965 the aim of which is to: "Extend the analysis of CYCLOPS II to include alternative scenario assumptions, planning factors and force deployments and their influence on the effectiveness of programmed forces; . . ."

February 5, 1965: The Deputy Secretary of Defense replies to the Secretary of the Navy, emphasizing that ". . . the sensitivity of the outcome to variations in Soviet and allied capabilities must be measured" and requesting the Secretary of the Navy to: ". . . concentrate on this work, making use of available exercise data on our ASW capabilities so that we may resolve the maximum number of issues about ASW forces this year."

January 22, 1966: The Secretary of Defense informs the Secretary of the Navy: "It is essential that we analyze a [nonnuclear war limited to the sea]. . . . I want to have this work completed in the near future so that results can be incorporated in the Presidential Memoranda this year."

April 27, 1966: The Chief of Naval Operations forwards report on the War-at-Sea study to the Secretary of the Navy, stating: "The War-at-Sea study forwarded herewith is a useful first step in an on-going study of conflict at sea." He also states that: ". . . I believe that any conclusions drawn from the study must be approached with caution. . . . Force level variations, as calculated, have little validity for planning."

April 29, 1966: The Secretary of the Navy forwards the War-at-Sea study to the Secretary of Defense stating: "I believe the effort to date has been productive of a good start in attacking the overall problem. . . . I share the CNO's concern about interpretation of the force variations."

July 8, 1966: The Vice Chief of Naval Operations forwards a report of CYCLOPS III ASW study to the Secretary of the Navy stating that: "The study makes a substantial contribution to our understanding of the ASW problem of overseas transport." He also states: "CYCLOPS III does not provide data to assist in judgments on force levels."

August 3, 1966: The Secretary of the Navy forwards the report of CYCLOPS III to the Secretary of Defense stating that he generally agrees with VCNO's comments and that: "I believe that it makes a useful contribution to our understanding of the ASW problems of overseas transport."[3]

As this series of quotations from the official correspondence between the Secretary of Defense and the Secretary of the Navy indicates, the Navy was indeed caught in the dilemma of wanting to believe the very high performance figures credited to its new systems when defending R&D programs, but not wanting to accept the implications of these beliefs when arguing for more forces. The studies, in effect, were forcing the Navy to face up to this dilemma by putting the performance claims and the force levels together in the same set of calculations. This was and still is a serious problem. In fact, by the end of 1968, the Navy did not have an authoritative set of performance factors for its weapon systems; that is, a set of performance factors that its leaders agreed were realistic, reliable estimates for use in deciding on R&D programs and making judgments on force levels.

If this were the situation in all military areas, rational defense planning would be impossible. Consider what would happen, for example, if there were no accepted performance factors for strategic offensive systems. Suppose that the Secretary of Defense wanted to be able to destroy a Soviet ICBM site: he would, of course, ask the Air Force what it would take to do the job. Suppose, hypothetically, that the Air Force replied that one Minuteman missile costing $10 million would have a 0.7 single-shot kill probability (SSPk) against such a site. (The actual numbers depend on the particular model of Minuteman and the specific target.) How many Minuteman missiles should be bought for this job? There is no calculation that will answer this, no "optimum," no unique "point of diminishing returns"; a judgment has to be made.

One might argue that two missiles would be a good number, based on the following process of thought: (1) Two missiles give a 0.91 chance of killing the target, and that looks like enough. (2) The second missile adds 0.21 to the total kill probability, and that's worth $10 million; a third missile would add about 0.06 and that's not worth $10 million (diminishing marginal utility). (3) A 2 to 1 edge over the Soviets can be maintained; a 3 to 1 edge can't, if they decide to deny it to us (Soviet reaction). All three factors are important; a sensible judgment on requirements cannot be based on the achievement of a 0.91 kill probability alone. (Of course, numerous other factors, including the purpose for killing the target in the first place, are also relevant. But they need not enter this example.) Now suppose the Air Force said: "Oh, no, Mr. Secretary, that 0.7 SSPk factor wasn't realistic. That's just what we thought when we were selling the development of the Minuteman system to the Director of Defense Research and Engineering, or what we used when we made our study to show that the Air Force's Minuteman is better than the Navy's Polaris. But it's not a realistic figure for force level determination. For that purpose, the realistic SSPk factor is 0.3. Therefore, to get your 0.91 kill probability, you need seven missiles, not two. Two missiles will only get you a 0.51 kill probability, and that's not enough."

Before accepting that argument, the Secretary might want to raise some other questions. For example, are there other ways of meeting the broader purpose that destruction of the missile site was intended to serve? After all, there is nothing absolute about the requirement for a 0.91 kill probability; it may be worth $20 million, but not $70 million. Moreover, at what point does the cost of the next missile outweigh the benefit it adds? If the SSPk is 0.3, the second missile adds 0.21 to the total kill probability; the third, 0.15; the fourth, 0.10; the fifth, 0.07; the sixth, 0.05; and the seventh, 0.04. It might appear that the third and fourth missiles—not to mention the fifth and sixth—do not add enough to justify their cost. If the SSPk is 0.3 and the objective of 0.91 implies a 7 to 1 edge over the Soviets, can this be maintained if they decide to deny it to us? It is obvious that the cost leverage would be very favorable to them if they did not want us to have this ratio and we persisted in trying to achieve it. Finally, would we get more for our money by buying five extra missiles than by spending it on R&D to push the SSPk back up to 0.7 or higher?

What is the relevance of this hypothetical example to ASW force levels? It illustrates, in a nutshell, why, as of the end of 1968, the Secretary of Defense had neither an agreement with the Navy on ASW force levels nor an "agreement to disagree" (a mutual understanding of the judgments leading to the disagreement).

Still there had been a sharpening of the major issues. The uncertainties to which the outcome of an antisubmarine campaign is sensitive had been well defined. The likelihood that the marginal utility of more forces would be low had been demonstrated repeatedly by the Navy's own studies. The importance of maintaining U.S. technological superiority had been made clear. All of these strongly suggested—but unfortunately did not prove—the Systems Analysis office's contention that if ASW forces needed to be improved, we would get more for our money by spending millions on R&D rather than billions on larger forces. If the kill probabilities of our weapon systems really are much lower than the Navy originally estimated them to be, we ought to work on raising them instead of buying more forces with low kill probabilities.

Strategic Mobility Forces

How many airlift aircraft does the United States need? How many Navy cargo ships? How many cargo ships in the commercial fleet? How many overseas bases? How much prepositioned or prestocked inventory of equipment in overseas locations? Where should it station its forces? How ready should these forces be? All these questions are interrelated elements of the same general problem. In 1961, each of these elements—the airlift, the sealift, the bases, the prepositioned equipment, the planned deployments, and the readiness—was the responsibility of a different group of people in the Defense Department. The elements were seen as separate and unrelated entities.

Yet formulating the problem in terms of an integrated whole was later to lead to several important analytical advances. Gradually all interested parties began to recognize that all these programs were, to a significant degree, alternative ways of achieving the same objective: deploying and supporting U.S. general-purpose forces. Even more important, we recognized that different systems may complement each other—that transport aircraft and ships working in tandem, for example, are more efficient than working alone.

It was not easy, however, to get comprehensive and accepted estimates of how many forces we wanted to move, where we wanted to move them, and how fast. Such estimates are necessary because the size, the cost, and the composition of our mobility posture depend on the answer. To move sizable forces rapidly to any of several possible contingency areas, the United States needs large numbers of expensive cargo aircraft and ships in a costly high-readiness posture. On the other hand, if we want to move our forces more slowly, are prepared to accept the greater risks, and are willing to give up some flexibility to achieve economies, we need a much less expensive force of aircraft, ships, and prepositioned equipment. The basic question is: Do we want to get there quickly and in larger numbers and pay the extra cost, or do we want to take our time, save money, and accept greater risks?

A series of landmark studies conducted in 1963 and 1964 under the leadership of the Chairman of the Joint Chiefs of Staff's Special Studies Group, working closely with the Systems Analysis office, addressed this question. The first of these studies looked at alternative deployment strategies for countering an enemy assault on any of several key theaters around the world, with particular emphasis on Europe, Korea, and Southeast Asia. In each case, it was assumed that the enemy attacked in full force and that our job was to defend and restore the *status quo ante*. To do this, the study compared three strategies, each requiring alternative speeds of deployment: (1) a "forward" strategy, emphasizing a capability to put fully equipped fighting men into action in a few days; (2) a "defensive" strategy, emphasizing only enough immediate capability to maintain a foothold; and (3) an "intermediate" strategy, emphasizing a capability somewhere between the first two. The forward strategy required what we now call rapid deployment; the defensive strategy, slow deployment; and the intermediate strategy, a medium rate of deployment.

This study confirmed a common-sense conclusion derived from World War II and Korean experience. During the first few months of each war, the enemy swept down quickly over a lot of territory, and American and allied forces had to spend many months painstakingly pushing him back. If we had been able to reinforce rapidly and stop the enemy before he captured this territory and dug in, we could probably have ended the war more quickly at less cost in lives and resources.

The reasons for this conclusion are fairly obvious. By rapidly deploying U.S. forces to reinforce allied indigenous forces, it is less likely that these forces will be destroyed or badly disorganized; thus, they can be more effective in pursuing the war. In addition, rapid deployments permit the launching of counterattacks before the enemy has a chance to consolidate and fortify his positions. In terms of the cost to fight a major conventional war, the forward strategy was estimated to save more than $10 billion over the defensive strategy. This suggests that a rapid-deployment capability is worth buying in large amounts.

As a result of these studies, it was generally accepted that there was very great value to having the ability to deploy forces rapidly to reinforce allied and U.S. forces in overseas theaters. It could mean shorter wars, fewer casualties to ourselves and our allies, less destruction of the attacked country, and a smaller total force requirement. This conclusion was expressed numerically in the form of tables such as Table 13, showing the desired deployment objectives in each theater of interest versus time (where "D" is the date of the initial enemy attack):

Table 13. Hypothetical Mobility Planning Objectives for Country X

Closure Time (days)	Rapid Deployment		Medium Deployment		Slow Deployment	
	Division Forces	Tactical Air Squadrons	Division Forces	Tactical Air Squadrons	Division Forces	Tactical Air Squadrons
D+10	1	15	⅓	10	⅓	10
20	3	30	⅔	25	⅔	10
30	5	40	1⅓	30	1	15
60	7	45	4	30	1⅔	20

Through the joint efforts of the Services, the JCS, and the Systems Analysis office, a mathematical representation of the situation—a model—was developed which, by 1968, tied together some 3,000 separate factors relating to the cost, capabilities, and limitations of each major component of U.S. mobility forces. With this model, we could perform a number of useful calculations. For example, we could calculate the combination of ships, aircraft, and inventories of Army equipment prestocked in overseas locations which would enable the United States to meet any of these deployment objectives at the least total system cost. This calculation was made repeatedly, using many different sets of assumptions about types of forces, deployment objectives, readiness, and the like. In this way, all interested parties were able to compare systematically the total cost of achieving successively faster (or slower) movements with JCS estimates of the military advantages (or disadvantages) accruing to these strategies. On the basis of these calculations, the responsible defense officials then reached judgments as to the combination of ships and aircraft and prepositioned equipment which the United States should have.

Several years of analyses of this kind suggested that a balanced mix of airlift, sealift, and equipment prepositioning to meet U.S. deployment objectives consisted of six C-5A squadrons, 14 C-141 squadrons, and 30 Fast-Deployment Logistic Ships (FDL's); prepositioned equipment in Europe and the Pacific; a Civil Reserve Air Fleet; and 460 commercial general-cargo ships.[4] Such a posture would provide the capability of simultaneously reinforcing allied forces in Europe and rapidly deploying U.S. general-purpose forces to counter a major conventional attack in Asia, as well as meeting a minor contingency in the Western Hemisphere. Again, these force levels were reached only after a lengthy examination of many alternative ways of achieving U.S. objectives and a careful comparison of their costs. Each major component of the program was carefully studied in the context of total mobility requirements and costs.

Another set of calculations using this model concerned the most effective use of any given set of resources. That is, assuming a certain fleet of ships and aircraft, certain readiness standards, and a certain deployment schedule around the world, we could calculate the best operational strategy. By such calculations, we determined the most efficient way to use these forces in a given situation. Under some circumstances, we found that it would be best to operate the FDL's and the C-5A's in tandem; that is, to have the FDL's carry the matériel by sea to ports and then have the C-5A's, operating within the theater, fly it from the ports to the combat zone. In other situations, it would be best to operate the two systems independently, or in combination with other mobility forces.

As the model grew more refined, we used it to calculate the possible effect on U.S. total world-wide rapid-deployment capability of deleting an overseas base, or set of bases. Such contingency analysis can, of course, be very important. For example, the status of Okinawa has been in question. When it reverts fully to Japan, we may well be able to use it as a military base on the same terms as our military bases in Japan; but under some circumstances we may not. Okinawa has a number of military uses, of course, but one of its main ones is as a logistic installation for the deployment and support of U.S. forces in Asia. However, it could be released from this role if we were to maintain a larger number of ships and aircraft and inventories, or to use other bases. The strategic mobility model enabled us to calculate what it would cost to meet our rapid-deployment objectives or our total logistic needs if access to Okinawa were denied.

Once the requirements and forces for a U.S. strategic mobility posture had been determined, the final step in the analysis was to tie together deployment capability and force readiness. There is no point in being able to deploy, say, eight Army divisions within a month or in buying the ships and aircraft and inventories that enable us to move eight divisions within a month, if, in fact, they are not ready to move. Alternatively, there is no point in keeping the manpower, training, and other readiness factors in the Army divisions at a high state if, in turn, we lack the resources to move them. There is an intimate relationship between the readiness of the forces to move and the capability of moving them. The importance of this relationship led us into a detailed analysis of the readiness of U.S. land and tactical air forces. This analysis was tied in with an important management information system for the Secretary of Defense: a monthly report on the readiness of all active and reserve units. These readiness reports were then used in the continuous updating of the strategic mobility calculations.

During the past few years, a combination of factors seems to have put the need for rapid deployment and the systems that would provide it under a cloud. Disenchantment with the Vietnam war has led to a growth in isolationist sentiment. In addition to the opposition of powerful maritime industry and labor interests, the FDL program ran into opposition from certain Congressmen who feared that it would only provide the United States with more capability to act as the world's policeman and thus increase the possibility of our getting involved in more "Vietnams." Counterarguments were, first, that having an efficient capability should be separated from the question of political wisdom about when to use it; and, second, that as long as the United States adheres to a policy of fulfilling its treaty commitments, it should do so with minimum risks and minimum costs in lives. But these arguments proved insufficiently persuasive. As a consequence, the FDL program did not receive the necessary appropriations from the Congress.

For a number of reasons, mainly a 60 percent cost overrun, the giant C-5A cargo aircraft has become a dirty word, a lightning rod for many pent-up resentments. Those who dislike the McNamara management controls, and want a return to a more informal and less controlled environment are using the C-5A as an example of the evils of "total package procurement."[5] Those who want to attack the military, their Congressional supporters, and the military-industrial complex use it as "yet another example of Pentagon waste and mismanagement." Still others use it for partisan advantages.

We are not going to defend cost overruns. We are already defending enough unpopular causes. The costs of the C-5A were underestimated by the Systems Analysis office, the Air Force, and others. It was an honest mistake; nobody in the Pentagon needed to underestimate the costs of the program to get it approved. Nor can we plead that the problems that arose in the contracting and management of the development program, which were the responsibilities of the Air Force, have no implications for the wisdom of going ahead with the program in the first place—a position actively supported by the Systems Analysis office. But before overreacting to the cost overrun and concluding that the program itself is not a good one, some reflection should be given to three relevant points.

First, cost overruns of 60 percent or more are not unique to the Defense Department. Other organizations also experience cost overruns, as many people who have built a home, many universities that have built medical centers, and utility companies that have built nuclear power plants can testify.

Second, a cost increase of 60 percent would be a highly successful program by pre-1961 Defense Department standards. As noted in Chapter 1, studies done at The Rand Corporation and at the Harvard Business School found that, during the 1950's, the typical weapon system ended up costing 200 to 300 percent more than originally estimated, and some cost even more. As one study put it: "Cost increases on the order of 200 percent to 300 percent and extensions of development time by ⅓ to ½ are not the exception, but the rule."[6] Viewed against this background, a 60 percent overrun represents a

substantial improvement. Total package procurement and other procurement techniques introduced by McNamara did not eliminate cost
overruns; far from it. They did, however, substantially reduce them;
and they did give them a clear visibilty that they did not have before.
If it had not been for techniques like total package procurement,
nobody would have been able to document an overrun on the C-5A
because there wouldn't have been a firm agreed point of departure.
McNamara's innovations in this field were an important step in the
right direction; they should be extended and improved upon, not
abandoned.

Third, an excess of actual cost over contract target cost is not the
same thing as an excess of actual cost over what the program should
cost or over what it is worth. For one thing, competition for the
contract often drives the contractors to bid on the basis of a target
cost that is below what they actually expect the cost to be. This
squeezes their profit margins. Ironically, in most circumstances—and
to a great extent in this one too—that is just what competition is
supposed to do for the taxpayers. The objection comes in weapons
procurement when the contractors and the Services work together to
introduce changes that raise the target cost to a realistic level and let
the contractor off the hook. This is a tough problem to control; some
of the changes do improve the product, some are justified, some are
desirable but not necessary. The C-5A contract was an attempt to
control this, and it contained ingenious provisions for this purpose.
As it turned out, apparently it also contained a provision that would
let the contractor recoup any losses on the second lot of aircraft that
he had suffered on the first lot—contrary to one of the main ideas of
total package procurement, and unknown to the Secretary of Defense.

We do not know what the actual cost of the C-5A should have
been. Because of the competitive factor described above, probably it
was higher than the contract target cost. But we do know that even at
the higher cost, the C-5A still results in a substantial reduction in the
cost of airlift capability. The cost per ton-mile of airlift capability is
still lower with the C-5A than with any other cargo aircraft. In other
words, the C-5A is not an example of cost escalation without a
commensurate increase in effectiveness—one of the most serious
problems in the defense business.

The need for systems such as the FDL and the C-5A was thoroughly analyzed and carefully thought out, and the design of each was carefully matched to the mission. The plans for them were part of an over-all strategic mobility plan that systematically tied together the theaters to be defended, the forces to be moved, the timetables on which they would move, readiness objectives, and all the complementary and alternative means of strategic mobility. These systems appeared then, as they do now, as necessary and economical parts of a sensible over-all strategic mobility posture that the United States ought to have. Whether we prefer it or not, a peaceful world order does depend in substantial part on the United States' having large military forces ready and able to oppose aggression in many parts of the world. It is true that our allies ought to do more and that we ought to persuade them to do more, but much of our persuasiveness depends on our doing *our* part.

In this regard, a good rapid-deployment capability is preferable to keeping large forces overseas. It certainly is better for the U.S. balance of payments if the forces are kept here. Also, the costs are generally less, and we get more flexibility. The same division that can be ready to go to Korea in a week can also be ready to go to Europe in a week. Thus, in an important sense, we realize better world-wide coverage by having the division here and deployable. If the division is stationed in an overseas theater, it is, in practical and political terms, tied to that theater, even though in theory it is available for use elsewhere. The inability to use the two U.S. divisions stationed in Korea for the Vietnam war is the most recent example of this problem. Also, psychologically it is better not to station large forces overseas, since the U.S. presence contributes to the feeling on the part of our allies that their security is mainly our business. Finally, we hark back to the original rationale of our studies and to World War I, World War II, and Korean war experience. Whether one believes we should do it or not, it is highly probable that if one of our allies were attacked we would go to its defense. If we had a good rapid-deployment capability, we could do so much more effectively. And if the enemy knew that we had such a capability in readiness, he would be more likely to be deterred from launching such an attack. It has taken years of painstaking analysis to define, in terms of force size and mix, what such a capability should be. Now that it has been so defined, we think that it can be defended as being in the national interest and as an economical posture for meeting our commitments.

Only a First Step

As the first OSD organization explicitly charged with the job of analyzing force requirements, the Systems Analysis office worked over the years to develop rational ways of determining military needs. It is obvious from the preceding discussion that the office was far from totally successful, especially in some key areas of general-purpose forces. Considerable work remains to be done in land forces; naval escort, replenishment, and amphibious assault forces; theater nuclear forces; logistic and support forces; as well as the areas discussed above. We badly need more publicly defensible yardsticks of sufficiency and more public insistence that they be used as the basis for designing and measuring the adequacy of major defense programs. Nevertheless, enough analytical progress was made between 1961 and 1969 that extreme views—such as deciding requirements solely on the basis of authority or deciding them on the basis of predetermined and arbitrary budget ceilings—are no longer being heard so frequently. Moreover, while the office did not succeed in developing adequate yardsticks of sufficiency for each major defense area, it did lay some important groundwork for future efforts. Finally, and more importantly, it helped prove repeatedly the utility of analysis as an aid to judgment.

CHAPTER

7

Three Controversial
Program Decisions

The B-70 Bomber

In Chapter 2, we discussed the fundamental idea behind the Planning-Programming-Budgeting System (PPBS) as it was used in the
Defense Department: to define explicitly, where possible, the national
interest in defense programs and to insist that the national interest
take precedence over local or institutional interests. Assured destruction and damage limiting are excellent examples of explicit criteria of
the national interest which have been publicly stated and used as a
measure of what defense planners have been trying to accomplish in
the design of strategic forces. While recognizing the many qualitative
factors that also must be considered, we believe that it is important to
develop and use, where possible, such explicit criteria of the national
interest in making major defense program decisions. The first prominent casualty of this management approach was the Air Force's
proposed B-70 bomber.

The development of the B-70 (or RS-70, as it was later called)
was one of the first issues McNamara had to face. The specific point
in question was not the future of manned strategic aircraft; rather, it
was whether this particular aircraft, in any of its configurations, could

add enough to already programmed capabilities to make it worth its very high cost. While we doubt that any responsible military or civilian official would now say that the United States should have gone ahead with the B-70 program, at the time it precipitated a major fight so intense as to lead to a constitutional crisis.

The purpose of the B-70 was to replace the B-52 as the principal U.S. bomber. It was designed to fly at 2,000 miles an hour at an altitude of 70,000 feet and to drop nuclear bombs on predesignated targets. In conception, the B-70 was really little more than a manned missile, as attested to by the fact that a book about it was published under this precise title. The B-70 system offered none of the advantages of flexibility often attributed to manned bombers in the rhetoric of the bomber advocates. Because of its high speed and altitude, it could not look for new targets; nor could it find and attack mobile targets or targets of uncertain location. It offered no capability beyond preplanned attacks against previously identified and located targets—a mission that could be more effectively performed by missiles.

Moreover, the B-70 had important disadvantages when compared with ballistic missiles. It would have required from two to three hours to reach most targets; a missile would require only 15 to 30 minutes. On the ground, it would have been much more vulnerable if a surprise missile attack caught it at its base. It would not have been dispersed in underground silos like Minuteman, or kept continuously mobile and concealed like Polaris. It would have had to depend instead on warning and ground-alert response for survival—a method of protection far less reliable, for example, than submarines.

In answer to these arguments, Air Force leaders claimed that the B-70, like other manned bombers, could be launched subject to positive control (that is, could be recalled after launch) in response to warning—a property not possessed by missiles. But this property was not the important point; rather, it was that the B-70 would *have* to be launched on warning because it would be vulnerable and could not ride out an attack. By contrast, it is not critical that Polaris missiles be launched subject to positive control, because our national leaders are under no compulsion to launch them until the point of a final decision.

Air Force leaders also argued that the B-70, and later the RS-70, could be maintained on a very high state of ground alert in a widely dispersed posture. Indeed, claims were made that as many as two-thirds or three-fourths of the aircraft could be maintained on a three-minute ground alert. Yet nothing like such a posture could have been achieved at the time for the B-52, and there was good reason to believe that the problems that effectively prevented such a posture for the B-52 would have been more serious for the B-70. Moreover, the size of the Soviet ICBM force and the prospect of MIRV makes it clear (or the small cost of an ICBM compared with an air base should make it so) that the U.S. bomber force cannot be dispersed to enough bases to make dispersal an effective long-run solution to the bomber vulnerability problem.

Finally, the B-70 was poorly designed to penetrate the enemy defenses of the late 1960's and 1970's. Its design for high speed at high altitude might have been good for outrunning enemy interceptor aircraft, but against surface-to-air missile defenses it was clearly the wrong way to go. For years, studies had shown that the best way to penetrate enemy defenses was to fly at low altitudes *under* the reach of the enemy's radars, and this was reflected in Strategic Air Command (SAC) practice at the time. Moreover, the B-70 had a large radar cross section, making the job of effective jamming difficult; and it would have emitted large amounts of infrared radiation, making it easily detectable.

In short, missiles were better than the B-70. They could be made to be less vulnerable; they could destroy their targets more quickly, they could deliver their warheads with comparable accuracy; and they would cost much less to do the same job, regardless of what it was. They were even less technically complex than the B-70. For these reasons, the B-70 program was killed.

Even before the official demise of the program, however, the Air Force had shifted its B-70 proposal from a bomber configuration to a "reconnaissance-strike" configuration—the RS-70—thus implicitly admitting the correctness of some of the arguments above. The RS-70 claimed two capabilities not possessed by the B-70: reconnaissance during and after a missile attack and reconnaissance strike or the ability to examine targets and attack them with air-to-surface missiles if desired. This would be a way of attacking any Soviet nuclear delivery sites remaining after a U.S. missile attack, or after the Soviets had launched most of their forces, if the war began with a Soviet first strike.

The advantage of having a strike capability in a reconnaissance aircraft was timeliness. If the reconnaissance data could be processed and interpreted rapidly enough, effective strikes could be made immediately against the targets. Thus, targets could be attacked within a few minutes after being reconnoitered, as compared with times approaching an hour (or more) if the strikes were made by ICBM's. Quick attack is not always important; but in cases where it is, and where it can be accomplished, having a strike capability in the reconnaissance aircraft appeared to be an advantage.

But just how urgent was the military requirement for such reconnaissance strikes? The Air Force contended that there were many situations where such a strike capability would be of significant value. But as General Maxwell Taylor argued at the time: "Is it worth several billion dollars of national resources to be able to overfly Soviet targets with a few score of manned bombers looking for residual weapons capable of inflicting additional damage on the U.S. after each country, the United States and the USSR, has already exchanged several thousand megatons of nuclear firepower on their respective target systems?"

If the strike missile were in the reconnaissance aircraft, postattack reconnaissance and subsequent strike by air-to-surface missiles might be used against three categories of targets:

1. Fixed bases of known location.
2. Fixed bases of imprecisely known location.
3. Mobile launchers.

Analysis showed that either missiles or the RS-70 could effectively attack targets in the first category, but that missiles had the important advantages of shorter time to target, lower cost, and higher survival potential. The only particular advantage claimed for the RS-70 against these targets was in the "mopping up" operation after a missile attack. However, since, with planned capabilities, we already would be able to set damage probabilities against such targets as high as desired by a combination of missiles, indirect bomb-damage-assessment techniques, and postattack aircraft reconnaissance, it was not clear that the RS-70 would be needed for mop-up operations. The required damage probability would have to be inordinately high—

much higher than the level then set by the JCS—before the RS-70 would become a cheaper way to increase it. Thus, in this mission, the RS-70 would be assigned to squeeze out, at very great cost, the last surviving Soviet bases and missile sites of a particular kind (known and fixed, with missiles not yet launched).

By the early 1970's, the number of targets in the second category —fixed bases of imprecisely known location—would be very small, perhaps nonexistent. And, to the extent desired, these targets could be attacked by ICBM's after postattack reconnaissance by purely reconnaissance aircraft (such as the SR-71). The only potential advantage of the RS-70 would have been in attacking some of these targets sooner. To make this potential advantage actual, however, would have required solving some difficult technical problems. The key question was whether the RS-70 crew would be able to gather and process data rapidly enough to fire the air-to-surface missile before the aircraft, flying at 30 miles a minute, moved out of missile range. Achievement of the ability to "recognize" or to analyze damage on important types of targets was beyond any known technique at the time. As McNamara pointed out:

Picture the RS-70 flying at 70,000 feet and moving at 2,000 miles per hour. The proposed mission would require the gathering of radar reconnaissance data on the presence of new targets—or known targets which may not have been destroyed or neutralized, and the prompt processing and analysis of these data in flight. The proposed radar, moving with the aircraft at 2,000 miles per hour, would be seeing new areas at the rate of 100,000 square miles per hour or 750 million square feet per second. We cannot state today with any assurance that satisfactory equipment to perform this processing and display function in an RS-70 can be made operational by 1970, let alone by 1967, on the basis of any known technology, or whether the human interpretation job required of the operation can ever be done.[1]

Even if all these technical problems could have been overcome, it was doubtful that this capability would provide any meaningful increase in effectiveness. Such targets could always be programmed for reattack by ICBM's, and the time lag for this type of attack (as compared with attack by air-to-surface missiles) was not significant in the context of the over-all results of a nuclear exchange. Generally, for time-urgent targets the critical period is the first hour. A difference of 60 minutes could make a great deal of difference at the beginning of a war. Put another way, the time interval between three hours and four hours is less critical than that between zero hours and one hour. (It would be three hours before the RS-70 could be over a target.) Further, by attacking these targets with ICBM's, the decision as to whether a reattack was necessary could be made with more data than would be available to the RS-70 crew and with more time to assimilate and analyze those data.

The third category of targets—mobile launchers (including submarines)—could be expected to be extensive. The same means that the United States was using to achieve a secure, protected retaliatory force able to survive any Soviet attack and still strike back were also available to the Soviets. These included mobile weapon systems (sea and land) and effectively concealed systems. The Soviets already had a submarine-launched ballistic missile (SLBM) force, which, if unopposed, would have permitted the launching of nearly 100 missiles against the continental United States; and intelligence projections indicated that a substantial Soviet build-up in that force was to be expected.

The RS-70, as a general rule, could not locate, identify, and strike previously unknown targets, once a nuclear war had begun. Its effectiveness depended on good peacetime intelligence; if this was not available, the prospects for wartime recognition of new targets were poor. Thus, attacking mobile targets simply could not be accomplished with an RS-70, and in fact the Air Force did not propose such a role for it.

The only particular advantage of the RS-70, then, would have been its ability to mop up after an initial missile attack. But, we have seen, this ability appeared to mean very little. More detailed analysis confirmed this point. Assuming that the Soviets struck first in a countermilitary attack using 90 percent of their ICBM force, using the maximum number of bombers that could reach the United States, and using one-half of their SLBM's, they could at that time have killed between 30 and 100 million Americans, depending on the condition of U.S. civil defenses. (The higher amount assumed that there was no civil defense; the lower, that the administration's civil defense program was carried out.) If the remaining 10 percent of Soviet ICBM's and the remaining half of the deployed SLBM's were used in an attack on U.S. cities, the estimated number of American deaths would have been between 80 and 150 million, again depending on the amount of civil defense. Even if the United States succeeded in destroying all the remaining ICBM's so that only the Soviet SLBM's were available for the countercity attacks, the U.S. dead would still have numbered between 70 and 135 million.

Alternatively, assuming that the United States struck first and destroyed 90 percent of the Soviets' ICBM's and all their bombers and that the Soviets retaliated against U.S. cities with the surviving 10 percent of their ICBM's and all their available SLBM's, Systems Analysis' studies showed that between 60 and 90 million Americans would be killed. Even if the United States successfully destroyed *all* Soviet ICBM's before they could be launched, the SLBM's alone would be able to kill between 45 and 75 million Americans.

These calculations were, to be sure, very rough—based on approximations and on uncertain assumptions. (At that time, there had not yet been developed any agreed numerical representations of the outcome of a nuclear war under various assumptions.) Nevertheless, they strongly suggested that, for practically any reasonably plausible set of circumstances and assumptions, the value of a mop-up capability was not likely to be very great.

The cost to complete the RS-70 program was then estimated to be at least $10 billion (excluding the cost of the required tankers and the annual operating costs), in addition to the $1.35 billion that had already been approved. In actuality, the cost would probably have been considerably more than $15 billion. Yet only a small increase in over-all capability would be achieved—reducing the time interval between "reconnaissance" and "strike"—by placing air-to-surface missiles in the reconnaissance aircraft. It was McNamara's judgment that this increase was not worth the large costs required to achieve it, and so the RS-70 program was also terminated.

The B-70/RS-70 decisions illustrate several important points. Most significant perhaps is the fact that few people today would claim that we should have gone ahead with either program. Nearly everyone now agrees that to have done so would have been a terrible waste, that the B-70/RS-70 would have been the wrong plane at the wrong time.

The B-70/RS-70 story also illustrates a common error in requirements planning; that is, basing new weapon system requirements on the simple extrapolation of such characteristics as altitude, speed, and range, in the belief that progress always means going higher, faster, and farther. This represents a failure to grasp and respond to the implications of new and different situations (a failure, of course, not confined to weapons planning). In particular, the B-70/RS-70 proposals failed to take account of the severe vulnerability of the bombers on the ground, once the enemy had ICBM's. They failed to take account of new Soviet surface-to-air missiles. They ignored the fact that by flying high and fast, penetrating bombers only helped solve the enemy's detection and tracking problem. These proposals tried, at enormous cost, to achieve a high speed to target that could be achieved more easily and at much less cost with missiles.

In this respect, at least, the B-70/RS-70 controversy did result in progress. Air Force bomber proposals since then, including the current AMSA proposal, have been very different from the B-70 proposal. Although they still do not solve the critically important problem of vulnerability on the ground to Soviet ICBM/MIRV and submarine-launched missile attacks, they do emphasize development of an aircraft with flexibility and good low-altitude capability. Aircraft speed is no longer treated as if it were the only decisive military characteristic. It is much more important for manned aircraft today to go in at low altitudes, to carry good penetration aids, including electronic countermeasures, and to carry a good standoff missile. The point is that such weapon system characteristics as speed and altitude have to be related to pay-off—to target destruction. Thus, the B-70/RS-70 story also shows the importance of analysis as a way of revealing the implications of changing technology for weapon systems.

Finally, the experience with the B-70/RS-70 proposals indicates the value of having civilians participate in force planning. The Air Force, led by General LeMay, pushed the B-70 and then the RS-70 programs with all the political force they could muster. The Senate, in fact, was so oversold on the need for the RS-70 by the Air Force that it voted 99 to 1 to proceed with its development over the Secretary of Defense's objection. It was also largely Air Force testimony that almost provoked a constitutional crisis when Representative Carl Vinson, then Chairman of the powerful House Armed Services Committee, proposed a resolution that would have ordered the Secretary of the Air Force to go ahead with full-scale development of the

RS-70. But the simple truth is that a great general and a leading military expert can be wrong, like experts in any other field. LeMay's judgments were based on assumptions that had been valid in the past, but were not valid for the future. The Air Force studies sent to the Secretary of Defense in support of the B-70/RS-70 proposals were filled with biased assumptions and exaggerated claims. Although many individual Air Force officers recognized the shortcomings of the B-70/RS-70 and privately expressed their reservations, it would have cost an officer his career to speak out, even within the confines of the Defense Department, against the views of his Chief of Staff. The B-70/RS-70 programs were pushed on the basis of meeting alleged military requirements, but these requirements could not be logically justified. Without analysis and review from an independent source, serious objections would probably not have been raised. Even in the face of the arguments above, the leaders of the Air Force persisted, noting in their last official correspondence to Secretary McNamara regarding the RS-70 that "the RS-70 development program promises a useful and versatile weapon system which will meet an essential military requirement of the 1968–1975 time period that can be met by no other weapon system."

Skybolt

Like the B-70/RS-70 decisions, the cancellation of the Skybolt missile program was a controversial decision at the time, made even more so because of the British interest in the program. Yet at the time the decision was made, it had become apparent that this very complex weapon system could not be completed within the cost estimates or the time limits that had been projected when the program was begun. It was also clear that Skybolt was as much a way to keep the Air Force's manned bombers usefully employed as a way to improve the U.S. deterrent. For these reasons, and because of the availability of proven alternative weapon systems, the Skybolt program was canceled. Within a year, practically everybody agreed that the Secretary of Defense had made the right decision and that Skybolt would not have been a good weapon system. Subsequent controversy centered on the diplomatic handling of the problem with the British, not on the substantive merits of the decision.

Skybolt was an air-launched ballistic missile system designed for a range of 1,000 nautical miles. Four Skybolt missiles were to be carried on each B-52 bomber. Except for its launch platform, there was no basic difference between Skybolt and any other ballistic missile system. Once launched, it would have been irrevocably committed. It would not have created a new and distinct defense problem for the Soviet Union, which was already confronted with the possibility of bombardment from many angles by Polaris, Minuteman, and other U.S. missile systems.

The nature of Skybolt's launch platform made it a more complex and hence more costly and inherently less reliable weapon than any we had developed until that time; it also made Skybolt a less versatile weapon. With respect to the versatility of competing systems (a point that will be dealt with below), it should be understood that, for operational purposes, primary strategic targets in the Soviet Union can be divided into three categories: (1) strategic threat targets (where quick destruction is essential); (2) other military targets (where time is a secondary consideration); and (3) cities (where an ability to hold them hostage is important). Of course, there are also other, less important targets, such as air defenses, which do not threaten the United States but must be suppressed to enable U.S. bombers to reach their primary targets.

Skybolt would not have been useful against targets in the first or third categories—against high-priority military targets or cities—and it would have been a less efficient weapon against targets in the second category—military targets of lesser urgency. On the other hand, the two systems already available, Minuteman and Polaris, that would form the principal part of the U.S. ballistic missile force from that time (1962) well into the 1970's, were more effective against targets in all categories.

It was the complexity of the Skybolt system which accounted for its high cost and lower reliability. The Skybolt missile was, in many ways, the most complex ballistic missile system ever to have been undertaken by the United States. It was to be launched not only from a moving platform, as Polaris is, but from a platform moving at a very high speed. It was not to be confined to a comparatively narrow range of launch "altitudes," as Polaris is, but was to be launched over an altitude range of thousands of feet. The missile itself would have been exposed to a great variety of rapidly changing environmental conditions. For example, it would have been subjected to shock, vibration, and noise environments far more severe than those in which any other ballistic missile had had to operate. Finally, the missile would have had to be integrated with the mother airplane in an entirely new way. Such a combination of difficult requirements was unique to the Skybolt concept.

Skybolt had originated in January 1959, when the Air Force issued a general operational requirement specifying the need for an air-launched ballistic missile of very advanced capabilities. The missile was to have a range of 1,000 nautical miles, 85 percent reliability, and an accuracy of about half a nautical mile. The Air Force estimated that R&D costs would be approximately $184 million, that the procurement of 1,000 missiles would cost $679 million, and that the missile would be operational not later than 1964.

During the spring of 1959, the Director of Defense Research and Engineering established an advisory committee, the Fletcher Committee, to assist in evaluating the proposed development program. By the fall of 1959, the Fletcher Committee, having reviewed Air Force and contractor plans, concluded that the system was excessively complex and that the time schedule for development was unrealistic. It recommended discontinuing the effort altogether. The recommendation was not followed. A total of $6 million was spent to finance exploratory investigations during the last nine months of 1959.

By January 1960, plans for Skybolt were extensively altered. For example, the accuracy requirement was relaxed considerably. The missile configuration was also greatly simplified, and the time schedules for development were stretched out by approximately six months. Despite these changes, the Fletcher Committee still reported serious concern about the technical complexity of the missile and predicted that the costs for both R&D and procurement would treble, while further slippages in the program schedules could be expected. Nevertheless, in February 1960 the revised Air Force plan for the development of Skybolt was approved.

The Skybolt program was then continued despite serious doubts regarding the growing vulnerability of U.S. bomber forces to missile attacks. At the time the Skybolt development plan was approved, the Atlas ICBM had been under development for nearly five and a half years, but the operational ballistic missile capability of the United

States consisted only of a single Atlas missile and a training squadron at Vandenberg Air Force Base. The second-generation Titan missile, the first to be deployed in hardened underground silos, was not scheduled for first deployment until mid-1961. The Polaris system had been under development for only three years, and it was not scheduled for deployment until the latter part of 1961. At that time, no more than approximately a dozen missiles of an operational configuration had been launched by the United States. Thus, even though the success of Skybolt seemed less assured than the success of other missile systems, its development was pushed on the basis that it provided additional "insurance."

In the meantime, it was known that the Soviet Union had made great progress in missile development. The Soviets were believed to have a small number of long-range missiles already operational, and intelligence estimates predicted Soviet deployment of a substantial number of ICBM's by the middle 1960's. These menacing facts and predictions, coupled with uncertainty over the ultimate success of the U.S. missile systems still in the development stage, further convinced defense officials that Skybolt development should be initiated to provide added insurance for the nation's deterrent force.

Expenditures and project costs rose quickly after inauguration of the program. Within six months, the Air Force requested an additional $70 million for fiscal 1961, though only a month earlier an initial $80 million had been apportioned for the same period in conformity with the approved plan. At about the same time, another independent scientific advisory group reviewed the project in detail, commented on its great technical difficulties, and recommended, like its predecessors, that serious consideration be given to its immediate cancellation. In the face of these difficulties—sharply mounting costs, increasing technical complexities, and additional recommendations against continuing the program—cancellation was seriously considered during the budget review in the latter part of 1960. The program was not canceled, however, and the $70 million that had been requested earlier was approved, although with the stipulation that the total $150 million would have to serve for both fiscal 1961 and 1962 program needs.

Early in 1961, Secretary McNamara reviewed the Skybolt project for the first time and ordered a special review by the Air Force. He concluded that the existing cost estimates were too low and that the program could not possibly achieve its objectives without a funding increase. However, because of the money spent to date, since the strategic situation was still highly uncertain, and since, even with its increased cost projections, Skybolt seemed competitive with other systems, he decided to continue it. A funding increase was authorized. Additional reviews of the Skybolt project were made from time to time after that. In September 1962, when additional problems were encountered in the program, Secretary McNamara visited the prime contractor, reviewed the program again, and approved a further upward revision on the grounds that cost estimates still made Skybolt competitive with other systems as a defense suppression weapon. It was recognized at that time, however, that Skybolt's ability to compete was becoming increasingly marginal and that if cost projections increased further and other systems were deployed successfully, continuation of the project would no longer be justified. McNamara made it clear that if the Air Force was not willing to assure him that the program would be satisfactorily completed on schedule at a total development cost of $492 million, he would reconsider his recommendation to the President.

Table 14 summarizes the changes that had occurred in Air Force cost estimates for Research, Development, Testing, and Evaluation (RDT&E) and for procurement. (Excluded are warhead costs in the hundreds of millions of dollars for 1,000 missiles.)

As the table shows, every aspect of program cost had increased two or three times over in the 34 months that had elapsed since initial approval. Moreover, it appeared probable at the time that the 1962 figures did not reflect still further increases that were likely to occur.

Table 14. Skybolt Cost Estimates

Date of Plan	RDT&E ($ Millions)	Investment ($ Millions)	Total RDT&E & Investment ($ Millions)	Total Number of Missiles
March 1960	214	679	893	1,000
June 1961	395	1,124	1,519	1,122
July 1961	395	1,259	1,654	1,319
December 1961	492.6	1,424	1,916.6	1,141
September 1962	492.6	1,771	2,263.6	1,077

Analysts in the Office of the Secretary of Defense were estimating the eventual program costs at over $3 billion.

Meanwhile, great changes had occurred in the development, production, and deployment of other strategic weapons. Before 1963, the entire Atlas program had been completed. All the Titan squadrons had been deployed, and the Titan II's would be in full operation before the end of 1963. The Polaris program had been further accelerated and was highly successful, with 9 sixteen-missile submarines already deployed and with a total of 41 submarines to be completed by mid-1967. The Hound Dog air-to-surface missile, which had gone into production just before Skybolt was approved, had been operational for two and one-half years. The Minuteman program had also been a success, with 20 missiles already operational and a full squadron of 50 to be operational by February 1963. Within a year, some 350 Minutemen would be deployed in hardened silos underground. More importantly, the survivability and reliability of these operational systems were high.

Throughout this same period (1959–1962), in contrast, major uncertainties regarding Skybolt continued unresolved—uncertainties relating to cost, to deployment dates, and to the effectiveness of the system when deployed. It became clear in December 1962 that funds additional to those estimated in September would be required to complete the development and to implement the planned procurement program. And there was nothing in the history of the Skybolt project to suggest that this was the end of its consistent pattern of rising costs. In all likelihood, the cost of R&D for Skybolt would not have stopped at the $492.6 million indicated in Table 14, but would have eventually reached at least $600 million—more than $150 million in excess of what had already been spent for RDT&E. The probability of R&D costs far in excess of the $492.6 million estimated by the Air Force was evidenced, for example, by the number of test firings completed by the end of 1962. Expenditures in 1962 were supposed to have permitted twenty-eight test flights. In fact, there were only six, though the over-all level of expenditures was as planned. Moreover, the total in-flight test time included in the Air Force cost estimates was only one-half to one-third of the in-flight test times necessary in the development of Hound Dog, a much less complex system.

Extensive deployment of the Skybolt, originally scheduled for 1964, was likely to be delayed until 1966. In addition to concern about the ultimate cost and the readiness date, there was uncertainty about the operational reliability of the Skybolt system. Among the principal problem areas were the guidance, data processing, and display systems. The Skybolt guidance system was by far the most complex and important component of the entire weapon system. Before the missile could be fired, it was necessary to know with considerable accuracy where it was at that instant, its heading, and its speed. A one-mile error in calculating the launch position would yield a one-mile error at the target. An error of one foot per second in measuring the aircraft velocity at the instant of launch—an error of approximately one-tenth of 1 percent of the aircraft speed—would result in an error at the target of approximately 1,000 feet at a range of 1,000 miles.

As mentioned earlier, there are three kinds of primary strategic targets: strategic threat targets of high time urgency, other military targets of lower time urgency, and cities. In addition to these, there are defense suppression targets. Minuteman, Titans I and II, Atlas F, and Polaris would all be effective against all four kinds of targets. All the land-based missiles could reach their targets in a matter of minutes; if "hardened"—buried, together with their control centers, in deep underground, reinforced silos—they could be made much less vulnerable to attack than Skybolt. Not one, but several enemy missiles, accurately directed, would be needed for a high confidence of destroying each of these U.S. missiles. Polaris had similar virtues.

Skybolt, however, could not have been used against high-priority nuclear threat targets, because it would have taken too long to get there (about eight hours from the time the B-52 left its base). By that time, follow-on launches of most of the Soviet missiles and bombers would have long been completed. Nor was Skybolt very suitable for programming against cities. The B-52's vulnerability on the ground required that it take off virtually at the outset of hostilities to avoid destruction. This meant that Skybolt would have to be committed, if at all, in the first hours of a war—perhaps before the President could determine whether an attack on Soviet cities would be advantageous to the United States. With respect to the second class of primary targets—the less time-urgent military targets, requiring neither the withholding option nor destruction by quick-reaction weapons—Skybolt suffered in comparison with the gravity bomb's larger warhead and greater accuracy.

Thus, the Skybolt system combined the disadvantages of the bomber with those of the missile. It shared the bomber's vulnerability on the ground and its slow over-all time to target; it had the poor accuracy and reliability and relatively low pay load of the missile. Therefore, it could qualify for inclusion in the strategic forces only if it were an inexpensive system for the defense suppression mission.

No one questioned at the time that a substantial defense suppression capability was required to get U.S. bombers through to their targets. The Soviets had spent large amounts for antibomber defenses. It was estimated that over 200 Soviet defense suppression targets would have to be destroyed to assure the penetration of U.S. manned bombers. These targets were completely vulnerable not only to ballistic missiles but also to Hound Dog, since neither the Soviet fighters nor their then widely deployed surface-to-air missile—the SA-2—was effective against Hound Dog approaching at low levels. There were, in fact, not enough productive defense suppression targets to occupy the entire alert force of Hound Dogs.

Nor was the total number of Soviet air defense targets which had to be destroyed to assure U.S. aircraft penetration expected to increase very substantially during the then current planning period of 1963–1968. It even appeared that there might be a net reduction in such targets, caused by an increasing Soviet allocation of funds to antimissile rather than to antibomber defense. However, Soviet air defense was being improved qualitatively by the deployment of a new surface-to-air missile, the SA-3, apparently designed to deal with the low-level threat. Capabilities of the SA-3 were not then known, but were believed to be marginal even against the Hound Dog. But even if the SA-3 was effective against the Hound Dogs and was widely deployed (an expensive proposition for the Soviets), the already programmed force would have been more than adequate to deal with that contingency. The number of Hound Dogs on alert status was scheduled to increase from 280 to approximately 400, and all of them could be assigned to defense suppression targets. This would have permitted multiple attacks against SA-3's. In addition, a certain portion of the missile force (the total force of approximately 2,000 projected for 1963–1968 had recently been increased by 100 Minutemen) would also be given defense suppression target options. The exact number allocated to this mission would, of course, have depended on the extent of Soviet antibomber defenses and on our own plans to use bombers, for which defense suppression would be required.

As far as could be foreseen at the time, these forces assured adequate destruction of all defense suppression targets, at a saving of at least $2 billion without Skybolt. Moreover, if intelligence information in later years were to indicate that these planned forces were inadequate, additional Minutemen could be procured, since facilities for rapidly expanded production of Minutemen already existed and the missile had been proven reliable by tests.

If Skybolt could have been completed within, or anywhere near, the cost estimates projected at the program's inception, it would have been an economical system for the limited strategic job of defense suppression. Unfortunately, Skybolt had priced itself out of the defense suppression market. And since, for reasons discussed earlier, it was relatively incompetent for the other necessary strategic jobs, there was no justification for its continued development. Thus, the program was canceled.

What conclusions can be drawn from the Skybolt story? First, it illustrates the importance of thinking through a weapon system before starting engineering development. Skybolt should never have been started. Even aside from the technical problems, it was conceptually a bad weapon system. Some weapon systems (for example, Polaris) are worth trying to develop, even though they involve substantial technical risks. But it should have been possible to know ahead of time that Skybolt was a bad idea, even if the enormous technical problems were overcome.

Second, Skybolt illustrates the importance of realistic cost estimates and the relevance of cost. Even if Skybolt had been worth while at $900 million, it certainly was not at $3 billion (the last estimate of OSD analysts before the program was canceled). Thus, the Skybolt development led to a great deal of waste and needless controversy and to political cost in the case of the British. If it had cost only $900 million to develop and procure, it might have paid its way as a defense suppression system. But, clearly, at the point where each alert Skybolt came to cost as much as an alert Minuteman (complete with blast-resistant silo), it was impossible to justify continuing the program. Realistic cost estimates are absolutely essential to good defense planning.

Third, Skybolt shows again the need for independent analytical staff assistance for the Secretary of Defense. Throughout the Skybolt development program, Air Force studies consistently claimed that Skybolt was not only a necessary but a "cost-effective" addition to our strategic arsenal. Memorandum after memorandum from the Secretary and the Chief of Staff of the Air Force pointed to the Skybolt as superior to other alternatives, such as the Hound Dog, Minuteman, and Polaris. According to their view, the B-52/Skybolt combination provided not the worst features of the bomber and the missile but the best: "the superior penetration capability of a ballistic missile with the inherent flexibility of the manned bomber, a combination which assures the highest degree of flexibility for our general war forces." Such beliefs, unfortunately, would not stand up under careful scrutiny and analysis.

It is unrealistic, perhaps, to expect that Air Force studies would have come to any other conclusion than that Skybolt was a necessary and desirable weapon system. Leaders in the Service had prematurely committed their prestige to the system. And, given its choice of scenarios and assumptions, the Air Staff had built an elaborate case for the system. The Secretary of Defense, faced with the Air Force's numerous supporting studies, needed independent staff assistance to review them, to question estimates, and to show how alternative scenarios and assumptions might change the Air Force's claims.

It is equally unrealistic to expect that the leaders of the Air Force at that time would not fight vigorously for a system that would help keep the manned bomber viable—a role that, in their eyes, obviously lay at the heart of the Air Force's *raison d'être*. Indeed, one of the most frequently heard arguments for Skybolt was that "it extends the usefulness of the manned bomber." In the sense that by suppressing defenses it would permit bombers to penetrate, this argument was correct; but Skybolt was by no means unique in this role. This task could be performed satisfactorily at much less cost in other ways. More importantly, in any other sense, such an argument is wrong. The most appropriate objectives for U.S. strategic retaliatory forces, then and now, are to deter war and if deterrence fails to be able to destroy the required number of targets at a minimum cost—not to propagate organizations or prolong the lives of particular weapon systems beyond the point where their continued operation is no longer compatible with those objectives. This is perhaps the great lesson of Skybolt.

Fourth, the Skybolt decision, with its adverse impact on U.S. relations with Great Britain, is frequently cited as an example of the political insensitivity of systems (or cost-effectiveness) analysis in particular, and PPBS in general. According to one Senate subcommittee, for example: "Skybolt presumably did not meet the Defense tests of cost-effectiveness, but one wonders whether, in estimating the costs of its cancellation, allowance was made for the impact on the British government and perhaps on French policies in Atlantic and West European affairs."[2] Others have criticized the decision on the grounds that British interests were not adequately considered.

Allowance was made for the impact on the British. The Secretary of Defense and his main advisers were keenly aware of the political implications of Skybolt for the British. (A special Draft Presidential Memorandum was prepared in OSD on this exact subject.) In fact, Skybolt was kept alive for many months longer, and with expenditures of millions of dollars more, than would otherwise have been the case, precisely because of the British interest. But, the point was finally reached where the expected effectiveness of Skybolt had fallen so low, and the projected costs had risen so high in relation to competing systems (such as Minuteman and Polaris), that President Kennedy and Secretary McNamara concluded that Skybolt would not be satisfactory for the British and would clearly be unsatisfactory for us. Continuation of Skybolt would only have postponed the political problem, not avoided it. Further, given the rising costs of Skybolt plus its decreasing performance, had we pursued the program, relations with Great Britain could easily have suffered more by our completing the program than by our canceling it.

Finally, the Skybolt decision (as well as that regarding the B-70/ RS-70) shows the role, utility, and limits of analysis in the defense decision-making process. It is a common belief that most defense issues are too complex to be understood. But the fact is that they *can* and *must* be understood. To do so normally requires a blend of

analysis and judgment. Of course, there are many questions that
analysis cannot answer (such as the probable Soviet reaction to U.S.
deployment of an ABM system); and these may turn out to be the
most important aspects of a decision. But there are also many questions that cannot be answered on the basis of judgment alone.
Judgment alone cannot determine how many ICBM's are needed to
destroy a given target system. In the strategic nuclear area—where
we all are (and hope to remain) inexperienced—analysis is essential
to help focus judgment on the most important aspects of the problem.

The TFX

No discussion of controversial program decisions in the 1960's
would be complete without some reference to the TFX, or F-111.
Few, if any, defense programs have been the object of such strong
and continuous criticism as this seemingly ill-fated aircraft. Unfortunately, we are not qualified to write a firsthand account of the main
TFX decisions in the early 1960's which sparked much of the controversy. As has been made clear more than once in the public record,
the Systems Analysis office was not involved in the early TFX decisions. Thus, at best, we can give only a kind of "inside-outsider's"
view.

At the risk of oversimplification, the early history of the TFX can
be described under the heading of three main decisions. The first was
a decision on performance requirements. The requirements set by the
Services were based on studies largely completed prior to 1961. As
one of the authors testified in September 1967:

The performance characteristics that were laid down were certainly established before the introduction of . . . Systems Analysis. I think they
were very ambitious, by far the most ambitious that had ever been projected. They were determined by the military services in 1961 without the
kind of careful analysis of need, feasibility, and alternatives we require
today.[3]

The main reason the TFX's performance requirements were not given
such an analysis was that in 1961 the Secretary of Defense did not
yet have an independent analytical staff. It was not until 1965 that
the Systems Analysis office had the charter and the manpower to

review systematically the requirements aspects of proposed engineering development programs. Had the office been fully staffed and functioning at that time, the history of the TFX might have been different. As Senator Henry M. Jackson remarked later in the same hearings:

> . . . I think that one can make the . . . argument that maybe if we had used systems analysis in connection with the TFX, some of the problems that we are now experiencing and have experienced since the procurement got under way might have been avoided. This might have been systems analysis' greatest triumph.[4]

In any event, McNamara's first basic decision about the TFX, which he worried about at the time, was to accept the recommendations of the Services on the plane's performance requirements. It is typical of the ironies of the defense business that McNamara was severely attacked later for overruling the Services, when, in fact, the troubles that were to beset the F-111—very high cost, failure to meet technical objectives, crashes in testing, and weight growth in the Navy version—stemmed not from McNamara's decisions but from the unjustifiably demanding performance requirements set for the aircraft by the Services.

McNamara's second main decision was that the Navy and Air Force would use the same basic aircraft. That decision was based on his belief that the cost of two new aircraft, one for the Air Force and one for the Navy, was not justified by the performance improvements over existing aircraft. Further, based on technical studies made by the two Services and the staff of the Director of Defense Research and Engineering, he concluded that the essential operational requirements of the two Services could be met with one plane and that a great deal of money could be saved in that way. Subsequent experience with the F-4 has shown that the Navy and the Air Force can, in fact, use the same plane very successfully and with great savings in cost. (Incidentally, the Secretary's decision in 1962 to stop the F-105 and to procure the Navy's F-4 for the Air Force—over the strong official objections of the Air Force—was based on a cost-effectiveness analysis.) Of course, the success of the Navy's F-4 in Air Force use does not prove that all "commonality" is a good thing. The key factor is the compatibility of the proposed missions of the aircraft. As it turned out, the Air Force's desire for a deep-interdiction tactical bomber and the Navy's desire for a fleet air defense interceptor did not prove to be a model of compatibility. The judgment that the Navy and the Air Force could use the same plane and that many hundreds of millions of dollars could thus be saved was sound, but the particular missions conceived by the two Services at the time made it very difficult for a single aircraft to do the job. Ironically, the Navy and the Air Force are now going their separate ways with the F-14 and F-15 aircraft, respectively, each an air-superiority fighter. Given the similarity in missions, perhaps some future Secretary of Defense will find that the needs of both Services can be met with one plane, and history will be repeated.

The third basic decision was the choice of a contractor. Fundamentally, this is a Service responsibility, with review by the Secretary of Defense. In any case, it was definitely outside the scope of Systems Analysis' responsibilities.

The source selection board, composed of Air Force and Navy officers and civilians, had found narrowly in favor of General Dynamics. General LeMay, the Chief of Staff of the Air Force, and Admiral Anderson, the Chief of Naval Operations, each preferred Boeing, but finally concluded that either contractor's proposal would meet the needs of both Services. It is perhaps understandable that General LeMay would have a preference for Boeing in view of the fact that Boeing had already built him two very successful bombers, the B-47 and the B-52, both of which had been produced in large numbers and had served the country well over a long period of time (continuing to the present in the case of the B-52). Boeing's proposal had a much lower percentage of parts common to the Navy and the Air Force versions than did the General Dynamics–Grumman proposal; therefore, it went farther toward giving the Navy its own plane, which is what Admiral Anderson and others in the Navy wanted in the first place. The Secretary of the Air Force, the Secretary of the Navy, and the Secretary of Defense overruled the two Service chiefs and went back to the findings of the original source selection board, because in their judgment the General Dynamics approach was simpler and appeared to have a better chance of meeting what they considered a high-risk objective at a reasonable cost.

Subsequent TFX history can be divided into two overlapping

phases: engineering development and procurement. The development phase was managed by the Services under the supervision of the Director of Defense Research and Engineering. During the procurement phase, several offices in OSD were involved, as a matter of course. The Comptroller reviewed the pricing aspects, which became extremely complex. The Systems Analysis office, beginning in late 1965, provided the Secretary of Defense with analyses and advice on how many aircraft should be bought each year and in total. The general thrust of Systems Analysis' recommendations was to cut back the planned procurement for all the Services from what they had been requesting, and this was done.

In the summer of 1968, the Systems Analysis office recommended that two of the programmed six Air Force F-111 wings be replaced with one A-7 and one F-4 wing, at a substantial reduction in over-all cost. This recommendation was not based on the popular criticisms of the plane, such as the unfortunate and overplayed crashes. As Secretary Clifford pointed out at the time, all new (and some older) fighter planes have crashes, and the F-111 did not compare unfavorably in this respect with previous successful developments. Systems Analysis' recommendation was based on (1) the belief that the deep-interdiction mission for which the plane was designed was not likely to be a productive use of resources and therefore should be reduced; (2) disappointment over the cost and performance of the plane in relation to alternatives; (3) recognition that the general financial situation of the country required a tougher scrutiny of all defense programs; and (4) realization that the cost and capability of U.S. tactical air forces had grown enormously in the past eight years without a sufficient reason.

It is impossible in any brief discussion to sort out the tangle of issues that came together in the TFX or to derive all the lessons to be learned from it. However, with the help of hindsight, we offer three general observations that ought to be included in a balanced appraisal. First, the program has not been a success. What went wrong? The most fundamental mistake was that the Services were not overruled on their basic concepts and requirements for the plane. In 1961, the Air Force was still thinking mainly of a tactical bomber for deep-interdiction missions—a sort of theater-sized strategic bomber. The Navy was still thinking mainly of a fleet air defense interceptor, a platform for long-range air-to-air missiles to protect the fleet from nuclear attack by massed Soviet bombers firing air-to-surface missiles. Neither was thinking seriously about the requirements of limited nonnuclear war. By 1967, after a basic change in military strategy from "massive retaliation" to "flexible response," and after a good deal of study, both Services decided that the need was for an air-superiority fighter. McNamara's failure to overrule the Services with respect to requirements is an understandable one. He was in his first months as Secretary of Defense; he had no independent staff capability to interrogate the Services effectively on their requirements; the general shift in military strategy that the President had decided on called for an increase in tactical air forces, and the TFX appeared to be a step in that direction; and he had many other decisions to make at the time. In short, the problem was not "too much McNamara"; it was too little.

Second, the power of the Secretary of Defense in such matters is largely negative. Within broad limits, he can stop the Services from doing something he does not want done. He can cancel or curtail programs by withholding funds. But, generally speaking, it is very difficult—often impossible—for him to get the Services to do something that they really don't want to do. He has to rely on persuasion and inter-Service rivalry and hope that if he sees a national need and is willing to spend the money for it, one or another of the Services will be willing to take on the mission of meeting that need. Although many men in both Services sincerely tried to make the project work, the incentives for doing so were not strong. There was a great deal of the "not invented here" feeling around, and antibodies to this foreign object started forming as early as 1961. In light of this, it is not surprising that by 1968 the Navy had succeeded in getting its version killed.

Finally, it is an interesting commentary on the validity of Marc Antony's dictum that McNamara should be so well remembered for his part in the TFX program, but that his far more important and courageous decisions on the B-70/RS-70 and Skybolt programs, not to mention Dynasoar, the nuclear-powered aircraft, and Nike X—decisions that later proved to be clearly right and decisions that saved the taxpayers many times the cost of the TFX—are now largely forgotten.

8

Some Problems in Wartime Defense Management

PPBS and Vietnam

This chapter discusses the Planning-Programming-Budgeting System (PPBS) as it relates to decisions on Vietnam. More specifically, it focuses on the Systems Analysis office and Vietnam. It deals only with the effort to analyze and manage force deployments and a few related questions, not with the basic political, strategic, or moral issues of the war.

PPBS was not involved in the really crucial issues of the Vietnam war. Should the United States have gone into Vietnam in the first place? Did we go in at the right time, in the right way, and on the right scale? What force levels should we have had there? How should these troops have been used? What timetable should we set up for withdrawals? How can we best achieve a speedy and just settlement? These are the really crucial questions. While PPBS can help, it cannot by itself answer such questions; nobody has ever claimed that it could. There are obvious limits to what any management system can accomplish. Still, the contributions of PPBS to the U.S. effort in Vietnam have been useful.

To begin with, the United States entered the war with balanced forces trained, equipped, and ready for combat. These forces were better prepared than at the beginning of any war in our nation's history. They were deployed as needed with few of the personnel or matériel shortages that have plagued all other such efforts. Massive call-ups of reserves were not necessary. Military tours did not have to be involuntarily extended on a large scale. The Planning-Programming-Budgeting System was an important factor in achieving this readiness.

With the deterioration of public support for the war effort, some have argued that this contribution of PPBS was really a disservice. If the United States had not had forces ready to fight, it would have been less likely to get involved. This is a curious argument: one that confuses political wisdom and defense management. Excellence or ineptitude in the one is not related to a similar quality in the other. Being unprepared has not prevented our entering wars in the past; it has only helped raise the initial costs in lives and resources. Moreover, if constraints on U.S. involvement are the goal, they should be achieved through our constitutional and political processes, not through poor management of billions of dollars in defense resources.

The quality of the forces deployed to Vietnam was much better than it had been a few years earlier. For example, the airmobile-division concept had been tested, and the division was ready when it was needed. New, modern conventional weapons and ordnance were available in quantity. Sufficient strategic and tactical airlift aircraft were available to meet deployment, battlefield, and evacuation objectives. PPBS played a major role in the design of these improvements.

As a part of the Vietnam build-up, some 500,000 men were temporarily added to the Army and about 100,000 to the Marine Corps to strengthen U.S. land forces. PPBS helped make possible the efficient and effective planning of these increases. As an extension of PPBS, a Vietnam deployment planning system was added to coordinate the force planning, budgeting, personnel planning, and procurement associated with the Vietnam operation. Thus, when the Secretary of Defense wanted to add another division to the Army, PPBS helped determine what should be added to the financial plan, the manpower plan, the procurement plan, and the like in a more balanced and coordinated way.

PPBS also brought about better, tighter financial planning during the build-up. A comparison with U.S. experience during the first two years of the Korean war illustrates the point (Table 15). As the table shows, from 1950 to 1952 Korean defense expenditures rose 220 percent, while new appropriations increased 320 percent. These increases are indicative of several facts. The U.S. armed forces were small and unprepared at the beginning of the Korean war. By today's standards, the force and financial planning during the resulting build-up was very disorderly. The increase in requested appropriations was all out of proportion to the increase in actual expenditures. In fact, much of the appropriated money was not used for several years. Clearly, at that time we did not have good estimates of our financial or matériel requirements. From 1965 to 1967, by comparison, both defense expenditures and requested appropriations rose by about 40 percent in a balanced and relatively orderly way. PPBS did not bring about perfection in this sort of planning; far from it. But the history of the Korean and Vietnam build-ups does show that requirements planning and associated financial planning were much more systematic this time than last.

PPBS provides the potential for better, less wasteful financial and force structure control as U.S. forces for Vietnam are phased down. Just as PPBS assisted in identifying and making balanced increases, so it can assist in making orderly and balanced decreases. Because it helps clarify the relationships between resources and force structures, PPBS facilitates the addition or deletion of resources, as required, without wasteful imbalances.

Table 15. Force and Financial Build-ups in the Korean and Vietnam Wars

	Korea		Vietnam	
	1950	1952	1965	1967
Defense spending (billions of 1966 dollars)	$15.9	$53.5	$48.7	$68.0
Defense new appropriations (billions of 1966 dollars)	20.6	86.1	51.9	72.8
Military personnel at end of fiscal year (thousands)	1,460	3,635	2,655	3,377
Forces in Korea (thousands)	—	309	50	50
Forces in Vietnam (thousands)	—	—	60	450
Forces in Europe (thousands)	120	355	357	350

The Role of the Systems Analysis Office

The Systems Analysis office did not have a prominent, much less a crucial, role in the Vietnam war. Prior to June 1965 it had no role at all, and afterward it was never closely involved with the development of strategy or operations. Such matters were largely outside its charter. Unlike the determination of peacetime force structures and the defense budget, in which the OSD staff was heavily involved, or even the determination of force deployments to Europe, which also involved OSD, decisions on force deployments to Vietnam were made largely by the President and the Secretary of Defense dealing directly with the U.S. military commander in Vietnam and the Joint Chiefs of Staff, with participation by only a few OSD civilians. The Systems Analysis office played no policy role in the decision to go into Vietnam, in the decision to bomb North Vietnam, in the determination of targets to be bombed, in the timing of bombing pauses, or in the development of strategy or tactics. It had no policy role in determining the over-all totals of men to send to Vietnam, or in figuring out what they should do when they got there.

Had the Washington-based Systems Analysis office had such a role, it is not clear that it could have helped to improve the U.S. military performance. The Vietnam war has been as much political as military; its dominant factors concern the allegiance of the people of South Vietnam. But systematic analysis and the application of program-budgeting concepts might have helped forestall the over-Americanization of the war, the pervasive optimism of official statements on how well we were doing, and the twisted priorities that developed in the expenditure of billions of dollars on various war programs. Systematic analysis was a major missing element in understanding what the United States was doing in and to Vietnam. In Vietnam, no one insisted on systematic efforts to understand, analyze, or interpret the war. If we make no other point in this book, we want it to be clear that the full value of systematic analysis in making decisions on the conduct of a war has yet to be tested.

While the Systems Analysis office was not asked to study questions basic to the key decisions, the office did do some useful pieces of work on the Vietnam war. This work consisted of (1) developing and maintaining a single, authoritative plan for manpower, logistics, procurement, and financial planning; (2) developing a model for estimating aircraft attrition; and (3) attempting to stimulate analysis by making pilot studies of various aspects of the war and publishing them (beginning in February 1967) in an unofficial monthly document called the *Southeast Asia Analysis Report*. All these items were aimed at improving the management of the war effort.

The Southeast Asia Deployment Plan

At the beginning of 1965, the United States had only some 23,000 men in South Vietnam, all advisers. By the end of June 1965, there were about 60,000, and General Westmoreland had asked for another 150,000 by the end of the year. No detailed advanced planning had been made for deployments of this size. The existing peacetime decision-making processes were too slow for the conditions of war. The established staff in DoD could provide the necessary fast action only by ignoring all other problems.

During the summer of 1965, Systems Analysis personnel worked with the Service and JCS planning staffs to convert the huge catalogue of units requested by General Westmoreland into crude deployment tables. Using these tables and drawing on experience with the Korean war, logistics planners in the other OSD offices and the Services then computed requirements for ammunition and other consumables.

In November 1965, a new request was received from Saigon for another 180,000 troops. Systems Analysis again helped build the deployment tables. At the same time, it produced a Draft Memorandum for the President (DPM) on the supplemental budget that would be required in January. The DPM included a series of tables that laid out systematically and in detail the proposed deployments to Vietnam and Thailand. In addition to manpower totals, they covered major combat units, such as artillery and maneuver battalions, and key combat support units, such as engineers. They also covered many types of fixed-wing aircraft and helicopters and ships. For the first time, planned deployments were displayed in a systematic, understandable manner for the benefit of top-level DoD managers as well as the Service staffs. In this series of tables, the Secretary and his principal assistants had the information they needed for controlling the planned deployments. Moreover, since the tables provided time-phased data, logistics and financial planners also found them useful.

Because of their wide usefulness, Secretary McNamara directed the Systems Analysis office to keep the deployment tables up to date, and a ten-man staff was set up in the office to handle this task. Subsequently, the tables were updated on a bimonthly, and later a monthly, basis. Normally, they included data on three types of planned deployment, displayed in three tabular rows: budget-plan, current-plan, and "actual." The budget-plan row displayed planned deployments as of the time the President's budget was prepared: December of each year. The current-plan row displayed the current status of planned deployments, reflecting all approved changes subsequent to the preparation of the budget. The "actual" row displayed the units and personnel actually in Vietnam at the end of each month. A simple visual comparison showed the additional units that had been approved, the deployments that had accelerated or had slipped, and other similar information. Thus, it was easy to calculate the budgetary and logistics impact of changes that had occurred since the budget had been prepared. The "actuals" also provided management with a view of how closely the Services were meeting the deployment schedules. Systems Analysis monitored the tables closely; as each month's "actuals" were incorporated, significant shortfalls or overages were identified and reported to the Secretary, or other appropriate officials, for action.

These tasks were aimed at monitoring the build-up of forces in Vietnam, ensuring that schedules were met, and helping tie the deployment planning to financial and logistical planning. Why did the job of monitoring deployment progress fall to an OSD office? It would seem that such a function belonged more naturally in the responsibilities of the JCS. But there were several problems with this. First, for reasons that OSD never understood well, the ability of the Joint Staff to manage numerical data, to present a consistent picture from day to day, and to control and reconcile changes was poor. The explanation is to be found, in part, in the inherent difficulties of managing such data when so many people are involved. At one time, even the OSD deployment figures had a 20,000-man discrepancy! Second, because the Services and the Joint Staff consistently tried to send more forces to Southeast Asia, some independent group responsive to the desires of the Secretary of Defense was needed to police the changes (were proposed increases merely meeting requirements that had already been met?), to bring issues to the attention of the Secretary of Defense, and to see to it that Presidential ceilings on total deployments were being observed. One might think that a ceiling on American military personnel in Vietnam would be a straight-forward matter: "549,500 men, and that's that." But when intelligent men, trying to get their job done, set about to deploy more men, a ceiling can become almost as complicated as the income tax. Does the ceiling refer to total authorized unit strength—that is, to "spaces" —or to actual men on the ground? What about men in transit to or from Vietnam? Or the wounded? Or prisoners of war? When is a man counted as "in Vietnam"? What about U.S.-based officers who are there on temporary duty? Vietnam-based officers on temporary duty elsewhere or on leave? Varying interpretations of such issues could easily mean a difference of 10 percent, or 50,000 men, or roughly $2 billion per year.

Further, OSD had to monitor the force build-up because the Services were concerned more with getting units to Vietnam as quickly as possible. Whether these units, or units previously shipped, were at full strength was a lower-priority item. Much of OSD's needling about deployments was directed at the Services' failures to send sufficient replacement personnel to keep deployed units at full strength.

Reporting deployments was one problem; reviewing them was quite another. The Systems Analysis office was not in the require-ments-review business in 1965. In March 1966, Secretary McNamara asked the office to review the large build-up of forces in Thailand, the Philippines, Okinawa, and Japan. The large expansion in Thailand was partially explainable by the deployment of attack and reconnais-sance aircraft there, together with their necessary support personnel. But the size of the requested build-up was alarming. Similar large expansions were being proposed for the Philippines, Okinawa, and even Japan. McNamara asked specifically for an analysis of a request by the Commander-in-Chief of Pacific Forces (CINCPAC) for 35,000 more men to be added to the 120,000 men already in Thai-land, the Philippines, and other western Pacific countries outside Vietnam. Our review enabled the Secretary to make a reduction of 18,000 men, saving about $500 million per year.

There was nothing mysterious about the review. It consisted mostly of asking questions: why the people were needed, how they related to those already deployed or others to be deployed, what would not get done if the request was denied, what the ratios were of support personnel to combat personnel, and the like. The answers had to make sense to Secretary McNamara, and he rejected the analysis twice until they did. The JCS and the Services had the right of appeal on every recommended denial. We believe it to be significant that only 6,000 of the 20,000 men recommended for deletion were appealed (2,000 of these were later approved for deployment).

The only "formal" OSD review mechanism used before 1967 was the irregular "Deployment Issue Paper." Most of these papers were concerned with apparent duplication in the units requested to do a particular job; very few questioned the requirement directly. Why did we need thousands of air defense personnel to defend against a handful of North Vietnamese light bombers? Why add more personnel to man automated telephone switchboards when these switchboards had been bought explicitly to reduce manpower needs? Questions of this sort were rarely asked.

The Deployment Issue Papers turned out to be, within their scope, a useful management device. Secretary McNamara forwarded them to the JCS for comment and review. The JCS, in turn, sent them to General Westmoreland's headquarters. Far too often we found that the basic request for more units had been only a stapling together of individual Service requests from the various components in Vietnam; this, in turn, had been rubber-stamped up the chain to the Secretary of Defense. (A notable exception to this process was General Westmoreland's personal interest in key combat and aircraft units.) No one had questioned why the specific units were needed. When such questions were finally raised, many alleged "requirements" were quickly and willingly deleted by the Military Assistance Command, Vietnam (MACV), and CINCPAC.

The "special study" and the Deployment Issue Paper were useful devices for analyzing requirements, but they did not and could not provide a systematic means of updating the approved deployment program for Southeast Asia. Most proposed changes in the program were submitted by the JCS or by the Service Secretaries. A means of consolidating these various changes and centralizing the management of deployments was missing. Systems Analysis' solution was the Deployment Adjustment Request system. Under this system all changes, regardless of origin, were channeled through the Joint Staff, with primary responsibility in the J-3 (Operations) division. At the recommendation of the Systems Analysis office, the Secretary of Defense directed that no deployment changes be considered official unless they had been taken through this channel. Even when the Secretary approved a program during budget review, the actual deployment authority had to come through the Joint Staff.

Later, thresholds for changes were established above which Secretary of Defense approval was required and below which the Joint Staff could approve. In general, the Secretary's approval was needed on changes that increased the total numbers of troops in any country in Southeast Asia and on changes in the approved totals that affected major units such as maneuver or engineer battalions, aircraft and helicopter units, or ships. In this way the Secretary was able to consider explicitly those changes with significant budgetary and logistical impact. All other changes could be approved by the Joint Staff.

By establishing a single official set of books and a workable system for keeping them up to date, the confusion that would have arisen from having each Service maintain its own unilateral plans was avoided. Because of this system, budget planning was coordinated with deployment planning with a high degree of efficiency.

A good management system gives all echelons incentives to use resources wisely. The over-all force levels for Vietnam were, of course, established by the President. Beginning in mid-1967, between major force level reviews, General Westmoreland's staff was expected to delete unnecessary units to make room for new and more pressing requirements. For instance, if the Army in Vietnam wanted another engineer unit, it would have to provide offsetting reductions, perhaps in other types of construction or logistical units. To motivate the Joint Staff to hunt for deadwood without being prodded, the Systems Analysis office developed what was called the "Debit/Credit Account," which permitted the accumulation of personnel spaces from deleted units as a credit to be drawn on as new requirements developed. This system provided an incentive to MACV to get rid of units that had outlived their usefulness, because as new requirements arose no justification for new personnel was needed so long as spaces were available in the account. (Although the Services normally kept a credit balance in the Debit/Credit Account, they were allowed to go in the hole from time to time. The only requirement was that at the end of each calendar quarter the accounts be brought into balance.) This system worked well, and we believe it helped to save millions of dollars in the support of U.S. combat operations.

Estimating Aircraft Attrition

A second area of Vietnam war management in which the Systems Analysis office participated was estimating future aircraft losses and planning aircraft procurement. In terms of costs, this was a major job. By 1968, the United States was losing some $1.7 billion worth of aircraft annually. Predicting aircraft losses was complicated by the great variety of aircraft types and models to be considered: 22 fighter/attack, 10 reconnaissance, and 30 other fixed-wing aircraft, and 20 kinds of helicopters. Moreover, because of the long budgetary and production lead times for aircraft, losses had to be projected forward over a three-and-one-half-year period to provide adequate budgetary and force planning data. (A December 1968 decision on the fiscal 1970 budget, though subject to modification later, would affect deliveries of aircraft through December 1971.)

The key equipment items projected in these forecasts were fighter/attack aircraft and helicopters—the former because of their huge cost and "visibility," and the latter because of the large numbers lost (almost 1,000 during fiscal 1968 alone) and the fact that the demand for helicopters consistently exceeded the production. Systems Analysis' "box score" in predicting fighter/attack losses was reasonably good. For example, in December 1966 we forecast a loss of 711 fighter/attack aircraft in 1967. In April, we reduced this estimate to 553; actual losses were 547. On the other hand, our helicopter loss estimates were consistently low.

Because of the large numbers of aircraft involved and the relatively long time period covered, the Systems Analysis staff developed a computer program to do the calculations. This program was used, as well, by the Services to test the sensitivity of the estimates to possible changes in major factors such as deployments. All our assumptions and factors were available for review, and uncertainties were clearly explained. Although the Service Secretaries and the Systems Analysis office usually came to an agreement on loss forecasts, there were often substantial disagreements to begin with. The Services tended to project higher losses than we did, for example, by using twelve-month instead of six-month moving averages in a period of declining losses. The difference reflected their desire to ensure enough replacement aircraft and our desire to save money whenever it appeared this could be done safely.

To illustrate the complexity of forecasting involving large procurements, which defense management must continually cope with, let us look at the job of projecting fighter/attack aircraft attrition. Thirteen different sortie (one plane, one mission) and loss rates were used for each of the 22 fighter/attack aircraft models (F-100, A-4, and the like) in the approved deployment program. They included sortie and loss rates for bombing and other sorties for various areas in Southeast Asia and rates for all other sorties and losses (including noncombat losses and losses on the ground). Each of these rates was based on historical experience, using the longest period possible but explicitly considering any recent trends. A weather cycle was introduced to apportion attack sorties among the areas in Southeast Asia in accordance with shifts in sortie patterns. The tropical monsoons affect North Vietnam in the winter and Laos and the southern part of South Vietnam during the summer months. The total sorties and losses per year were not influenced by the weather cycles, but, since month-by-month losses changed sharply, the weather cycle aided in following seasonal changes.

After the Systems Analysis staff had made a loss estimate, a second estimate was made based on some major policy uncertainty (such as a halt in the bombing of North Vietnam and later a resumption of the bombing north of the 19th parallel). The Service staffs were then given the estimates and the computer program for criticism and information on any changes in the deployment plans made necessary by the new attrition projections. After receiving their comments and making final adjustments, we prepared a memorandum for the Secretary of Defense outlining the methodology, results, and alternatives and the views of the Services. Rarely was there a dispute over the estimates themselves, once the system was in operation. When one did arise, the Secretary could quickly check the key assumptions underlying each choice. The aircraft-attrition estimating process provides an outstanding example of open and explicit analysis at work.

The system operated smoothly for three reasons. First, it was open and explicit. Everyone knew what the calculations included and why they came out the way they did. Second, it was a clear case of evenhanded justice. The same methodology was used for all the Services, avoiding many of the problems that would have arisen if each Service had estimated its own losses in its own way. And third, the major uncertainties about the future were accommodated primarily in the procurement decisions. In essence, all parties could agree on how many aircraft would probably be lost based on the best possible review of past history and future operational and deployment plans. The degree to which we should hedge against the unknown (inapplicabilities of the past and uncertainties in future plans) was determined separately when the Secretary of Defense decided how many aircraft to buy. But when he made that decision, he had before him as an aid to his judgment a consistent and impartial attrition prediction and the record of previous predictions.

Shortages

In November 1966, General Westmoreland told *U.S. News & World Report:*

Never before in the history of warfare have men created such a responsive logistical system—one that is capable of supporting a flexible strategy that creates sudden requirements from widely scattered points. Never has there been such zealous participation by logistical troops who believe in the importance of full and fast support for the combat elements. Not once have the fighting troops been restricted in their operations against the enemy for want of essential supplies.

In April 1967, he told a Joint Session of Congress:

Our President and the representatives of the people of the United States, the Congress, have seen to it that our troops in the field have been well-supplied and equipped. And when a field commander does not have to look over his shoulder to see whether he is being supported, he can concentrate on the battlefield with much greater assurance of success. I speak for my troops, when I say—we are thankful for this unprecedented material support.

Despite these and other statements supporting the fact that in terms of logistics planning, the Vietnam war effort has been far superior to any other, there were, nevertheless, the inevitable charges of "shortages." Between mid-1966 and mid-1968 a great deal of the time and effort of top-level DoD management, military and civilian, was taken up answering such charges, most of which originated from members of the Senate and House Armed Services Committees. Because they illustrate other important points about defense management as well as the difficulty of determining and explaining the facts concerning shortages, two of these alleged shortages—in pilots and tactical aircraft—are discussed below.

In 1967, four interrelated factors led Secretary McNamara to ask the Systems Analysis office and the Services to make a thorough analysis of pilot requirements and inventories. The Vietnam war greatly increased our pilot needs, especially because of the desire to minimize each pilot's combat exposure. Retention rates dropped off sharply as increasing numbers of pilots, especially the younger ones, resigned after their initial obligations were up. The costs of pilot training kept rising. By 1967, it cost roughly half a million dollars to train one pilot for a fighter aircraft. With a stated requirement for over 70,000 pilots, this posed a major and expensive management problem. Finally, the Senate Armed Services Preparedness Investigating Subcommittee publicly charged that there was a serious pilot shortage. A thorough review was clearly needed. Despite the huge sums involved in pilot training, this marked the first time that pilot requirements had been subjected to an intensive review by OSD.

The review revealed several things. To begin with, it showed that the Services' methods of determining pilot requirements were, at best, unsatisfactory. In essence, the Services established pilot requirements by counting, in peacetime, all flying and nonflying jobs that, in their judgment, required pilots. This approach had two serious defects. It failed to take explicit account of the fact that more pilots are needed in wartime than in peacetime—a "surge" capability to last until new pilots could be trained. And, since these billets (or personnel spaces) were originally counted at a time when, because of the World War II and Korean war "hump," the United States had more pilots than it needed, there was a natural tendency to count as pilot billets many jobs (almost 10,000) where it was desirable, but not essential, to have a pilot. Over the years, many of these types of billets had become, for largely institutional reasons, firmly identified as requiring pilots.

For example, we found that the Air Force alone had some 3,500 qualified pilots (Lieutenant Colonel and below) assigned to jobs that did not require pilot skills. Moreover, the Air Force had some 1,000 grounded pilots who, in theory at least, could have filled some of the nonflying jobs requiring the professional knowledge of a pilot, but were assigned to jobs not calling for pilots. Here alone were 4,500 pilots who were needlessly unavailable to do jobs for which they had been expensively trained. Further, the Air Force counted as pilot billets about 2,500 jobs calling only for "rated" officers. Any officer with an aeronautical rating (for example, navigators) could fill these jobs, and at the time the Air Force had an excess inventory of navigators. Similar management problems were uncovered in the other Services. In the Navy, for example, 40 pilots were "required" to operate fleet computer centers.

The review established that there was no "pilot shortage" in the sense of not having enough pilots to fly the planes. The fact that some peacetime billets calling for a pilot were temporarily unfilled did not necessarily mean that the United States had a pilot shortage. Nor did a shortage necessarily exist between the time a decision was made to buy additional aircraft (and thus pilots) and the time of actual delivery (even though planning documents would show such a paper shortage). In all cases, there were more than enough pilots to man all U.S. aircraft fully at approved crew ratios (generally 1.5 to 4 crews per aircraft), supervise and plan flying activities, and train new pilots.

But while confirming that there was no actual pilot shortage, the review revealed a number of serious management problems. Pilots were being used in jobs that didn't require pilots. More pilots than necessary were on proficiency flying (monthly flying to maintain aviation skills). Retention rates were dropping significantly, because large numbers of World War II and Korean war pilots were becoming eligible for retirement, because of the increased stress on pilots caused by the Vietnam war, and because of the substantial demand for pilots by the commercial airlines. More importantly, because small changes in retention rates necessitate large changes in training rates, management actions to improve retention rates promised large pay-offs at much less cost than increasing training rates. In terms of pilot-training capacity, some Services were not able to meet their training rates while operating at maximum capacity, and thus were requesting funds for increasing training facilities, while at the same time other Services had unused capacity and facilities standing idle. But these were all *management* problems, not "shortages"; training more pilots would not necessarily solve them.

Another point that this review drove home was the enormous expense involved in training a pilot. Undergraduate and advanced flight training was costing over $1.5 billion annually. The aircraft used for this training cost over $6 billion. The average cost to give one new pilot basic flight training was over $100,000 for the Navy, over $75,000 for the Air Force, and over $40,000 for the Army. Much of the advanced flight training cost between $1,000 and $2,000 per hour, and each pilot receives hundreds of hours of such training during his career. Obviously, the United States must have enough pilots to meet our requirements; but, just as obviously, these requirements should be determined as accurately as possible. The traditional billet-counting methods were inadequate for this. Relying on these methods, it would have cost $3.5 billion more than programmed over a five-year period to meet the Services' stated requirements.

As a result of this review, the Systems Analysis office, working closely with the Services, developed a model for calculating pilot requirements and training rates that tied the necessary supply of pilots to the kinds of wars which we planned to be able to fight and for which we bought aircraft and logistic support. The model explicitly considered a large number of planning factors such as crew ratios, pilot work loads, opportunities for career development, periods of separation from families, and short tours to limit combat exposure.

In contrast to the billet-counting method, this new approach to determining pilot requirements not only helped ensure enough pilots to man every aircraft, to train new pilots and other crewmen, and to provide supervision at all levels—the "core" requirement—but also explicitly provided for additional pilots to meet initial wartime surges and to fill the gap caused by wartime attrition until new pilots could be trained—the "supplement" requirement.

Where there were specific disagreements with the Services on a particular planning factor, such as the number of pilots per crew in an F-4 or P-3 aircraft, the Systems Analysis office challenged them on the specific merits of each case and worked with the Service to define the issue clearly for decision by the Secretary of Defense. In so doing, the office tried to gather evidence on the benefits and costs of having more pilots and to present the information in such a way that the Secretary of Defense could reach an informed decision.

During testimony before the Senate Armed Services Preparedness Investigating Subcommittee early in 1967, each of the Joint Chiefs of Staff had used estimates based largely on peacetime counts of "pilot billets" when asked about pilot requirements—numbers that, as a result of review during the spring and summer by Systems Analysis and the Service staffs and the resulting changes in methods of calculating pilot requirements, were now obsolete. Using the new procedures, by the end of the summer the necessary pilot inventories and training rates to meet U.S. requirements were agreed upon by most parties. The few significant differences remaining were clearly defined as issues for further analysis and decision.

In the fall, the Subcommittee held additional hearings on the question of a pilot shortage. The Subcommittee referred to the earlier statements by the Chiefs regarding pilot requirements and compared them with the actual numbers of available pilots given in later testimony by other witnesses. In this way the Subcommittee went on to "prove" that a shortage existed, since the earlier requirements stated by the Chiefs were not being met. Attempts by military witnesses to explain or back away from these earlier statements were sharply criticized. The Subcommittee appeared to be interested more in the source of the stated requirements than in the reasons for them. Subcommittee members did not challenge the billet-counting method. They did not question what the Chiefs had said earlier. They did not ask whether the value of manning the billet lists with pilots was worth the cost. They merely got the Chiefs' statement of requirements on the record and proceeded to use it to show that the requirement was not being met and therefore that a "shortage" existed.

The Subcommittee did not prove a pilot shortage. There was no such shortage, as careful analysis had demonstrated. Much of the problem was due to the fact that the Services, being under no pressure to do so before, had not taken the management steps to ensure that pilots were used in nonflying jobs only where they were clearly required. This is not surprising. Most large and busy organizations need outside prodding before changes are made. As the Secretary of Defense's interrogator, this was one of the jobs of the Systems Analysis office.

Indeed, we doubt seriously if these insights into pilot requirements would have been possible without the kind of independent view that the Systems Analysis office could bring to this problem. Largely for institutional reasons, the Services would have had great difficulty in producing an objective study of their own pilot requirements. For example, the number of pilots authorized for the Air Force is more than a technical matter. Pilots dominate the Air Force. The great majority of senior officers are pilots, and most believe that the model of an Air Force officer should be a pilot. This image can be maintained if 50,000 of the 150,000 Air Force officers are pilots; it is threatened, however, if the number falls significantly below this. In other words, the numerical difference between 30,000 and 50,000 pilots is an important factor governing whether the pilot is to be regarded as a minority specialist or as the archetype of the Air Force officer. In important ways, the whole *raison d'être* of the Air Force is tied up in pilot requirements; it would be difficult for its leaders to admit having "enough" pilot billets.

In the Navy, the number of pilot billets is intimately related to the internal power balance between aviation, surface ship, and submarine officers. It is reflected in an internal "treaty" of long standing.

This episode illustrates several other points. As we noted earlier, requirements must be placed in a total political, economic, and military context of what we want to do, what we need to do it with, and what we are willing to afford. Like those for pilots, many such "requirements," on close inspection, turn out to be based less on a systematic consideration of goals, needs, and costs than on arbitrary and narrow standards. It is hard to make a convincing case that the required number of pilots depends on a list of billets previously filled by pilots, particularly when many of the billets have nothing to do with flying, but rather provide staff and management jobs for men who happen to be pilots. Such a system tells one a great deal about how military "requirements" are generated in practice, but very little about actual pilot requirements.

Another point that this story illustrates is the unfortunate tendency for some Congressional committees to rely, uncritically, on authority rather than on analysis. The Senate Subcommittee showed little interest in why billet counting was an unsatisfactory basis for determining pilot requirements or in the fact that by using this method, the Services could easily waste hundreds of millions of dollars a year by training too many pilots, or, alternatively, could wind up with too few pilots at the beginning of a war. They appeared to be interested only in the "fact" that a stated requirement by the military experts had not been met. On the face of it, this constituted a shortage and suggested civilian mismanagement. In such an atmosphere, it is difficult to make progress toward developing better means of determining what our nation's military needs really are.

Finally, the pilot episode is one more example of the lack of acceptance of the relevance of cost in defense planning. As we have indicated, pilots are enormously expensive to train and keep proficient. During the review of pilot requirements, one issue concerned whether the Air Force F-4 would continue to be manned by two pilots (as the Air Force wanted) or by one pilot and one navigator (as the Navy and Marine Corps's F-4's had always been). Estimates of the difference in costs were about $100 million dollars annually, and there was no evidence that a second pilot (rather than a navigator) would provide substantial advantages. (It is to the credit of the Air Force that, when the evidence on these points was brought to their attention and thoroughly reviewed, they changed their position.) Given other defense needs and the high costs of training pilots, we cannot afford to train pilots for jobs where they are not really needed. Nor can we afford to train an excess of pilots beyond the substantial hedge already built into the training rates. Naturally, the Services want as many pilots as they can get, and the Subcommittee explicitly noted in its report that it was not concerned about training too many pilots. But someone has to be. A pilot surplus means that other programs have been shortchanged. Moreover, it offers a golden opportunity for someone to raise the specter of an "aircraft shortage."

Indeed, another alleged Vietnam shortage involved tactical aircraft. Like that of pilots, this was a "paper" shortage, not a real one. If one were careful to stick to objective facts only—the central one being that the United States has far more and better tactical aircraft than any other country—it would be extremely difficult to make a case that there was a shortage in any real sense.

As the United States began to deploy tactical air forces to Vietnam on a sustained basis, it became clear that there was more to the job than had previously been recognized. The build-up was slow, and there were serious problems with jams at port facilities and with air-base construction. It quickly became apparent that a large number of aircraft were needed for the advanced-combat-readiness training of new pilots. (For example, given their deployment and pilot-rotation policies, the Navy needed almost one aircraft in training for each one in combat.) Thus, it was not possible to deploy and sustain all the aircraft normally assigned to combat units. Moreover, the percentage of aircraft in overhaul or transit—the "pipe line"—continued to expand as aircraft were placed in the repair shop for longer and longer periods to repair combat damage and to incorporate innumerable modifications that the Services believed were required. This "down" status further reduced the number of aircraft available for deployment. Factors of this kind created a need for a larger training base and lay behind the public confusion and controversy during 1966 and 1967 over "shortages" of tactical aircraft, particularly Navy aircraft.

The confusion stemmed primarily from the aircraft accounting system. Secretary McNamara quite properly (but in contrast to the Services) based his force and procurement recommendations on the total inventory of aircraft he thought was needed to meet U.S. worldwide commitments. In displaying these decisions on force size and composition in the force tables of the Five-Year Defense Plan (FYDP), the total inventory was traditionally divided into several categories: unit equipment (UE), training, pipe-line, and other support functions. The UE is the planned number of aircraft to be assigned to combat units. For example, an Air Force tactical air wing is nominally assigned 72 UE aircraft, even though 100 aircraft are bought for it. A Navy fighter squadron is nominally assigned 12 UE aircraft, even though about 18 are bought for it. The force tables also listed nominal planning figures (25 percent) for combat-crew training and for the number of aircraft in repair (10 percent for the Air Force and 15 percent for the Navy). The crew-training and pipe-line numbers were used as arbitrary procurement planning factors to estimate inventory requirements. Because the actual factors would inevitably vary with each actual deployment situation, it was generally known and understood that no single set of planning factors could be universally valid.

The original rationale for these nominal planning numbers was that the main FYDP tables showed combat forces, and the Services described aircraft combat units in terms of unit equipment. Four groups of aircraft with supporting roles were deducted from the total inventory. These aircraft were (1) those in overhaul and repair; (2) those used for combat-readiness training; (3) those used for other supporting roles, such as target towing, radar operator training, research and development, and the like; and (4) those bought for advanced attrition. In the minds of many, however, the UE figure came to be synonymous with combat capability. Because it was the key number shown in the force tables, people tended to think of an Air Force tactical fighter wing as having 72 aircraft. This might have been a good system if the UE figures were a better measure of combat capability than total-inventory figures, but they were not, for several reasons.

For one thing, even when a unit had its full UE, that was not the number of aircraft that were combat-ready. As little as 71 percent combat-ready is good enough to earn an Air Force "C-1" rating, which is the highest level of readiness the Air Force itself credits to its own units. Thus, even at the beginning, the numbers shown in the FYDP force tables started to depart from the intended notion of indicating real capability.

Next, the deduction for aircraft in overhaul and repair was inaccurate in practice. In the Air Force these aircraft were called "command support," and they amounted to 10 percent of the UE. In the Navy and Marine Corps, they were called "pipe line," amounting nominally to 15 percent of the UE. The Army called them "maintenance float" aircraft and used a factor of 15 percent for units deployed in Southeast Asia and 10 percent elsewhere. These percentages were used arbitrarily across the board, whether the aircraft were new or old, transports or fighters, battle-damaged or not. While they were called "planning" factors, they did not reflect actual factors. Actual factors, depending on the Service accounting system, were almost always higher than even the Navy's 15 percent. In Southeast

Asia, some were around 35 percent. Thus, the force tables departed still further from the original purpose of indicating real capability, and one had to interpret Army and Navy force tables differently.

Further, the deduction for combat-readiness training aircraft was an arbitrary 25 percent. (For Marine Corps helicopter forces, lower factors ranging from 11 percent to 17 percent were used, depending on the complexity of the training program. The Army approached combat-readiness training quite differently, and no such allowance was authorized.) And, like the command-support and pipe-line percentages, this flat, across-the-board figure could not be right for all types of aircraft in all types of situations. Because some types of aircraft are more complicated than others and have a longer training syllabus, more may be required in the training role. Because some aircraft are being phased into the force, relatively more may be required for training (initially, all may be in that role). For aircraft that are being phased out, few, if any, may be required for training. In a sustained war like that in Vietnam, the numbers of readiness-training aircraft have to be increased to provide for pilot rotation. For example, during the bombing of North Vietnam, for every Air Force aircraft flying into North Vietnam there was another of like type in the United States to train a replacement pilot. The Navy took aircraft from nondeployed combat units to augment their crew training beyond the nominal 25 percent figure; and many Air Force squadrons, even though they were shown in the force tables as combat units, were really doing little more than training. All these actions were perfectly justified and represented intelligent use of available resources. Moreover, since defense officials will always want the freedom to manage aircraft in the best way, if the 25 percent figure was ever right, it would have been mere coincidence.

In addition, though the "non-UE" group was not shown in the force tables, it contained some combat-capable aircraft. As an illustration, there were a number of older F-8 fighters in this group which the Navy had been using as high-speed target tugs. These were later transferred to more important combat roles. But looking only at the force tables, one would never have known they existed.

Finally, as noted in Chapter 4, there was a tendency to compare U.S. unit equipment with the Air Order of Battle of potential enemies. The Communists, however, have fewer aircraft nominally allocated to the support of combat units. For example, the Air Order of Battle for the Communist countries in 1968 was about 80 percent of their total active inventory, while the UE for the United States and its allies was only about 60 percent. Comparing the Communists' Air Order of Battle with the United States' UE not only did not really measure the relative capabilities of the two forces but helped support the false claims that the United States was outnumbered in tactical aircraft.

Thus, the system suffered from a lack of realism. It did not measure combat capability. It led to considerable confusion. The Navy, for instance, interpreted UE as meaning "operating aircraft in combat units" and believed that it should always have this number of aircraft in operating units *regardless of the circumstances*. Using this interpretation, there would be a "shortage" whenever more than 15 percent of the aircraft were being repaired or modified outside of squadron facilities, or whenever more than 25 percent were being used for training. Given the Navy's mode of operation, its aircraft reporting and accounting system, and its definitions, there would always be a "shortage" in some units during wartime. But in terms of having sufficient aircraft in the total inventory to meet planned deployment objectives, there was no shortage—as the Navy later confirmed to the Secretary of Defense when asked if, because of its alleged shortage, the Navy's role in Vietnam should be reduced either by replacing Navy units with Air Force units and/or phasing out a carrier to balance the number of ships and aircraft.

One result of the alleged aircraft shortage was to force us to analyze the deployment capability for tactical air forces as a function of total inventory, attrition rates, sortie rates, pilot-rotation policies, and so on. This in turn indicated the desirability of abandoning the UE planning system.

While no single index can represent true combat capability over the wide range of contingencies for which the United States must plan, it is better to start with real hardware than with paper proxies. The best possible first approximation is the total inventory of aircraft (taking into account, of course, qualitative differences in the aircraft, pilot training, ordnance, and the like). Varying allocations of that total inventory can be made to combat units, to training, to odd jobs, and to pipe line according to the needs of the moment. The Army aviation and Marine Corps helicopter force tables had been changed in 1966 to avoid the problems of arbitrary allocations by simply showing total inventory. And while the parallel may not be exact, force tables for ships also showed total inventory. Everyone recognized that something like 20 percent of U.S. ships are in overhaul at any given time, but the force tables showed the full 15 attack carriers, not 12.

It was in recognition of these shortcomings that the Secretary of Defense decided to abandon the UE planning system in favor of a system based on total inventory. Under the new system, the "Authorized Active Inventory" (AAI) and the number of squadrons, instead of UE, were shown in the force tables. This did not mean that UE disappeared; the concept remained useful for certain aspects of the planning process. The system was changed only to the extent that (1) the force tables in the FYDP showed total inventory (AAI) instead of only part of it (UE) and (2) it was explicitly stated that the UE of a squadron represented only a nominal allowance, which would vary with the circumstances. In a long war, the number of UE aircraft could be smaller, because of larger pipe lines; in a short war, it could be larger, because of diversions of readiness-training units to combat.

The new accounting system did not change the way in which tactical air force needs were determined. The size and composition of these forces continued to be set on the basis of the world-wide deployment objectives of the United States. The only change was in the way in which decisions regarding force size and composition were displayed in the FYDP—and in the quieting of claims of shortages based on data showing fewer UE aircraft assigned to combat units than the arbitrary numbers shown in the FYDP.

The basic lesson of the tactical aircraft case is that there are "paper" shortages as well as real shortages. Often it is difficult for even DoD management, much less the Congress and the public, to recognize the difference. Planning factors, many of them quite arbitrary, are used in every defense program. In peacetime these factors are frequently changed to make improvements recommended by staff studies; in many cases they can be changed by commanders in the field. When the revisions are upward, an "instant shortage" is created as soon as the change is recorded on the planning documents. An Army division that was fully ready yesterday is made unready today by the stroke of a pen. Yet this fact is often buried in the details of day-to-day management.

In wartime or a peacetime crisis, these planning factors inevitably become "absolute minimum requirements," regardless of the fact that continuing to meet them all would represent an enormous waste of resources. However, individual commanders concerned with only a part of the total combat effort see only that their particular part has fewer resources than before, or fewer than the planning factor calls for, and thus a "shortage" exists. This is reported up the chain (and to the Congress), setting off the familiar cycle of charges, counter-claims, investigations, and explanations.

The heart of the Navy's alleged aircraft shortage was really a disagreement with the Secretary of Defense over force levels. The Navy's leaders were not reconciled to the Secretary's decision that the total number of aircraft required was less than what the Navy wanted. But rather than debate this issue, they turned to arguments based on planning factors. The Navy's planning factors (25 percent for training, 15 percent for pipe line, and so on) were based on peacetime requirements or those for a short war. When the United States got into a long war and needed more aircraft in training and pipe line, the Secretary of Defense's position was that changing circumstances required us to employ our adequate inventory in a different way; that is, to treat the inventory as a constant, the fraction in UE as a variable. The Navy's leaders argued that they were entitled to a given amount in UE in all circumstances; if the ratios changed, a shortage existed until they got more aircraft. (One trouble with this position is that no inventory could make a Service immune from shortages under some circumstances.)

A discerning public should learn to recognize the difference between a real shortage that might have occurred because of poor planning and a "paper" shortage that really is a surrogate for a disagreement with the Secretary of Defense over force levels. The cost to cure these "shortages" would have run in the billions of dollars each year.

Analysis of the War

One of the main lessons for government organization that should be drawn from U.S. involvement in Vietnam is that the President and the Secretary of Defense must have, but today lack, a reliable source of information and analysis of overseas operations that is independent of the military chain of command and Service interests, can get at the basic facts, is capable of self-criticism, and can give searching consideration to genuine alternatives without prior commitment to existing policies. Secretary McNamara was so conscious of this deficiency that in 1967 he asked the Central Intelligence Agency to set up a special unit to analyze the effectiveness of air operations over North Vietnam, and he requested a group of scientists to carry out some operations research on the war. The same reform that the establishment of the Systems Analysis office represented for peacetime force planning badly needs to be applied to wartime operations and strategy.

Another lesson of almost equal importance is that U.S. military commanders need, but for the most part either do not have or have and do not use, operations analysis organizations that provide them with a systematic method of learning by experience. There are organizations whose titles suggest such a responsibility—for example, in 1967, General Westmoreland formed an evaluation group in his headquarters—but they have not had a significant impact on the conduct of the war. On the contrary, U.S. military operations in Southeast Asia have been notable for a lack of systematic learning by experience.

If existing organizations are not meeting this need, what kind of organization would? First, a successful operations analysis organization must be an integral part of the military command, working with and accepted by all the other elements of the command. It must not be seen as an externally imposed group of outsiders. Second, its head must report directly to the appropriate military commander so that the organization's findings can be presented without prior compromise. Third, such an organization must have field representatives with the operating units, able to gather data and relay it back through their own channels. Fourth, it must be intimately tied into the real operational decision making so that there will be a systematic process of data gathering, analysis, conclusions, decisions, and dissemination of orders for new operating doctrines. Such a pattern was achieved by operations researchers working with American and British forces in World War II. It has not been achieved in Vietnam.

The leaders of the Systems Analysis office saw the need for both types of organization—an independent reporting and analysis group for the President and Secretary of Defense, and an operations analysis group for the U.S. commander in Vietnam—and we tried in several ways to encourage their development. But for a number of reasons, there were limits to what we could accomplish. What limited Vietnam analysis effort the office was making met with strong opposition from many military leaders. (For example, on at least two occasions, the Chairman of the Joint Chiefs of Staff "strongly" recommended to the Secretary of Defense that the unofficial *Southeast Asia Analysis Report,* published monthly by the Systems Analysis office as a stimulus to more analysis and discussion, "be limited for internal OSD use only" in order to "reduce the dissemination of incorrect and/or misleading information to senior officials of other governmental agencies, as well as our commanders in the field.") It was generally recognized that an attempt to give the Systems Analysis office a charter to analyze Vietnam operations and strategy, one that really tied the office into decision making, would meet with such strong military resistance as to make it politically impossible. We were not organized or staffed to provide the President and the Secretary of Defense with an independent source of information on Vietnam operations. Like everyone else in Washington, the Systems Analysis office lacked continuing firsthand contact with the problems in Vietnam. We were almost completely dependent on the data provided by U.S. military authorities in Saigon. We had no systematic independent source of information from the field. Moreover, while members of the office were trained in basic analytical skills, we did not have the specific knowledge that would have been needed to do analysis of combat operations. Finally, we already had our hands full doing the job for which the office had been created; that is, to provide the Secretary of Defense with independent analyses of force requirements.

Nevertheless, as a means of encouraging the development of such capabilities in the government, we carried on an unofficial, unsolicited, and small-scale effort consisting mainly of (1) making a number of pilot studies on various aspects of the war and (2) publishing the *Southeast Asia Analysis Reports.* With one or two possible exceptions, neither the *Reports* nor the studies had a significant impact on major Vietnam decisions. (The possible exceptions are our critique of MACV's attrition strategy in February and March 1968, and our work on pacification in the fall of 1968, after Ambassador Robert Komer took over this program in May 1967.) Although some of the studies were shown a polite interest by the MACV staff in Saigon, where there were officers who were both capable and desirous of doing effective analytical work, the conclusions were not acted upon, and the analytical approach did not take root in the Vietnam decision-making process.

Some of the pilot studies which were done by the Systems Analysis office are described below. We want to make it absolutely clear that these were only pilot studies; none claimed to be more; all conclusions were tentative and carefully qualified; all were based on data supplied by MACV; all urged additional analysis before any policy decision. We include them only to suggest what might have been accomplished had there been an organized analytic effort with respect to the Vietnam war. The controversy over basic strategy and tactics was never limited to those who opposed the war in principle. But without an organized analytic effort there was no legitimate place or procedure in the government to air disagreements, to build on pilot studies, and to provide objective information to inform the judgments that had to be made. As a result, this most complex of wars never got serious and systematic analysis.

Estimating the Costs of the War

Systems Analysis' first analytic effort was to develop a Southeast Asia cost model. In 1966, with the assistance of the Research Analysis Corporation, a model was developed to estimate the cost implications of additional deployments. Using this model, we were able to estimate the cost of various specific force increases and decreases. For example, if General Westmoreland requested an additional infantry division or tactical fighter squadron, the cost model could quickly give us a good approximation of the total financial impact. It could also tell us the cost of major U.S. combat activities, the air war in North and South Vietnam, ground combat operations, logistical support costs, the war at sea, and the like.

More importantly, the model permitted the Systems Analysis staff to develop a crude Vietnam "program budget." The purpose of this analysis was to provide a rough idea of what the various "output" programs (as opposed to the "input" programs—supplying men, ammunition, fuel, spare parts) in Southeast Asia were costing. These output programs included offensive land operations, border protection, air interdiction, security, pacification, and economic development. The budget resulting from this analysis included the total government cost, adding in expenditures by the Government of Vietnam (GVN), the U.S. State Department, the Agency for International Development (AID), the Central Intelligence Agency (CIA), and the like. It showed vividly that the overwhelming bulk of U.S. total resources was going into offensive operations, with relatively little into population security, pacification, and related programs designed to protect and influence the South Vietnamese population. For example, in fiscal 1968, almost $14 billion was spent for bombing and offensive operations, but only $850 million for pacification and programs designed to offset war damage and develop the economy and social infrastructure in South Vietnam. While this analysis was circulated in Washington and Saigon, it had no discernible impact on the key decisions.

Without systematic analysis of resource allocation, the United States tended to dissipate its resources on high-cost, low-pay-off operations that happened to be congenial to traditional Service missions in conventional warfare. Emphasis was focused on inputs; little attention was given to outputs. More attention to effectiveness in relation to cost might well have led to reductions in the billions of dollars spent on offensive operations and massive firepower displays —activities yielding small returns. Had even a modest part of these resources been used for activities which appeared to have higher pay-offs, such as providing security for the local population through expansion of the South Vietnamese Regional and Popular forces, or enhancing the effectiveness of the Vietnamese Army by reequipping and modernizing its forces (a South Vietnamese division force costs roughly one-twentieth as much to establish and operate as a U.S. division force), or providing the GVN with better pay and financial incentives in the hope of reducing the widespread corruption—things which were later to be given priority—the course of U.S. involvement in the war might have been altered sooner.

The Attrition Strategy

Some of the most important pilot studies done by the Systems Analysis office dealt directly with the strategy of attrition. From the beginning, the Vietnam conflict had been characterized as a "war of attrition," with heavy emphasis on enemy casualties, particularly the "body count." The concept of "body count" did not mean that every enemy corpse was viewed by a foot patrol at close range and recorded. Nor did it mean that every corpse that was counted was marked to prevent recounting. The regulations provided only for counting "males of fighting age and others, male or female, known to have carried arms." The regulations further provided that "body counts made from the air will be reported" if they met these criteria "beyond reasonable doubt." Errors could and did frequently creep in through double-counting, counting civilians (either bystanders or impressed porters), or counting graves, or through ignoring the rules because of the pressures to exaggerate enemy losses or the hazards of trying to count bodies while the enemy was still in the area.

The incentives for field commanders clearly lay in the direction of claiming a high body count. Padded claims kept everyone happy; there were no penalties for overstating enemy losses, but an understatement could lead to sharp questions as to why U.S. casualties were so high compared with the results achieved. Few commanders were bold enough to volunteer the information that they had lost as many men in an engagement as the enemy—or more. The net result of all this was that statistics regarding body counts were notoriously unreliable. Off-the-record interviews with officers who had been a part of the process revealed a consistent, almost universal pattern: in a representative case, battalions raised the figures coming from the companies, and brigades raised the figures coming in from the battalions. In addition, something had to be (and was) put in for all the artillery and air support, which the men on the ground could not check out, to give the supporting arms their share of the "kill."

The extreme emphasis on body count as *the* measure of success led to various attempts to lend credence to the reported data. In one such attempt, General Westmoreland's intelligence chief reported in mid-1967 that his search of 70 captured enemy documents confirmed the

1966 body count to within 1.8 percent. But the documents were far from precise and their interpretation and analysis far from convincing. A review of the same documents by the Systems Analysis office suggested that the enemy body count was overstated by at least 30 percent.

Another review suggested that in hit-and-run guerrilla fights and in ambushes the enemy typically lost no more troops than the United States did. Over half of the larger engagements (and virtually all the smaller ones) were of this kind. It also indicated that one-fifth to one-third of the U.S. deaths were caused by mines and booby traps, for which few enemy were killed in exchange. The only type of engagement in which the United States consistently achieved a highly favorable kill ratio was enemy attacks on entrenched U.S. units. But such attacks accounted for less than one-fourth of the large engagements in 1966, and after learning that he could not overrun a dug-in U.S. unit as large as a company or more, the enemy for all practical purposes quit trying until Tet.

Moreover, body counts (as well as other numerical indicators, such as supplies and weapons captured), even if believable, had to be tied to Vietcong and North Vietnamese Army (VC/NVA) replacement capabilities in order to be meaningful. This relationship required a sophisticated analysis based on data of hopelessly unequal reliability. Body counts were "known." Prisoners of war, ralliers (Chieu Hoi), and deserters captured by friendly forces were reported, but except for ralliers no distinction was made between soldiers and political operatives and civilians. Deserters who returned to their villages and soldiers who died or were disabled by wounds could be estimated only by digging through mountains of scrap notes and low-level enemy reports, euphemistically called "captured documents." Enemy manpower resources had to be estimated by census techniques and models applied to the North and South Vietnam populations, of which we knew very little.

For these reasons, estimates of enemy losses and manpower resources from whatever sources were always suspect. Nevertheless, by late 1968, it seemed clear from various studies, based on even the most optimistic assumptions, that the North Vietnamese were capable of replacing annual losses as high as 200,000 men for years. Moreover, even this figure may have understated the enemy's "surge" capability because Hanoi could choose to use some of its long-term-war-sustaining manpower to provide short-term (two- to three-year) political gains. In any event, the enemy's ability to sustain losses of 200,000 men per year was of critical importance to any U.S. strategy that called for defeating the enemy through a war of attrition.

In 1966, VC/NVA losses had been estimated at 55,000 to 75,000 men; at the time, our commanders had felt that the enemy could not possibly sustain such losses. In 1967, enemy losses had been estimated at 100,000 to 140,000: "victory was just around the corner." But even in the first half of 1968, when the bloodshed of the enemy Tet and spring offensives shocked Americans and South Vietnamese alike, estimated enemy losses had never approached 200,000 per year. In other words, the VC/NVA forces appeared to have the manpower to sustain the war for years at the intense level of the first half of 1968, including launching major country-wide offensives such as Tet. The United States could not hope to win a war of attrition, within any reasonable period of years, even when the enemy was willing to fight on a massive scale.

More important, a Systems Analysis study of representative fire fights during 1966 suggested that the enemy could control his losses within a wide range and thus keep them below a level that was unacceptable or unsustainable. Enemy losses mounted only when he chose to fight, and, by and large, he chose to fight only at times and places favorable to him. Correlations between enemy attacks and enemy losses were very high; similar correlations between friendly force activity and enemy losses were close to zero. In other words, regardless of the level of allied activity, the VC/NVA lost significant numbers of men only when they decided to stand and fight. And in 1966 they had the choice of time and place in over 85 percent of the fire fights in Vietnam. When the enemy did not choose to fight, he simply faded into the jungle and across the borders to sanctuaries. If he did not want to be found, he could not be, as U.S. commanders repeatedly stated.

The VC/NVA strategic objective in fighting was more political than military: they wanted to influence U.S. and South Vietnamese public opinion by inflicting unacceptable allied casualties, in areas of highest psychological value, but always with the intention of outlasting the United States. Systems Analysis' studies suggested that they had an excellent chance of succeeding. In short, these studies concluded that the enemy could continue fighting for years, even if his losses reached 200,000 men per year—a level that was highly unlikely, since he could control his casualty rate within a wide range by choosing where and when to fight. If this conclusion was true, the notion of winning the war by wearing down the enemy was untenable. This was the essence of the first memorandum on Vietnam sent by the Systems Analysis office to the new Secretary of Defense, Clark Clifford. That memorandum is reproduced below:

20 March 1968

MEMORANDUM FOR MR. CLIFFORD

SUBJECT: Vietnam

One important fact about the war in Vietnam is that the enemy can control his casualty rate, at least to a great extent, by controlling the number, size and intensity of combat engagements. If he so chooses, he can limit his casualties to a rate that he is able to bear indefinitely. Therefore the notion that we can "win" this war by driving the VC/NVA from the country or by inflicting an unacceptable rate of casualties on them is false. Moreover, a 40% increase in friendly forces cannot be counted upon to produce a 40% increase in enemy casualties if the enemy doesn't want that to happen.

In a conventional war for territory, with a front, we can force the enemy either to accept higher casualties or to yield territory by attacking with greater intensity. But this analogy does not hold in Vietnam.

In Vietnam, to a great extent, the enemy can control how much he fights. If he wants to suffer fewer casualties per month, he can fall back into the jungles and remote areas. If we go after him, we must accept combat on less favorable terms. Or he can melt into the population, and the combination of his coercive power and our poor intelligence can prevent us from destroying him without destroying the population.

Studies of combat engagements in 1966 showed that the enemy had a choice as to whether or not to fight in the majority of cases. Although data collection in 1967 was poor, what data we have indicates no change in this basic fact.

A better analogy than conventional land war would be our air campaign against NVN [North Vietnam]. The enemy can influence the attrition rate per sortie by the amount and quality of his defenses. But we control the number of aircraft lost per month—which we trade-off against damage to NVN—by controlling the number of sorties. If we wanted to lose fewer aircraft per month, we could fly fewer sorties.

And if the VC/NVA want to lose fewer troops per month, they can make fewer attacks. They can trade-off lower U.S. casualties for lower VC/NVA casualties, and time.

/s/ Alain Enthoven

Why were similar analyses not performed by U.S. military and civilian leaders in Vietnam who had access to much more data and had far more experience? First, the leaders in Vietnam were not studying "theoretical" questions of this kind. They were extremely busy with the enormous day-to-day operating problems posed by the massive American build-up, the ubiquity and effectiveness of the VC/NVA attacks, and the condition of the South Vietnamese allies. In the beginning, staving off defeat was such a clear purpose that there seemed to be no need for a searching evaluation of long-range objectives. Unfortunately, this pattern was to persist. Second, typically, the environment of a military staff, especially one serving a field commander, is not conducive to a self-critical evaluation of alternative strategies. Rather, the whole spirit of such an operation stresses teamwork. An officer who articulates and defends a policy different from the official position can expect to suffer in his fitness reports and subsequent promotions. Third, military staff and field commanders had a one-year tour and usually more than one job within the year, so that there was little time to assimilate the lessons of the war. Fourth, the leaders had no alternative strategy and so no incentive to make calculations that would call into question the strategy of attrition. Alternatives suggested from outside the command, such as General Gavin's "enclave strategy," were received by many in Saigon (and in Washington) as threatening criticisms to be rebutted rather than given serious analytical consideration.

Why did the Joint Chiefs not perform such analyses and report such conclusions to the President and the Secretary of Defense? Largely because the JCS made virtually no independent analysis of the Vietnam war. They viewed their role as supporters of the commanders in Vietnam and the Pacific. They used the vast flow of data from Vietnam as input material for keeping themselves informed of daily events in the war so that they could better argue General Westmoreland's case to top civilian officials. They did not attempt to organize the data for systematic assessment of strategy. They did not even establish an analysis group until late in 1967, and then denied it the leeway necessary to analyze basic questions. In short, the JCS had no desire to second-guess General Westmoreland. The President and Secretary of Defense always consulted the JCS before making decisions, but the advice was absolutely predictable: do what General Westmoreland and Admiral Sharp ask, and increase the size of the remaining forces in the United States.

Pacification

Analyses of "pacification" and popular support for the GVN were much tougher to make than analyses of the military side of the war. The numerically analyzable aspects of progress were even fewer and less significant than those used for military operations, and meaningful analysis was difficult to do from Washington. Changes in popular support were being reported, but real progress required that they be tied to ultimate objectives and specific time frames. For example, the total population in government-controlled areas was a poor indicator of the percentage of the population really supporting the allied side (or at least not supporting the other side). We could achieve 100 percent with population control statistics, and the United States would still be in very bad shape in Vietnam. To be significant, the changes had to indicate improvements in the ability of the South Vietnamese to protect and govern themselves with progressively less U.S. help and intervention. They had to show that the Vietnamese in the villages and hamlets were less subject to assassination and kidnaping by the VC. They had to demonstrate that the United States knew where it had been, where it was now, and where it was going.

From 1964 through 1966, the basic system for measuring progress in pacifying and securing the people of Vietnam was a set of pacification statistics developed primarily by the GVN (but with considerable U.S. advice and assistance). United States advisers in the field were supposed to make their own independent assessment of the degree of security and governmental administrative control in their districts. The results were aggregated into four or five categories, ranging from "Secured" to "VC Controlled," and widely publicized (when the trends were favorable) in such statements as "the VC control only 25 percent of the Vietnam population while the other 75 percent either is secure or is being secured."

The pre-1967 pacification-statistics system was bad for three main reasons. First, U.S. advisers (who with rare exceptions didn't speak Vietnamese) had no way of analyzing security status independently of their Vietnamese counterparts, who had no interest in telling the Americans that things were going badly. Second, the advisers had every reason to bias the assessments upward, since they were in effect rating their own progress in helping to secure the people from the VC. They tended to report changes resulting from ongoing work, while ignoring deterioration in areas worked previously. Third, since the system was not very good, constant changes in the methods of reporting were made to "improve" it, thus breaking comparability with the past. This happened at least five times between December 1964 and January 1967; many of the changes had the effect of making progress appear rapid, when actually only the bookkeeper's pencil had moved.

The obvious answer to the problem of improving the continuity of the data was to adjust the previous numbers for the changes in criteria to make them comparable. The Systems Analysis office attempted to do this in September 1967. The result was that while the official numbers had indicated an increase of three million Vietnamese in the "Secured" category from December 1965 to June 1967, our retrospective estimate was about two million. Furthermore, as was confirmed by Ambassador Komer, most of the increase in secure population did not result from significant expansion of territory protected by friendly forces, but rather from the movement of people (refugees and job seekers) from VC-controlled and contested areas into areas already controlled by allied forces, and from natural population growth. Less than one-sixth of the three million people reportedly made secure in the first eighteen months of U.S. fighting in Vietnam lived in rural areas more secure than before.

The reluctance to correct the pacification numbers is not surprising. The reason most widely given was that the public would never understand why numbers being used now differed from those used in the past. Considering the "credibility gap" problems of officials in Saigon and Washington, this was understandable, even though the gap was widening in part *because* the corrections were not made. More fundamental, however, was the lack of interest in, or sensitivity to, the importance of good historical data prior to 1967. This failing is a perennial one in the intelligence community and among operational military personnel concerned only with today and tomorrow.

Even retrospectively adjusted, the pre-1967 pacification data were inadequate, because they failed to get at the heart of the pacification problems. The most important problems were reflected in the belief of the rural Vietnamese that their government officials would not remain when they came into an area, but that the VC would; that the VC would punish cooperation with the government; that the government was indifferent to the people's welfare; that low-level government officials were tools of the local rich; and that the government was excessively corrupt from top to bottom. Success in changing these beliefs, and thus in pacification, depended on the interrelated jobs of providing physical security, destroying VC organization and presence, motivating the villager to cooperate, and establishing effective local government.

Physical security was the essential prerequisite to a successful pacification effort. The security had to be permanent to have meaning for the villager. It had to be established by a well-organized "clear and hold" operation, continued long enough to really clear the area, and conducted by competent military forces trained to show respect for the villager and his problems. This prerequisite had not been shown by late 1966, so we did not trust the pacification statistics that glowingly reported progress.

A new statistical system was needed to measure progress in both securing the people and developing the nation. Secretary McNamara asked the CIA to devise a new system for measuring pacification progress: the Hamlet Evaluation System (HES), instituted in January 1967. Through an arrangement with U.S. authorities in Saigon, the Systems Analysis office became the official repository in Washington for this highly detailed computerized data system. This system, tied to quantitative data on military operations, enemy activity, and friendly/enemy force locations, allowed a much more systematic understanding of the impact of pacification activities in Vietnam.

The HES started with a new gazetteer of hamlets and new estimates of population wherever possible. Each adviser rated each hamlet on eighteen different criteria, nine each on security matters and matters of economic and political development. The system was specific enough to show that pacification had expanded only slowly in the first half of 1967 and lost ground in the second half. For example, on analysis, the new system showed that 60 percent of the Saigon-reported 1967 gain came from "accounting changes" in the HES system rather than from actual pacification progress. In the area that really counted, the moving of VC-controlled and -contested populations in hamlets to relatively secure status, there had been a small net decline between June and December 1967. In short, by the end of 1967 pacification still had not gotten very far off the ground. But at least the new pacification program seemed better attuned to the political nature of the Vietnam conflict than many of the conventional military operations, and it did get moving in the fall of 1968.

Tactics and Operations

In addition to wrestling with the statistics on body counts and pacification and trying to make sense out of them, the Systems Analysis office made several interesting pilot studies of military operations in Vietnam. Again, none of these studies claimed to be definitive; all were based on data supplied by the military authorities in Saigon; all urged more study before any change in policy. One of them concerned the effects of the bombing campaign in North Vietnam. While there was considerable controversy over just what the objectives of the bombing campaign were, most supporters of the campaign included these two in their lists:

1. To reduce or limit the flow of men and supplies from North to South Vietnam below the level the enemy would otherwise maintain, and thereby to reduce its force or activity levels in South Vietnam.

2. To increase the cost to North Vietnam of supporting the war in South Vietnam, thereby providing an incentive for Hanoi to negotiate a settlement.

The study strongly suggested that the bombing campaign was contributing very little toward meeting either objective (not to mention more ambitious objectives proposed by others). This conclusion coincided with the findings of similar studies done in other parts of the government. (The Systems Analysis study was not unique.) In the face of steadily intensified bombing, the flow of men and supplies from North Vietnam had continued to increase. While the bombing may have destroyed roughly 10 percent of the men and supplies in a given flow going to the south, the enemy was able to replace these losses and still maintain or increase the desired flow. Moreover, the bombing did not greatly reduce North Vietnam's road, truck, railway, watercraft, or manpower capabilities. While it placed an additional strain on North Vietnam's management capacity and resources, the strain was not severe enough to prevent significant increases in the rate of infiltration such as those that occurred in 1968 in the face of the heaviest U.S. bombing efforts.

Similarly, the study indicated that the U.S. bombing in North Vietnam had little observable effect on enemy force or activity levels in South Vietnam. Between 1965 and 1968, U.S. attack sorties against North Vietnam increased about fourfold. Over the same period, the enemy's main force increased its strength levels by 75 percent, its attacks fivefold, and its over-all activity level ninefold. For example, in the critical I Corps area (the area immediately south of the Demilitarized Zone [DMZ] dividing North and South Vietnam), VC/NVA attacks increased eightfold between 1966 and 1968. Over the same period, interdiction sorties in the DMZ and immediately to the north increased fourteenfold; and tactical sorties in the I Corps itself doubled.

What about costs? Between 1965 and 1968 the bombing campaign was estimated to have caused North Vietnam about $600 million of damage in terms of the destruction of capital stock and military facilities and the losses in economic production. During the same period, however, North Vietnam received over $2 billion in foreign aid. In fact, as the United States intensified the bombing campaign, North Vietnam's Communist allies steadily increased their economic and military aid. At the same time, the campaign had cost the United States about $6 billion in destroyed aircraft alone.

One of the important lessons of the Vietnam war, we believe, is that deep-interdiction bombing appears far less effective in this kind of war than its advocates claim. Although there was much complaint about them, the bombing restrictions under which U.S. forces operated in 1967 were reasonable and of small significance for the military effectiveness of the operation. If we had bombed and destroyed the Haiphong docks, the North Vietnamese would have been able to bring in equivalent supplies by land and over the beaches, just as they did after the bombing of their oil installations. The optimistic claims for what could be accomplished by unrestricted bombings were based on far too narrow a view of the problem. Proponents of the bombing campaign give too little consideration to what the enemy could do to counteract the effects of the bombing. A thorough and objective study comparable to the Strategic Bombing Survey after World War II is needed to establish the facts of the bombing campaign and make them available to the public.

Another Systems Analysis pilot study examined the effectiveness of small, long-range patrols versus large, battalion-sized search-and-destroy sweeps. Based on a statistical analysis of after-action reports on engagements during 1966, the study concluded that small patrols were much more effective and much less costly in casualties than big sweeps. Small-unit operations produced enemy losses ranging from ten to almost forty times the friendly losses, compared with a multiple of less than seven for battalion-sized operations. Thus, the study suggested that the expanded use of small-unit operations, particularly patrols, would be advantageous. On the basis of past results, such a shift in emphasis promised to bring about a decline, or at worst no increase, in friendly losses while significantly increasing enemy losses. From Washington, we could not be sure whether these conclusions were correct or not. But it did seem clear that more analyses of this kind should have been done in Vietnam, their conclusions tested, and, if proved valid, acted upon.

Still another such study concerned the utility of unobserved air and artillery strikes. In 1966, some 65 percent of the total tonnage of bombs and artillery rounds used in Vietnam was expended against places where the enemy *might* be, but without reliable information that he *was* there. The purpose of these unobserved strikes was to harass, discourage, and drive off the enemy if he happened to be around.

While the available evidence was fragmentary, the study suggested that (1) in 1966, such unobserved strikes probably killed fewer than 100 VC/NVA; (2) the 27,000 tons of dud bombs and shells from such attacks provided the enemy with more than enough material for mines and booby traps (the cause of death for over 1,000 U.S.

soldiers in 1966); (3) the effects of such strikes on civilians in VC
and friendly areas were often undesirable, probably creating more
VC than they eliminated; (4) the more than $2 billion a year the
United States was spending for such strikes could probably be spent
with greater effectiveness elsewhere; and (5) the subject deserved
more analysis and top-level consideration. Not long after the study
was circulated, U.S. forces captured a Vietcong training film that
showed recruits how to dismantle American dud bombs, recover the
explosive material, and make grenades out of it. The combination of
study and film led only to an effort to improve the reliability of fuses
and to the discontinuance of some particularly unreliable types of
munitions.

These examples should not be allowed to obscure the basic fact
that *there was no organized critical analysis of the strategy and
operations of the Vietnam war—cost-effectiveness or otherwise.*

The Need for Integrating Over-all Operations

One of the most fundamental deficiencies in the management of the
Vietnam war has been the lack of integration of the military aspects
with the political and economic aspects. The Communists have been
able to use their military operations very shrewdly for political
purposes, but it has been politically impossible for U.S. leaders to do
so. As a result, the Vietnam operation has been filled with internal
contradictions. Often, we have destroyed with the left hand what we
were building with the right. For example, one of the basic U.S. goals
in Vietnam has been to establish strong armed forces and an honest
civil service. Yet the heavy deployment of American forces contributed directly to inflation, eroding the economic position of both
the Vietnamese officer corps and the supporting civil servants and
making them more susceptible to corruption and disunity. Similarly,
U.S. policies of saturation bombing and almost unlimited use of
firepower helped create large numbers of homeless refugees, thus
further undermining the social fabric of South Vietnam.

If nothing else, Vietnam has clearly shown the need for better ways
of tying together total national security policy and operations. One of
the most significant contributions of PPBS in the Department of
Defense was to help integrate related functions in an intelligible way.

An implementation of these ideas at the national policy-making level would seem to offer a promising means of avoiding the internal policy contradictions that Vietnam so vividly demonstrates.

The Need for More Analysis

If the highest officials in Washington and Saigon were blinded by the deluge of statistics showing only change and activity, it was largely because of a deep resistance to trying to run the war from Washington. The problem was not overmanagement of the war from Washington; it was undermanagement. The problem was not too much analysis; it was too little. The President and his key advisers sought candid assessments of the war, but they would not pay the political costs in terms of friction with the military to get them. There was no systematic analysis in Vietnam of the allocation of resources to the different missions of the war and no systematic analysis of the effectiveness and costs of alternative military operations. Little operations analysis was being conducted in the field or in Washington. And even if all these analyses had been made, there was no good program budget or over-all organization in the Executive Branch of the government to put the findings to use, on either the military or the civilian side.

Analysis is no substitute for judgment, and analysts cannot do the final judging. But judgment can be a poor substitute for fact and analysis. Policy should result from a combination of judgment and analysis. And the best analysis usually comes from adversary proceedings, with all interested parties participating. Only then are policy makers likely to see clear alternatives before them, each with its benefits and costs stated as explicitly as possible.

The President and the Secretary of Defense cannot get this kind of analysis simply by asking for it. They have to establish competent, independent analytical staffs in their own offices and create competent, independent reporting systems in the field. Had this been done in Vietnam, the military and civilian leaders there would probably also have established competent analytical staffs of their own, if for no other reason than self-defense. This is the process that occurred after Secretary McNamara set up the Systems Analysis office in DoD in 1961 to analyze the regular defense program. It became accepted for the Secretary of Defense to control the peacetime defense budget, and he had a fighting chance to establish systematic analysis as one of the main instruments for doing this. But it was not accepted that systematic analysis should be an important criterion in the strategy or conduct of military operations in Vietnam. Thus, decisions were largely made on the basis of judgment alone.

9

Unfinished Business, 1969

The work of improving the national defense program decision process calls for continuing effort. We have described the unfinished business of 1961. There was also much unfinished business when we left the Pentagon at the beginning of 1969. We have grouped the main items on the agenda under four general headings: (1) Need for More Effective and Balanced Outside Review and Interrogation, (2) Improving the Quality of Information Presented to the Secretary of Defense, (3) Lack of Adequate Financial Discipline, and (4) Strengthening Some Procedural Links. In what follows we make no pretense of treating *all* the many aspects of these areas, but only some of those affecting strategy, force, and financial planning. Nor do we presume to prescribe detailed changes for the problems noted. Rather, in each case we have sketched some possible next steps in what appears to us to be the right direction for further improvement. As noted in the concluding section, some of these steps have already been taken (some voluntarily, others in response to public and Congressional demand) by the Nixon administration.

Need for More Effective and Balanced Outside Review and Interrogation

During 1968 it became apparent to most observers that there was widespread dissatisfaction with the over-all size of the defense budget

309

in relation to other national needs. Although much of this was related to Vietnam spending, a substantial part was directed at the non-Vietnam part of the defense budget. This dissatisfaction intensified in 1969. The sharp debates and sharp attacks on the Safeguard ABM system, the C-5A, and other programs were clearly fueled by concern over the total level of spending.

The problem of balancing defense spending and other national needs cannot be solved by the Defense Department alone. The President, the Congress, and ultimately the public set the context in which defense decisions are made. In discussing the national defense program decision process, one must look to this context as well as to the Department's own management system. And it is in this broader context that we find one of the main elements of unfinished business: the need for more balanced debate on basic defense issues outside the Department of Defense, and more balanced and effective interrogation of the Department from outside. Such debate and interrogation are needed to clarify the context in which key assumptions and judgments are made by defense officials. *In particular, Congressional debate and interrogation of military strategy and needs should be more balanced, and more informed participation by the interested public should be encouraged.*

Between 1961 and 1969, there was a pronounced tendency on the part of the Congress, particularly some members of the Armed Services Committees, to rely solely on appeal to authority—to insist that the military leaders must be followed on matters of military strategy and need because they are the experts. As McGeorge Bundy noted, following the appearance of the Senate Preparedness Subcommittee's summary report in 1967, which recommended a larger bombing compaign in North Vietnam:

The Senators appeal not to evidence but to authority. They set a group of generals and admirals against Secretary McNamara, and their position is that the generals and admirals are right simply because they are professionals. The Subcommittee does not demonstrate the military value of the course it urges; it simply tells us that the generals and admirals are for it. It is true that both sides in such a public argument are hampered by problems of security, but Secretary McNamara, in his powerful public statement before the Subcommittee, offered extensive evidence—facts and figures—in support of his position. The Subcommittee answers only with a repeated appeal to the opinions of officers it heard.

Nothing is less reliable, in hard choices of this sort, than the unsupported opinion of men who are urging the value of their own chosen instrument—in this case military force. We must not be surprised and still less persuaded, when generals and admirals recommend additional military action—what do we expect them to recommend? The interesting question is always whether their supporting argument is strong or weak, and on this critical point the summary report tells us nothing. There is literally no evidence at all, in this report, for the Subcommittee's sweeping conclusions that the restrictions currently in effect are "vital to the success of the air war."[1]

The approach taken in the report was taken all too frequently in the review of defense programs. From 1961 to 1968, there was not enough balanced Congressional debate and interrogation of the defense program. More often than not, the procedure was to get the Joint Chiefs on the record with their requests and then criticize the civilian leaders for not buying or doing everything the Chiefs wanted. If the Secretary of Defense was ever seriously importuned by the Congress to buy less of a military program, it was a rare exception (and usually explained by the fact that the Chiefs didn't want the program because it was a substitute for something they did want). In such an atmosphere, the civilian leaders of DoD were forced to concentrate on building defenses against attacks from those favoring more defense spending. When any given factor was uncertain, the tendency was to pick a value that could not be easily attacked by the Congressional proponents of more defense spending. This was reflected, for example, in such judgments as how great the greater-than-expected threat should be. Moreover, the efforts by DoD's civilian leaders to get the Services to do better studies in justification of programs were often undermined by the knowledge that detailed justifications and studies would not be demanded by the Congress. On the contrary, the situation encouraged the Services not to do good studies, but to assert that they needed more, because such assertions would be sufficient.

Equally significant, the Congressional debate that did occur during this period focused almost entirely on narrow weapon systems issues: the B-70, TFX, Nike-X, Skybolt, and nuclear-powered frigates. But the defense budget is the product of a chain of factors: foreign policy (including treaties and commitments), military strategy to support it (including judgments as to which threats and contingencies the

United States should meet and how), military forces to implement the strategy, and weapon systems to arm the forces. Many billions of dollars turn on decisions made much further up the line than weapon systems. For example, the difference in cost between a "2½ war" and a "1½ war" planning assumption for general-purpose forces could be $10 billion per year. Yet, to the best of our knowledge, the Congress has never seriously considered this broader issue, although Secretary McNamara discussed such planning assumptions in his annual budget statements. Nor has it seriously debated such broad questions as why we should spend some $1.5 billion per year to maintain 15 rather than 12 attack carriers in the fleet, or why we should keep 300,000 rather than 200,000 men in Europe, or why we should spend roughly $1 billion to maintain 50,000 troops in Korea. This is not to say that we believe the force levels in Europe and Korea, or the extra carriers, could not stand up in a debate. It is only to say that such broad military priorities ought to be tested in debate against domestic priorities.

More balanced Congressional interrogation and debate, as a regular procedure, could have a tremendous impact on the cost and quality of the defense program. A continuing pattern of serious debates would be a strong stimulus to DoD to do better analysis and planning. It would undoubtedly help produce a more balanced defense program.

More public debate of major defense issues, for example, along the lines of the 1969 ABM debate (but hopefully of higher quality), and more independent study of such issues by groups outside the government (such as the Council on Foreign Relations and the Brookings Institution), would also contribute to clarifying the broad judgments involved and to enlarging the context of defense decisions. For such debate and study to be very useful, however, the public must have access to at least the basic analytical material used in making those decisions. In the annual Secretary of Defense statements to the Congress, it was the policy of both McNamara and Clifford to release this material as an aid to public understanding. (Indeed, most of the numerical material in this book first appeared in these statements.) Such information enables the interested public not only to see the rationale for a decision but to check that rationale for logic and reasonableness. We hope this policy will be continued by Secretary Laird.

More outside interrogation and debate from the above-mentioned sources would go a long way toward forcing the military and civilian participants involved directly in the strategy and force planning process to take a larger view. The Defense Department, in particular, includes many vigorous and dedicated men who are pushing their own programs very hard and who see the whole defense of the United States as being tied up with these programs. These men are often personally affronted and publicly outraged when their programs are questioned or cut back. Too few people in DoD appreciate the problem of getting a total defense program that makes sense. But the perspective appropriate to a project officer or individual unit commander is simply not appropriate to the development of the total national defense program.

In the military planning staffs, conservatism is the rule. Each echelon tends to hedge against uncertainties. This is understandable, but since the hedging is rarely made explicit, the result can be serious imbalances in forces or equipment. The military commander sees all of his unit's shortcomings, but none of the enemy's. He sees the whole Soviet army aimed at his particular division, the entire Soviet air force directed at his air wing, or all the Soviet submarines bearing down on his ship. And since he gets most of his resources in kind, not money, he has little concept of or interest in total cost. Quite understandably, what he wants is more. But his view must be balanced by a different point of view—from men who want the totals to make sense.

Part of the problem also results from the fact that the "national security community" (the Defense and State Department civilians, the Services, the Central Intelligence Agency, and the Armed Services Committees) as a whole tends to accept its own assumptions, almost all of which have a pro-defense bias. What is needed is to open up some of these assumptions to broader scrutiny.

Improving the Quality of Information Presented to the Secretary of Defense

There is a need for great improvement in the quality and usefulness of information that comes to the Secretary of Defense and other top defense officials (and ultimately to the President and the Congress). Looking back at the major decisions made during 1961–1968, we see a strong correlation between the eventual success or failure of a decision by the Secretary of Defense and the quality of information available to him when the decision was made.

Operations in the Field

As noted in Chapter 8, more and better information on and analysis of actual military operations is needed if defense planners are to have a satisfactory grasp of the real effectiveness of U.S. forces and programs. In most cases the effectiveness of these forces is simply not known. What is worse, in the past there has been little systematic effort to find out. In Vietnam, for example, no military evaluation group was even formally established until 1967, and, as a part of the military chain of command, it could not have the independence necessary to ask fundamental questions.

The Secretary of Defense and the President need an evaluation group that is independent of the military chain of command and can do for them with respect to military performance what the Systems Analysis office did with respect to force requirements. It is unreasonable to continue to ask the military (or any other group) to critique objectively and systematically its own performance. In the field, in particular, there is neither the necessary time, trained manpower, nor incentives to do so. But if Washington-based leaders are to know what is happening in the field, they must have independent, objective, and systematic evaluations made at the source.

Cost and Performance Data

A related problem area is the lack of realistic cost and performance data on new and existing weapon systems—particularly, operating and support costs, and performance data for employment conditions approximating actual combat.

(1) PROCUREMENT COSTS

A series of greatly overoptimistic cost estimates can have a disastrous impact on defense planning. It can cause the Defense Department to go ahead with programs that would not have been approved with more realistic estimates and that have to be canceled when the true costs become apparent, after much waste of time and money. Alternatively, it can cause the Department not to approve comparatively inexpensive but effective items to improve existing forces because it looks better to wait for the marvelous new system that unfortunately never arrives. To a large extent, rational force planning is impossible without realistic cost estimates.

The two basic lines of attack used during 1961–1968 on the problem of cost growth were (1) developing better estimating procedures, such as statistical methods for correlating aggregate costs with key performance characteristics, and (2) developing better management controls, such as total package procurement and the Development Concept Paper, described earlier. These helped to reduce cost overruns substantially from the 200–300 percent average of the 1950's, but not by enough to resolve the problem.[2] (Indeed, in an important sense, these changes made the existence of the problem more apparent, since because of them the original cost estimates for new weapon systems were explicitly documented, so that, if they were exceeded, it was clearly known.)

We know of no easy answer to the problem of cost growth. Congressional and public expectations of what can be accomplished in this respect are probably too high. As we have indicated, the estimation of requirements is far from an exact science. The same is true of cost estimates. If the Department of Defense ever reached the point where actual costs were within 25 percent of the original estimates, it would be doing remarkably well (and much better than many other organizations). Continued work on developing better estimating methods, finding better management controls that clearly identify agreed cost and performance estimates and fix responsibility for overruns, and tougher scrutiny of new proposals by the Office of the Director of Defense Research and Engineering are all steps in the direction of reaching such a goal. And the Secretary of Defense's willingness to cancel programs that do not stay within reasonable limits is a key to progress in controlling costs.

(2) OPERATING COSTS

The budgeting system in DoD provides for fairly clear-cut decisions and control over the procurement of major equipment items (tanks, ships, planes, and the like) and over military construction projects. The categories of expenditure are reviewed and decided upon for specific projects (by "line item," in Pentagon jargon), in both the planning and the budgeting process. The currently approved status of many of these items is given for several years in advance in the Five-Year Defense Plan. Various Congressional committees scrutinize these expenditures very carefully. Yet these major procurement and construction items account for only about a third of the total defense budget. The remaining two-thirds go for operating costs, including pay and allowances for military personnel, pay for the more than one million civilians employed by the Defense Department, and expenditures on millions of small procurement items such as ammunition, spare parts, petroleum, and other supplies needed to operate the forces. The management of these vast outlays has not been adequately integrated with top-management decisions or the over-all planning process of the Department. Some of these costs have been allocated to wings and divisions to make the Secretary aware of the implications of decisions concerning major units, but the real decisions on operating costs are made in the final budget review, mainly by adjusting each Service's previous year's budget. Each Service then parcels out operating budgets to its component elements. The "actual" operating costs of a division or a supply depot are not really known anywhere in the system. Nor is there adequate feedback in the system to inform top-level decision makers of the financial results of their decisions.

These defects in the system create two kinds of problems. First, the top management of the Department cannot make good decisions when the costs, other than procurement, are unknown—possibly half the total costs associated with a decision. There is no assurance that decisions made on operating budgets are the "right" ones to support the major over-all forces and strategy decided upon; and whether right or not, there is no system for telling what actually happened as a result. Any deficiencies or overages are absorbed in the massive Service budgets in one place or another.

The right amount of operating funds for a unit depends on the desired degree of effectiveness and readiness for that unit. With a few exceptions, the Defense Department has not developed criteria explicitly relating operating and maintenance (O&M) funds (input) to effectiveness or readiness (output). For example, in 1967 there was a major disagreement between the OSD and the Navy over O&M funds for Naval aviation. But neither side was able to offer a set of re-producible calculations relating different levels of O&M funds to different levels of readiness. An unsatisfactory compromise had to be made. Such standards could and should be worked out. Much of the groundwork has already been laid in the development of more explicit readiness standards.

Second, incentives for efficient operations in the field are badly distorted. For example, field commanders frequently strive hard to save money from their own budgets, often finding ingenious ways to reduce costs. However, the system allows these commanders to con-trol only a fraction of the costs they affect (their operations and maintenance costs) and excludes from their budget such major items as military personnel, equipment, and real estate, which are given to them in kind. Any economies made by the commander with assets given to him in kind simply result in a decrease in the assets available to him and an increase for someone else; by contrast, economies made in his dollar budget are available to him for other uses. This anomaly often leads to situations where inefficient use is made of resources allocated in kind, such as military personnel or major equipment, in order to save on the dollar operating budget.

The defense budgeting and accounting system should be revised to control operating costs in output-oriented terms, both to improve the incentives in the field and to provide better data to top management. The reforms recommended by Robert Anthony, the DoD Comp-troller, in 1967, under Project PRIME (Priority Management Effort) go a long way toward doing this. The basic objectives of PRIME are to develop better information on the actual use of operating resources and to integrate DoD's programming, budgeting, and accounting more effectively. Essentially, PRIME attempts to accomplish these objectives by providing an accounting procedure to follow up on the spending of funds in the same output-oriented categories in which the decisions to approve them were originally made.[3] These changes should eventually involve giving information to field commanders on the actual costs of forces under their control, including military personnel costs, and greater freedom to reallocate within approved operating budgets to achieve greater efficiency. This action would be especially useful to rear area support activities, which account for a major fraction of total defense costs, such as the costs of operating supply depots, transportation and maintenance facilities, administrative centers, and the like. Even the huge training centers operated by the Services could be managed under this concept. In sum, we believe that PRIME represents a major step in the direction of closing the loop on operating expenses and should be vigorously carried through.

(3) EQUIPMENT PERFORMANCE DATA

The consequences of a lack of reliable equipment performance data, acquired under realistic conditions, are equally severe. Some of the most important program decisions in DoD concern the introduction of new equipment. Realistic estimates of performance must be available if the choices are to be good ones. Indeed, the problem of reliable performance estimates has become more significant in the past ten years, as complex electronic components have become key elements in the effectiveness of many new weapon systems.

As an illustration of the importance of highly technical gear, over 60 percent of the total ten-year system cost for the A-6 aircraft, the Navy's newest all-weather tactical bomber, goes toward buying and maintaining its electronic systems. The comparable figure for Navy aircraft purchased in the late 1950's was around 20 percent. The worth of the A-6 as a system thus depends heavily on the ability of its electronic gear to permit the accurate delivery of weapons at night or in bad weather, or more accurate delivery in clear weather than by purely visual means. If it really works, the increase in military effectiveness can be very good, clearly enough to justify the cost. But if it does not, as has been the case with some comparable systems, there would be little reason to buy such an expensive system with all the attendant maintenance and operating problems. Similarly, the Army, having retired most of its antiaircraft guns, has been relying for air defense mainly on surface-to-air missiles. The wisdom of this decision depends on the ability of these missiles to destroy airplanes that are maneuvering and electronically jamming, just as U.S. tactical fighters did over North Vietnam.

In view of this trend, much more needs to be done to make sure that reliable and accurate performance information on new weapons is obtained and brought to the attention of the Secretary of Defense and other top officials. Frequently, the only performance data available on a new system come from the contractors who are developing or producing it, or the officers who are managing the project. Even with the best intentions, these sources are frequently too optimistic in their estimates. It is important to understand that the contractors and project officers have potentially much to gain from selling their system and thus incline toward optimistic performance estimates, but that no one has a strong incentive in the opposite direction.

Too little emphasis, incidentally, has been placed on the testing of prototypes before a decision to procure. Even where prototypes have been developed, the time allotted for testing has frequently been too short to do the job thoroughly. The philosophy of "concurrency"—concurrent development and procurement—was adopted in the 1950's in the atmosphere of urgency created by the apparent Soviet lead in intercontinental ballistic missiles. It may have been justified in some cases then, but generally it has led to a waste of money and time. According to the theory of concurrency, money and time can be saved by starting production while development is still under way. The work force trained to build the R&D prototypes can be kept on the job, and their valuable learning can be applied to building production articles during the period of prototype testing. This is fine if the testing does not disclose unanticipated deficiencies. But it usually does, necessitating costly retrofits. Also, the approach generates undue pressure to shorten the test period. This pressure has contributed substantially to the long series of weapon systems that have been introduced into production before it is discovered that they do not work. Very few systems are so urgently needed as to warrant a production decision before being fully tested.

As a way of obtaining more systematic and objective data, we recommend the establishment of an independent group directly under the Secretary of Defense to test and evaluate the performance of operational equipment and prototypes of new systems. Such a group would attempt to do for the Secretary of Defense in the R&D area what the financial auditors do in the area of financial performance. The rationale for the group would be similar to that for quality-control groups in industry: separating the producers of a product from those who judge it. This group, whose members could be drawn from several existing offices in OSD and the Services, would verify and evaluate the operational performance of both new and existing systems, using comparable, objective ground rules under realistic conditions. Much of the data could be obtained from exercises and troop tests, many of which are now conducted with little systematic guidance or follow-up aimed at deriving useful performance data. The cost of these tests and exercises, much of which would be incurred anyway, would be a small price to pay for realistic performance information on multibillion-dollar systems affecting national security. This group would, in effect, be an objective source of information on the actual performance of equipment.

Such a group, if it is to be successful, would have to be independent of Service and contractor interests and directly responsible to the Secretary of Defense. It would not substitute for the technical or military judgment of the Secretary's other advisers in the Office of the Director of Defense Research and Engineering. Its sole function would be to provide objective information on the actual performance of equipment under operational or realistic test conditions. These data would be used by other staffs in formulating analyses and recommendations. If it were properly set up, we believe that such a group would be welcomed by most military officers as a direct channel of information on the many practical problems they face in operating complex modern equipment.

Such a group could go a long way toward preventing the production of ineffective equipment and toward encouraging the production of equipment that actually works. It could also contribute to the preparation of the Development Concept Papers, providing benchmarks against which to measure new and competing systems. In effect, we would be closing the loop in R&D, comparing estimated performance with actual performance, then using the results to make future estimates.

Defense Studies

While there was substantial improvement in the general quality between 1961 and 1969, particularly in the level achieved by the best analyses, there is still considerable room for improvement of the study effort on defense programs.

Ideally, the large-scale study effort in the Services, the Joint Staff, and the major contract study organizations should provide a fund of knowledge which can be drawn on when specific program decisions are being considered. Yet, while hundreds of studies of force requirements were turned out each year, few were of any real use in decision making at the Secretary of Defense level. For example, major studies of total U.S. tactical air force requirements produced by the Services and by contract study organizations between 1963 and 1968 numbered in the dozens. Many involved large study groups and complex computer models. All came up with recommendations and conclusions. None shed much light on the important questions of force size or mix. In fact, the few conclusions that could be confidently drawn on these subjects came from much simpler analyses, mostly made by the OSD staff. Much the same can be said for studies of naval and land forces requirements.

One key reason for the poor quality of many defense studies, particularly studies of general-purpose forces, is that much of the basic input information is suspect. Most of this information is supplied by sources that cannot be considered totally objective. Moreover, not enough basic research has been done on underlying or component-performance areas (ordnance effectiveness, target acquisition, the impact of tactics and training, and so on) that bear on most of these studies. Basic data on intelligence and technical performance are too frequently accepted without question.

This is not necessarily a criticism of the individuals—many of them highly capable—who participate in these studies. In part, the problem stems from the fact that nearly all such studies are oriented to near-term program decisions. Few attempt research on underlying areas, where basic data and knowledge are lacking. Moreover, most such studies have fairly short deadlines and specific terms of reference, established by the Service that commissioned the study. Normally, the study group is not authorized to investigate or question basic data supplied by other agencies, such as data on intelligence and technical performance.

A more basic explanation of the poor quality of many defense analyses is the fact that their authors often begin with a predetermined conclusion—usually a Service position—and make the analysis, in effect, a sophisticated sales pitch. This occurs, in large part, because of the strong institutional pressures discussed earlier.

A related point concerns the fact that far too few studies in a given mission area (for example, NATO, antisubmarine warfare, or tactical air forces) are done on the basis of consistent sets of assumptions. Given its choice of scenarios and assumptions, a Service can make a plausible case for any weapon system. A great deal of the work of the Systems Analysis office over the years consisted of trying to enforce the use of consistent sets of assumptions, so that the Department would not end up buying one weapon system on the basis of a set of assumptions particularly favorable to it and another on a different set particularly favorable to it. What is needed is a systematic look at several consistent sets of assumptions applicable to competing weapon systems to build a balanced posture that will be effective under a broad range of circumstances. Reaching this goal is doubtful, however, so long as each new study group starts with its own particular set of assumptions. In brief, the need for an "analytic policeman" in the study effort that supports the strategy and force planning process is as great as ever.

Far too many defense studies are so complex that they are hardly understood by anyone except (and sometimes including) their authors. The most compelling reason to make analyses understandable is to make them useful to decision makers. We all recognize that decision makers usually add judgment to the facts they consider. This is as it should be; analysis is the servant of judgment, not a replacement for it. However, in cases where the decision maker does not personally understand at least the basic logic of the analysis, he may be forced to rely on judgment entirely. In view of the importance of defense decisions and the enormous costs they involve, few would argue that this is a desirable situation.

We know of no way to guarantee that a study group will produce a useful analytical product. However, the following suggestions might help. First, the instructions to study groups should make clear that their goal is to identify the important questions and to get the answers roughly right. Too many groups spend too little effort defining the problem they are working on and developing a logical way of relating data to it. The design phase of a study is by far the toughest and most critical. It may take up most of the total time. But there is little to be gained from charging off to gather data and make detailed calculations until one knows what is really needed and how the parts of the problem fit together. Basically this means setting more realistic deadlines to allow sufficient time for thoughtful problem definition and allowing more freedom to question basic assumptions and basic input data.

Second, continuity of personnel is essential. Every important study should be seen as a step in a continuing study effort. Millions of dollars worth of study time has been wasted because of the disbanding of study groups upon completion of the group's report, for often the first report only serves to define some of the major questions. A frequent practice of the Services is to meet a study request by calling in a group of officers from the field on temporary duty for a crash effort and then to disband the group immediately upon completion of the study. Nobody stays around to answer follow-up questions. A similar result is caused by the high turnover in Pentagon staff jobs. To understand a problem such as antisubmarine force levels or tactical air force levels is likely to take years of full-time effort. A six-months, quick-and-dirty effort is probably a waste of time, except for whatever value the officer personally realizes by being read into the problem. Yet, current career assignment patterns often penalize the officer who stays in such a staff job for longer than the normal two- or three-year tour. Much more needs to be done by the Services to encourage the continued development of their own analytical capability.

Third, the studies should be honestly tied into the process of program decision making. They should not be considered a part of Service advocacy. The most effective motivating factor for Systems Analysis studies was the knowledge that they would be seriously considered in the real decision-making process, not merely referred to in the after-decision advocacy phase. Good systems analysts were willing to work for McNamara and Clifford because they knew that when they did good work it would be acted upon and would influence decisions. While they have greatly improved in quality, the analytical staffs in the Services have not yet been effectively meshed with the actual decision-making process.

Finally, in the past, one effective way of ensuring better studies in the Services has been for the Systems Analysis office to do a pilot study in a particularly sensitive area and then send it to the Services for comment and review. The zeal with which Service staffs can uncover errors in such studies and come up with better ways to approach the problem is impressive. In this important sense, the mere existence of an office like Systems Analysis exerts pressure for better staff work throughout DoD. Indeed, much of the impetus for the improvement in the Service's own analytical capability can be attributed to this fact.

Yardsticks of Sufficiency

The need for better yardsticks of sufficiency against which to measure the need and adequacy of major components of the defense program has been discussed in Chapter 6. In some areas, particularly strategic nuclear forces and strategic mobility forces, requirements were thoroughly analyzed. In these areas, while considerable disagreement remained about the selection of valid assumptions, few argued that important assumptions were being ignored, or that the calculations based on the selected assumptions were inaccurate. In other areas—tactical air forces, antisubmarine warfare forces, and land forces, for example—real progress toward developing good requirements analysis was just beginning in 1967–1968. Mainly, this progress consisted of simple indicators of force capability and means of making objective comparisons with potential enemy forces. While these indicators and comparisons held promise for improving our ability to analyze requirements in these areas, much more work remained to be done before any confident statements could be made about needs and adequacy. As we noted in Chapter 6, comparing U.S. forces with an enemy's can be helpful, but may not be a good test of adequacy. In still other important areas—communications and intelligence programs, in particular—we were far from having satisfactory principles for determining aggregate requirements. Considering the large sums of money spent in these areas, it is imperative that more effort be devoted toward understanding explicitly what the expenditure of these resources is contributing to national security.

Lack of Adequate Financial Discipline

The lack of adequate financial discipline by the Services constitutes another important area of unfinished business. While there appears to have been some recent progress, the Services are still reluctant to set priorities and make hard choices. General Eisenhower's description of this problem is still appropriate:

Words like "essential" and "indispensable" and "absolute minimum" become the common coin of the realm, and they are spent with wild abandon. One military man will argue hotly for a given number of aircraft as the "absolute minimum," and others will earnestly advocate the "indispensable" needs for ships, tanks, rockets, guided missiles, or artillery, all totaled in numbers that are always called "minimum." All such views are argued with vigor and tenacity, but obviously all cannot be right.[4]

In reaction to the failings of the system used in the 1950's, President Kennedy decided there would be no arbitrary budget ceilings on the defense budget. The President's two basic instructions to Secretary McNamara were to "develop the force structure necessary to our military requirements without regard to arbitrary budget ceilings" and to "procure and operate this force at the lowest possible cost."[5] McNamara's idea was that the nation's foreign policy, military strategy, military forces, and defense budget would be brought into balance, and Service and JCS proposals would be considered on their merits on a case-by-case basis. The problem was that the Services could and did flood OSD with proposals for more of everything, and the Secretary of Defense and his staff could not possibly do justice to them all. More important, the Services made little attempt to face up to hard choices, since they could avoid choice by simply adding all "requirements" together. For example, the Navy argued for more nuclear-powered aircraft carriers, with the support of the other Joint Chiefs, without having to specify whether the total defense budget should thus be increased (with appropriate reasoning and evidence to support that conclusion), or whether the greater cost of nuclear carriers should be paid from a reduction in the total number of carriers. In fact, if nuclear carriers are really more effective, their advantages should permit a corresponding reduction somewhere else, possibly in the total number of Navy ships. But neither the Navy nor the JCS addressed this question. As a result, the burden of choice in judging Service proposals rested almost entirely on the Secretary of Defense and his staff. And since the analysis of complex defense issues is almost never clear-cut and provable one way or the other, this meant that the pressure on the Secretary for continuous budget increases was very great.

A number of other factors also contributed to high defense costs—

and still do. For a variety of political and institutional reasons, it is very difficult to reduce the numbers of major force units: divisions, air wings, and capital ships. These units are the most widely known aspect of the Services' structure; their number has remained relatively fixed for some years. (Indeed, the Navy has maintained a minimum requirement of fifteen capital ships—once battleships, now attack carriers—since the Washington Naval Treaty of 1921.) The tendency has been to keep the same number of units and replace older, cheaper equipment on a 1 for 1 basis with more capable and more expensive items. The conventionally powered carrier *John F. Kennedy,* launched in 1967, cost $280 million; the nuclear powered *Nimitz I* is now reported to cost over $600 million. Yet, in the face of this cost differential, the Navy recommends that the attack carrier force level remain the same. The cost to buy and operate an A-6 Navy attack bomber is eight times that of an A-1, so that the replacement of A-1's with A-6's means a major cost (and performance) increase, because the Navy proposes that the nominal force structure in terms of air wings remain constant. The Services have not emphasized the development of simple, low-cost equipment that could be introduced in larger numbers and possibly with far greater effectiveness per dollar.

Modern technology generates even more possibilities for new weapons. Consider, for example, long-range bombardment. The progression from the B-17 to the B-52 was straightforward and apparently obvious. But now we have the possibility of literally dozens of distinctly different strategic nuclear delivery systems, not to mention the endless array of other weapon systems. And the number expands almost daily. There are aerodynamic missiles and ballistic missiles that can be based and launched from fixed land bases, mobile land bases, and platforms on the surface of the sea, under the sea, and in the air. There are missiles launched from aircraft, aircraft launched from missiles, missiles launched from submarines, and so on in endless progression.

The enormous menu of new systems that technology makes possible is matched by the number of possible contingencies which military planners would have us prepare for. And, of course, ever more complex and expensive weapon systems bring on ever more contingencies to plan against.

Moreover, in adding new weapon systems to our forces and new

contingencies to our plans, there is a strong tendency to treat everything new as an add-on. New contingencies are added without cutting
back the old ones. Korea is still largely treated as if the South Korean
army were in the same shape as in 1953. Existing weapon systems
are treated as if they were "in the bag," and the debate focuses on
proposals for expensive new systems.

The problem of how to provide the Services with incentives to face
up to hard choices and get the most capability for the money they
spend does not lend itself to simple solution. Certainly, management
procedures alone are not the solution. Part of the answer lies in
maintaining a political climate that demands that they (and the entire
Defense Department) do so. More effective and balanced outside review and interrogation from the Congress and from the interested
public promotes such a climate. Part lies in moving the Department
toward the middle ground between the positions that (1) the Services
should ask for anything they think is needed, and (2) the Services
should be given a financial total and be left free to spend it as they see
fit. We have explained at length what is wrong with the latter position.
Perhaps it is combat fatigue from serving so many years on that particular firing line, but it seems to us that the general climate outside
the Department and the anticeilings rhetoric caused the Department
to spend too much time near the former. Finally, part of the answer
lies in continued efforts by the Secretary of Defense to build up the
"case law" of equal cost trades (adding a given quantity of a new item
and taking out an equal dollar amount of some other item or items)
and equal effectiveness trades (adding only enough of a new item to
replace the performance or effectiveness of the items dropped out).
Such an approach would be an extension of the efforts made in the
second half of the 1960's to force the burden of choice back onto the
Services—in those cases where the choice affected only one Service
and the Service in question had the necessary information with which
to make a good choice.

For example, in late 1967, the Army was pressing hard for the
inclusion of funds in the fiscal 1969 budget for production of the
Cheyenne armed helicopter (or AAFSS, for Advanced Aerial Fire
Support System). The Director of Defense Research and Engineering
supported the Army and advised the Secretary of Defense that the
key technical problems had been or would be solved. The Systems

Analysis office opposed AAFSS on the grounds that (1) there was little evidence to support the need for such a costly system in comparison with cheaper systems and (2) its cost and performance estimates appeared overly optimistic. Secretary McNamara's decision was to approve AAFSS for production if the Army was willing to agree to an equal cost trade. In other words, if the Army would agree to "pay for AAFSS" by deleting older units having similar missions and costing as much as AAFSS from their approved force structure, they could go ahead. In this way AAFSS would not be simply an add-on to the fiscal 1969 and future defense budgets; while at the same time, if it were as effective as claimed, there would still be a net gain in the Army's over-all effectiveness. While much less ardent for AAFSS on this basis, the Army agreed. The Systems Analysis office then worked with the Army to identify the units to be deleted and to make sure the costs were equivalent. An agreed list was developed and approved.

When the AAFSS later ran into technical problems and increasing costs, the Army showed an unprecedented toughness and canceled the production contract on its own initiative. In part, at least, we suspect this toughness was prompted by a clear understanding of what would have to be given up to add AAFSS to the Army's force structure.

While the suggestions above can help to get the Services to make hard choices and manage more effectively within limited resources on their own initiative, we are not optimistic that they would be sufficient. In the long run, particularly as the political climate changes, the Services' conceptions of their roles and missions and their internal power balances are likely to be more powerful influences on force recommendations than any procedural arrangements or economic incentives. In the final analysis, there is no easy way for the Secretary of Defense to get out from under the heavy burden of his responsibility to make the decisions.

Strengthening Some Procedural Links

The fourth area of unfinished business in the national defense program decision process concerns improving the procedures for (1) making an aggregate analysis of the budget and (2) integrating national security policy and operations.

Few activities in the U.S. government are as important as the annual determination of the defense budget. Roughly half the money available to the federal government is up for decision. When one considers that taxes are hard to change and that most nondefense expenditures are relatively inflexible, it is apparent that small percentage changes in the defense budget can vastly alter the discretionary money available for all other government programs. In addition, the size of the defense budget determines many U.S. strategic and foreign policy options. If we want to maintain various degrees of strategic nuclear balance with the Soviet Union, defend Northeast and Southeast Asia, maintain a major conventional war capability in Europe, and at the same time protect political interests world-wide and control the seas, we must be willing to pay the price. Each of these capabilities costs large sums of money, and each has powerful advocates. The size and composition of the annual defense budget constitute the principal form that these hard choices take. The system should, as a regular procedure, encourage top government leaders to focus explicitly on broad options for various levels of defense spending and on the range of military capabilities that would go with each.

This objective could be served by developing an explicit procedure for determining a budget total based on an aggregate analysis of the defense program in relation to foreign policy and domestic needs. Participants in such an analysis would include, at a minimum, the JCS, OSD, and appropriate members of the White House staff. Such an analysis would focus on broad judgments such as the number and size of simultaneous nonnuclear contingencies, readiness and rapid deployment goals, how much of the greater-than-expected threat to ensure against, the value of long-range tactical air interdiction capability, the damage-limiting program, and so on, using average aggregate cost factors and adjusting for pay increases, inflation, changes in deployments, and the like. The domestic and foreign political implications, and the economic impact on the rest of the U.S. budget, of the alternative budget levels flowing from these judgments would be explicitly considered. Other means of meeting broad foreign policy objectives, such as economic aid, technical assistence, and military assistance, would also be considered and compared with military options before a military program and budget were decided upon. Such an analysis could be summarized for the President in a presentation of perhaps three alternative budgets, one at the current level, one substantially higher (perhaps 5 to 10 percent), and one substantially lower; an analysis of the military capabilities that could be provided by each; and an analysis of the extent to which these capabilities meet various military objectives. For example, each budget would be accompanied by a list of the combat units that could be supported and a summary of their readiness and estimated effectiveness. These alternatives would then be considered by the President and his advisers. The process would culminate in a decision by the President on the required military capabilities and the defense budget needed to provide them. These decisions would then be sent back to the Defense Department for preparation of detailed plans for implementation.

Such an approach is not radically different from that followed by Secretaries McNamara and Clifford and Presidents Kennedy and Johnson. Although the formal defense program and budget reviews addressed items individually without explicit reference to the totals, both the Presidents and the Secretaries had their ideas as to what constituted a reasonable total. And their ideas were based on fact and analysis, though a substantial part of the analysis was not explicitly or formally stated and debated. For example, McNamara discussed the reasonableness of the budget total with his staff, describing major changes from the previous year in the threat, deployments, prices, and other pertinent factors and estimating how much they ought to affect the total. But, by 1968 the analytical techniques had not yet been developed to the point that such a procedure could be formalized, although a good start had been made in this direction. For example, in 1968 the Systems Analysis office started an over-all analysis of general-purpose forces along these lines which, in 1969, became the basis for a Presidential review. But approximately two more years would have been required to develop such an over-all analysis to the point that it could serve as a regular tool for Presidential decision making. Work along these lines ought to be continued.

It should be stressed that, under such a procedure, the budget level decided upon would not in any sense be an arbitrary ceiling. It would be a reasoned and considered ceiling reached by open and explicit analysis and debate. This procedure would also be a far cry from determining a ceiling and then turning it over to the Services to spend "their money" as they chose. For one thing, the military capabilities to be provided would be given at least as much emphasis as the budget level. The budget review would focus on detailed implementation, on finding ways of providing the required capabilities at lower cost, and on finding ways of spending the approved budget more effectively. The most important divisions of the budget for decision-making purposes would still be military missions, not military Services.

Finally, one of the most significant contributions of PPBS in the Defense Department has been the integrating of related items in an intelligible way. But the problem is at the next level up, at the broader level where defense policy and other national security programs and operations come together—a problem that Vietnam clearly revealed. Examples abound of the lack of coordination among various U.S. military and economic efforts in that country. We are not well organized to oppose Communist insurgencies. Overt military action is only part of the total threat we face in such wars. Various ideas—such as consolidated country programming, putting the Ambassador in charge of all U.S. programs in an area, and program budgeting by country or region—have been proposed for moving in this direction, but none has received more than lip service thus far. One of the greatest challenges in the national security field remains the development of effective procedures for integrating all the many U.S. operations and programs affecting national security in overseas areas. While we will not presume to spell out the details, we believe that an imaginative and vigorous application of the ideas underlying PPBS at the national policy-making level offers one promising approach to meeting this challenge.

Will the changes improve the chances that the national interest will be better served? This, we would argue, should be the basic question behind the procedural changes we have suggested, or any other defense management reforms. The centrifugal forces pulling for a variety of parochial interests in the Department of Defense are strong, well established, and persistent. The forces centering on the national interest in defense programs—getting the needed amount of effective military power at minimum cost—are small and must be maintained and strengthened.

Postscript: Full Cycle?

In terms of both national security policy and defense management procedures, 1969 and early 1970 have seen a number of changes. Strategic Arms Limitations Talks, an elusive goal sought for several years, were started in Helsinki and were scheduled to resume in Vienna. The reversal of the course of U.S. involvement in Vietnam, a process begun in 1968, has continued. Under current plans, the Nixon administration will have reduced the number of American troops there by over 250,000 by April 1971. More emphasis and insistence that, with American economic and military aid, our allies do more than they are now doing in their own defense appears to be part of the administration's over-all national security strategy as well as the cornerstone of its "Vietnamization" policy. The rise in defense spending has been halted, at least temporarily. The fiscal 1971 defense budget forecasts expenditures of $71.8 billion. If achieved, this would represent a decrease of almost $7 billion since fiscal 1969, the last year of the Johnson administration. This reduction is largely accounted for by reduced expenditures reflecting reduced activity rates and manpower levels in Vietnam and cutbacks in a number of expensive but ineffective weapon systems (for example, B-58 bombers and the antisubmarine carrier fleet) which the Services had held on to in the hope that they could trade them in for new systems on the familiar 1 for 1 replacement basis.

A number of changes have also occurred in defense management procedures both within and outside the Defense Department. The National Security Council (NSC) has been made the focal point for reviewing alternatives and formulating broad national security policy. The NSC staff has been expanded and strengthened. This staff appears to be trying to do for the President at the national level what the Systems Analysis office did for the Secretary of Defense. A Defense Program Review Committee has been established, reportedly to assist the President in determining the costs and benefits of alternative national security budgets and in reviewing resource allocation between defense and nondefense needs. Formal procedures have been devised for giving the Department of Defense strategy and fiscal guidance approved by the White House early in the annual planning cycle.

With respect to management procedures in the Department of Defense, one change expected in 1969 did not occur. The Systems Analysis office was not abolished. In view of the many pressures to kill it, the survival of the office was a substantial accomplishment. As a candidate, Nixon had promised to "root out the whiz kid approach at the Pentagon." Early in 1969, the JCS and the Services all recommended (in varying degrees) that the office be cut back drastically in power and size, if not abolished. Later, however, they gradually modified their views, eventually agreeing to a "treaty" that essentially reaffirmed the office's original charter, but without the initiative it had formerly exercised in carrying it out.

The Chairman of the House Armed Services Committee included language in the fiscal 1970 defense authorization bill, which passed the House, that would have abolished the office. He made it clear that it was not the personalities or the views of the office that were at issue; it was the fact of having civilian analysts review JCS and Service recommendations on strategy and forces. In effect, his position went much further than the official views of the Joint Chiefs and the Services. His attempt to abolish the office was blocked, however, by the Senate Armed Services Committee. The principal reason was that some of the Committee's most influential members, while not necessarily agreeing with the specific findings and recommendations of the office, felt that the Secretary of Defense should have the kind of independent staff assistance provided by the office.

Thus, by the beginning of 1970, it was clear that the office would survive at the same level and with the same charter, but not the same role, as before. A new Assistant Secretary was nominated by the President and confirmed by the Senate without incident.

But the formal existence of the Systems Analysis office is much less significant than what the office actually does and how it is used by the Secretary of Defense. The important question is whether the defense program will be substantially different as a result of its efforts. Here the picture is much less encouraging. Secretaries McNamara and Clifford used the Systems Analysis office as an important instrument of their concept of active management. Through the office, both

Secretaries and their Deputies took the initiative in shaping the defense program. Secretary Laird and Deputy Secretary Packard apparently have chosen more passive roles for themselves with respect to the shape of the defense program, and this has had its impact on the role of the office. In a "treaty" signed by Deputy Secretary Packard, the Service Secretaries, and the Chairman of the Joint Chiefs of Staff in July 1969, it was agreed that the "Secretary of Defense will look to the Joint Chiefs of Staff and the Services in the design of forces" and that the Systems Analysis office would limit itself to "evaluation and review" and, by implication, would not put forward independent proposals of its own. Since the Secretary of Defense looked to the Joint Chiefs of Staff and the Services (as well as the Systems Analysis office) in the design of forces from 1961 through 1968, and neither group showed any lack of initiative in pressing its views, we can only conclude that the intent was to limit the role of the Systems Analysis office to that of passive commentator on JCS and Service proposals. If this proves to be the pattern, the ability of the office to recruit and retain first-rate talent will inevitably suffer, and an important force for the national interest in defense programs will be lost.

While there was considerably less doubt, the Planning-Programming-Budgeting System (PPBS) also survived, if in somewhat altered form. Similarly, the Development Concept Paper was continued as the principal management tool for making decisions on new weapon systems. On the other hand, the Five-Year Defense Plan (FYDP), which McNamara considered one of the main instruments by which the Secretary of Defense can keep the defense program balanced, had been suspended (albeit only temporarily, according to Secretary Laird); and the Draft Presidential Memorandum, the main vehicle by which the Secretary can exercise initiative in shaping the strategy and the forces, had been abolished outright.

But the continuation of something called PPBS and the survival of the Systems Analysis office and the other tools that make the system work are not the important thing. The important question is the substance of DoD management, not the appearance. Here, as of early 1970, the signs were mixed.

On the basis of broad strategy guidelines set earlier, a proposed fiscal 1972 budget was divided about equally among the three Military Departments, with the *Service* breakdown replacing the *mission* breakdown, as the item having primary importance. This "fiscal guidance" was then sent to the Services for comment and review. "Participatory decision making" apparently means the Services are allowed to determine how they will apportion their fractions, with review by OSD. While we hope that the OSD review will be effective —and reflect substantial participation by the Secretary of Defense and his staff—at this writing it is not clear that it will be. The theory seems to be, "We'll give the Services broad guidance and review their implementation." It will be interesting to see how many significant changes actually emerge from the OSD review and how many "prestige items" replace needed but unglamorous military capabilities in the Service budgets. In any event, the initiative for shaping the strategy and the forces is no longer in the hands of the Secretary of Defense and his staff.

If by now we have not made our case for why the defense budget should not simply be turned over to the Service bureaucracies to spend as they think best, we are not going to succeed here. But it may be useful to summarize again the main reasons.

Most major defense program issues transcend individual Service programs. How many ICBM's and bombers the Air Force should deploy is related to the numbers of Polaris and Poseidon submarines deployed by the Navy and to the Army's Safeguard deployment. All come back to the national nuclear strategy, an issue whose scope is far beyond that of an individual Service. Similarly, decisions on the number and kind of tactical air forces that the Air Force should deploy depend on comparable decisions with respect to the Navy and Marine Corps tactical air forces. More importantly, they depend on national policy with respect to the number and kind of limited war contingencies that the United States should be prepared to meet and the speed or readiness which we should be able to meet them with. Likewise, the size and readiness of the Army must be related systematically to the Air Force's airlift and the Navy's sealift capability. It is wasteful to have Army divisions that cannot be moved, or airlift capacity in excess of that needed.

Of course, the JCS is supposed to integrate these interdependent Service parts. But history has repeatedly shown that a committee like the JCS does not act this way. If not forced to make hard choices between Service interests, the JCS staples together Service requests. If forced to make hard choices, the JCS tries to negotiate a compromise —one that often bears little relationship to the best mix of forces from a national or a military point of view. If the Joint Chiefs fail to agree, they hand the problem back to the Secretary of Defense. It is the Secretary's job to see that there is no unnecessary duplication in glamour areas and underfunding in others. But more than that, he is the only one in a good position to shape the program in terms of the whole—in terms of the national interest.

The history of the 1950's shows clearly that under financial pressure the Services will seek to keep the prestige items—the major combat units and the glamorous weapon systems—and cut back the unglamorous support items essential to readiness. The result is the hollow shell of military capability, not the substance.

Finally, if they are not compelled to plan and justify their forces systematically on the basis of explicit criteria of the national interest, the Services, like any bureaucracy, will tend to perpetuate existing missions and capabilities. This is a fact of bureaucratic life in any organization. The horse cavalry and the battleships took a long time to die after they had outlived their usefulness. If the Secretary of Defense does not do it, who is going to shift the spending on strategic forces from Air Force bombers to the Navy Polaris? Who is going to cut back the continental air defense forces when their size and cost can no longer be justified? Who is going to insist that the size and composition of the antisubmarine forces be clearly related to national need? Who is going to see that the interdependent parts fit together?

Much has been made of the apparent decline in dissatisfaction among the Services as more initiative is turned over to them. In the long run, however, handing the budgets back to the Services is unlikely to assure job satisfaction and high morale among military leaders. It might seem so in the initial enthusiasm over "rooting out the whiz kid approach." But the record shows as much military dissatisfaction in 1960 as in 1968—perhaps more.

More Presidential guidance on strategy and budgets earlier in the annual planning cycle and more Service responsibility for making the hard choices can be valuable additions to the Defense Department's management system. But they must be additions to the system; they cannot be substitutes. For if the pattern of carving up the budget by

Service fractions and turning the pieces over to the Services to spend as they see fit were to persist, within a few years, as the logic of the over-all shape of the defense program erodes, as the readiness of the general-purpose forces deteriorates, as new Taylors and Howzes come up with the 1970's counterparts of flexible response and the airmobile division and find themselves underrepresented at JCS and Service bargaining tables, one can be sure that the expressions of legitimate dissatisfaction will increase.

It happened in the 1950's. The lessons learned then and applied in the 1960's should not have to be relearned in the 1970's.

Source Notes

Chapter 1: Unfinished Business, 1961

1. Robert S. McNamara, *Remarks before the American Society of Newspaper Editors,* Washington, D.C., April 20, 1963 (hereinafter cited as DoD Press Release, No. 548–63).
2. Rockefeller Brothers Fund, *International Security: The Military Aspect* (Garden City, N.Y.: Doubleday, 1958), pp. 58–59.
3. Maxwell D. Taylor, *The Uncertain Trumpet* (New York: Harper, 1959), p. 123.
4. Senate Preparedness Investigating Subcommittee, *Hearings on Major Defense Matters,* 86th Congress, 1st Session, May 20, 1959, p. 207.
5. House Committee on Appropriations, *Report on Department of Defense Appropriations Bill, 1960,* Report No. 408, 86th Congress, 1st Session, 1959, p. 11.
6. For an excellent discussion of the defense budget process in the 1950's, see Samuel P. Huntington, *The Common Defense* (New York: Columbia University Press, 1961), pp. 47–122.
7. Taylor, *op. cit.,* pp. 82–83.
8. *Ibid.,* p. 70.
9. Senate Subcommittee on the Air Force of the Committee on Armed Services, *Study of Airpower,* 84th Congress, 2nd Session, April 16 and 20, 1956, pp. 69, 105.
10. House Appropriations Committee, *Report on Department of Defense Appropriations Bill, 1961,* Report No. 1561, 86th Congress, 2nd Session, 1960, p. 25.

11. Senate Subcommittee on National Policy Machinery, *Organizing for National Security*, 87th Congress, 1st Session, October 16, 1961, pp. 4–5.
12. Reproduced in Charles H. Donnelly, *United States Defense Policies in 1957*, House Document No. 436, 85th Congress, 2nd Session, 1958, p. 83.
13. House Appropriations Committee, *Report on Department of Defense Appropriations Bill, 1961, op. cit.*, p. 25.
14. *Ibid.*
15. Taylor, *op. cit.*, pp. 93–94.
16. *Ibid.*, pp. 94–95.
17. Senate Subcommittee on National Policy Machinery, *Organizing for National Security, op. cit.*, p. 8.
18. See, for example, Merton J. Peck and Frederic M. Scherer, *The Weapons Acquisition Process: An Economic Analysis* (Cambridge: Division of Research, Harvard Business School, 1962); A. W. Marshall and H. W. Meckling, *Predictability of the Cost, Time, and Success of Development*, The Rand Corporation, P-1821, December, 1959.

Chapter 2: New Concepts and New Tools to Shape the Defense Program

1. Robert S. McNamara, *The Essence of Security* (New York: Harper & Row, 1968), pp. 87–88.
2. *Ibid.*, p. 88.
3. For the best exposition of these arguments, see Senate Subcommittee on National Security and International Operations, *Hearings on Planning-Programming-Budgeting, Parts I–IV* (Washington: Government Printing Office, 1967–1968), and the three-volume compendium by the Joint Economic Committee entitled *An Analysis and Evaluation of Public Expenditures: The PPB System* (Washington: Government Printing Office, 1969).
4. DoD Press Release No. 548–63.
5. Senate Subcommittee on the Air Force of the Committee on Armed Services, *Study of Airpower*, 84th Congress, 2nd Session, April 16 and 20, 1956, p. 230.
6. House Armed Services Committee, *Hearings on Military Posture*, 87th Congress, 2nd Session, 1962, p. 3306.
7. Senate Subcommittee on National Security and International Operations, *Planning-Programming-Budgeting: Interim Observations* (Washington: Government Printing Office, 1968), p. 5.
8. Senate Subcommittee on National Security and International Operations, *Hearings on Planning-Programming-Budgeting, Part 1* (Washington: Government Printing Office, 1969), p. 46.
9. House Subcommittee of Committee on Appropriations, *Hearing on*

Department of Defense Appropriations for 1969, Part 6 (Washington: Government Printing Office), p. 58.

10. Brock Brower, "McNamara Seen Now, Full Length," *Life,* May 19, 1968, p. 80.

11. Similar memorandums on important support areas—called Defense Guidance Memorandums (DGM's) because their subjects were not important enough for White House review—were also prepared beginning in 1967. In 1968, DGM's were prepared covering Indirect Support Aircraft; Manpower; Shipbuilding Policy; and Pilot and Navigator Requirements, Inventories, and Training.

12. Senate Preparedness Investigating Subcommittee, *Hearings on Major Defense Matters,* 86th Congress, 1st Session, May 20, 1959, p. 206.

13. Maxwell D. Taylor, *The Uncertain Trumpet* (New York: Harper, 1959), p. 69.

14. Brower, *op. cit.,* p. 80.

15. See, for example, E. S. Quade and W. I. Boucher, eds., *Systems Analysis and Policy Planning* (New York: American Elsevier, 1968); C. West Churchman, *The Systems Approach* (New York: Delacorte Press, 1968); and Bernard H. Rudwick, *Systems Analysis for Effective Planning* (New York: Wiley, 1969).

16. Robert S. McNamara, "Managing the Department of Defense," *Civil Service Journal,* Vol. 4, No. 4 (April–June 1964), p. 13.

17. This belief does not represent a latter-day conversion. From the beginning, leaders of the systems analysis effort in DoD have repeatedly called attention to the subordination of analysis to judgment. See, for example, the excerpts from various speeches and writings between 1960 and 1965 by Charles J. Hitch and Alain C. Enthoven, reprinted in Senate Subcommittee on National Security and International Operations, *Hearings on Planning-Programming-Budgeting, Part II* (Washington: Government Printing Office, 1967), pp. 132–134, and in Samuel A. Tucker, ed., *A Modern Design for Defense Decision: A McNamara-Hitch-Enthoven Anthology* (Washington: Industrial College of the Armed Forces, 1966).

18. Senate Subcommittee on National Security and International Operations, *Planning, Programming, Budgeting: Initial Memorandum* (Washington: Government Printing Office, 1967), p. 4.

19. Thomas C. Schelling, "PPBS and Foreign Affairs," Memorandum prepared at the request of the Senate Subcommittee on National Security and International Operations (Washington: Government Printing Office, 1968), p. 1.

Chapter 3: Why Independent Analysts?

1. House Armed Services Committee, *Report Authorizing Appropriations for Military Procurement, Research and Development, Fiscal*

Year 1961, and Reserve Strength, Report No. 1645, 90th Congress, 2nd Session, July 5, 1968, pp. 41–42.

2. Department of Defense Directive 5141.1, September 17, 1965.
3. *National Security Organization,* A Report with Recommendations, Prepared for the Commission on Organization of the Executive Branch of the Government by the Committee on the National Security Organization, January 1949 (Washington: Government Printing Office, 1949), p. 57.
4. General Thomas D. White, "Strategy and the Defense Intellectuals," *Saturday Evening Post,* Vol. 236 (May 4, 1963), p. 10.
5. General Curtis E. LeMay, *America Is in Danger* (New York: Funk and Wagnalls, 1968), pp. viii, x.
6. House Subcommittee of the Committee on Appropriations, *Hearings on Department of Defense Appropriations for 1969,* 90th Congress, 2nd Session (Washington: Government Printing Office, 1968), pp. 54–55.
7. Samuel P. Huntington, *The Soldier and the State* (New York: Vintage Books, 1957), pp. 449–450 (emphasis added).
8. Winston S. Churchill, *The Gathering Storm* (Boston: Houghton Mifflin, 1946), pp. 467–468.
9. LeMay, *op. cit.,* p. xiii ((emphasis added).
10. Many military officers have been penalized for unorthodoxy, over the years, by nonpromotion. The most celebrated case perhaps is Hyman Rickover, whose promotions to Rear Admiral and Vice-Admiral had to be forced by civilians outside the Navy—that is, the Congress.
11. Senate Subcommittee on National Security and International Operations, *Hearings on Planning-Programming-Budgeting,* 90th Congress, 1st Session, September 27 and October 18, 1967, pp. 125–127.
12. As an example of this problem see the chronology regarding Navy antisubmarine warfare studies shown on pp. 230–232.
13. Senate Preparedness Investigating Subcommittee, *Hearings on U.S. Tactical Air Power Program* (Washington: Government Printing Office, 1968), pp. 170–171.

Chapter 4: NATO Strategy and Forces

1. See Robert E. Osgood, *NATO: The Entangling Alliance* (Chicago: University of Chicago Press, 1962), pp. 34–40.
2. Arthur H. Vandenberg, Jr., ed., *The Private Papers of Senator Vandenberg* (Boston: Houghton Mifflin, 1952), pp. 495–496.
3. From a speech to the House of Commons on May 12, 1949 (*Parliamentary Debates* [Commons] CDLXIV, 2016).
4. London *Times,* February 26, 1952, p. 5.

5. *U.S. Department of State Bulletin,* Volume XXX, No. 761 (January 25, 1954).

6. New York *Times,* November 30, 1954, p. 13.

7. SACEUR, *Second Annual Report* (Paris: SHAPE, 1953), p. 21.

8. John F. Kennedy in *The Strategy of Peace,* edited by Allan Nevins (New York: Harper, 1960), p. 184.

9. Joint Senate Committee on Foreign Affairs and Armed Services, *Hearings on Assignment of Ground Forces of the U.S. to Duty in the European Area,* 82nd Congress, 1st Session, 1951, p. 79.

10. B. H. Liddell Hart, *Deterrence or Defense* (New York: Praeger, 1960), p. 20.

11. Bernard Brodie, "What Price Conventional Capabilities in Europe?" *Reporter,* May 23, 1963, p. 29.

12. This conclusion was not new. As early as 1952, two-sided war games in the Seventh Army in Europe had shown the same thing. As General James Gavin reported: "One over-all conclusion stood out clearly, although for several years it was the basis for considerable argument: more rather than less manpower would be required to fight a nuclear war successfully." James M. Gavin, *War and Peace in the Space Age* (New York: Harper & Bros., 1952), p. 139.

13. William W. Kaufmann, *The McNamara Strategy* (New York: Harper & Row, 1964), p. 131.

14. See Maxwell D. Taylor, *The Uncertain Trumpet* (New York: Harper, 1959), pp. 136–139.

15. Ironically, at about the same time this memorandum was being completed, a book by the former Air Force Chief of Staff, General Nathan Twining, was published claiming that the nation was rapidly approaching a serious airplane gap. As General Twining put it: "The United States actually faces two very real gaps in its combat inventory for the future. This is an 'airplane gap' in both fighter and bombardment types, and there is a very large yield warhead gap in this nation's follow-on ballistic missile program. If these two deficiencies are not corrected with the utmost speed, the announced policies of 'flexibility' and 'Multiple-options' of the Johnson nee Kennedy Administration cannot be implemented by our future fighting forces." Nathan F. Twining, *Neither Liberty nor Safety: A Hard Look at U.S. Military Policy and Strategy* (New York: Holt, Rinehart, and Winston, 1966), p. 257.

16. The center region is, of course, not the only area of military concern in Europe. NATO's northern flank (Norway) and southern flank (Greek and Turkish Thrace) are obviously important, and a definitive comparison of NATO and Warsaw Pact conventional forces should consider the forces in the flanks as well. For two main reasons, our discussion does not. First, the center region is by far the most critical to determining U.S. force requirements for NATO.

344 Notes to Pages 147 to 152

Second, including the flanks would not alter our fundamental point of a rough balance between NATO and the Pact in existing forces. As McNamara noted in his 1968 posture statement: "In all regions except Norway, the NATO-Pact forces are about equal in manpower. NATO has about 900,000 troops deployed in all regions of Continental Europe, compared to 960,000 for the Warsaw Pact. While manpower comparisons, alone, are not conclusive measures of military strength, I believe they are reasonable first approximations of relative ground force capabilities." Secretary of Defense Robert S. McNamara, *Statement before the Senate Armed Services Committee on the Fiscal Year 1969–73 Defense Program and the 1969 Defense Budget* (Washington: Government Printing Office, 1968), p. 80.

17. For further amplification of the data in this table and those appearing in Tables 4 and 5 as well, see Annex IV, *Report of the United States Delegation to the Fourteenth Meeting of Members of Parliament from the North Atlantic Assembly Countries*, U.S. Senate, 91st Congress, 1st Session, pp. 50–59. See also Alain C. Enthoven, "Arms and Men: The Military Balance in Europe," *Interplay* (May 1969), pp. 11–14.

18. We are reminded at this point of one of Churchill's memorandums to General Ismay, the Chief of Staff to the Minister of Defense during World War II, which shows the timeless nature of this problem: "The statement that one division could not be transferred from Great Britain to Ireland in less than eleven days, no matter how great the emergency nor how careful the previous preparations, is one which deserves your earnest attention. When we remember the enormous numbers which were moved from Dunkirk to Dover and the Thames last May under continued enemy attack, it is clear that the movement of personnel cannot be the limiting factor. The problem is therefore one of study. Let me see the exact program which occupies the eleven days, showing the order in which men, guns, and vehicles will embark. This would show perhaps that, say, nine-tenths of the division might come into action in much less than eleven days. Or, again, a portion of the mechanical transport, stores, and even some of the artillery, including Bren-gun carriers, might be found from reserves in this country and sent to Ireland in advance, where they would be none the less a reserve for us, assuming no need in Ireland arose. Surely now that we have the time some ingenuity might be shown in shortening this period of eleven days to move fifteen thousand fighting men from one well-equipped port to another—the voyage taking only a few hours. If necessary some revision of the scale of approved establishments might be made in order to achieve the high tactical object of a more rapid transference and deployment.

"We must remember that in the recent training exercise 'Victor' five German divisions, two of which were armoured and one motorized, were (supposed to be) landed in about forty-eight hours in the teeth of strenuous opposition, not at a port with quays and cranes, but on the open beaches. If we assume that the Germans can do this, or even half of it, we must contrast this with the statement of the eleven days required to shift one division from the Clyde to Belfast. We have also the statement of the Chiefs of Staff Committee that it would take thirty days to land one British division unopposed alongside the quays and piers of Tangier. Perhaps the officers who worked out the landings of the Germans under 'Victor' could make some suggestion for moving this division into Ireland via Belfast without taking eleven days about it: Who are the officers who worked out the details that this move will take eleven days? Would it not be wise to bring them into contact with the other officers who landed these vast numbers of Germans on our beaches so swiftly and enabled whole armoured divisions and motorized troops to come into full action in forty-eight hours?"—Winston S. Churchill, *The Grand Alliance* (Boston: Houghton Mifflin, 1950), p. 731.

19. Alastair Buchan, *NATO in the 1960's* (London: Institute for Strategic Studies, 1960), pp. 10–11.
20. *Economist,* February 10, 1968, p. 115.
21. For a fuller discussion of this point and the problem of burden sharing, see Alain C. Enthoven and K. Wayne Smith, "What Forces for NATO? And from Whom?," *Foreign Affairs* (October 1969), pp. 80–96.
22. "Europe: A Time of Testing for the Power Blocs," *Time,* December 12, 1969, p. 32.

Chapter 5: Nuclear Strategy and Forces

1. John F. Kennedy in *The Strategy of Peace,* edited by Allan Nevins (New York: Harper, 1960), pp. 37–38.
2. See, for example, A. J. Wohlstetter, "The Delicate Balance of Terror," *Foreign Affairs* (January 1958), and A. J. Wohlstetter, F. S. Hoffman, R. J. Lutz, and H. S. Rowen, *Selection and Use of Strategic Air Bases,* The Rand Corporation, R-266, April 1954.
3. The terms "strategic retaliatory forces" and "strategic offensive forces" refer to those forces the United States maintains for the intercontinental delivery of nuclear weapons (ICBM's, bombers, and missile-launching submarines). The term "strategic defensive forces" refers to the continental air and missile defense forces (interceptor aircraft, surface-to-air missiles, antiballistic missile systems, radars and control systems) intended to protect the United States from nu-

clear attack. We use the terms "strategic forces" and "strategic posture" to refer to the sum of all these forces and their essential command and control systems.

4. House Appropriations Committee, *Hearings on Department of Defense Appropriations for 1959,* 85th Congress, 2nd Session, April 29, 1958, p. 356.

5. A part of the Army's strategy for asserting its right to the ABM defense mission was to give all its defensive missile systems the same or similar names. Thus, its surface-to-air missiles were called Nike-Ajax and Nike-Hercules. The Army wanted to call the new ABM system Nike-Zeus to stress the continuity with the existing program. The administration, wanting a new name to distinguish the new weapon system, asked the Army to come up with a new name, and used "Nike-X" as an interim name until the Army did so. It wasn't until 1967 that the Army came up with "Sentinel," so Nike-X became the system's name for five years.

6. We would have welcomed it even more two or three years earlier. Indeed, it is somewhat ironic that so much national attention and intense debate have been given to the initial Safeguard system—a light, relatively inexpensive, assured-destruction measure—when so little were given to the Nike-X system—a heavy, very expensive, damage-limiting measure. Those who publicly expressed skepticism over questions of need and cost at the time when the JCS were unanimously recommending full-scale deployment of Nike-X found little public support or interest in their position. Yet few people today believe that Nike-X would have worked with enough confidence to justify the enormous expenditures involved.

7. Within those boundaries, of course, there have been and remain important areas of uncertainty. For example, what are the exact limits of deterrence? No one really knows. What happens if deterrence should fail? No one can be sure. In short, a note of caution is in order. In the discussion above, we have tried to simplify something that is inherently very complex. We have also concentrated on strategic force *planning* (how much is enough?)—not strategic force *operations* (what is the best way to use the available forces?).

Chapter 6: Yardsticks of Sufficiency

1. DoD Press Release No. 548–63.
2. Maxwell D. Taylor, *The Uncertain Trumpet* (New York: Harper, 1959), p. 118.
3. House Armed Services Committee, *Hearings on Military Posture,* 90th Congress, 2nd Session, April–June 1968, pp. 8896–8897.
4. When it became evident in 1968 that the C-5A was going to cost substantially more than originally estimated, the Systems Analysis of-

fice did calculations that showed that, at the new price, the required amount of airlift capability could be obtained at less cost by buying fewer C-5A's and planning to fly the whole airlift fleet more hours per day in an emergency (necessitating more crews, spare parts, and the like), and thus the office recommended cutting back the planned force to three or four squadrons.

5. The C-5A was one of the first examples of total package procurement, an important McNamara reform that required contractors to submit bids for a binding contract that would hold them responsible for development, production, and certain aspects of operating costs. Under the previous approach, contractors could deliberately underbid ("buy in") to get a development program, knowing that having completed the development they would be in a near monopoly position and could bargain to make up the losses during the production phase. One of the main ideas of total package procurement was to make the contractor responsible for the whole project and to make him submit firm bids for the production price while the competition is still on.

6. A. W. Marshall and W. H. Meckling, *Predictability of the Costs, Time, and Success of Development,* The Rand Corporation, P-1821, December 1959, p. 22.

Chapter 7: Three Controversial Program Decisions

1. Robert S. McNamara, *Statement on the RS-70,* Department of Defense Press Release, March 15, 1962.
2. Senate Subcommittee on National Security and International Operations, *Planning-Programming-Budgeting: Initial Memorandum,* 90th Congress, 1st Session, August 11, 1967, p. 6.
3. Senate Subcommittee on National Security and International Operations, *Hearings on Planning-Programming-Budgeting, Part II* (Washington: Government Printing Office, 1967), pp. 81–82.
4. *Ibid.,* p. 91.

Chapter 9: Unfinished Business, 1969

1. McGeorge Bundy, "A Communication," Washington *Post,* September 11, 1967.
2. According to one study, cost overruns in the 1960's (between estimated and actual) have averaged about 40 percent for complete programs and 90 percent for development programs. See R. L. Perry *et al., System Acquisition Experience,* The Rand Corporation, RM-6072-PR, November 1969.
3. For additional information, see "A Primer on Project PRIME," Department of Defense, November 1966, and "Defense Resource

Management Systems: Project PRIME," National Security Monograph Series, 1967, Industrial College of the Armed Forces, Washington, D.C.

4. "The Eisenhower Tax Program," *U.S. News and World Report,* May 29, 1953, p. 98.

5. Secretary of Defense Robert S. McNamara, *Statement before the Senate Committee on Armed Services on the Fiscal Year 1963–67 Defense Program and 1963 Defense Budget* (Washington: Government Printing Office, 1962), p. 1.

Index

MLF (Multilateral Force), 131
Montgomery, Field Marshal Bernard, 120
MRBM (medium-range ballistic missiles), 169
Multilateral Force (MLF), 131
Multiple, Independently Targetable Reentry Vehicle (MIRV), 44, 178, 208
  effectiveness of, 181, 183
  Soviet, 250
    ABM and, 188, 192, 193
    B-70 and, 245
  Soviet ABM and, 193
Mundt, Karl, 42
Mutual Defense Assistance Act (1949), 119
Muzzling the military, 99; see also Military, the

National Military Command System, 168–69
National Policy Machinery, Senate Subcommittee on, 20, 24–25
National Security Act (1947), 2
National Security Council (NSC), 14, 332
National Security Organization, 77
NATO, see North Atlantic Treaty Organization
Navy, see Services
Nike-Hercules (missiles), 15
Nike X (antiballistic missile), 44, 266
  Congressional debate on, 187, 311
  developing, 184–88, 190
Nike-Zeus (antiballistic missiles)
  approved (early 60s), 16
  disapproved (late 60s), 184–87, 190
  ICBM's and, 169–70
  JCS recommended, 110–11
Nimitz I (carrier), 326
1958 Act (Department of Defense Reorganization Act), 2–4, 31
Nitze, Paul, 122
Nixon, Richard M., administration of, 309
  Safeguard system and, 191
  Systems Analysis office and, 79, 333

Nixon Doctrine of "self-help" for Asians, 194
North Atlantic Treaty Organization (NATO; 1949), 117–64
  budget of, 151–52
  "complex" in, about conventional forces, 118–19
  defense studies for, 321–22
  division strength of, 68–71
    Soviet division compared with, 147–49
  force goals of (1952), 119–21
  lessons from strategy debate in, 157–64
  manpower in (1968), 151
  nuclear weapons and, 117–32, 159–61
    limited role of weapons, 121–32
  power of, in center region of Europe (1968), 147–56
  size of Soviet Army and, 117–18, 132–42
    cost of maintaining, 134–41
  tactical air force of, 142–47, 154–56, 217–20
North Korea, infiltration by, 212–13; see also Korea
North Vietnam, 277
  air war in, 293
  bombing of, 277, 287, 304–6, 310–11
  U.S. pilots and surface-to-air missiles of, 220
  See also Vietnam war
Norton, Col. John, 100, 103
NSC (National Security Council), 14, 332
NSC-68 (Nitze; document), 122
Nuclear forces
  calculating requirements for, 108–9
  strategic, 207–10
Nuclear strategy, 165–96
  ABM and, see Antiballistic missile system
  reappraising, 165–72
  theory of requirements, 172–84, 194–96
Nuclear superiority, meaning of, 183–84

Tet offensive (1968), 296, 297
TFX (F-111; aircraft), 7, 58, 221, 262–66, 311
Thailand, 271, 273
Think tanks, 106–7
Thor (intermediate-range ballistic missiles), 22, 169, 170
Time (magazine), 164
Titan (missiles), 170
  developing, 254, 256
  fuels for, 168
  I, 27, 257
  II, 27, 256, 257
TO&E, *see* Tables of Organization and Equipment
Total package procurement, 239–40
Total systems cost, year-to-year planning and, 18–19
Trade-off, land/air, 216–17
Truman, Harry S., administration of budgeting practices, 13
  nuclear weapons and, 122

Uncertain Trumpet, The (Taylor), 12, 193
"U.S. force plus options," 178
U.S. News & World Report (magazine), 278
U.S.S.R., *see* Soviet Union

Vandenberg, Arthur, 118
Vietnam war, 4, 7, 267–308
  airmobile warfare and, 100
  analysis of, 290–93, 314
  build-up for, 93, 151, 268–74
  calculating who is winning, 212
  deep interdiction in, 222–23
  estimating cost of, 293–308
    attrition strategy, 276–78, 295–300
    bombing and offensive operations, 294
    need for integrating over-all operations, 306–7
    pacification, 294, 300–3
    tactics and operations, 303–6
  force requirements for, 268–69

Vietnam war (*Continued*)
  "forty odd," 214–15
  the military's view of, 98–99; *see also* Military, the
  need for more analysis of, 307–8
  nuclear war and, 128
  PPBS and, 267–69, 306–7
  redeployment of forces in Korea and, 241
  Services and, *see* Services—Vietnam war and
  shortages in, 278–90
    of aircraft, 286–90
    of pilots, 279–83
  Southeast Asia Deployment Plan and, 271–76
  strategic rapid deployment and, 238
Vietnamization, 194, 332
Vinson, Carl, 41, 250
VSX (aircraft), 110
VTOL (Verticle Take-off and Landing aircraft), 102, 105
Vulnerability
  minimum-deterrent and, 171
  problem of (1960's), 166–69

War
  airmobile, 9, 100–4
  ASW, *see* Antisubmarine warfare
  Arab-Israeli (1967), 200–1
  armored, 106
  Clemenceau and Eisenhower on, 116
  conventional, *see* General-purpose forces
  nuclear, *see* Nuclear war
  principles of, defined, 89–90
  strategy of, *see specific strategies; for example:* Flexible response strategy; Nuclear strategy
  U.S. objectives in hypothetical war with Soviet Union, 83–84
  Vietnam, *see* Vietnam war
  See also Deployment; First-strike capability; Weapons systems
War-at-Sea study (1966), 231
Warsaw Pact (1955)
  budget of, 151–52

About the Authors

Alain C. Enthoven

ALAIN C. ENTHOVEN is the Marriner S. Eccles Professor of Public and Private Management (Emeritus) in the Graduate School of Business at Stanford University. He holds degrees in economics from Stanford, Oxford, and MIT. His career has included positions as an economist with the RAND Corporation, Assistant Secretary of Defense, and President of Litton Medical Products. In 1963, he received the President's Award for Distinguished Federal Civilian Service from John F. Kennedy. In 1977, while serving as a consultant to the Carter Administration, he designed and proposed the Consumer Choice Health Plan, a plan for universal health insurance based on managed competition in the private sector. He is a member of the Institute of Medicine of the National Academy of Sciences, a member of the Research Advisory Board of the Committee for Economic Development, and a fellow of the American Academy of Arts and Sciences. He is Chairman of Stanford University's Committee on Faculty/Staff Human Resources; a consultant to Kaiser Permanente; and the former Chairman of the Health Benefits Advisory Council for CalPERS, the California state employees' medical and hospital care plans. He has been a director of the Jackson Hole Group, PCS, Caresoft Inc., and eBenX, Inc. He was the 1994 winner of the Baxter Prize for Health Services Research and also the 1995 Board of Directors Award, Healthcare Financial Management Association. In 1997, Governor Wilson appointed him Chairman of the California Managed Health Care Improvement Task Force. Commissioned by the state legislature, the task force addressed health care issues raised by managed care. In 1998–1999, he was the Rock Carling Fellow of the Nuffield Trust of London and also visiting professor at the London School of Hygiene and Tropical Medicine. He is author, coauthor, or editor of numerous publications, including (with Laura Tollen) *Toward a 21st Century Health System: The Contributions and Promise of Prepaid Group Practice* (Jossey Bass, San Francisco, 2004).

K. Wayne Smith

K. WAYNE SMITH served as President and Chief Executive Officer of OCLC (Online Computer Library Center, Inc.), Dublin, Ohio, from January 1989 until May 1998; he is now President Emeritus. OCLC is a nonprofit, membership-based, library service and research organization whose international computer network and database link more than 50,000 libraries and other educational organizations in the United States and 94 other countries. He holds degrees in political science from Wake Forest University and Princeton University. He holds honorary degrees from Ohio State and Ohio University and was named an honorary consulting professor by Tsinghua University in Beijing, China, in 1996—one of only six so honored in the university's 85-year history at that time and the first U.S. citizen to be so named. He was a Captain in the U.S. Army; Special Assistant to the Assistant Secretary of Defense (Systems Analysis); Program Manager for defense studies at the RAND Corporation; Director of Program Analysis for the National Security Council (NSC); President and CEO of Dart Properties Group, one of five operating groups of Dart Industries; Group Managing Partner, Washington DC operations for Coopers & Lybrand; and Chairman and CEO of World Book Encyclopedia, Inc. He also served as assistant professor at West Point and as university professor at Wake Forest University. He is author or coauthor of numerous works on management systems, systems analysis, planning, and national security affairs.